Hollywood: *The Movie Lover's Guide*

Movie Lover's L.A.

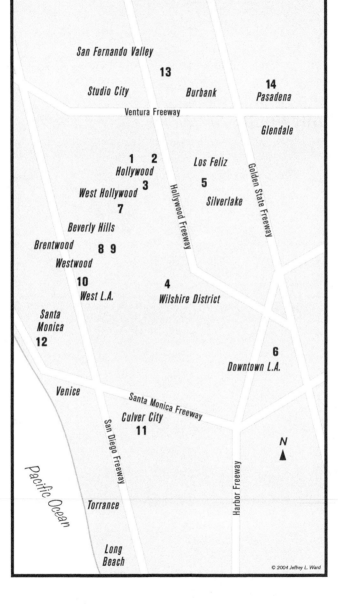

Numbers refer to corresponding chapters

San Fernando Valley

13

Studio City · Burbank · 14 Pasadena

Ventura Freeway

Glendale

1 · 2 · Los Feliz

Hollywood · 5

West Hollywood · 3 · Silverlake

7

Beverly Hills

Brentwood · 8 · 9

Westwood

10

West L.A. · 4 · Wilshire District

Santa Monica

12

6

Downtown L.A.

Venice

Santa Monica Freeway

Culver City

11

Hollywood Freeway

Golden State Freeway

San Diego Freeway

Harbor Freeway

N

Pacific Ocean

Torrance

Long Beach

© 2004 Jeffrey L. Ward

Hollywood:
THE MOVIE LOVER'S GUIDE

THE ULTIMATE INSIDER TOUR OF MOVIE L.A.

RICHARD ALLEMAN

BROADWAY BOOKS
NEW YORK

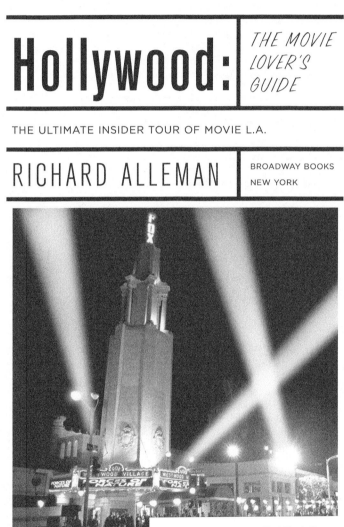

THE MOVIE LOVER'S GUIDE TO HOLLYWOOD. Copyright © 1985, 2005 by Richard Alleman. All rights reserved. No part of this book may be reproduced or transmitted in any form or by any means, electronic or mechanical, including photocopying, recording, or by any information storage and retrieval system, without written permission from the publisher. For information, address Broadway Books, a division of Random House, Inc.

Pages 493–495 constitute an extension of this copyright page.

PRINTED IN THE UNITED STATES OF AMERICA

BROADWAY BOOKS and its logo, a letter B bisected on the diagonal, are trademarks of Random House, Inc.

Visit our website at www.broadwaybooks.com

First Broadway Books trade paperback edition published 2005

Book design by Caroline Cunningham

Maps by Jeffrey L. Ward

Library of Congress Cataloging-in-Publication Data:

Alleman, Richard.
   Hollywood : the movie lover's guide : the ultimate insider tour of movie
L.A. / Richard Alleman.—1st Broadway Books trade pbk. ed.
      p.   cm.
   Rev. ed. of: The movie lover's guide to Hollywood.
   Includes index.
   (alk. paper)
      1. Motion picture locations—California—Los Angeles—Guidebooks.
2. Motion picture industry—California—Los Angeles—Guidebooks.
3. Los Angeles (Calif.)—Guidebooks.   4. Los Angeles (Calif.)—
Description and travel.   I. Alleman, Richard. Movie lover's guide to
Hollywood.   II. Title.
PN1995.67.C2A44 2004
791.4302'5'0979494—dc22

2004054476

ISBN 978-0-7679-1635-6

11

To the memory of my mother, Kaye Alleman,
who first took me to the movies—
and my father, R. B. Alleman,
who first took me to California

Contents

Acknowledgments

Again, there are many people to thank. First of all, all the people who helped with the original edition, including my then agent Paula Diamond, legendary editor Larry Ashmead, and the late Roy Barnitt, Eleanore Phillips, Ronald Haver, Billy Wilder. And, for their help with the new edition, I'm especially grateful to Charles Conrad at Random House for letting me return to the scene of the crime, and to Alison Presley for her hard work in making everything come together. In addition, I couldn't have written this without the help and superior research of Bruce Kingsley, David Dedeaux, and Bill Brown. Thanks also to David Garth, Robert Bierley, Mark Decker, Bryan Harper, and Ed Klein for their help on site (and in the car) in Los Angeles, and to so many others, including Anna Martinez at the Hollywood Chamber of Commerce; Honorary Mayor of Hollywood Johnny Grant; Marc Wanamaker at Bison Archives; Kristine Krueger and Leslie D. Unger at the Academy of Motion Picture Arts and Sciences; Michelle Blaya for the Beverly Hills Convention and Visitors Bureau; Wendy Schnee at the Beverly Hills Hotel; Dinah Hoven at the Huntington Library and Museum; Alec Layattien-akoff at the Argyle Hotel; Holly Fazio at Sony Pictures; Joanna Erdos at John Marshall High; Catherine Lucas at Warner Bros.;

Lori Falco at Occidental College; Nadia Balaz at the L.A.
County Arboretum; Jennifer Westfell at Pacific Theatres; Tammy
Lyn Phillips for the Fairmont Miramar; Lisa Melou at Mount St.
Mary's College; Mike Malone at the National Park Service; Mar-
lene Armas-Zermeno at the Millennium Biltmore; Imee Gacad
for the City of West Hollywood; Gary Gadson at tla Video; Jim
Heimann; Candice Carstensen; Christina Hart; Jane E. Lasky;
Mike Salazar; Jennifer Green; Jack Sayer; Dick Lovell; Planeria
Price; Russell Leland; Lucy McIntyre; Trey Walkey; Skye Lacerte;
Lydia Pogorzelski; Donna Reyes; Jan Davis; Pat O'Donoghue;
Lynette Falk; Robert Gitt; Kelly Granlon; J. Duncan Trussell;
Marsha Feldman; Julie Lugo Cerra; Sami Chow; Andy Ulloa;
Laurel Lambert; Dana Bromley; Barrie Perks; Debbie Lee; Adri-
ana Daunt; Stephanie Senter; Robert Keser; Rabecca Faez;
Lorena Parker; Lynda Bybee; Peter Deming, Ian Schrager Hotels;
the *Queen Mary*; and Mikael T. Zielinski.

Introduction

One of the most delightful periods of my life was the year I spent in Los Angeles in the mid-1980s researching the original *Movie Lover's Guide to Hollywood.* I had always been attracted to Los Angeles for all the usual reasons—the weather, the beach, the palm trees, and naturally the movies. And with my first book contract ever, I now had this wonderful opportunity to explore the city in depth, tracking down the vestiges of L.A.'s legendary film past. Indeed, at times I felt like a Raymond Chandler detective, following leads about long-lost studios, splendid movie palaces, secret cemeteries, and little-known locations for classic films like *Double Indemnity, Sunset Boulevard,* and *A Star Is Born.* Meanwhile, the icing on the cake was that during my wanderings I wound up meeting a number of Hollywood legends— from director Billy Wilder to actress-photographer Jean Howard to Mary Pickford's actor husband Charles "Buddy" Rogers—all of whom were wonderfully supportive of my project and generous with their time and stories.

The mid-1980s was a critical time for Hollywood—and by Hollywood I mean any area of L.A. with a connection to the movie industry (in other words virtually *all* of Los Angeles). For it was a period when many historical landmarks were being torn down in the name of progress, which usually meant yet another strip shopping center. At the same time, however, preservationists were finally getting organized and becoming serious about fighting developers and sometimes even city hall to save L.A.'s endangered past. In addition to the buildings that were saved back then, perhaps the greatest legacy of this period was the fact that it raised the consciousness of many Angelenos to the wisdom of preserving the city's rich cinematic legacy. And I'd like to think that *The Movie Lover's Guide* played a small role in that process.

For personal and professional reasons, I spent most of the last decade far from L.A. In fact, when I was approached to revise the *Movie Lover's Guide to Hollywood* two years ago, it had been almost seven years since I had spent any time at all in the city I had come to know so well and love so much. Seven years is a long time—so I was concerned anew about just how much of the movie lover's Los Angeles remained. Happily, I discovered that not only were most of the sites from my original book still standing, but many had been rehabilitated, often as museums or, in the case of movie palaces, as clubs, churches, or legitimate theaters.

In addition to the thrill of revisiting old sites, returning to this project after so long meant I had almost two decades of film history—not to mention film locations—to catch up with and uncover. So once again I switched into Philip Marlowe mode, slightly older but no less enthusiastic than I had been in the 1980s. In the process, I rekindled old friendships and fell in love with L.A. all over again. Talk about happy Hollywood endings.

For readers not familiar with the original *Movie Lover's Guide to Hollywood,* this book is meant not just for armchair travelers, but to be as actively used as any travel guide. To help orient sightseers, a numbered site map precedes each chapter. Not necessarily drawn to scale, these maps are included to show landmarks and sites as conveniently as possible. It is therefore recommended that serious sightseers consult an additional, more detailed map—especially when setting out for some of the more distant areas covered in the guide. Let me also stress that many of these places are private property. Needless to say, the privacy of the owners and tenants should always be respected. A final note: Whereas you'll need a car to best see many of the places in this book, thanks to L.A.'s cool new subway system, it's now possible to do a movie lover's tour—especially to the areas covered in the first six chapters—by Metro! Raymond Chandler would have loved it.

—Richard Alleman

Hollywood: *The Movie Lover's Guide*

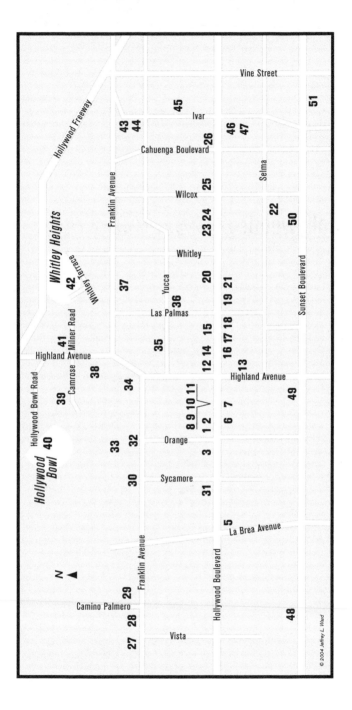

Hollywood: Birth of a Boulevard

Hollywood Boulevard—from Vista to Vine

In the 1880s, there were ranches, bean fields, orange and lemon groves. It was a peaceful, pastoral place—a far cry from the big city called Los Angeles that was growing up just five miles to the southeast. Staunchly conservative, early Hollywood was populated mostly with transplanted midwesterners. One of these, a

777 HOLLYWOOD BOULEVARD, HOLLYWOOD, CALIF.

prohibitionist from Kansas named Harvey Wilcox, had some 120 acres that his wife had christened "Hollywood" because, so the story goes, she had met a woman on a train who had spoken in glowing terms of her summer home back East called Hollywood. When the Wilcoxes subdivided their property in 1887, the name that Mrs. Wilcox had so fancied was printed on the map advertising the lots the couple was selling for $150 an acre. Hollywood—like so many communities in Southern California—was officially launched as a real estate development.

The little community grew steadily, if not dramatically. By 1897, Hollywood had its own post office, and in 1903, the citizens (the population was now close to 700) voted to be incorporated as a city. One of the first things that the officials of this new little "sixth-class" city did was to enact a number of ordinances. Ranging from limiting the hours that billiard and pool rooms could be open to banning the sale of alcoholic beverages, Hollywood's laws reflected the essential conservatism of its citizens. When this same citizenry voted in 1910 to have Hollywood annexed by the city of Los Angeles, it wasn't out of any particular fondness for their worldly metropolitan neighbor; it was simply because they needed L.A.'s water and sewer system.

Needless to say, when the first movie folk came to town in 1911, these Eastern outsiders of questionable moral character were not exactly welcomed with open arms by Hollywood's straitlaced locals. Indeed, in many ways, this Midwestern town that happened to be in Southern California was, except for the weather, an unlikely candidate to become the movie capital of the world.

Ironically, it was Hollywood's conservatism that was indirectly responsible for its first movie studio. For when the Centaur Film Co. of Bayonne, New Jersey, arrived in California in 1911, they found a perfect setup for moviemaking in a former Hollywood tavern that had fallen on hard times owing to the town's tough liquor laws. Besides its main building, the tavern property offered a barn and corral that would facilitate the shooting of Westerns, a group of small outbuildings that could be used as dressing rooms, and a bungalow for additional office space. Within a matter of days, the company was turning out three films a week from what they called the Nestor studio.

Universal's founder, Carl Laemmle, was next on the Hollywood scene. Arriving in 1912, Laemmle set up his first West Coast base of operations on the southwest corner of Gower and Sunset, just across the street from the Nestor studio. A year later, a trio made up of Cecil B. DeMille, Jesse Lasky, and Samuel Goldfish (later Goldwyn) also settled in Hollywood and shot the town's first feature-length film, *The Squaw Man,* based in a barn at the corner of Vine and Selma. As more and more movie people came, the locals who had at first looked down on the film business suddenly found themselves either directly in its employ or involved in businesses—from rooming houses to restaurants—that were making money thanks to motion pictures. In a word, Hollywood was booming—and the little Midwestern town in Southern California would never be the same again. By 1920, Hollywood's population had grown to 36,000. By the end of the twenties it would swell to over 150,000.

As Hollywood made the transition from village to metropolis, a great boulevard kept pace with the new city's growth and came to be the center of its wealth, power, and glory. Edged with movie palaces, stately hotels, glamorous restaurants and apartment buildings, Hollywood Boulevard was, in its heyday, one of the most dazzling thoroughfares in the country. The glamour started to wane in the late 1950s, however, and by the time the 1980s had rolled around this once great main street had lost much of its luster and parts of it had become home to punks, prostitutes, and panhandlers. It was then that concerned citizens and the local business community started taking action, realizing that the Boulevard's ultimate glory lay in its past. Although there were differing visions of how best to revive the area, everyone agreed that something had to be done. In some ways, too, Hollywood Boulevard was unique because, owing to its long period of decline in the sixties and seventies, many architecturally distinguished buildings and theaters had not been torn down, as they had been in more thriving areas of Los Angeles. In other words, Hollywood Boulevard was a remarkably intact, if somewhat down-at-heels, monument to the city that would always be considered the motion picture capital of the world.

Happily, the last decade has been one of revival, with many of the Boulevard's historic buildings now either restored or slated for restoration. Some have been turned into museums, whereas others are back to their original uses as theaters, restaurants, cafes, and nightclubs. At the same time, Hollywood Boulevard has welcomed a couple of new large-scale projects such as the Kodak Theatre, built to host the Academy Awards ceremonies, and the Hollywood & Highland complex, an entertainment mall designed in the spirit of a famous Old Hollywood movie set.

All this is not to say that Hollywood Boulevard has been totally sanitized. The old souvenir shops, fast-food outlets, tattoo parlors, and T-shirt emporiums are still very much a part of the mix—and the street's funky charm. But whereas twenty years ago, when this book was originally published, finding the history that lurked on the movie capital's main street was not easy. Today, it's visible everywhere. And since so much of this history is connected with the film industry and its larger-than-life personalities, Hollywood Boulevard is a logical first stop in the movie lover's Los Angeles odyssey. Here, a look at Hollywood's main street and its new splendor, plus trips to some fascinating places beyond the Boulevard—from the legendary barn where *The Squaw Man* was shot back in 1913 to a secret enclave of Mediterranean houses where silent films stars once lived. Welcome to Hollywood—as it is now . . . and as it was then.

For convenient sightseeing, this first chapter covers Hollywood Boulevard and the vicinity from Vista to Vine Street. The best way to tour the Boulevard proper is on foot. To reach some of the places mentioned on Franklin Avenue and in the hills behind the Boulevard, a car is suggested.

1. GRAUMAN'S CHINESE THEATER
6925 Hollywood Boulevard

Built by Hollywood developer C. E. Toberman for theater magnate Sid Grauman in 1927, the Chinese is the most famous movie house in the world. Reason? No other picture palace has ever come up with a publicity stunt as clever or successful as Grauman's hallowed ritual of having movie stars leave their footprints, handprints, and autographs in the cement of the theater's forecourt.

There are all sorts of stories as to how the custom began. The one most widely told is that silent screen star Norma Talmadge stopped by to tour the construction site and accidently stepped into some wet cement as she was getting out of her car. Another version says Grauman got the idea from Mary Pickford, who told him how her dog Zorro had gotten into some wet cement at her driveway up at Pickfair. "Now, we'll have Zorro with us forever," Pickford reportedly said to Grauman. Two days later, Grauman invited Pickford, her husband, Douglas Fairbanks, and Norma Talmadge to come celebrate the construction of his new theater with their prints and signatures. As these proved too faint upon drying, Grauman invited the same three stars as well as a few reporters back for an "official" ceremony. It made good copy—and indeed it still does.

Since that time, some 240 celebs have cemented their fame in the forecourt of the Chinese. Not all of the celebs have left just hand- and footprints: silent film star Harold Lloyd's trademark glasses have been immortalized in cement here—as have Sonja Henie's ice skates, John Wayne's fist, Harpo Marx's harp, Jimmy

Cementing their fame: Marilyn Monroe and Jane Russell at Grauman's Chinese Theater in 1953

Grauman's Chinese Theater

Durante's nose, and one of Betty Grable's "million-dollar" gams. Besides real-live people, Edgar Bergen's dummy Charlie Mc-Carthy has signed in at the Chinese; Roy Rogers's horse Trigger and Gene Autry's Champion have left hoofprints; *Star Wars* robots R2D2 and C3PO have rolled over the cement into immortality; and in 1984 Donald Duck marked his fiftieth birthday at the Chinese with two giant webbed-foot prints.

While movie lovers might question the credibility of some of the "legends" represented in the forecourt of the Chinese, few star presences have ever been publicly protested. A notable exception was Ali MacGraw's December 1972 appearance at the theater, which was met by a small band of chanting and placard-carrying demonstrators who felt Ms. MacGraw's lackluster four-film (at the time) career did not merit the full concrete treatment. (So far, though, Ms. MacGraw's prints are still in place and have not wound up in the basement of the theater—the fate, according to insiders, that a number of the prints of some lesser legends are said to have met.)

There is more to the mystique of the Chinese Theater than footprints. Throughout its history, the theater has been one of

Hollywood's premier premiere places—ever since Cecil B. De-Mille's *King of Kings* opened the Chinese on May 27, 1927. Besides premieres, the theater hosted the Academy Awards in 1944, 1945, and 1946. The Chinese is also a treasure of movie theater architecture and interior design—and happily, after a $7 million restoration in 2001 by Mann Theatres, which has owned the Chinese since 1973, this 1920s picture palace is almost as splendid as it once was. Outside, the theater's façade is a wonderful fantasy of a Chinese temple—complete with huge stone guard dogs on either side of the entrance and a sky-soaring pagoda roof. Inside, the lavish lobby and auditorium have marvelous murals, columns, Oriental vases, furniture, and carpets. It's the kind of theater they just don't build anymore—and simply being here makes up for anything that might be up on the screen.

Visit www.manntheatres.com.

2. MANN'S CHINESE 6 THEATERS
6801 Hollywood Boulevard

Opened by Mann Theatres in 2001 to coincide with the debut of the restored Chinese Theater next door, this upscale multiplex features a stylish minimalist version of its legendary sibling's Chinese decor as well as twenty-first-century amenities such as stadium seating, digital THX sound, and VIP lounges.

3. HOLLYWOOD ENTERTAINMENT MUSEUM
7021 Hollywood Boulevard

There's something for everyone in this vast (32,000 square feet) exhibition hall's assemblage of movie and television props, costumes, sets, and hands-on exhibits. TV fans can check out the *Cheers* barroom, the *Star Trek* Starship *Enterprise* control room, and Agent Mulder's *X-Files* office. Sci-fi nuts can ogle forty years' worth of monsters and scale models—from a Gort robot from *The Day the Earth Stood Still* (1951) to the alien spacecraft from *Independence Day* (1996). Among the interactive exhibits, the Foley Room has visitors adding sound effects to a film sequence. In addition to its permanent displays, the museum features excellent special shows such as "Marlene Dietrich: Treasures from the Estate Collection"; "Smoke, Lies, and Videotape," which documented Hollywood's role in glamorizing smoking; and "USO Presenting Hollywood Salutes the Troops," focusing on legendary USO shows from World War II up to the war in Afghanistan.

For current museum hours and information on special exhibitions, call 323–465–7900 and visit www.hollywoodmuseum.com.

4. THE WALK OF FAME

If Grauman's Chinese Theater could achieve world renown through its sidewalk—why not all of Hollywood? At least, that's what a group of local business people thought in the late 1950s when they concocted a scheme to turn the sidewalks of a deteriorating Hollywood Boulevard into a vast star-studded terrazzo commemorating the legends of the film, radio, television, and recording industries. Shop and property owners along the proposed walkway were asked to contribute $85 per front foot and $1.25 million was raised to begin the project that initially immortalized 1,558 personalities and continues to do so at the rate of about fifteen to twenty stars a year. (There are now more than 2,200.)

Sidewalk superstar: Harrison Ford on the Walk of Fame

In 1983, theater was added as a fifth Walk of Fame category and Mickey Rooney, then starring in *Sugar Babies* at Hollywood's Pantages Theater, became the first "two-star" celebrity when he was given his second star for his recent theatrical success. To make the Walk of Fame, new stars must be sponsored—by their agents, their producers, their fan clubs, or a local business—for the honor. A special committee of the Hollywood Chamber of Commerce then votes on the candidate's acceptability, taking into consideration professional as well as humanitarian achievements. If the candidate fulfills the requirements, the sponsor pays approximately $15,000 to cover the cost of the star, the ceremony that goes along with it, and the Walk's ongoing maintenance and repairs.

The Walk of Fame extends for some two and a half miles from La Brea to Gower along both sides of Hollywood Boulevard and from Sunset to Yucca along Vine Street.

Dedication ceremonies for the Walk of Fame are usually held at noon on the third Thursday of each month. Check with the Hollywood Chamber of Commerce for exact times and locations by calling 323-469-8311.

5. HOLLYWOOD GATEWAY SCULPTURE
Hollywood Boulevard/La Brea Avenue

Erected in 1993 on the strategic corner of Hollywood Boulevard and La Brea Avenue—often considered the western "gateway" to downtown Hollywood—this striking installation by artists Catherine Hardwicke and Hari West pays politically correct homage to four screen goddesses, each from a different ethnic background. The women, their gigantic stainless-steel images holding up a 30-foot gazebo, are Mae West, Dorothy Dandridge, Anna May Wong, and Delores Del Rio. The whole concoction is topped by a tiny Marilyn Monroe weathervane.

6. HOLLYWOOD ROOSEVELT HOTEL
7000 Hollywood Boulevard

A 1927 newspaper ad touted its grand opening as "the dominant social occasion of the year." "Don't wait," it enthused. "You will see the greatest number of stage and screen stars ever assembled." Among those invited were: Mary Pickford, Douglas Fair-banks, Norma Talmadge, Constance Talmadge, Pola Negri, Richard Barthelmess, John Gilbert, Harold Lloyd, Greta Garbo, Gloria Swanson, Rod La Rocque, Janet Gaynor, Will Rogers, Clara Bow, Sid Chaplin, Sid Grauman, Wallace Beery, Charles Chaplin . . . and scores of others. And most of them came—not only because, at twelve stories and four hundred rooms, this was the most impressive hotel ever to be built in Hollywood, but also because the syndicate that built it included such movieland nota-bles as Douglas Fairbanks, Mary Pickford, Joseph Schenck, Louis B. Mayer, and Marcus Loew.

Throughout its history, the Hollywood Roosevelt has had a strong connection with the motion picture industry. The Acad-emy of Motion Picture Arts and Sciences had its first Merit Awards dinner in the Roosevelt's Blossom Room on May 16, 1929. Marking the second anniversary of the founding of the Academy, this was the first time the Academy Awards were pub-licly presented. Today, the Blossom Room—with its Moorish columns, tiled walls, and muraled ceiling—is one of the hotel's most beautiful spaces.

Hollywood Roosevelt Hotel, 1984

The Roosevelt has also been a radio and television studio. In the 1930s, Russ Columbo broadcast a national radio show from the Roosevelt's Cinegrill—and in the 1950s and 1960s TV's *This Is Your Life* came live from the hotel. The famous hotel has also been a location for numerous films, including *Beverly Hills Cop II* (1987), *Internal Affairs* (1990), and *Charlie's Angels 2* (2003). It is especially memorable in the 1998 version of *Mighty Joe Young,* where the monster ape climbs atop Grauman's Chinese Theater while police helicopters circle the Roosevelt's landmark Cinegrill neon sign.

Back on the ground, the Roosevelt's 1950s-style pool with its tropical patio is one of Hollywood's most famous. Not only was it where starlet Marilyn Monroe posed for her first print ad (for suntan oil), but it served as the prototype for the pool patio at the Hollywood hotel that housed Lucy, Ricky, Fred, and Ethel when the gang went west in the original *I Love Lucy* series. And when Leonardo DiCaprio headed to L.A. as con man Frank Abagnale Jr. in *Catch Me If You Can* (2002), he wound up at this same pool patio, which provided the perfect 1960s setting for the sequence where he is confronted by his bumbling FBI agent nemesis (Tom Hanks).

Besides the pool (which artist David Hockney, famous for his paintings of swimming pools, turned into his largest pool painting, covering the bottom and sides with fat white squiggles in 1987) and the historic Blossom Room, movie lovers should check out the Roosevelt's exotic Moorish lobby, its mezzanine (where a permanent exhibition documents Hollywood's early history), and the famous Cinegrill nightclub, recently reopened and often featuring live entertainment.

The ultimate way to experience this Old Hollywood icon, however, is to check into a room. But beware of the ninth floor, where, it is reported, the ghost of actor Montgomery Clift roams the corridor outside his old room—number 928.

For reservations, call 800–950–7667 and visit www.hollywoodroosevelt.com.

7. EL CAPITAN THEATER
6838-6840 Hollywood Boulevard

In 1926, a year before the debut of Grauman's Chinese Theater, a lavish legitimate theater opened on Hollywood Boulevard across the street from the Grauman's construction site. Called the El Capitan, the theater featured an opulent East Indian interior—the creation of famous theater designer/architect G. Albert Lansburgh—and was housed in a magnificent building with an intricately carved façade decorated with characters from literature and drama. The first production at the El Capitan was a British revue starring Bea Lillie, Gertrude Lawrence, and Jack Buchanan.

In 1942, the El Capitan was converted to a movie house and its name was changed to the Paramount. The first film shown at the new Paramount was Cecil B. DeMille's answer to *Gone With the Wind,* a southern epic called *Reap the Wild Wind.* Over the years, uninspired remodelings turned the once grand theater into a very ordinary Hollywood Boulevard movie house. In 1991, however, the Paramount got a new lease on life from the Walt Disney Company, which in partnership with Pacific Theatres, bought the property, completely restored it, and changed its name back to El Capitan. The reborn movie palace began its new life with the premiere of Disney's *Beauty and the Beast,* complete with a live stage show. Since then, this magnificent theater, the flagship of the Disney empire, has been used mainly for first-run Disney films.

Visit www.disney.go.com/disneypictures/el_capitan.

8. KODAK THEATRE
Hollywood Boulevard/Highland Avenue

After some seven decades of bouncing around Los Angeles at various ballrooms, theaters, and civic auditoriums, Oscar finally has a permanent home for its annual Academy Awards ceremony. Just a block away from the Hollywood Roosevelt, where the first Oscars were handed out in 1928, the spectacular new $94 million Kodak Theatre—designed to Academy requirements by noted architect David Rockwell—opened in late 2001 as the

Oscar's new home base:
Kodak Theatre

star anchor of the new Hollywood & Highland development and hosted its first Oscarcast the following March. With its flexible seating—from 2,200 to 3,600 (3,300 for the Academy Awards)—the five-level theater is one of the largest in the United States. It is also one of the most technically advanced, with all backstage areas underground, a hydraulically controlled "media cockpit" that rises from the center of the orchestra seating area, and the latest in sound and lighting equipment. The Kodak also has numerous Academy Awards–friendly innovations—such as the grand spiral staircase with steps that are extra low and wide in deference to high heels and gowns. There's also a handy secret passageway between the theater and the glamorous new Renaissance Hotel (where many stars book rooms on Awards day to do their hair, makeup, and wardrobe) located just behind the Hollywood & Highland complex.

In addition to the Academy Awards, the Kodak hosts concerts, Broadway musicals, plays, TV specials, and other awards shows such as the Latino Grammys and the American Film Institute's Lifetime Achievement Awards. For movie lovers, however, the best news is that the theater offers a fascinating insider's walking tour of the facility. So you don't need to wait for your Academy Award nomination for a chance to see where it all happens.

For details on the guided tours, currently offered daily, call 323–308–6363, and visit www.kodaktheatre.com.

9. HOLLYWOOD & HIGHLAND
Hollywood Boulevard/Highland Avenue

Of all the positive changes that have taken place along Hollywood Boulevard recently—the Metro, restored theaters, new museums—the most spectacular is this $615 million enclave of shops, cafes, restaurants, cinemas, public courtyards, and performance spaces. For several decades, various plans for a major entertainment complex to help revitalize a dying Hollywood Boulevard had been put forward. The most ambitious—and most controversial—was one in the mid-1980s that called for high-rise office and hotel towers to anchor a rather uninspired retail mall to be built around Grauman's Chinese Theater. Fought by preservationists, conservationists, and many Hollywood residents, the scheme was eventually done in by the economic downturn that followed the 1987 stock market crash.

Thus, the fact that the Hollywood & Highland development has happened at all is somewhat remarkable. An added surprise is that it has been done with a great deal of taste as well as with a sense of fun and fantasy. Inspired by nothing less than pioneer director D. W. Griffith's monumental Babylonian temple movie set for his 1916 epic *Intolerance,* which stood as a Hollywood landmark on Sunset Boulevard and Vista Street for almost thirty years, Hollywood & Highland stuns with its grand staircases, massive columns, exotic frescoes and friezes, and most of all, its 33-foot-tall elephants that stand some 73 feet above the plaza, weighing in at 13,500 pounds each. The pièce de résistance is the colossal arch at the rear of the complex, perfectly positioned to frame the Hollywood Sign and now the hottest photo-op in town.

Despite its distinctive design, Hollywood & Highland initially delivered a fairly run-of-the-mill array of shops and eateries—

Remembering Old Hollywood: Hollywood & Highland's Babylon Court

and it was not a financial success. New owners—who took over in late 2003—hope to change that. One of H&H's biggest hits thus far has been the slick new Lucky Strike Lanes, a high-tech bowling alley/lounge/restaurant, which has become one of Hollywood's coolest hangouts. Hollywood & Highland is also drawing crowds with a lively series of special events in its Babylonian court. These include Ryan Seacrest's *On Air* TV show plus rock and folk concerts, mixed-media happenings, and good old-fashioned Hollywood movies—all for free.

Visit www.hollywoodandhighland.com.

10. HOLLYWOOD HOTEL SITE
Hollywood Boulevard/Highland Avenue

A century ago, in 1903, a Spanish Colonial–style hotel was built on the corner where the Hollywood & Highland entertainment complex now stands. Created to accommodate the growing number of visitors from back East who found Hollywood, with its pepper trees, orange groves, and mild climate, an ideal place for a winter vacation, it was called simply the Hollywood Hotel. About ten years later, another—and very different—group of Easterners discovered Hollywood . . . the moviemakers. And suddenly the once staid Hollywood Hotel became *the* place where many of the early stars and directors stayed and played. Rudolph Valentino was the most famous of the regulars and often tangoed at the hotel's Thursday tea dances. He also spent, by all accounts, a perfectly dreadful honeymoon at the Hollywood Hotel in 1919 with his first wife, Jean Acker, who had a suite there. One story about their wedding night has an overzealous desk clerk refusing to allow Valentino into his new wife's suite until the great screen lover dramatically produced his marriage license. Another story has Jean Acker refusing to allow Rudy into her suite. Seems Jean wanted to keep things platonic. Whatever happened, the marriage was over a month later.

The hotel achieved its greatest fame through legendary gossip columnist Louella Parsons, who broadcast a popular radio program called *Hollywood Hotel* from the premises in the 1930s. Inspired by Parsons's successful show, Warner Bros. made a mu-

Long-gone landmark: Hollywood Hotel, 1944

sical in 1938 that was based loosely on the Hollywood Hotel. Directed by Busby Berkeley, *Hollywood Hotel* was a forgettable film that starred Dick Powell and featured a rather awkward Louella Parsons playing herself. Also in the cast was a good-looking young sportscaster-turned-actor named Ronald Reagan. What did turn out to be memorable about the film was the Richard Whiting–Johnny Mercer song it unleashed upon the world—a little ditty that would go on to become the classic musical embodiment of Hollywood. The song? "Hooray for Hollywood." The hotel—demolished in 1956 to make way for a parking lot and bank, which in turn were leveled to build Hollywood & Highland—is gone, but the melody lingers on.

11. HOLLYWOOD AND HIGHLAND METRO STATION
Hollywood Boulevard/Highland Avenue

They said it couldn't be done, yet after years on the drawing board and a delay- and accident-fraught decade in the building, Los Angeles finally has a subway, at least for 17.4 miles between North Hollywood in the San Fernando Valley and Union Station downtown. Each of the new Metro's sixteen stations makes a unique architectural statement and the one at Hollywood and Highland is no exception with its theater-style lighting and its gigantic "rib cage" of blue metal arches above the tracks. The station made its film debut in the recent remake of *The Italian Job* (2003), where Mark Wahlberg, Charlize Theron, and Jason Statham drive a trio of Mini Coopers down the steps of its entrance and onto the tracks. For the scene, two blocks of Hollywood Boulevard were shut down for a week, which caused a traffic nightmare. "I got calls from friends on their way home from work, blaming me for getting stuck," said the film's director F. Gary Gray at the time.

12. HOLLYWOOD FIRST NATIONAL BANK BUILDING
6777 Hollywood Boulevard

Designed by the firm of Meyer and Holler, this impressive Hollywood Boulevard landmark—with its distinctive neo-Gothic tower—was the second-tallest building in Los Angeles when it

High-rise on Highland:
Hollywood First National Bank
building

debuted in 1927. But Meyer and Holler would be far better remembered—especially by movie lovers—for two low-rise Hollywood Boulevard buildings that they designed: Grauman's Egyptian (1922) and Grauman's Chinese (1927) theaters. Today, the building, which was often seen as a lofty Gotham City springboard for Superman in the 1950s TV series, is being restored and is currently advertising for prospective tenants.

13. HOLLYWOOD HISTORY MUSEUM/MAX FACTOR BUILDING
1660 North Highland Avenue

Of all the new museums that have opened on and off Hollywood Boulevard recently, this is one of the best. First of all, there's the setting: the historic former headquarters of the legendary Max Factor company.

It is impossible to imagine Hollywood without makeup—and makeup without Max Factor. Born in Czarist Russia, this cosmetics pioneer began his career as a makeup artist with the Russian Royal Ballet. He emigrated to the United States in 1904 and by 1909 had set up shop in downtown Los Angeles. Among his many contributions to the film industry was his 1914 invention of the first motion picture makeup to be packaged in a sanitary collapsible tube; he also developed panchromatic makeup to be used with the new panchromatic film of the late 1920s, for which Factor received a special Academy Award in 1929.

It was also in the late 1920s that Max Factor moved his base of operations from downtown Los Angeles to Hollywood. And when continued prosperity necessitated major renovations of his Hollywood offices, Factor commissioned the famed designer of motion picture palaces, S. Charles Lee, to create the Regency Moderne jewel of a building that still glitters on Highland Avenue.

The building—with its four-story pilasters and green marble base—became the Hollywood History Museum in the summer of 2003. On the first floor, four sumptuous former makeup consultation rooms—designed to duplicate the most splendid of movie-star dressing rooms of the 1930s—are now each dedicated

Max Factor building—now the Hollywood History Museum

to a different Hollywood type: blonde, redhead, brunette, and brownette. On view here are vintage beauty products and priceless photos and adverts featuring some of the biggest stars of the day. Beyond these salons, another main-floor gallery displays hundreds of historic photos of Hollywood that span the decades from the 1910s to the 1960s.

The vast second-floor show-space mainly celebrates individual stars—such as Mae West, Marilyn Monroe, Lucille Ball, and Judy Garland—with costumes, posters, stills, and other memorabilia from their lives and their films. The third floor focuses on individual films—and features sets and costumes from such hits as *Men in Black, Gladiator, Moulin Rouge,* and various sci-fi epics. Another highlight of the third floor is a full-size reproduction of the guest powder room from the late Roddy McDowall's L.A. home. Crammed with personally autographed movie-star photos—many of them campy poses such as Bette Davis done up as a nun!—this little lavatory was famous among Hollywood insiders, all of whom wanted to be invited to McDowall's just to check out the loo.

And speaking of invites, down in the basement of the museum—reached via a secret elevator—visitors can join the infamous Dr. Hannibal Lechter for dinner in his jail cell. Just don't ask too many questions about the menu.

For information on opening times for the Hollywood History Museum, call 323-464-7776 and visit www.hollywoodhistorymuseum.org.

14. HOLLYWOOD WAX MUSEUM
6767 Hollywood Boulevard

If you strike out and don't spot any real-life movie stars while visiting Hollywood, you can always find a whopping 180-plus lifelike waxen facsimiles at this popular attraction. Granted, some of the figures are less successful than others—Marilyn, her white dress billowing in the air from the infamous *Seven Year Itch* scene that may have cost her her marriage to Joe DiMaggio, resembles a great big Barbie Doll . . . and Ronald Reagan could be a double for Howdy Doody. But the tackiness of it all is part of the fun. Besides movie stars, the museum features TV people (the casts of *Seinfeld, M*A*S*H,* and *Baywatch* for example), recording artists, and athletes. There're also a Hall of Presidents, a Chamber of Horrors (shades of Vincent Price and Carolyn Jones in Warners' 1954 3-D film *House of Wax),* and a wax re-creation of Leonardo da Vinci's *The Last Supper.* If all this isn't enough, a short film on the history of the Academy Awards—featuring vintage footage of Oscar-winning films and perfor-mances—runs continuously in the museum's Academy Awards Movie Theater.

On a Hollywood historical note, the Spanish Colonial Revival building housing the wax museum was built in 1928. In the 1930s, its second story was taken over by the Embassy Club, a private dining club for celebrities who wanted to avoid the crowds at the very popular Montmartre Cafe next door. A secret passageway connected the two glamour spots.

Visit www.hollywoodwax.com.

15. MONTMARTRE CAFE SITE
6763 Hollywood Boulevard

Designed in the style of an Italian Renaissance palazzo, this little Boulevard building originally housed a bank on its ground floor and one of early Hollywood's most glamorous nightspots—Montmartre Cafe—on its second story. The Montmartre opened in 1923 and quickly became *the* place to go for a wild night on the town in the Roaring Twenties. When the Charleston was the rage, Joan Crawford was the star who danced it best—often atop a table. Tango honors went to Rudolph Valentino.

Looking back at the Montmartre, the late Buddy Rogers re-membered white-tie evenings and violins, whereas the late Eleanore Phillips, longtime West Coast editor of *Vogue* maga-zine, recalled the Montmartre's maître d'—"tanned and hand-some and always in a white linen suit." He became Bruce Cabot, the star of *King Kong.* Open for lunch as well as dinner, the Montmartre was a favorite haunt of Louella Parsons who, in the early days of her career, often went table-hopping asking any-one and everyone the question, "Any news, dear?" In 1930, the Montmartre was one of the first clubs to book a young crooner who had recently left the Paul Whiteman orchestra. The singer

Montmartre Cafe, 1930

was Bing Crosby, and it was also at the Montmartre where he wooed his first wife, Dixie Lee.

The historic watering hole has had many incarnations since its glory days, including a stint as the Lee Strasberg Institute, the famed acting school known for teaching the Method, in the 1970s. The good news today is that the Montmartre has been rehabilitated and turned back into what it was originally—a Hollywood nightspot. Called Club Day After, it features a special section named the Montmartre Lounge.

Call 323-465-5369.

16. GUINNESS WORLD RECORDS MUSEUM/HOLLYWOOD THEATER SITE
6764 Hollywood Boulevard

Until the late 1980s, the former Hollywood Theater, which now houses the Guinness World Records Museum, was the oldest extant movie theater in Hollywood. Originally a nickelodeon, the Hollywood dated back to 1911. Of particular interest to movie

Hollywood Theater, ca. 1970

lovers today, however, is the historic theater's beautiful 1930s neon marquee. Now being used to advertise the museum, this was one of the first marquees to be designed with large side panels that were angled to catch the eyes—not of pedestrians—but of passing motorists. And if you visit the museum, don't miss Michael Jackson's "Bad" jacket, valued at $40,000 and loaded with 12 pounds of gold trim.

Visit www.guinnesssworldrecords.com.

17. PIG 'N WHISTLE RESTAURANT
6714 Hollywood Boulevard

For most of the 1980s and 1990s, this site was a pizza parlor, with little to distinguish it other than its wrought-iron marquee and the fresco of dancing pigs embedded above the entrance. Back then, paneling concealed the sculpted wood ceiling by the famed architects Morgan, Walls, and Clements (who did the nearby El Capitan Theater). Once one of the most popular restaurants on the Boulevard, the original Pig 'n Whistle was a frequent stop before or after a show at the adjacent Egyptian Theater. In 2001, however, restaurateurs Chris Breed and Alan Hajjar took over the 1927 landmark, restored it, and reopened it as a full-service bar and restaurant under its original name. So, today, movie lovers can dine (on pizza, pastas, sandwiches, and salads) and have drinks at the same smart spot where Shirley Temple, Clark Gable, Spencer Tracy, and Loretta Young were once regulars.

Call 323–463–0000 or visit www.pignwhistle.com.

18. EGYPTIAN THEATER
6712 Hollywood Boulevard

Another Sid Grauman extravaganza, the Egyptian opened in 1922 with the gala premiere of *Robin Hood* starring Douglas Fairbanks. The Egyptian was the first real movie palace to be erected in Hollywood and its architects—Meyer and Holler— were the same ones that Grauman would use for his Chinese

Egyptian Theater, today

Hollywood Egyptian Theater

Theater five years later. Like the Chinese, the Egyptian is characterized by a large forecourt, which in its heyday was edged by Middle Eastern shops and by guards in ancient Egyptian costumes. No wonder Cecil B. DeMille premiered his original *The Ten Commandments* here in 1923. Inside the theater, hieroglyphic murals, a sunburst ceiling, and a giant scarab above the proscenium continued the Egyptian theme—especially popular in the early 1920s when major archaeological finds were being made in Egypt, culminating in Howard Carter's discovery of Tutankhamen's, or King Tut's, tomb in 1922.

By the time the 1980s rolled around, the Egyptian was in sorry shape, a victim of remodelings rather than restoration, not to mention marginal maintenance. But in 1998, the American Cinemathèque, a nonprofit organization dedicated to the preservation and exhibition of classic and forgotten films as well as works of little known and emerging talents, acquired the theater and set to rehabilitating it. Today, the Egyptian has two screens: a main house seating 650 people, and a smaller theater, which Steven Spielberg financed. Both are used for the Cinémathèque's regular programs as well as its many mini-festivals, which can focus on anything from the works of a specific director to short subjects, indies, gay and lesbian, developing world, and even 3-D films, and often feature guest celebrities. 2003's Film Noir festival, for example, brought in Patricia Hitchcock O'Connell (Alfred's daughter and a star of his *Strangers on a Train*), Jan Sterling, Nancy Olson, Peter Graves, and Kevin McCarthy.

Movie lovers can not only see films in this historic survivor of Hollywood Boulevard's golden age, they can have an insider tour of the place, offered several times a month. The tour includes the 55-minute documentary *Forever Hollywood,* which features fascinating archival footage and celebrity interviews on the film capital's history and mystique. But even if you can't make the tour, just a walk around the Egyptian's exotic Pharaonic court-yard off Hollywood Boulevard is a pleasure, as is the exterior view from McCadden Place, with the theater's long slanted beige wall looking like that of an ancient temple.

For program and tour information, call 323–466–3456 or visit
www.americancinematheque.com.

19. LARRY EDMUNDS BOOKSHOP, INC.
6644 Hollywood Boulevard

This is where the Library of Congress paid $12,500 for Bernard Herrmann's original score for the soundtrack to the 1941 film *Citizen Kane;* it's also where the late French filmmaker François Truffaut headed first whenever he was in L.A. It is Hollywood's best-known source for film books, scripts, stills, posters, lobby cards, magazines, and memorabilia. Its catalogue is so vast that it encompasses three volumes and its collection of motion picture still photos—more than 1 million—is said to be one of the largest in the world.

Hours are 10 a.m. to 6 p.m., Monday to Saturday. Call
323–463–3273 or visit www.larryedmunds.com.

20. MUSSO & FRANK GRILL
6667 Hollywood Boulevard

Opened in 1919, it claims to be the oldest restaurant in Holly-wood. And at first everybody—Gloria Swanson, Mary Pickford, Douglas Fairbanks, Jesse Lasky, Cecil B. DeMille, Barbara La Marr, John Barrymore—came because there weren't too many other places to go to at the time. Eight decades later, celebrities and industry people (Sean Penn, Tom Cruise, Demi Moore, Tom Hanks) still come—from as far away as Malibu and Santa Mon-ica—not for the glamour, but for the experience of dining in an old-fashioned, uncomplicated American restaurant. If restaurants were movies, Musso's would be a 1940s Andy Hardy musical.

Remodeled in 1937, the restaurant—with its two large din-ing rooms, beamed ceilings, long counter, red banquettes, wooden booths with coat racks—has changed little since those days in the late 1930s and early 1940s when F. Scott Fitzgerald, Robert Benchley, and William Faulkner were regulars. Possibly they were drawn to Musso's because the place reminded them more of the East than of the West Coast, where they never felt at home. Also, it was next door to Stanley Rose's bookshop—

Musso & Frank Grill, 1936

an important hangout of the Hollywood intelligentsia at the time.

Musso's menu has also changed little over the years—with no-nonsense entrees like chicken pot pie, beef goulash, steaks, and chops seeming strangely anachronistic in today's nouvelle Los Angeles. But Musso & Frank will probably still be around long after the chic places—the Spagos, Mortons, and Michaels of the moment—have closed their kitchens. Portions are enormous, prices moderate.

For reservations, call 323-467-7788.

21. FREDERICK'S OF HOLLYWOOD
6608 Hollywood Boulevard

Purveyors of naughty nighties to the world since the late 1940s, this Hollywood Boulevard landmark occupies a beautiful 1935 Art Deco building that was formerly home to a posh leather and luxury goods shop. Inside, besides racks and racks of R- and X-rated undies, movie lovers will also discover, at the rear of the store, a Museum of Lingerie. On view here are all sorts of kinky celebrity kit, highlighted by Greta Garbo's slinky black slip from *Camille* (1937), Marilyn Monroe's *Let's Make Love* (1961) brassiere, Madonna's bullet-nosed bustier from her Blonde Ambition (1988) tour and video, and even the bra that turned Tony Curtis into a woman in *Some Like It Hot* (1957). The museum is free.

22. HOLLYWOOD WILCOX HOTEL
Wilcox Avenue at Selma

An example of humble beginnings, this unprepossessing hotel across from the post office was the first Hollywood address of an eighteen-year-old MGM contract player named Ava Gardner, who shared a small flat here with her sister Beatrice, called Bappy, in the early 1940s. Recalling those early Hollywood days, Miss Gardner had this to say in 1984: "I was getting $35 a week—I thought I'd be making $50. Bappy and I stayed at the Wilcox—a little bed, a little kitchen. For the first three weeks we were there, I didn't get paid at all—so Bappy got a job at I. Magnin selling bags. I had to take two buses to get to the studio." Today, the former Hollywood home of Gardner, who died in 1990 in London, where she had resided for several decades in that city's posh Knightsbridge neighborhood, is now owned by the Church of Scientology Celebrity Center International. (Celebrity Centers provide training and services for Scientology members.)

23. JANES HOUSE
6541 Hollywood Boulevard

Standing at the rear of a rather shabby little shopping mall off Hollywood Boulevard is a curious turreted Queen Anne dwelling. A cause célèbre for preservationists in the 1980s, the Janes House is of interest to Hollywood history buffs, since it was typical of many of the homes that edged the Boulevard at the beginning of the twentieth century. Built in 1903, when Hollywood Boulevard was a dusty byway called Prospect Avenue, the Janes House was the family residence of three sisters who ran a school on the premises between 1911 and 1926. During those years, the Janes ladies taught the progeny of C. B. DeMille, Charlie Chaplin, Douglas Fairbanks, Carl Laemmle, and producer Thomas Ince. The last surviving sister lived in the house until 1982 before being moved to a nursing home, where she died the following year. Meanwhile, the house, which narrowly escaped demolition, was restored and repositioned as part of the mall that went up at the end of the 1980s. Currently unoccupied, both it and the mall are slated to be redeveloped as an upscale restaurant and wine court.

24. HILLVIEW APARTMENTS
6531–6535 Hollywood Boulevard

Since many early Hollywood rooming houses refused to rent to actors ("No Actors, No Dogs" signs were frequently posted in front of many buildings), pioneer producers Jesse Lasky and Samuel Goldwyn built the Hillview Apartments in 1917 with the express purpose of providing housing to silent-film folk who bounced back and forth between the East and West Coasts much as actors still do today. Among the early stars who resided in what was then a handsome pink Mediterranean apartment building on Hollywood Boulevard were Mae Busch, a fixture in many Laurel and Hardy films, and Viola Dana, a Brooklyn-born beauty whose star faded fast with the advent of talking pictures. As the years went by, Hillview's glamour faded as well and by the mid-1980s, the place was overrun with drug addicts, runaways, and hookers. In 1994, the building was severely damaged by the Northridge earthquake and was pretty much left to whatever squatters were brave enough to live there. A fire in 2002 nearly finished off the place, but in its darkest hour, Hillview was saved by developer-preservationist Jeffrey Rouze, who redid the El Capitan office building farther up the Boulevard. The revived building is very similar to the 1917 original, right down to the folding Murphy beds in a number of studio apartments. The aim, once again, is to provide affordable housing to, among others, young Hollywood hopefuls.

25. PACIFIC HOLLYWOOD THEATER
6433 Hollywood Boulevard

When it opened in 1927 with the premiere of *Glorious Betsy*, starring Conrad Nagle and Dolores Costello, it was called the Warner Bros. Theater and the opulent Moorish palace was the largest movie house ever built in Hollywood. Over the years,

Warner Bros. Theater, 1935

the theater lost its original marquee, its name, and was subjected to that late-twentieth-century engineering technique/economic necessity known as "tri-plexing." Even so, it was still showing movies well into the 1990s and many of the original interior details—such as the sculpted white walls and wood-beamed ceiling of the lobby—could still be admired. But in 1994, severely damaged by both the Northridge earthquake and Metrorail tunneling, the former Warner closed down completely. Today, it stands abandoned and locked up and the only evidence movie lovers can see of its former glory is by peeking through the gates and looking up at the crumbling coffered ceiling and down at the fading terrazzo floor. Take a look, too, at one of the Walk of Fame stars in front of the theater. Honoring comedian Carol Burnett, the star was placed here to commemorate the fact that in the late 1940s, the Warner employed Burnett, then a student at Hollywood High, as an usherette. A child of alcoholic parents, Burnett lived with her grandmother up the street from the theater in a tiny apartment at 6434 Yucca Street.

26. SECURITY BANK BUILDING
6381-6385 Hollywood Boulevard

Fans of films noir and detective fiction consider this 1921 pink granite office building hallowed ground, because it was here, on the sixth floor, that one of America's most famous fictional detectives had his office. The detective was Philip Marlowe and his creator Raymond Chandler is remembered outside with a plaque designating the intersection of Cahuenga and Hollywood Boulevard as Raymond Chandler Square. Without Chandler and Marlowe, we would have been deprived of such memorable films as *Murder My Sweet* (1945), *The Big Sleep* (1946 and 1978), *Lady in the Lake* (1947), *The Long Goodbye* (1973), and *Farewell My Lovely* (1975), to name just a few.

27. *REBEL WITHOUT A CAUSE* HOUSE
7529 Franklin Avenue

Who can forget James Dean, drunk, crawling like a baby on his hands and knees, playing with a little mechanical monkey, on the street outside that nice upper-middle-class home with the columned entryway at the opening of *Rebel Without a Cause* (1954)? For this dramatic slice of 1950s dysfunctional family life, director Nicholas Ray went outside the studio and shot on a real street. The house, now seriously updated, is still recognizable. Ironically, it stands just a few blocks from perhaps the ultimate symbol of idealized 1950s American family life, *The Adventures of Ozzie and Harriet* house (see item 29).

28. ANITA STEWART HOUSE
7425 Franklin Avenue

In the teens, Anita Stewart was one of the biggest names at Vitagraph Studios. Enter Louis B. Mayer and his newly created Louis B. Mayer Pictures in 1917. In need of a big star to add class and clout to his new company, Mayer went after, and got, Miss Stewart. Not only would he match the $3,000 a week that she was getting at Vitagraph, he would even throw in a unique perk for the period: an automobile! The only hitch to the whole deal was the fact that Miss Stewart's Vitagraph contract had not yet run its term. The result? Vitagraph sued and won a landmark breach of contract case that proved, for the moment at least, that movie studios were stronger than movie stars. The suit is said to have cost Mayer some $123,000. After it all died down, Miss Stewart went on to make a number of successful pictures with Mayer—but the Brooklyn-born actress was smart enough to exit the picture business just as talkies were coming in. This massive Franklin Avenue mansion with the ten columns and two balustrades was Anita Stewart's onetime Hollywood home. Today, it stands abandoned, a crumbling hulk with an uncertain future in a no longer fashionable neighborhood.

29. THE OZZIE AND HARRIET HOUSE
1822 Camino Palmero Drive

This is where Ozzie, Harriet, David, and Ricky Nelson lived while they were portraying the ideal American family in their popular 1950s television series. A pleasant upper-middle-class dwelling, it fit the Nelsons' screen image so well that their television house was modeled after it—and occasionally the real house would be used

Ozzie and Harriet Nelson's Hollywood home

for exterior long shots. When the Nelsons went to work in the morning, they didn't have far to go since the Hollywood General Studios where *The Adventures of Ozzie and Harriet* was shot were just five minutes away on Las Palmas. Ozzie and Harriet Nelson were still based in their Camino Palmero home when Ozzie died of cancer in 1975. Harriet sold the house and moved out several years later. She died in 1994, nine years after her son Ricky Nelson was killed in a plane crash. All three are buried at the Hollywood Hills branch of Forest Lawn Cemetery in Burbank.

30. HIGHLAND GARDENS HOTEL
7047 Franklin Avenue

On October 4, 1970, rock star Janis Joplin was found dead of a drug overdose in this Hollywood hostelry. Known as the Landmark Motel at the time, it is now called the Highland Gardens. Famed for drinking Southern Comfort onstage and for espousing the virtues of getting and staying "stoned," Janis was a child of the 1960s who just barely made it into the seventies. Her greatest moment professionally was her gut-wrenching performance of "Love Is Like a Ball and Chain" at the 1967 Monterey Rock Festival—a performance that was immortalized in the film *Monterey Pop*. Later, Joplin would again be remembered on screen—in the film *The Rose*, which starred Bette Midler in a role patterned after Joplin. Actress Renée Zellweger is currently slated to play Joplin in a biopic called *Piece of My Heart*. Often questioned by the press about her wanton life and singing style, Janis Joplin once answered: "Maybe I won't last as long as other singers . . . but I think you can destroy your *now* worrying about tomorrow." Her death in Hollywood at age twenty-seven came less than three weeks after fellow rock star Jimi Hendrix, also twenty-seven, OD'd in London.

Today, the former Landmark Motel is a well-maintained seventy-one-room mid-century-Moderne hotel that caters to tourists. There are photos of celebrities in the lobby, but none of Miss Joplin.

Call 323–850–0536 or visit www.highlandgardenshotel.com.

31. *ALIAS* APARTMENT BUILDING
1731 North Sycamore Avenue

This classic Hollywood-Mediterranean courtyard apartment complex, called El Cadiz after the famous Andalusian city in the south of Spain, is the original TV home to college student/under-

El Cadiz: home to *Alias* agent Sydney Bristow

cover CIA agent Sydney Bristow (Jennifer Garner) and her un-suspecting roommate Francine (Merrin Dungey) in the popular series *Alias*.

32. THE MAGIC CASTLE
7001 Franklin Avenue

This splendid Gothic mansion on Franklin Avenue was erected in 1909 as the family home of a banker named Rollin S. Lane. Later, in the early 1930s, it was home to actress Janet Gaynor and her then husband, attorney Lydell Peck. Since 1963, how-ever, the mansion has been the clubhouse of the five-thousand-member Academy of Magical Art, said to be "the only club in the world devoted to magicians and lovers of magic." Frequently used as a location by TV news shows doing Halloween features, the beautifully restored "castle" is made up of bars, dining rooms, theaters, and secret chambers. In the Houdini Séance Room, the ghost of master magician Harry Houdini returns

Magic Castle

twice nightly. In the Invisible Irma Room, a phantom pianist named Irma plays requests. Fittingly, this private club keeps its membership list top secret. But Hollywood's most famous part-time master of prestidigitation, the late Orson Welles, was supposedly a member as were other celebrity dabblers in the Magical Arts such as Johnny Carson, Muhammad Ali, Cary Grant, Steve Martin, Tony Curtis, and Bill Bixby. Rumor has it that Harry Potter is an honorary member.

To experience the Magic Castle's magic, nonmembers need an invite from a member—or they need to be a registered guest at the adjacent forty-two-room Magic Castle Hotel. Call 323-851-0800 or visit www.magiccastle.com.

33. YAMASHIRO
1999 North Sycamore Avenue

Called Yamashiro ("mountain palace"), this is one of Holly-wood's most surprising sights—an authentic replica of a Japanese palace perched almost 300 feet above Hollywood Boulevard. Surprisingly, this architectural treasure of teak and cedar with gold-lacquered rafters was not the fantasy home of an early film star but was built between 1908 and 1912 by two brothers named Bernheimer who were dealers in Asian antiques. Yamashiro's connection with the movie business began in 1923 when the mansion became the clubhouse for the Club of the Hollywood Four Hundred. This organization of the Hollywood film elite was formed partially as a response to the cool reception motion picture people received at many of Los Angeles's old-moneyed and very restrictive private clubs. The prejudice against movie people went back to the days when they first arrived in Hollywood. At the time (1911), Hollywood was basically a small Midwestern town that happened to be in California. Nicknamed "movies," early film people were discriminated against to such an extent that many rooming houses refused to accommodate them.

As times changed and Hollywood film stars were elevated to the status of royalty, there was less and less a need for the Club of the Hollywood Four Hundred and it was eventually disbanded.

Yamashiro, 1912

Yamashiro then passed through various hands and had various incarnations—from military academy to brothel. The building was also in the news in the early 1940s, when it was targeted and trashed by anti-Japanese mobs after Pearl Harbor. In the late 1940s, developer Tom Glover Sr. bought the dilapidated property, restored it, and opened it as a restaurant, which it still is.

Often used as an instant Asian location for films and television shows, Yamashiro "appeared" as the American Officers' Club in *Sayonara,* the 1958 film starring Marlon Brando, Miiko Taka, Red Buttons, and Miyoshi Umeki. Recent films to capitalize on Yamashiro have been *Playing God* (1997), where it is Timothy Hutton's mansion and the site of the film's final shootout, and producer Jerry Bruckheimer's Nicolas Cage–Angelina Jolie thriller *Gone in 60 Seconds* (2000). Recently, too, Yamashiro provided the suitably Asian background for a *Turner Classic Movies* interview with Tom Cruise, director Ed Zwick, and writer John Logan on the making of the 2003 epic *The Last Samurai.* And needless to say, this romantic locale—with its Japanese gardens, six-hundred-year-old pagoda, and an authentic teahouse— is constantly used for TV commercials and print ads.

For a close-up look at this exotic Hollywood spot, movie lovers can stroll the grounds, or better yet, have lunch or dinner. At night, the view of the lights of Hollywood looks like the one James Mason showed Judy Garland during the first reel of *A Star is Born*.

For reservations, call 323–466–5125, and visit
www.yamashirorestaurant.com.

34. FIRST UNITED METHODIST CHURCH OF HOLLYWOOD
6817 Franklin Avenue

This handsome house of worship at the busy corner of Franklin and Highland Avenues features a clean neo-Gothic exterior and a wood-beamed ceiling that's a scaled-down replica of the one in Westminster Abbey. Dedicated in 1929, the church has appeared in a number of famous Hollywood films. In David O. Selznick's 1932 *What Price Hollywood?*—directed by George Cukor—Constance Bennett plays a Hollywood hopeful who finds that success in tinseltown does not bring happiness. Her mid-picture marriage to a polo-playing socialite takes place at the First

First United Methodist Church

United Methodist Church. In 1941, Warners' Academy Award–nominated *One Foot in Heaven* featured Fredric March, Martha Scott, Beulah Bondi, Gene Lockhart—and the First United Methodist Church as, of all things, a Methodist church! Science-fiction fans may also remember the church as one of the places where the terrified inhabitants of Los Angeles sought shelter during the invasion of their city by Martian spaceships during the climatic ending of the 1952 classic, *The War of the Worlds*. More recently, the church was used in *Sister Act* (1992) and *Anger Management* (2003). It's also a frequent location for the TV soap opera *Days of Our Lives* and was often seen in *Murder, She Wrote*.

Besides its importance as a location, the First United Methodist Church of Hollywood has had a number of famous members through the years. Among them: Robert Taylor, Busby Berkeley, Barbara Britton, and Bob Barker. Today, too, the church is home to the First Stage theater company, which develops new material for the stage and screen.

35. VILLA CAPRI SITE
6735 Yucca Street

Now a gated, nondescript office complex, this Hollywood-Elizabethan bungalow once upon a time was an Italian restaurant called the Villa Capri. Run by the D'Amore family, the Villa Capri had a friendly family atmosphere—which is perhaps the reason it became "home" to James Dean. First introduced to the place by Pier Angeli (the actress who broke Jimmy's heart when, at her Italian Catholic family's insistence, she married Vic Damone), Dean continued coming to the Villa Capri restaurant even after the breakup of their romance. In fact, he was so at home here that he entered through the kitchen—and even rented a house from one of the Villa's maître d's.

On the evening of September 29, 1955, Hollywood columnist James Bacon remembers seeing Dean "doing 80 miles an hour" up McCadden Place and screeching to a halt in front of the Villa Capri. As Dean got out of his brand-new special-model Porsche Spyder, Bacon admonished the young actor, saying: "Jimmy, that's a good way to keep from growing old." Replied Jimmy,

"Who wants to grow old?" The next day Dean died at the wheel of the same Porsche.

After Dean's death, the Villa Capri became a shrine to his legend. Fans would arrive, try to sit at their hero's table, and order his favorite dishes. The place also was a hangout for Hollywood's famous Rat Pack in the late 1950s, and frequently saw the likes of Frank Sinatra, Sammy Davis Jr., Humphrey Bogart and Lauren Bacall, and Judy Garland and Sid Luft drinking and dining here. (From 1960 to 1962, Sinatra even hosted the radio show *Live from the Villa Capri*, from the restaurant.) The restaurant closed in 1982 and went on to house the offices of the KFAC radio station for a decade after that.

36. LAS PALMAS HOTEL
1738 North Las Palmas Avenue

"Daily . . . Weekly . . . Color TV . . . phone." That's what this three-story hotel, bordered by parking lots on both sides, promises. For Vivian Ward, the ingenuous runaway/Hollywood Boule-

Las Palmas *(Pretty Woman)* Hotel

vard hooker played by Julia Roberts in *Pretty Woman* (1990), the Las Palmas was her humble home base (she kept her cash in the toilet bowl) before she landed much better accommodations, thanks to Richard Gere, in the posh penthouse of the Regent Beverly Wilshire Hotel in Beverly Hills.

37. THE MONTECITO APARTMENTS
6650 Franklin Avenue

Built in the early 1930s, this Art Deco classic of zigzag-moderne architecture is reported to have been Ronald Reagan's first Hollywood home. According to legend, young Reagan, upon his arrival in Tinseltown, hotfooted it to the Montecito because he wanted to live in the same building where his idol Jimmy Cagney had lived. Mickey Rooney and Don Johnson also reportedly lived here. Particularly popular with the New York crowd in the 1950s and early 1960s, the Montecito provided accommodations for Geraldine Page, Rip Torn, Julie Harris, George C. Scott, and Ben Vereen. In those days it was a place where, according to a former resident, "No one ever bought their beer by the six-pack—since no one ever knew how long they'd be staying."

For Raymond Chandler fans, the Montecito was the prototype for the Chateau Bercy apartment building in Chandler's Philip Marlowe detective novel *The Little Sister.* Despite its historied past, by the 1980s, the Montecito had hit the skids and stood boarded up for a number of years on Franklin Avenue, seeming a casualty of a dying Hollywood. Now restored and listed on the National Register of Historic Places, the Monty is an apartment building for senior citizens.

38. THE AMERICAN LEGION
2035 North Highland Avenue

Hollywood Post 43 was the late President Ronald Reagan's until 1982, when he transferred his membership over to Pacific Palisades, where he owned a house at the time. Post 43 can also boast a batch of other star legionnaires among its former ranks. Among them: Gene Autry, Clark Gable, Conrad Nagle, old-time cowboy star Art Acord, and Adolphe Menjou—one of Hollywood's most notorious "squealers" during the McCarthy witch hunt of the early 1950s. The American Legion building—a dazzling neo-Mesopotamian temple designed in 1929 by architect Eugene Weston Jr.—ranks with the best of Hollywood's fantasy architecture.

During the late 1980s, the building doubled for several years as an Italian villa for the avant-garde theatrical event *Tamara,* during which the audience followed the actors from room to room, choosing which scene and actors they wanted to view.

39. THE HIGH TOWER
End of Hightower Drive

Are you in Hollywood—or Bologna? One of Hollywood's most enchanting architectural oddities, this Italian-looking tower actually conceals an elevator that services the houses on the top of the hill. Built in the 1920s as part of a development known as the Hollywood Heights, the area and its "high tower" were used extensively as locations in United Artists' *The Long Goodbye*

Hollywood Heights sight:
the High Tower

(1973) starring Elliott Gould and Nina Van Pallandt. Directed by Robert Altman, the film was based on the Raymond Chandler novel of the same title. In 1991, the Tower and one of the cliff-hanging houses above it were featured in the climactic finale of another thriller, *Dead Again*, which paired the then hot British acting duo Emma Thompson and Kenneth Branagh, who were at the time married to each other.

High Tower Drive is off Camrose Drive, which lies just west of Highland Avenue, not far from the Hollywood Bowl.

40. HOLLYWOOD BOWL
2301 North Highland Avenue

The sylvan setting for this world-famous outdoor amphitheater was originally known as Daisy Dell. In early Hollywood, it was often used by silent filmmakers as a location for low-budget Western movies. Its location days were interrupted in 1919, however, when a Mrs. Christine Witherill Stevenson of the Pittsburgh Paint fortune felt Hollywood needed a little "serious" culture and went about forming a group that purchased Daisy Dell with the idea of presenting religious plays there. Bickering over the cost of a proposed theater structure for the site quickly brought about the dissolution of Mrs. Stevenson's high-minded group and a new organization acquired the Dell and began using it for public concerts as well as for sunrise services on Easter. Today, the Easter services and the concerts continue at what is now known as the Hollywood Bowl.

The dramatic concrete band shell that most people associate with the Bowl was built in 1929; it was preceded by various other structures, two of them designed by Frank Lloyd Wright's architect son, Lloyd Wright, who is credited with inspiring the Bowl's concentric-circle shape. One of the classic symbols of "Hollywood," the Bowl has appeared in a number of films set in the city. In the 1937 version of *A Star Is Born*, Esther Blodgett (Janet Gaynor) meets a very drunk Norman Maine (Fredric March) at a Bowl concert near the beginning of the film. In *Anchors Aweigh* (1945), sailors Gene Kelly and Frank Sinatra come across José Iturbi practicing before a Bowl concert.

Hollywood Bowl, 1985

While many assumed that the current Bowl would always be around, by the year 2000, the seventy-year-old structure was starting to show signs of serious decay and the County of Los Angeles decided to replace rather than restore the band shell. Needless to say, the news instantly raised concerns in the pre-servationist community—especially when it came out that the replacement might be rectangular in order to improve the acoustics. But, happily, a new design, inspired by the 1929 model, was ultimately approved, so the new Hollywood Bowl, which bowed in 2004, did not have to be rechristened the Hollywood *Rectangle*.

Open year-round on the Bowl grounds, the Hollywood Bowl Museum celebrates the architectural, musical, and cinematic history of this famed amphitheater. For information on opening times, call 323–850–2058. For concert information and to book tickets, call 323–850–2000. Visit www.hollywoodbowl.com.

41. HOLLYWOOD HERITAGE MUSEUM/DEMILLE BARN
2100 North Highland Avenue

In 1913, a New York film company decided to make a feature-length cowboy movie "on location." The site chosen for the production was Flagstaff, Arizona—but upon arriving there, the film's director was said to have found the territory a little too realistic, what with warring cattlemen and sheep ranchers taking potshots at one another. Instead of returning East, the intrepid director continued westward and wound up in Hollywood, California. There, he set up headquarters in a horse barn that he rented from a local named Jacob Stern. That director went on to become a legend in the motion picture business—he was Cecil B. DeMille. His partners in the project did pretty well, too. One was Jesse Lasky and the other was Samuel Goldfish (later Goldwyn). And their Western, *The Squaw Man*—the film that DeMille directed while using a horse barn as a studio—is consid-

DeMille Barn/studio—now the Hollywood Heritage Museum

ered to be the first feature ever shot within the borders of the town of Hollywood.

Jacob Stern's barn might have gone the way of most of the makeshift "studios" used in Hollywood's early silent days were it not for the foresight of DeMille and Lasky who, in 1927, had it moved to the back lot of Paramount Studios. At Paramount, the barn's exterior was often used for Western films—and its interior became the studio gym, where stars like Fred MacMurray, Gary Cooper, Cornel Wilde, Burt Lancaster, and Kirk Douglas stayed in Paramount-perfect shape.

As long as DeMille or Lasky were at Paramount, the barn was safe. But after they were gone, then what? DeMille, realizing how quickly Hollywood forgets, managed to have the barn declared a California Historic Landmark in 1956—a designation that would make it difficult for later generations to tear it down. In 1979, however, Paramount decided that, historic landmark or no, the barn had no place in the renovations it was planning for the studio. So it gave the barn to a division of the Hollywood Chamber of Commerce known as the Historic Hollywood Trust, which moved it to a parking lot on Vine Street until someone could come up with something more interesting to do with it.

To the rescue came a vital new organization—dedicated to preserving the landmarks of Hollywood's past—called Hollywood Heritage. Through a great amount of effort, this enthusiastic group of private citizens found a permanent home for the barn on Highland Avenue across from the Hollywood Bowl. Today, Hollywood's oldest extant movie studio has been restored and is the town's first museum dedicated to the history of silent motion pictures. Among the treasures inside are vintage photos of early filmmaking and screen stars, exhibits of ancient cameras and other moviemaking equipment, even a working nickelodeon. The museum also has numerous temporary exhibits as well as lectures, play readings, and chats with historians and film world VIPs.

For museum hours and special events information, call 323–874–2276 or visit www.hollywoodheritage.org; then click on museum.

42. WHITLEY HEIGHTS

For a feeling of what Hollywood was really like in the 1920s, perhaps no other neighborhood expresses it better than this little-known hilltop enclave of Mediterranean houses just north of Hollywood Boulevard and east of Highland Avenue. Built by an important Los Angeles developer of the early twentieth century named H. J. Whitley, Whitley Heights was to be his dream development, the final achievement of his career. Here, smack in the middle of Hollywood, he would create an authentic Italian hilltown—and, in order to get it just right, he sent his chief architect to Italy to study the age-old secrets of hillside construction and landscaping. Ground was broken for the project in 1918 and the building of Whitley Heights continued feverishly for the next eight years.

Immediately popular with the silent set, Whitley Heights became Hollywood's first "Beverly Hills," if by that we mean a rather exclusive area with an unusually heavy concentration of celebrities. In fact, screenland's first movie-star house tours started bringing sightseers up to Whitley Heights in the early

Venice in Whitley Heights: Villa Vallambrosa

Rudolph Valentino and Natacha Rambova outside their Whitley Heights home in the 1920s

1920s. Among the many stars who lived here at the time, the biggest of them all was Rudolph Valentino who, at the height of his career between 1922 and 1925, resided at 6770 Wedgewood Place with his second wife, Natacha Rambova. The house was torn down in 1947 to make way for the Hollywood Freeway.

It is not what is gone but what remains in Whitley Heights that makes the neighborhood so fascinating. Awarded National Historic Register status in 1982, Whitley Heights preserves beautiful tile-roofed Mediterranean houses that were home to everybody from Richard Barthelmess, whom Lillian Gish described as "the most beautiful man who ever went before a camera," to Barbara La Marr, who was known as "the girl who was too beautiful" and who died of "nervous exhaustion" at the age of twenty-nine.

The Barthelmess house—where Norma Talmadge was a frequent visitor, even though she was married to powerful producer Joe Schenck at the time—sits above Whitley Terrace at 6691, fronted by a balustrade topped with pineapple-shaped finials.

Next door to where Barthelmess lived, the large villa at 6697 Whitley Terrace was once owned by director Robert Vignola. William Randolph Hearst is said to have handpicked Vignola to direct many of the films made by Marion Davies in the 1920s since Hearst knew that Vignola was a homosexual and could therefore be trusted with Miss Davies. Hearst is also rumored to have built the Vignola house as a hideaway for himself and Miss Davies.

The Barbara La Marr house—suspended above the hillside at 6672 Whitley Terrace—is said to have had a secret passageway between the chauffeur's quarters and Miss La Marr's boudoir.

Farther along Whitley Terrace, at 6660, an odd but attractive house that resembles a fat round tower was home to, at various times, character actor Joseph Schildkraut, *Lost Horizon* author James Hilton, Rosalind Russell, and, last and longest, character actress Beulah Bondi, who resided there from 1941 until her death in 1981.

Mediterranean magic:
Whitley Heights mansion

Continuing along Whitley Terrace, the pretty house with terraced gardens and various balconies at 6621 was—according to local lore—used as a location in Bette Davis's 1942 film classic *Now Voyager*. (Bette was also a former Whitley Heights resident—her house, however, was torn down in 1962 to make room for a Hollywood Museum that was never built.)

Still farther along Whitley Terrace, steep Whitley Avenue may seem familiar to many filmgoers since it often doubles for a San Francisco street in movies as well as in television shows. The street where Burgess Meredith sold his miracle medicine in *The Day of the Locust* (1975) was Whitley Avenue. Beyond the intersection of Whitley Terrace and Whitley Avenue, the house with the massive fortresslike garage at 2015 Whitley Avenue was once Jean Harlow's.

On the other side of the Heights, Janet Gaynor and her husband, costume designer Adrian, lived at the end of Watsonia Terrace (number 2074) in the beautiful three-story villa that looks as though it should be in Venice. Called Villa Vallambrosa, it was built in 1922 by socialite Eleanor De Witt—who leased it over the years to Dame Judith Anderson, Danny Thomas, and Leonard Bernstein. A few houses away, at 2058 Watsonia Terrace, there's another villa with an impressive rental history: William Faulkner, in Hollywood to write screenplays for Columbia, lived here—as did Gloria Swanson, who took the place in 1949–1950 and resided here with her mother while making her great screen comeback in *Sunset Boulevard.*

The best way to see Whitley Heights is on an organized walking tour of the area. These are given several times a year by the Whitley Heights Civic Association and provide a chance to go inside a number of historic houses. For information on when tours are given, write: Whitley Heights Tours, P.O. Box 1008, Hollywood, CA 90078. For those who want to explore the area on their own, the easiest way to reach Whitley Heights is to head up Whitley Avenue from Hollywood Boulevard or to go north on Highland Avenue and turn right onto Milner Road. Whitley Heights can be seen both by car (there's virtually no parking, however, so a drive around is recommended) or by foot (steep climbs involved). Also see www.whitleyheights.com.

William Holden's *Sunset Boulevard* digs: Alto-Nido Apartments

43. ALTO-NIDO APARTMENTS
1851 North Ivar Avenue

This hill-topping California-Spanish apartment building is where we see unemployed screenwriter Joe Gillis (William Holden) working at his typewriter in the early part of Billy Wilder's classic 1950 film about Hollywood, *Sunset Boulevard*. Gillis soon finds "employment" as writer/gigolo-in-residence with aging silent-film star Norma Desmond (Gloria Swanson). And we all know how that arrangement played out. Today, the little apartment building, overlooking the Hollywood Freeway (which wasn't there when *Sunset Boulevard* was made), advertises "Old World Charm . . . Superb Views."

44. PARVA SED APTA APARTMENTS
1817 North Ivar Avenue

Author Nathanael West moved into this odd-looking Hollywood-Tudor apartment building with the equally odd name (it means "small but suitable" in Latin) in 1935. From this base, he got to know the neighborhood prostitutes, hung out at nearby Musso & Frank Grill on Hollywood Boulevard, wrote screenplays, and made notes for what would be one of the greatest novels ever written about Hollywood: *The Day of the Locust*. Ironically, the book was not a commercial success at the time of its publication in 1939. West died a year later in a car crash that also killed his wife, Eileen McKenney, sister of Ruth McKenney, the author of *My Sister Eileen*. At the time, more was made of her death than of his, and it was another ten years before Nathanael West was "discovered" by the literary establishment. The film version of *The Day of the Locust,* directed by John Schlesinger in 1974, met with as little initial success as the novel that inspired it. Today, however, it is a cult classic.

45. HOLLYWOOD KNICKERBOCKER HOTEL
1714 North Ivar Avenue

By the 1920s, the flourishing film industry was turning small-town Hollywood into a city that would have a population of more than 150,000 by the end of the decade. To meet the needs of these boom years, a number of big hotels like the eleven-story Knickerbocker were built in downtown Hollywood. The Knickerbocker opened in 1925 and was popular with celebrities between coasts, between marriages, and between studios. Early guests included Rudy Vallee, Gloria Swanson, Dick Powell, and Bette Davis. When Errol Flynn arrived in Hollywood, he made the Knickerbocker his base. Later, Frank Sinatra and Elvis Presley would also stay here early in their careers.

The hotel has been the scene of a number of Hollywood's more bizarre happenings. In 1936, the widow of escape artist Harry Houdini held a well-publicized séance on the Knickerbocker's roof, during which she tried to contact her dead husband. Then, in 1943, the hotel found itself in the news when police broke into the room of low-on-her-luck "Paramount

Pretty" Frances Farmer. Claiming she had failed to report to her parole officer for an earlier drunk driving/disorderly conduct conviction, the police dragged the unfortunate Frances half-nude and screaming obscenities across the Knickerbocker lobby. (Actress Jessica Lange re-created this harrowing scene in the 1982 biopic *Frances.)*

In 1962, the hotel again was part of lurid headlines when famous MGM costume designer Irene *(Gaslight, State of the Union, Easter Parade)* registered at the Knickerbocker in the morning, tried unsuccessfully to slash her wrists later in the day, and then leapt to her death from the eleventh floor. Newspapers attributed her suicide to depression over business problems as well as the recent death of her husband. Two days before, she had displayed her latest collection at a fashion show in Beverly Hills.

Another tragic event connected with the hotel took place in July 1948 when pioneer silent film director and producer D. W. Griffith suffered a fatal cerebral hemorrhage in his rooms at the Knickerbocker, where he lived alone. Griffith, seventy-three years old at the time, had not made a film since 1931 and was ignored by the industry he helped found. Nonetheless, his funeral service at the Hollywood Masonic Temple a few days later brought out some three hundred film industry celebrities. In his eulogy, Charles Brackett, a producer and then vice president of the Academy of Motion Picture Arts and Sciences, said: "It was the fate of David Wark Griffith to have a success unknown in the entertainment world until his day, and to suffer the agonies which only a success of that magnitude can engender when it is past. There was no solution for Griffith but a kind of frenzied beating on the barred doors. Fortunately, when he is dead, a man's career has but one tense. The laurels are fresh on the triumphant brow. He lies here, the embittered years forgotten."

Today the Hollywood Knickerbocker is a retirement hotel.

46. THE HOLLYWOOD USO SITE
1641 North Ivar Avenue

Now home to a film company, this Ivar Avenue building was formerly what was unofficially called the Bob Hope USO Club from 1973 to 1988. A caricature of the late comic's distinctive profile (and proboscis) adorned the club's façade. Hollywood's connection with the USO (United Service Organization) is a long one, going back to 1940 when it opened the first club of its kind where servicemen and -women on leave could hang out, dance, and be entertained. Bob Hope's connection with the Hollywood USO went back almost as far, beginning in 1941, when he first put together a Christmas show for U.S. servicemen at the March Air Force Base east of Los Angeles. The following Christmas saw Hope and his troupe entertaining the troops in Alaska—and in 1943, he went overseas for the first time. From then on his USO shows became legends of the entertainment industry and starred almost every major movie sex goddess from Betty Grable to Marilyn Monroe to Raquel Welch.

What many thought would be Bob Hope's last overseas USO show was his final visit to Vietnam in 1972—but in 1983, at age eighty, he once again revived the tradition of entertaining outside of the United States by taking Ann Jillian, Cathy Lee Crosby, Vic Damone, George Kirby, Julie Hayek (Miss USA), and Brooke Shields to the Eastern Mediterranean where the performers did a number of shipboard shows for U.S. forces stationed in Lebanon. And if that wasn't enough, at age eighty-eight, he hit the road one final time in 1991 to entertain Desert Shield troops in Bahrain.

Today, although the Bob Hope USO is closed in Hollywood, another branch of the organization bears the late comedian's name at the Los Angeles International Airport.

47. FRANCES HOWARD GOLDWYN HOLLYWOOD REGIONAL LIBRARY
1623 North Ivar Avenue

Named for the wife of mogul Samuel Goldwyn—whose charitable foundation came across with $3 million to fund a replacement for Hollywood's 1940 library, which was destroyed by arson in 1982—this unusual 1986 building is the work of world-famous L.A.-based architect Frank O. Gehry. With its stark straight lines and steel-and-glass façade, the library is a far cry from Gehry's later and more news-grabbing buildings, such as the Guggenheim Museum in Bilbao, Spain, and the new Disney Concert Hall in downtown L.A., which feature curvy asymmetrical metallic shells.

48. HOLLYWOOD GUITAR CENTER/ROCK WALK
7425 Sunset Boulevard

A prime pilgrimage stop for the rock 'n' roll crowd, the Hollywood Guitar Center not only sells the latest in guitars, key-
boards, and sound equipment, but since 1988 has been
immortalizing music-industry legends with its collection of handprints and signatures out front along its Rock Walk. Currently,
there are some 150 rock stars and groups represented—from
Aerosmith to ZZ Top. Induction ceremonies take place frequently and the public is welcome.

*For information on Rock Walk inductions, call 323-874-1060 or
visit www.rockwalk.com.*

49. HOLLYWOOD HIGH SCHOOL
1521 North Highland Avenue

When it opened in 1904, it was bounded by bean fields and a
lemon grove—and some students arrived on horseback. As one
of the oldest high schools in Los Angeles, it counts among its distinguished graduates Norman Chandler, former publisher of the
Los Angeles Times; Nobel Prize winner (for co-inventing the
transistor) William Schockley; 1960s activist Episcopal Bishop
James J. Pike; and former Secretary of State Warren Christopher.
Not to mention all of the show-biz people who have been part
of Hollywood High's student body through the years. Among
them: Mickey Rooney, Judy Garland, Fay Wray, Gloria Grahame, Nanette Fabray, Marie Windsor, Marge Champion, Jason
Robards Jr., Alexis Smith, Ruta Lee, Sally Kellerman, Linda
Evans, Ricky and David Nelson, Carol Burnett, Yvette Mimieux,
Stephanie Powers, Mike Farrell, James Garner, Joel McCrea,
Anita Louise, Tuesday Weld, Barbara Hershey, Swoosie Kurtz,
John Phillip Law, John Ritter, and Lana Turner (who was not
discovered at Schwab's Drugstore but at the Top Hat Malt Shop
across the street from Hollywood High on the southwest corner
of Sunset and Highland; the site is now a fast-food restaurant).

Today, Hollywood High has three thousand students. The
school's administration building, at the corner of Highland and
Sunset, is a 1936 landmark of Streamline Moderne architecture,

whereas the enormous, celebrity-studded *Portrait of Hollywood* mural on the auditorium building on Highland is a contemporary reminder of this institution's unique history.

Visit www.hollywoodhighschool.net.

50. HOLLYWOOD ATHLETIC CLUB
6525 Sunset Boulevard

This imposing 1924 Spanish-style hulk—built by Meyer and Holler, the same firm that did Grauman's Chinese and Egyptian theaters—began its life as Hollywood's ultimate health club. Indeed in the 1920s and 1930s, every major male star in town was a member of this ultra-exclusive swim-and-gym organization. Johnny "Tarzan" Weissmuller and Buster Crabbe did laps in the club's huge pool, John Wayne tossed billiard balls from the roof at passing cars on Sunset, and Walt Disney, after a nervous breakdown, worked out in the club's gym at the suggestion of his doctor.

Among the many stars who stayed here at one time or another

Hollywood Athletic Club

were Charlie Chaplin, Rudolph Valentino, Bela Lugosi, Bud Abbott, and Lou Costello. The Club's grandest "digs" were the five rooms that made up its penthouse suite. These were often leased (under assumed names) by Hollywood's early playboys—and although women were not allowed in the penthouse tower, security guards were rumored to have been somewhat lax when it came to enforcing this rule.

In 1949, the Athletic Club was used for the first televised Emmy Awards broadcast. From the mid-fifties until the late seventies, the building was taken over by a religious school and uninspired remodelings did away with much of its original splendor. In 1978, however, local entrepreneur Gary Berwin took over this Hollywood landmark and began a long and expensive restoration process that turned the place into an office/entertainment complex. The early 1990s saw the ground floor of the building become a trendy billiard hall and nightclub. It has since closed but is available for film shoots. Among the films and TV shows that have used it recently have been *Introducing Dorothy Dandridge* (1999), the TV series *Profiler,* and PBS's *Unsolved Mysteries.* In 2003, director Quentin Tarantino staged the premiere party for his film *Kill Bill: Volume 1* here, which saw all of young Hollywood converge on this Old Hollywood landmark.

Call 323–462–6262 or visit www.hollywoodathleticclub.com.

51. CINERAMA DOME/ARCLIGHT THEATERS
6360 Sunset Boulevard

Four decades after the era of Hollywood's great movie palaces—characterized by Grauman's Egyptian (1921), Grauman's Chinese (1927), the Warner (1927), and the Pantages (1930)—along came the Cinerama Dome. The year was 1963 and the Dome's premiere attraction, *It's a Mad Mad Mad Mad World,* seemed an appropriate offering to introduce this bizarre bit of 1960s theater architecture. Built in a decade when America was mesmerized more by technology than by motion pictures, the Dome boasted not only a futuristic geodesic shell but an ultrawide Cinerama screen and stereo sound system.

Always a great place to see spectacle films that came off best the bigger the screen, the eight-hundred-seat Dome got a shot in the arm when it was completely restored in 2002 as part of the exciting new ArcLight cinema complex that was built behind it. The updated Dome now has cushy new seats, an enormous new concave screen, and an amazing twenty-first-century sound system with forty-four computerized surround sound speakers strategically positioned throughout the house. Best of all, for die-hard movie buffs, the theater has been equipped with three restored vintage Cinerama projectors, all of which are called on for special showings of the early three-strip/three-projector Cinerama films, including a restored version of the original *This Is Cinerama* (1952) travelogue, with the famous roller-coaster ride.

Meanwhile, the adjacent ArcLight complex ushers in a bold new era as arguably the first true movie palace of the twenty-first century. A courtyard set off by fountain-like walls of water gives way to the enormous, stylishly minimalist lobby—with a bookstore, sleek restaurant/cocktail lounge, balcony cafe, and frequent museum-quality exhibits on film and filmmaking. Toward the back of the lobby, a grand staircase leads to ArcLight's fourteen "Black Box" auditoriums, where ushers in black escort

Cinerama Dome Theater

patrons to their luxurious, reserved business class–style seats and where no one is admitted after the feature has begun. The only downside is the price of admission—$14 a pop on weekends—which some movie lovers find exorbitant. (And at least one movie star, Faye Dunaway, reportedly felt the same way. When told the price, the diva supposedly tried to cop a comp, saying "Don't you know who I am?" Although the ticket seller recognized the living legend, she still had to fork over the full amount.)

In addition to first-run films, ArcLight has an impressive on-going program of film festivals and celebrity-hosted screenings of classic movies. Among the stars who have appeared here have been writer-producer Sidney Sheldon, actress Julianne Moore, actor Gary Sinise, director Rob Marshall, and writer/director Kevin Smith. But so far not Miss Dunaway.

For information on ArcLight films and special programs, visit www.arclightcinemas.com.

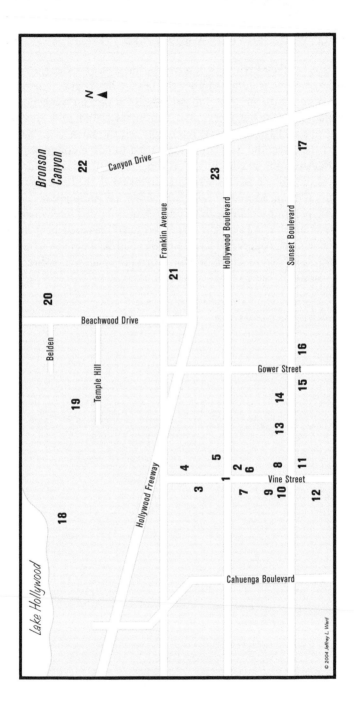

Lake Hollywood

Bronson
Canyon

Canyon Drive

Franklin Avenue

Hollywood Boulevard

Sunset Boulevard

Beachwood Drive

Belden

Temple Hill

Gower Street

Vine Street

Hollywood Freeway

Cahuenga Boulevard

N

18

20

22

21

23

17

19

16

15

14

13

5

4

2

6

8

11

1

3

7

9

10

12

© 2004 Jeffrey L. Ward

Hollywood: Beyond the Boulevard

Central Hollywood—
Between Vine and Western

Starting with Vine Street and heading east, most of Hollywood's major sights are no longer on Hollywood Boulevard. Instead, they turn up on Sunset Boulevard, Franklin Avenue, and on Vine Street itself. (The two great exceptions to this generalization are the new Hollywood and Vine Metro Rail Station and the spectacular Pantages Theater, both of which are on Hollywood Boulevard just east of Vine.) On Sunset Boulevard, the attractions range from historic motion picture studios to the vestiges of Hollywood's once great radio industry to fabulous 1940s nightclubs, many of which are today enjoying renewed popularity as part of L.A.'s thriving club scene.

Franklin Avenue—the main street that is north of both Sunset and Hollywood boulevards—is more residential. Of particular interest to movie lovers are Franklin Avenue's spectacular château apartment houses that were built in the 1920s to accommodate the many motion picture people who commuted between New York and Hollywood. And since most of these imposing structures have been restored in the last decade, their essential splendor can now be appreciated as never before, as can their juicy histories. Other attractions in the area include the exclusive housing development that the famous Hollywood Sign was built to promote, secret spots used as locations in classic films, a landmark house created for a silent superstar who met a tragic end in the 1960s, an early residence of Charlie Chaplin, and, last but not least, one of Hollywood's greatest unsolved mysteries.

The first seventeen sites listed in this chapter can be seen on a walking tour. The last group are best visited by car.

1. "HOLLYWOOD AND VINE"
Intersection of Hollywood Boulevard and Vine Street

Everyone's heard of it—but in person, it may be the most disappointing intersection on earth. Indeed, an ongoing debate among local history buffs centers around how Hollywood and Vine came to symbolize the movie capital at its most glamorous. The most plausible theory attributes Hollywood and Vine's notoriety

Bob Cummings and Marsha Hunt crossing Hollywood and Vine, 1936

to the fact that many of Hollywood's important radio studios were located on and around Vine Street in the 1930s. Historians go on to argue that since "brought to you from Hollywood and Vine" was a familiar opening to many an early broadcast, the intersection came to be thought of as glamorous because it *sounded* glamorous—especially to the millions of radio listeners who had never actually seen it.

Today, the intersection, which has historic 1920s office buildings on three of its four corners, seems to be lagging behind in Hollywood's current revitalization flurry. But ambitious plans call for major renovations of these buildings, a Motion Picture Hall of Fame within one of them, and even a trendy three-hundred-room hotel just down the block at Hollywood Boulevard and Argyle Avenue. As they used to say on the radio, stay tuned.

2. HOLLYWOOD AND VINE METRO RAIL STATION

For the moment, the most exciting development on Hollywood and Vine is underground. Designed by Chicano artist Gilberg "Magu" Lujan, the new Hollywood and Vine Metro Rail Station is a whimsical celebration of Hollywood's film history.

Star stop: Hollywood and Vine Metro station

The fun starts aboveground where stretch limo– and brown derby–shaped pavilions provide shelter from the elements and where a mini-movie marquee stands above the elevator entrance. Taking the escalator down to the trains, passengers come across a veritable art gallery of 240 tile paintings, depicting Hollywood and L.A. scenes. Continue along the "Yellow Brick Road" through Egyptian-columned corridors and find a dramatic installation created from gigantic 1930s-era movie projectors. Down by the tracks, the ceilings are studded with recycled film canisters, and those squashed-automobile sculptures are actually benches. The station is even equipped to show videos and films for special events. Worth a visit, even if you aren't going anywhere.

3. AVALON/HOLLYWOOD PALACE SITE
1735 North Vine Street

With its handsome Spanish-baroque façade and its gleaming Art Deco lobby, it came on the Hollywood scene back in 1927 as a legitimate theater called the Hollywood Playhouse. Then came the Depression and the Works Project Administration took over the place and continued to use it for plays and shows until 1939. After that, the Hollywood Playhouse was occasionally used as a radio studio (CBS's *Baby Snooks,* starring Fanny Brice, originated from here) until 1942 when a new owner changed the theater's name to El Capitan, and Ken Murray came along with his famous *Blackouts* revue. When it closed in 1949, *Ken Murray's Blackouts* had become the longest running show in U.S. entertainment history—playing 3,844 performances at El Capitan.

Next came television: the Bob Hope *Chesterfield Sound Off Time* show, *This Is Your Life,* and the *Jerry Lewis Show* were among the shows telecast from El Capitan. Then, in 1964, ABC changed the theater's name to the Palace and began beaming the *Hollywood Palace* variety show from here. Bing Crosby was often a host of this very successful series and an unknown beauty named Raquel Welch was a card-carrying *Hollywood Palace* showgirl. After the series ended in 1970, the Palace continued to be used for television productions, the most famous being the *Merv Griffin Show,* which was based here for four years.

Today, the historic theater, now known as Avalon, is a key player in Hollywood's emergence as L.A.'s nightlife capital, hosting rock and pop groups, hip-hop, and house parties. It's also used for television specials and music videos. On the feature-film front, the former Palace was a location for *Against All Odds* (1984) and the Tina Turner biopic *What's Love Got to Do with It?* (1993).

To check what's on at Avalon, call 323–462–8900 or visit www.avalonhollywood.com.

4. CAPITOL RECORDS TOWER
1750 North Vine Street

Used in countless films and television shows to "establish" the fact that we are in Hollywood, the Capitol Records Tower is a symbol not just of Hollywood but of the city's powerful role in the recording industry. Rising thirteen stories and standing 150 feet tall, the Capitol Records Tower was (on account of a 1905 Los Angeles building-height-limit law that had more to do with aesthetics than with earthquakes) as high as any building in Los

Capitol Records Tower

Angeles could be back in 1955. Some have said the building's whimsical, stack-of-records shape was the idea of then Capitol superstar Nat King Cole and Capitol songwriter/cofounder Johnny Mercer. The architect of this Hollywood landmark, which even though it's pushing fifty still looks as fresh as tomorrow, was Welton Becket who, a decade later, would build another local landmark—the Music Center complex in downtown Los Angeles.

For years, music lovers could go inside the Capitol Records building's lobby and check out the gold and platinum records displayed inside. Alas, in today's security-conscious environment, that is no longer possible.

5. PANTAGES THEATER
6233 Hollywood Boulevard

One of the most splendid Art Deco theaters in the world, the Pantages opened in 1930 with MGM's *The Floradora Girl* starring Marion Davies. In addition to the film, the "mixed bill" included an edition of Movietone News, a Walt Disney cartoon, a stage piece, and Slim Martin conducting the Greater Pantages Orchestra. The real star attraction, however, was the theater itself—with its lavish auditorium, lounges, lobbies, staircases, and restrooms. A theater where the comfort of the moviegoer came before economics, the Pantages gave over 40 percent of its interior space to public areas, and every detail—from the tiled water fountains to the stylized exit lights—was a work of art.

Originally built by the great theater-circuit mogul Alexander Pantages, the Pantages actually opened as a Fox theater since Pantages was serving a jail sentence at the time for a rape conviction that was later overturned. In 1949, the theater was acquired by Howard Hughes, who changed its name to the RKO Pantages. It was during its RKO era that the Pantages was the site of the Academy Awards presentations (1949 to 1959). Pacific Theatres bought the Pantages in 1967 and a decade later joined forces with the Nederlander theater organization to turn it into a legitimate playhouse for road companies of Broadway musicals such as *The Lion King, The Producers,* and *Hairspray*—all based on successful films, by the way. Major refur-

Lobby luxe: Pantages Theater

bishing and renovations have brought the Pantages back to its original dazzle and today it is still one of the most spectacular theaters on earth.

Next door to the theater, movie lovers may recognize the Frolic Room, with its distinctive neon sign, from the 1997 film *L.A. Confidential,* as a Hollywood bar where Kevin Spacey leaves a $50 tip.

To find out what's on at the Pantages, call 213-365-3500 or visit www.nederlander.com/wc.

6. BROWN DERBY SITE
1628 North Vine Street

When Hollywood lunched in the 1930s and 1940s, the Brown Derby was the place to go to see and to be seen. In those days, crowds would jam the Derby's entrance waiting to be seated at what was Hollywood's most famous restaurant—and head waiter Bill Chilios would just let them stand until all of the regulars were seated. Chilios took good care of the regulars. Occa-

sionally he went too far. Once, for example, when Groucho
Marx arrived at the Derby in the company of the wife of radio
producer Carroll Carroll, Chilios refused to seat them until he
was sure everything was on the up and up. For the Brown Derby
was a very public place—a place where news was made (Clark
Gable proposed "officially" to Carole Lombard in booth 54),
photographs taken, interviews given, and the more times you
were paged and had a telephone brought to your table, the better it looked. You didn't do any serious business at the Derby—
you confirmed (or tried to confirm) your status as an important
member of the Hollywood establishment.

Although the Vine Street Brown Derby called itself the "original" Brown Derby, it was actually the second of what was ultimately a chain of four restaurants started by a former husband
of silent-screen queen Gloria Swanson (and father of her daughter Gloria), Herbert Somborn. His first venture, a lunch counter
on Wilshire, opened in 1926; this was the Brown Derby in the
shape of the hat. The Vine Street branch opened in 1929 and was
followed by a Beverly Hills operation in 1931 and a little-known
Los Feliz branch in 1941. While the Derbys are often confused,
it is the Vine Street Brown Derby that became the most famous
because of its proximity to the movie and radio studios. It was
here, for example, that Lucy Ricardo famously grappled with her

The Brown Derby, 1937

Infamous lunch: Lucy with William Holden at the Brown Derby

spaghetti while ogling William Holden seated in an adjacent booth in a classic episode of *I Love Lucy* in the 1950s.

In the sixties, the Brown Derby, along with many businesses in central Hollywood, started to decline. The restaurant managed to hold on until 1985, when it closed abruptly, to reopen briefly at a different location on Hollywood and Vine. But it wasn't the same and this venture ultimately failed. Today, most of the original Brown Derby building has been torn down, but Hollywood archeologists recognize that a tiny section of it survives as the Star Hair Nails salon.

7. PLAZA HOTEL/IT CAFE SITE
1637 North Vine Street

One of many 1920s Hollywood hotels turned old-age homes, the Hollywood Plaza was, in its day, especially popular with radio people since most of the broadcast studios were either on, or just off, Vine Street.

In 1937, silent films' hottest Jazz Baby, Clara (the "It Girl") Bow, her film career long over, opened a nightclub adjacent to the Plaza and called it, appropriately, the It Cafe. Alas, the It was a short-lived affair—yet another of Miss Bow's comeback tries

The original "It" Girl:
Clara Bow

that didn't pan out. One of the main reasons for the demise of Miss Bow's film career was a major Hollywood scandal of 1930 that forever shattered her reputation—and her peace of mind. Miss Bow's troubles started when a secretary whom she fired got back at her by selling the "secrets" of her former employer's love life to a sleazy New York tabloid. Of all the revelations that sprang from this newsmaking affair, the most spectacular was one that had Miss Bow "entertaining" the entire starting lineup of the University of Southern California football team—including a tackle named Marion Morrison who would later achieve screen fame as John Wayne. Even though Clara took her secretary to court and won, the story of Clara Bow and the USC Trojans remains one of Hollywood's most enduring myths.

As for the term "it," it was taken from Bow's 1927 film of the same name, penned by racy novelist/screenwriter Elinor Glyn. In the 1930s, "it" pretty much went the way of Clara's career, but it came back into vogue in the Swinging Sixties, when Brit model Twiggy and actress Julie Christie were at the top of the It list. Then in 2000, It surfaced again, when *Vanity Fair* magazine christened a whole new generation of It Girls, proclaiming Gwyneth Paltrow not just an It Girl but an Uber-It Girl. Just what is It? Most agree it's that indescribable something that separates the person who has it from the rest of the pack. Call it star quality—or just call it It.

8. WASHINGTON MUTUAL BANK
1500 North Vine Street

This massive bank building—a 1970s American version of Mussolini-Moderne architecture—celebrates Hollywood's past with the names of hundreds of movie stars inscribed on its white-marble façade. Accompanying the names are colorful mosaic images of legends like Garbo, Valentino, Pickford, Fairbanks, Chaplin, Davis, Cooper—even Nanook of the North! Inside, the Hollywood theme goes on—with huge murals depicting scenes from Cecil B. DeMille's 1913 film *The Squaw Man.*

The first feature-length motion picture ever made in Hollywood, *The Squaw Man,* was shot a block away, near the corner

Washington Mutual Bank:
Mary Pickford mosaic

of Vine and Selma. With the film's success, Jesse Lasky, one of its producers, was able to expand his studio to include the present-day location of the Washington Mutual Bank (formerly the Home Savings and Loan Association). Ultimately, Lasky's Feature Players Company occupied the entire block between Sunset and Selma from 1914 to 1926. (A plaque marks the spot—incorrectly—at the northeast corner of Vine and Selma.)

Lasky's was the studio that became Paramount, and it was on this site that Mary Pickford made some of her first Hollywood films and Rudolph Valentino made many of his. After Paramount moved to Melrose Avenue in 1926, the Sunset/Vine studios became everything from a rental lot to a miniature golf course. Then, in 1938, NBC Radio leveled the works to build its massive Moderne Radio City—which was a major Hollywood landmark until it was torn down in 1964.

9. RICARDO MONTALBAN THEATER
1615 North Vine Street

Renamed in 2004 for former MGM Latin Lover and later the star of the hit TV series *Fantasy Island,* the Ricardo Montalban is now owned and managed by Nosotros, a nonprofit organization founded by Montalban to promote positive images of Latinos in the performing arts. This theater has had many lives. It opened in 1927 as a legitimate house called the Vine Street Theater. By the mid-1930s, it was taken over by Hollywood's burgeoning radio industry and became the CBS Playhouse Theater. It was from here that the famous *Lux Radio Theater*—hosted by C. B. DeMille and featuring major stars in radio versions of current movies—emanated. In 1954, the theater once again went "legit" and was named the Huntington Hartford, after the millionaire A&P heir who bankrolled its renaissance. For the next forty years, the Huntington Hartford (and after yet another name change, the James E. Doolittle Theater) was used for local productions as well as road companies of Broadway plays. In its newest life, it will feature mainly, but not exclusively, shows of interest to the Latino community.

Call 323–465–4167 or visit www.nosotros.org.

10. SUNSET & VINE
1555 North Vine Street

Another instance of New Hollywood paying homage to its past, this mixed-use complex sports updated Streamline Moderne architecture and features three hundred apartments as well as 85,000 square feet of retail space. For movie lovers, the most exciting commercial tenant at Sunset & Vine is Schwab's, being touted as a nostalgic remake of the drugstore/soda fountain of the same name that stood for decades at 8024 Sunset Boulevard in West Hollywood, where it was a popular hangout for "under-employed" actors, writers, and directors, until it closed down in 1983 and was eventually torn down to make way for a mall. In the film *Sunset Boulevard* (1950), Schwab's appears frequently, referred to as "headquarters" by out-of-work screenwriter Joe Gillis (William Holden). Movie lore also credits Schwab's as the soda fountain where Lana Turner was discovered. That event actually took place at the Top Hat Malt Shop across the street from Hollywood High School, where Lana was a student, on the southwest corner of Sunset and Highland. It, too, bit the dust decades ago and today is a Burger King.

Call Schwab's at 323-462-4300.

11. SUNSET AND VINE TOWER
6290 Sunset Boulevard

Standing twenty stories tall, this is Hollywood's loftiest structure. Built in 1963, when improved construction techniques allowed earthquake-prone Los Angeles to reach heights it never dreamed possible, the L.A. Federal Savings and Loan Building was nonetheless one of the skyscrapers that almost bit the dust in the 1974 Universal film *Earthquake*. Ironically, the building suffered serious real damage in the 1994 Northridge earthquake and has been closed down ever since. Current plans call for it to be turned into an apartment tower.

12. PICKFORD CENTER FOR MOTION PICTURE STUDY
1313 North Vine Street

Besides handing out Oscars, the Motion Picture Academy of Arts and Sciences is deeply involved with a number of other film-related activities. One of the most important of these is preservation—and with the opening in late 2002 of the Pickford Center, the Academy has a new high-tech home for its extensive film archive. Named for Mary Pickford, one of the world's first movie stars as well as one of the founders of the Academy, the Center is housed in a historic mid-century Moderne building that was erected in 1948 for the Don Lee Mutual Broadcasting Network. Today, it is the oldest surviving structure in L.A. that was built specifically for television. In the 1950s, it was the site of many early TV shows, including the long-forgotten *Carson's Cellar,* starring guess-what-fledgling-talk-show host. Today, seven of the original eight concrete TV studios have been turned into state-of-the-art film vaults, where the temperature is a carefully monitored 45 degrees Fahrenheit. The remaining studio is now a three-hundred-seat screening room used for private and public film showings. The Center also administers something called the *Academy Players Directory,* an annual publication listing thou-

Don Lee Mutual Broadcasting Studios—now Pickford Center for Motion Picture Study

sands of Screen Actors Guild members, who pay $75 to be included along with their photo in this industry bible that goes to all the major and minor casting directors in the country.

Visit www.oscars.org/facilities/pickford.html.

13. WORLD PALLADIUM
6215 Sunset Boulevard

During the big band days of the 1940s, this was where they all played and where all of L.A. came to listen and to dance. Originally built by *L.A. Times* publisher Norman Chandler, the Palladium opened in 1940 with Tommy Dorsey, who was featuring, at the time, a skinny young vocalist from New Jersey named Frank Sinatra. Among the many stars who were regulars at the Palladium, two lovely ladies—Alice Faye and Betty Grable—wound up marrying boys in the band (Phil Harris and Harry James, respectively).

By the 1950s, the big bands played less frequently and the Palladium started doing more private parties and banquets. But Lawrence Welk changed the Palladium picture at the beginning of the 1960s when he began broadcasting his immensely popular television show from here. Besides the *Lawrence Welk Show,* the Palladium has also been used for numerous Emmy, Grammy, and Golden Globe Awards telecasts. The famous club has had a minor movie career, too—and has appeared in everything from *The Day of the Locust* (1975) to *F.I.S.T.* (1978) to the 1979 clunker *Skatetown, U.S.A.,* in which its vast dance floor was turned into a roller-skating rink, but which is more notable for being Patrick Swayze's film debut. Today, rock groups and stars—from the Rolling Stones to Billy Idol—are frequently booked into the Palladium, and it is still used for television specials as well as for major Hollywood bashes. It's also big on the Latino music circuit.

14. KNX COLUMBIA SQUARE
6121 Sunset Boulevard

When the Centaur Film Co. of Bayonne, New Jersey, came to Hollywood in 1911, they found an old roadhouse called the Blondeau Tavern on the northwest corner of Sunset and Gower

Street. A victim of a recent prohibition ordinance passed by the ultraconservative residents of early Hollywood, the tavern proved to be a suitable—and available—place for the company to set up their operations, which they called the Nestor studio. The Eastern filmmakers wasted no time and within a matter of days started churning out the first films ever produced in the town of Hollywood. Mostly one-reel Westerns and comedies, these early films were directed by a man named Al Christie, who, with his brother Charles, continued to produce Christie Comedies at the corner of Sunset and Gower up until the beginning of the 1930s. After that time, their studio became a rental lot.

CBS entered the picture in 1936 when it razed the old Nestor/Christie studios and broke ground for its Columbia Square radio complex. Among the many famous radio broadcasts that originated from these CBS studios were *Burns and Allen, Beulah, Edgar Bergen and Charlie McCarthy, The Saint, Our Miss Brooks,* and the *Lucky Strike Hit Parade.* Still standing in the same spot, the CBS building, despite renovations, is an architectural classic—designed with the clean bold lines and great simplicity that exemplified an offshoot of Art Deco known as the International Style. Today, Columbia Square is home to the CBS-owned news radio station KNX.

Visit www.knx1070.com.

15. GOWER GULCH
Corner of Sunset Boulevard and Gower Street

In the 1920s, there were so many small storefront movie studios along Gower Street that the area came to be known as Poverty Row. At the same time, the corner of Gower and Sunset got the nickname Gower Gulch because of the large numbers of celluloid cowboys and Indians who hung out here—often in costume—waiting for bit parts or extra work in the low-budget one- and two-reel Westerns that many of the Poverty Row studios produced. Today a small shopping center occupies a corner of what once was Gower Gulch. Built in 1976, a time when Hollywood was starting to take its own history seriously, the Gower Gulch Shopping Plaza resembles a back-lot Western street with board-

Movie cowboys at Gower Gulch in the 1930s

walks and frontier-town façades. In its own way, this little mall pays homage to the past whereas so many other shopping centers and parking lots built over historic Hollywood sites have not.

16. SUNSET-GOWER STUDIOS
1438 North Gower Street

Today, this vast studio is a thriving rental lot—affiliated with Paramount-Viacom—where HBO's *Six Feet Under* is the current star tenant. It's also been home to *General Hospital* and *Days of Our Lives*, although they are now shot elsewhere.

For film-history buffs, however, the Sunset-Gower Studios are noteworthy because from 1926 until 1972 they were the headquarters of the Columbia Pictures Corporation. Columbia started out as a small independent studio in the early 1920s when the Cohn brothers—Harry and Jack—and a third partner named Joe Brandt began making short comedies under the banner of the CBC Film Sales Company. By the time they took over the California Studios at 1438 North Gower in 1927, they had changed their company's name to the classier-sounding Columbia. Gower

Queen of Columbia:
Rita Hayworth

Street at the time was known as Poverty Row since it was the center of numerous small and often fly-by-night studios. Columbia, however, turned out to be Poverty Row's only real success story and the studio quickly increased in size through taking over a number of failing Poverty Row operations.

During the 1930s, Columbia came to fame largely through director Frank Capra's string of successful comedies that often used stars borrowed from other studios. The first and still one of the most famous of these Capra classics was *It Happened One Night* (1934) with Clark Gable (on loan from MGM) and Claudette Colbert (on loan from Paramount). The picture won Columbia its first Academy Award.

By the time the 1940s rolled around, Columbia had manufactured its own great star. When she was discovered in the late 1930s, this young castoff from Fox had a widow's peak, a weight problem, and an ethnic last name (Cansino)—and she hardly seemed a candidate for the superstar status she would attain. But Columbia boss Harry Cohn played his hunches and ordered the studio to put the young woman under contract, on a diet, and to fix her hairline as well as her name—and thus Rita Hayworth was born. In the mid-1950s, she handed over the title of resident glamour goddess to another Columbia beauty and Cohn creation: Kim Novak. In 1958, Harry Cohn—one of the last of the old-time studio bosses—died and an era ended. He was buried a few blocks away at Hollywood Memorial Cemetery in a plot that he had specially selected so that he could keep an eye on his studio.

Since Cohn's day, Columbia has bounced around Hollywood and corporate America quite a bit. In 1972, after a major reorganization several years earlier, the company moved across the Hollywood Hills to Burbank, where it shared Warner Bros.' studios for many years. The years 1977–1978 saw Columbia weather one of the greatest scandals in the history of the entertainment industry. The problems began when it came out that David Begelman—the president of Columbia who had turned the company around with films like *Funny Lady* and *Close Encounters of the Third Kind*—had forged some $75,000 worth of checks. To make matters worse, it was alleged that a number of other studio bosses had attempted to cover up the incident. In 1982, Columbia was purchased by the Coca-Cola Corporation and then changed hands again in 1989, when the Sony Corporation bought it for a whopping $3.4 billion. This eventually involved yet another move, this time to the former MGM lot in Culver City, which had been taken over by Sony in 1991. Somehow it was all simpler back in the Cohn era.

17. KTLA
5800 Sunset Boulevard

This handsome Greek Revival building was erected in 1918 by a quartet of movie-mogul brothers named Warner. It was here that Warner Bros. perfected a technique that would change the course of motion picture history—namely synchronized sound. Contrary to popular belief, Warners' 1927 *The Jazz Singer* was not the first commercial sound film. That honor goes to Warners' 1926 *Don Juan*, which featured a synchronized track of musical accompaniment by the New York Philharmonic Orchestra. Then came *The Jazz Singer* in 1927 with synchronized songs and some synchronized dialogue. The first true "all-talking" picture, *The Lights of New York*, was released by Warner Bros. a year later.

In 1929, Warner Bros. took over the former First National

Studios in Burbank and made them its main base of operations. The Sunset Boulevard facilities were subsequently used for the production of Warners' animated cartoons—Porky Pig, Bugs Bunny, and Daffy Duck. In 1942, Warners' Sunset studios were acquired by Paramount; after that, they were converted into one of the world's largest bowling centers—with fifty-two lanes. In the early 1960s, back in show business again, the lot was used by CBS Television, which shot episodes of hit series such as *Gunsmoke, Have Gun Will Travel,* and *The Twilight Zone* here. Star cowboy and media mogul Gene Autry (1907–1998) bought the property in 1964 as headquarters for his Golden West Broadcasters company. Today his former radio station, KMPC, and television station KTLA are based here. And coming full circle, KTLA TV is now part of the WB (as in Warner Bros.) Network.

Visit www.ktla.com.

18. *DOUBLE INDEMNITY* HOUSE
6301 Quebec Street

"It was one of those California Spanish houses everyone was nuts about ten or fifteen years ago—this one must have cost

Double Indemnity house

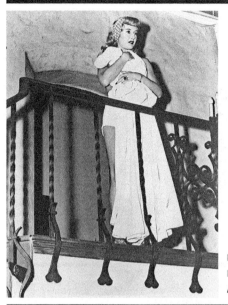

Dressed to kill:
Barbara Stanwyck in
Double Indemnity

somebody about thirty thousand bucks." So speaks Fred Mac-Murray as insurance investigator Walter Neff at the opening of Billy Wilder's classic 1944 film, *Double Indemnity*. And as soon as MacMurray utters the line, the audience in the revival cinema breaks into gales of laughter because the house up there on screen would easily cost thirty times that much in the booming real estate market of today's Los Angeles.

In the film, the house belongs to Barbara Stanwyck's character, Phyllis Dietrichson, and to the husband (played by Tom Powers) she and MacMurray plot to kill. It appears in many scenes, the most memorable being the one in which Stanwyck helps her husband—he's on crutches owing to an unforeseen accident—down the front steps to the garage where MacMurray is hiding in the backseat of the LaSalle ready to strangle him to death.

The house, which sits on a quiet corner up in the Hollywood Hills, is not easy to find. Movie lovers should consult a good map to get to Quebec Street—and take care not to disturb the occupants.

The Home of Charles Chaplin, Beverly Hills, California.

Charlie Chaplin's Hollywood (not Beverly) Hills house

19. CHARLIE CHAPLIN HOUSE
6147 Temple Hill Drive

According to a 1923 postcard, this enchanting little castle was once the home of Charlie Chaplin. The house is not in Beverly Hills, however, as the postcard says. It is in the lower Hollywood Hills on Temple Hill Drive north of Franklin Avenue and west of Beachwood Drive. Mary Astor is another movie person who is said to have lived here.

Temple Hill Drive is a marvelous pocket of early Hollywood fantasy architecture; a quick spin around it will reveal a number of other exotic villas, castles, and tiny Arabian palaces.

20. HOLLYWOODLAND AND THE HOLLYWOOD SIGN
Beachwood Drive at Westshire Drive

High in the Hollywood Hills and visible from almost anywhere in the Hollywood "flats," the Hollywood Sign has come to symbolize the city of Hollywood in much the same way as do Grauman's Chinese Theater, the intersection of Hollywood and Vine, and the Marathon Street Gate of Paramount Pictures. Unlike these other Hollywood landmarks, however, the sign has no connection with the entertainment industry. Instead, it originally represented the one Hollywood business that is—and always has been—even bigger than showbiz: real estate.

When the Hollywood Sign was erected in 1923, it didn't spell Hollywood—but rather "Hollywoodland," which was the name of the urban utopia that *L.A. Times* publisher Harry Chandler and two other local big-businessmen were developing in the Hollywood Hills. Their dream development (where silent movie producer Mack Sennett had his lot all picked out but never built) boasted architectural styles that included Norman castles, Elizabethan cottages, Moorish mansions, and Spanish haciendas. All were advertised as being "above the traffic congestion, smoke, fog, and poisonous gas fumes of the Lowlands." (It would seem that air pollution was a Los Angeles problem even in the idyllic 1920s; it would be christened "smog" some two decades later.)

While perhaps not the utopia promised by its developers, the Hollywoodland/Beechwood Canyon area remains one of Hollywood's loveliest neighborhoods. It is approached by driving north on Beachwood Drive and continuing through the handsome Hollywoodland Gates at Westshire Drive. The storybook

Hollywood Sign

cottage to the right is the original—and still functioning—office of the Hollywoodland Realty Company. To the left, the intersection of Beachwood and Belden was immortalized in the original *Invasion of the Body Snatchers* (1956) as the center of the small California town whose zombielike populace Kevin McCarthy and Dana Wynter tried to escape. A large still of this scene from the 1956 Allied Artists film hangs above the produce counter of the Beachwood Market at 2701 Belden Drive.

A drive up Beachwood will reveal the intriguing architectural diversity of the area, an area that remains much as it was in the 1920s and 1930s and one that has been traditionally favored by screenwriters as a quiet place to live and to write. Looming over this beautiful fantasyland, the famous sign has had a life of its own quite separate from the real estate development it was built to advertise. The most famous event associated with the sign was the suicide jump of Peg Entwistle, a young actress who tried to parlay her success on the Broadway stage into a Hollywood film career. Unfortunately things didn't work out "just like in the movies" and in September 1932, Miss Entwistle climbed to the top of the *H* and jumped to her death 50 feet below.

Despite this tragic event, life went on in Hollywoodland. But as the development prospered, its huge emblem was allowed to deteriorate until all maintenance of the sign was discontinued in 1939. Finally, the dilapidated structure was deeded to the Hollywood Chamber of Commerce, which removed the last four letters in 1945 in an attempt to make the sign represent the whole city of Hollywood. In subsequent years, the sign has been restored several times, the most extensive restoration being that of 1978 when a major Save the Sign campaign succeeded in raising enough money to create a brand-new, super-reinforced version of the famous 45-foot-tall, 450-foot-long, 480,000-pound sheet-metal landmark.

21. CELEBRITY CENTRE INTERNATIONAL/CHATEAU ELYSEE
5930 Franklin Avenue

Of all the "château" apartment buildings erected in Hollywood during the booming 1920s, none was more impressive than the Château Elysée. Built in 1928 by the widow of the famous early movie producer Thomas Ince, the Château Elysée—sometimes known as Château Ince, but usually just as "the Château"—was designed by prominent architect Arthur E. Harvey as a luxury hotel in the form of a gigantic seven-story Norman castle. Originally this grand hotel had seventy-seven apartments, and the celebrities who resided here, both short- and long-term, included some of the most famous names of the 1930s. Cary Grant was a former tenant, and in the early 1980s he returned to the Château to show his old apartment to his new wife, Barbara Harris. According to Château records, Gable and Lombard also lived here in the 1930s and hid away (they weren't yet married) in apartment 604; George Burns and Gracie Allen spent some of their early Hollywood days in 609; Ginger Rogers shared 705 with her mother, Lela; and Lily Pons had an opulent multilevel suite (416) that had three bedrooms and three baths but no kitchen. No need for that, as a dazzling "European" dining room served meals and also provided room service.

The center of the film world's "château life" in the 1930s, the Elysée was often the scene of glamorous parties and saw frequent visits by Hollywood nobility dwelling in nearby "castles." Hum-

Scientology's Château Elysée

phrey Bogart, for example, is said to have once lived a few blocks away in the Hollywood Tower (6200 Franklin Avenue) and often came over to the Château to play tennis. Another neighbor was Gloria Swanson—who is rumored to have shared luxurious secret quarters at Castle Argyle (1919 Argyle) with her mentor/lover Joseph Kennedy.

Like all fairy stories, there was a dark side to some of the glamour at the Château Elysée, for there was always talk that the hotel may have concealed one of Hollywood's greatest unsolved mysteries. The secret of the Château was that it was not Mrs. Ince's money that built the castle but rather that of newspaper heavyweight William Randolph Hearst. The basis for this story goes back to the mysterious sudden death of Thomas Ince while on a weekend outing aboard Hearst's yacht *Oneida* in 1924. The official version of *l'affaire Ince,* as it came to be known, was that Ince suffered an acute attack of gastritis aboard the boat and was quickly taken to his home in Beverly Hills, where he died. A far juicier account of the incident purports that Ince was shot aboard Hearst's yacht and suggests that the person who pulled the trigger was none other than William Randolph Hearst! The reason for the supposed shooting is even more bizarre. It seems that Hearst suspected his movie-star girlfriend, Marion Davies, of having a fling with Charlie Chaplin. Both Chaplin and Davies were aboard the *Oneida* and when Hearst found Davies alone in a cabin with a man he thought to be Chaplin, he fired. The man, however, was not Chaplin but Ince. Everyone on board was then sworn to secrecy, including a young Hearst columnist named Louella Parsons, whose career supposedly started to soar once *l'affaire Ince* blew over.

Meanwhile, poor Mrs. Ince was out a mate, and many people have speculated that Hearst financed Château Ince because of his guilt over having killed the woman's husband by mistake. It is also speculated that Hearst built the Villa Carlotta across the street from the Château at 5959 Franklin Avenue for the same reason. (Louella Parsons was an early Villa Carlotta resident.) So the story goes . . . and goes. Peter Bogdanovich's 2001 film *The Cat's Meow*—released in 2004—takes on the Ince affair with Edward Hermann as Hearst, Kirsten Dunst as Davies, Eddie Izzard as Chaplin, Jennifer Tilly as Parsons, and Cary Elwes as Ince.

In 1952, the Château Elysée was turned into a luxury retirement hotel called Fifield Manor. In 1973, the building was acquired by the Church of Scientology of California. Today, after a long and thorough restoration process, Scientology—whose high-profile members include John Travolta, Tom Cruise, Kirstie Alley, and Lisa Marie Presley—has returned the Elysée to its former splendor and has also opened its glittering Renaissance dining room to the public. Visitors, even if not dining here, are welcome to take a quick peek inside at what is once again the grandest of Hollywood's châteaux.

For reservations at the Renaissance Restaurant, call 323-960-3100 or visit www.celebritycentre.org.

22. BRONSON CANYON
Griffith Park and Canyon Drive

Before it became fashionable—and feasible—to shoot films on location all over the world, movie studios stayed as close to home as possible. After all, what were all those soundstages and back lots for, anyway? There's an old Hollywood story about a young director who told producer Sam Goldwyn that he needed an out-of-town location for the picture he was working on.

Made in Bronson Canyon: *The Cyclops*

Replied Goldwyn: "A rock's a rock, and a tree's a tree. Shoot it in Griffith Park!" And with some 4,000 acres of pastoral scenery, Griffith Park was not only the largest municipal park in the country, it was a godsend to early moviemakers as a location.

A prime Griffith Park location has always been Bronson Canyon, which was used for such early swashbuckler epics as Douglas Fairbanks's *Robin Hood* (1922) and *The Three Musketeers* (1933), which starred John Wayne. Since the canyon looks like everyone's fantasy of the Wild West, it has furnished backgrounds for countless Westerns—from Gene Autry's old Saturday matinee series *The Phantom Empire* to numerous episodes of *Gunsmoke, High Chaparral, Bonanza, The Lone Ranger,* and *Little House on the Prairie,* to name but a few television series that have shot episodes here. Especially popular as a setting for science-fiction films are the nearby Bronson Caves. Batman stored his Batmobile in one of these caverns in the 1960s TV series; Kevin McCarthy and Dana Wynter hid out in another at the end of *The Invasion of the Body Snatchers* (1956); and all manner of extraterrestrial creatures and monsters have lived and died in the Bronson Caves in 1950s' films such as *Night of the Bloodbeast, Robot Monster, The Cyclops,* and *It Conquered the Earth.* The caves can also be seen in *Star Trek VI: The Undiscovered Country* (1991), cult director Sam Raimi's *Army of Darkness* (1993), Robert Altman's *Short Cuts* (1993), and *The Scorpion King* (2002), the sword-and-sandals spinoff of *The Mummy,* starring pro-wrestler the Rock.

To reach Bronson Canyon, drive north on Bronson Avenue until it turns into Canyon Drive. Continue north on Canyon until you enter Griffith Park; then follow the sign to Bronson Canyon. From there, the caves are a short hike to the east.

23. FLORENTINE GARDENS
5951 Hollywood Boulevard

Never one of Hollywood's most glamorous nightspots, this 1940s club featured Italian food and a tacky, often risqué floor show. It was the kind of place where working people went for a night on the town. And when sixteen-year-old Norma Jean Baker

Hollywood hot spot: Florentine Gardens

married twenty-two-year-old factory-worker Jim Dougherty in June 1942, the wedding party celebrated the event at Florentine Gardens. The couple never had a honeymoon, and the marriage ended four years later as Norma Jean Baker Dougherty was starting a new life with a new name . . . Marilyn Monroe.

After numerous owners and lives (one of which featured stripper Lili St. Cyr as the headliner and another saw the building used as a Salvation Army post), Florentine Gardens is currently thriving as a rock club, which, in addition to live groups, frequently features some of L.A.'s hottest DJs.

To find out what's on, call 323-464-0706.

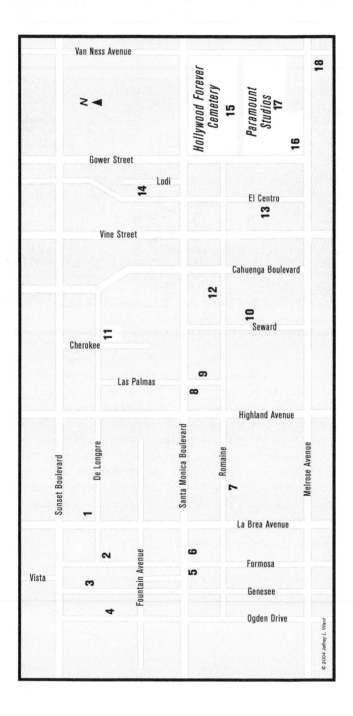

Van Ness Avenue

N

Hollywood Forever Cemetery 15

Paramount Studios 17

16

18

Gower Street

Lodi 14

El Centro 13

Vine Street

Cahuenga Boulevard

12

10

Seward

Cherokee 11

9

Las Palmas

8

Highland Avenue

Sunset Boulevard

De Longpre

Santa Monica Boulevard

Romaine

Melrose Avenue

1

7

La Brea Avenue

2

Fountain Avenue

6

Vista

3

5

Formosa

4

Genesee

Ogden Drive

© 2004 Jeffrey L. Ward

Hollywood: The Factory Town

Central Hollywood —
South of Sunset Boulevard

South of Sunset Boulevard lies a great flat section of Hollywood where massive moviemaking installations share space with tiny streets of Spanish bungalows and Craftsman-style cottages fronted by neatly tended lawns and gardens. This is the center of Hollywood, the factory town—but from the look of things, this is a factory town straight out of the movies. It's all surprisingly attractive, especially on the side streets, where the feeling is often one of a small Southern California community. It's all a little strange too, since the great studios and film processing plants that cover the area seem to have almost no architectural relationship to their environment. The studios, the dream factories, stand like alien, private worlds that appear to be outside the scheme of things. Yet, they are the heart of things.

Today, little has changed in this part of Hollywood. The little streets with their bungalows and cottages are still here, many now housing Latino and Asian families. The movie plants are still here as well. In fact, the area—now officially called the Hollywood Media District—continues to have one of the world's greatest concentrations of movie-related industries, and even though many historic early movie lots have changed owners and names a number of times over the years, the lots themselves continue to flourish, turning out not only films, but television shows, commercials, and music videos.

Of all the studios in this part of Hollywood, the most famous still in operation is Paramount—which has been in exactly the same spot since 1926. But for the movie buff, much of the fun involved with discovering this neck of the Hollywood woods will no doubt have to do with seeing what's become of vanished studios like RKO, Charlie Chaplin, and United Artists. Another of the treats in store for the movie lover south of Sunset is the Forever Hollywood Cemetery. Built smack in the middle of studioland, this wonderfully theatrical cemetery is where some of the greatest names in the motion picture industry have been laid to rest amid an exotic setting of palms, obelisks, and temples worthy of a Cecil B. DeMille epic. No wonder Mr. DeMille himself chose to be buried here.

This chapter covers a lot of ground and the sites mentioned here should be seen by car.

1. THE JIM HENSON COMPANY/CHAPLIN STUDIOS
1416 North La Brea Avenue

A statue of Kermit the Frog now stands at the entrance of this row of fairy-tale Tudor cottages, announcing that it is now the domain of Jim Henson Productions. Kermit is dressed, however, as the Little Tramp, the character made famous by the studio's original owner, Charles Chaplin, who built the lot as part of the independent production company he founded in 1918. For a while, Chaplin lived at the studio in a large Tudor mansion off Sunset that had a tennis court and stables. Today the house is long gone, but inside the Jim Henson complex many of the original Chaplin Studios' buildings remain, notably the main soundstage (Chaplin's "duckwalk" footprints are embedded in the cement in front of this structure)—plus dressing rooms, carpentry shop, and stables. Chaplin had the studio until the early 1950s and made most of his classics here. Among them: *A Dog's Life* (1918); *The Kid,* with Jackie Coogan (1920); *The Gold Rush* (1925); *City Lights* (1931); *Modern Times* (1936); and *The Great Dictator* (1940).

Chaplin Studios, 1929

After Chaplin sold the studio and left the country—having been targeted by the McCarthy witch hunt for his leftist leanings—it changed hands numerous times. Subsequent owners included American International, Red Skelton, and CBS. From 1952 to 1957, many episodes of the popular TV series *Superman,* starring the late George Reeves, were filmed on this lot. *Perry Mason* was also made here, and Raymond Burr (taking a cue from Chaplin?) is said to have had his own apartment on the property. In 1966, A & M Records, headed by Herb Alpert, took over the premises, restored them, and made them its headquarters. During the A & M era, Charlie Chaplin's original soundstage was often used for the taping of music videos (the Police's "Every Breath You Take," Ray Parker Jr.'s "Ghostbusters," and the Stevie Wonder sequences of his duet with Paul McCartney "Ebony and Ivory," among them) as well as for filming commercials and TV specials. The Muppets entered the picture in 2000, but in early 2004, they became part of another famous show business family, the Walt Disney Company, which bought the Jim Henson Company. So far, however, Kermit—not Mickey Mouse—still reigns at the studio entrance.

Visit www.henson.com.

2. COURTYARD APARTMENTS
1328–1330 North Formosa Avenue

There are so many stories associated with this little cluster of rose-covered "Hansel and Gretel" cottages that we may never know the truth about them. Some people say the buildings were constructed by Charlie Chaplin as a movie set; others say that Chaplin built them as stables; still others insist that Chaplin used them as dressing rooms and guest quarters. Given the proximity of Chaplin's studios, a Chaplin connection would seem plausible—although neither the building permits nor the assessor's records make any mention of the man.

More Hollywood stories center on the famous people who have lived in the cottages over the years. Naturally, Valentino heads the list (he did get around!), followed by the Munchkins who supposedly stayed here during the filming of *The Wizard of Oz*. (In truth, these little folk were put up at a full-sized hotel over in Culver City near the MGM Studios where the movie was filmed.) Marilyn Monroe is another name one hears in connection with this location—and the stories go on and on. No matter who lived here, these 1923 buildings are historic from an architectural point of view—since the original building permits list the name Zwebell as the architect. Zwebell was actually the last name of a husband and wife, Arthur and Nina, architect team who later were responsible for a number of notable Los Angeles courtyard apartment buildings, the most famous being the Andalusia (1926) in West Hollywood. Built in 1923, the Formosa Avenue Zwebell apartments would appear to be one of the couple's earliest works.

3. *A NIGHTMARE ON ELM STREET* HOUSE
1428 North Genessee Avenue

With an M.A. in philosophy, former professor of humanities Wes Craven has a surprising background for a man whose name has become synonymous with some of Hollywood's scariest films. His first big hit, *A Nightmare on Elm Street* (1984), dealt with a group of teenagers plagued by intensely terrifying dreams that involved a monstrous-looking man named Freddy Krueger with a hideously burned face and a brown floppy hat. Most of the

A Nightmare on Elm Street house

teens—including a nineteen-year-old Johnny Depp in his first major screen role—were no match for Freddy, and they wound up dying horrific deaths. (Or did they?) Only a young woman named Nancy (Heather Langencamp) figured out how to face up to Freddy. In the film, Nancy lived in a pretty Dutch Colonial–style house on tree-lined Elm Street. Her rather undersexed boy-pal Glenn (Depp) lived across the street. Both the street and Nancy's abode saw a lot of action in the film—what with Glenn's climbing in and out of the upstairs window, not to mention Freddy's frequent comings and goings. Today the house and the leafy West Hollywood street where *A Nightmare on Elm Street* was shot look exactly as they did in the 1984 film.

As for *Nightmare*'s creator, Craven, he went on to produce and often direct a whole slew of further Freddy Krueger flicks as well as a series of *Scream* horror films. So who said a philosophy degree would get you nowhere?

Lucille Ball's first Hollywood home

4. LUCY'S FIRST HOLLYWOOD HOUSE
1344 North Ogden Drive

Twenty-two-year-old Lucille Ball had been trying to break into show business in New York for almost five years when she finally got her big chance. The year was 1933 and Ball had been bounding around Manhattan studying acting, doing the occasional bit part in a road show, but mainly modeling. Then, one July afternoon, she just happened to run into an agent who told her about an open call for showgirls for a six-week job in Hollywood to be "background" in producer Samuel Goldwyn's latest RKO musical, *Roman Scandals*. Ball, who had recently been a Chesterfield cigarette poster girl, was chosen as a backup and ultimately got the job when another young woman's mother refused to let her travel to California.

Lucille liked L.A.—and she ultimately parlayed her gig as a Goldwyn Girl into a full-fledged RKO contract. But she also missed her family, so when she realized that Hollywood was going to be her home, she convinced her mother, DeDe, her brother,

Fred, and her grandfather, Fred Hunt, to move west as well. For their home, she rented a cozy little columned cottage on tree-shaded Ogden Drive between Sunset Boulevard and Fountain Avenue in Hollywood. Ball lived with the family for several years, until moving to her own, much more private apartment on nearby Laurel Avenue. Her family stayed on on Ogden, however, and it was here that her socialist grandfather held Communist Party meetings and got Lucy and her mother and brother to register to vote as Communists. Needless to say, this surfaced during the McCarthy Era, and at the beginning of the great success of *I Love Lucy,* Miss Ball was called to testify before the dreaded House Un-American Activities Committee. Luckily, the committee bought her explanation that she had registered to please her grandfather and that she had never been a Communist at any time in her life. In fact, in her later years, she would be much better known for her right-wing leanings.

5. THE LOT
1041 North Formosa Avenue

One of the town's most historic studio facilities, the Lot dates back to 1918, when producer Jesse D. Hampton turned out pictures here starring a well-known silent actor named W. B. Warner. Then in 1922, Mary Pickford and Douglas Fairbanks, who in 1919 along with Charlie Chaplin and D. W. Griffith had formed United Artists in order to free themselves of studio contracts and constraints, took over the Hampton lot and renamed it the Pickford-Fairbanks Studios. This is where Fairbanks turned out such swashbuckling classics as *Robin Hood* and *The Thief of Bagdad* and Pickford did *Tess of the Storm Country* and *Rosita.* Photos from the period show the mammoth sets of many of these early epics towering above Santa Monica Boulevard.

In 1928, with the addition of Samuel Goldwyn to the United Artists team, the Pickford-Fairbanks facility was renamed United Artists Studios and Goldwyn made the lot his permanent base. By 1936, the studio came to bear Goldwyn's name, although Mary Pickford retained principal ownership. Among the Goldwyn productions of this era were *Roman Scandals* (1933), *Nana* (1934), *Barbary Coast* (1935), *Dodsworth* (1936), *Stella Dallas* (1937),

United Artists: Mary Pickford and Douglas Fairbanks inaugurate their new studio, 1922

Wuthering Heights (1939), *The Little Foxes* (1941), *The Best Years of Our Lives* (1946), *Hans Christian Andersen* (1952), and *Guys and Dolls* (1955). The studio also saw Billy Wilder's *Some Like It Hot* (1959) shot here, with Marilyn Monroe, Tony Curtis, and Jack Lemmon. Goldwyn bought out Pickford in the mid-1950s and headed the studio until his death in 1974. The property was sold to Warner Bros. in 1980, who operated it for almost two decades, using it for both television series (Aaron Spelling's *Dynasty* and *Love Boat*, for example) and feature films such as *Basic Instinct* (1992) and *The Green Mile* (1999).

In 1999, the studio was sold again—to a company called BA Studios, which turned it into a rental lot and renamed it simply the Lot. An important tenant continues to be Warner Bros., which has its postproduction sound facilities here. Recent film production includes *Scary Movie II* (2002) and *The Majestic* (2002), which saw Jim Carrey cavorting on the same historic movie lot as Douglas Fairbanks did some eight decades earlier.

Visit www.warnerhollywood.com.

6. FORMOSA CAFE
7156 Santa Monica Boulevard

Since 1945, this little Chinese/American bar and restaurant has
served as unofficial commissary for the various movie studios in
the area. The closest of these studios was Samuel Goldwyn
(which became Warner Hollywood and is now the Lot), which
was literally a stone's throw away across Formosa Street. Inside
the long dinerlike building of the Formosa Cafe—created from a
trolley car that once traveled the long-lost Red Line along Santa
Monica Boulevard—practically every inch of wall space is taken
up with photos of the many stars who have dined here at one
time or another. Most of the photos are are signed with best
wishes to the Formosa's longtime owner Lem Quon, who died in
1994. (His grandson Vince Jung now runs the place.) Among
them are Orson Welles, Clark Gable, Marilyn Monroe, John
Wayne, Frank Sinatra, Bogey and Bacall, and Elvis Presley, who,
reportedly, gifted a Formosa waitress with a pink Cadillac. Current customers include Jodie Foster, Nicolas Cage, Matthew
Perry, Christian Slater, Kevin Spacey, Jim Carrey, and Shannon
Doherty, who, while having a bad-hair day, was arrested for

Formosa Cafe, 1985

smashing a bottle against a customer's car in the Formosa parking lot.

Over the years, the Formosa has had several brushes with the wrecker's ball. In 1991, Warner Bros., which owned the land occupied by the cafe, tried to evict the Formosa to make way for a parking lot. Regulars and preservationists joined forces, however, and managed to save the property by getting it declared a historic landmark. This status again helped protect it when the rest of the block it sits on was leveled in 2003 to make way for the humongous new West Hollywood Gateway shopping center.

Hollywood insiders have not only hung out at the Formosa but sometimes have used it as a location, most memorably perhaps in *L.A. Confidential* (1997), where detective Wendell White (Russell Crowe) meets up with gangster Johnny Stompanato and mistakes his gal-pal for a hooker lookalike of Lana Turner. It turns out, however, that it's the real Lana—and it also turns out that the *real* real Lana and her real mobster boyfriend Stompanato (whom her daughter famously stabbed to death in 1958) frequented the Formosa on a regular basis. Other Formosa screen appearances include Jim Carrey's *The Majestic* (2002), Vince Vaughn's *Swingers* (1996), and Brendan Fraser's *Still Breathing* (1998), in which Fraser dreams of meeting his future wife in Formosa, which turns out to be not an island off China but a restaurant in Tinseltown!

7. HOWARD HUGHES HEADQUARTERS SITE
7000 Romaine Street

A massive Babylonian-Moderne fortress was the longtime Hollywood headquarters of eccentric millionaire Howard Hughes. It was from here that Hughes controlled a vast empire that, at various times, encompassed film studios, movie theaters, aircraft factories, and Trans World Airlines. (He sold his stock in the latter for a cool $546 million in 1966.)

Hughes moved into 7000 Romaine Street in 1927. At the time he was involved with his Caddo Pictures company, which produced *Hell's Angels* (the 1930 film that unleashed Jean Harlow) as well as the original *Scarface* (1932), starring Paul Muni. Both films were edited on Romaine Street as was Hughes's controversial Jane Russell film, *The Outlaw,* which was completed in 1943

Howard Hughes's former Hollywood headquarters

but not released until 1946. The reason for the long interval between the picture's completion and its release was partially because of the censors and partially owing to Hughes's perverse personality: He would make the public want to see his film by withholding it from them as long as possible!

Hughes's legendary eccentricities were also responsible for the special film printing room at Romaine Street that had a series of doors in order to keep any dust from contaminating his precious film. Anyone entering the room was under boss's orders to vacuum their clothing ahead of time. There's another story about Hughes that had him experimenting with carrier pigeons at Romaine Street—and it is said that the cagelike structure still attached to the building was used during Hughes's pigeon period. Hughes died in 1976. Today, his former fortress is just another Hollywood office building, although many of the tenants are connected with the film business.

8. EASTMAN KODAK CO.
1017 North Las Palmas Avenue

Although a shadow of its former self—Kodak's current global payroll is 62,000 workers versus a peak of 136,500 in 1983—

this venerable company is still the world's premier maker and supplier of a certain commodity that Hollywood can't do without: film. Things are changing fast, however, what with the rise and constant perfecting of digital technology, which accounts for Kodak's recent downsizing. Since 1928, the company's classy Hollywood base for its Motion Picture Film Division has been this elegant Spanish Colonial palace. Behind the main building, a recent addition is an $8 million facility devoted to—guess what?—digital imaging technology. Over the years Kodak has won eight Academy Awards for scientific and technical excellence. Kodak is also the major backer of the new $94 million theater that bears its name on Hollywood Boulevard, where the annual Academy Awards ceremony is now held.

9. HOLLYWOOD CENTER STUDIOS
1040 North Las Palmas Avenue

Producer/director/screenwriter Francis Ford Coppola was the last big name to head this studio. Coppola had a dream: He wanted to create in the New Hollywood of independent producers and production companies a studio that would be run along the lines of the great Old Hollywood studios of the 1930s. For his Zoetrope Studios, Coppola would have a stable of contract players (Teri Garr and Raul Julia were among the actors he signed), writers, directors, technicians. Zoetrope would be a place where creative people would find a hospitable filmmaking environment rarely found in Hollywood. It would be a breeding ground for new talent as well as a place where veterans like writer/director Michael Powell *(The Red Shoes)* would have a chance to pick up their careers.

It was all a lovely idea—but, alas, Zoetrope's Hollywood studio was a financial disaster. Aside from *Hammett, One from the Heart,* and *The Escape Artist* (all 1982), the studio produced little in the way of motion pictures and even less in the way of profits. By 1983, money problems forced Coppola to sell the studio and return to the commercial realities of Tinseltown.

The studio where Coppola indulged his dream was founded in 1919 as a rental lot called Jasper Studios. In the mid-1920s, when comic Harold Lloyd split from producer/director Hal

Lucy and Desi
at work

Roach, Lloyd made this lot headquarters for his own production company. In 1929, Howard Hughes produced and directed *Hell's Angels* here and detonated blond bombshell Jean Harlow in her first major role. Another important independent who used the same studio was Alexander Korda, who lensed *That Hamilton Woman* here with Laurence Olivier and Vivien Leigh in the early forties.

By the time the 1950s rolled around, the Las Palmas lot was known as Hollywood General Studios and it became an important center of television production. Hollywood General (later known as General Service Studios and now called Hollywood Center Studios) was the home of *The Adventures of Ozzie and Harriet, Love That Bob, The George Burns and Gracie Allen Show, Our Miss Brooks, The Lone Ranger, The Beverly Hillbillies, Green Acres, Petticoat Junction, Mr. Ed, The Addams Family, Baretta,* and *The Rockford Files.* The studio also saw a lot of the most famous TV series in history, *I Love Lucy,* which shot at Hollywood General for much of its lifetime, from 1951 to 1957.

Today, the historic studio is one of Hollywood's busiest rental lots. Besides being home base for the country's current number-

Hollywood Canteen

one sitcom, *Everybody Loves Raymond,* Hollywood Center has leased stages to the following features: *The Running Man* (1987), *When Harry Met Sally* (1989), *The Player* (1992), *A Walk in the Clouds* (1995), *Scream 2* (1997), *Con Air* (1997), *Spawn* (1997), and *X-Men* (2000).

Visit www.hollywoodcenter.com.

10. HOLLYWOOD CANTEEN
1006 North Seward Street

With laminated wood walls, a low silver-leaf ceiling, and Streamline Moderne lighting fixtures, this stylishly updated diner sits in the heart of movie-studio Hollywood and could be the setting for a 1940s Raymond Chandler film noir. The food is also retro—chili, burgers, steaks, lamb chops, mashed potatoes, and world-class Cobb salad, which was invented at that long-gone Hollywood watering hole, the Brown Derby. A popular lunch spot for working film actors and crews, the place heats up at night with a celebrity crowd that since its 1990 debut has included Robert Downey Jr., Rob Lowe, Richard Gere, Lenny

Kravitz, Cindy Crawford, and Madonna. If you go, don't miss checking out the back garden, where a restored shiny Airstream trailer is the VIP lounge.

For reservations call 323-465-0961.

11. DELONGPRE PARK
Cherokee Avenue at DeLongpre Avenue

Strange bedfellows: In the middle of a little municipal park, Latino and Asian preschoolers play and shout, an occasional burned-out hippie relaxes on a park bench, and movie lovers will find a memorial to Hollywood's greatest screen lover—Rudolph Valentino. Erected in 1930 (four years after Valentino's death) by "friends and admirers from every walk of life, in all parts of the world, in appreciation of the happiness brought to them by his cinema portrayals," the memorial statue—entitled *Aspiration*—is of a nude male with head thrust back and looking up to the sky. Next to this statue, a bronze bust of Valentino completes the picture.

Rudolph Valentino in DeLongpre Park

12. HOLLYWOOD TELEVISION CENTER/
TECHNICOLOR SITE
6311 Romaine Street

From 1930 to 1975, this impressive Art Deco building housed the offices and laboratories of Technicolor, Inc., the company that made color a permanent part of the Hollywood picture in the early 1930s. The original Technicolor process was developed between 1914 and 1922 by Dr. Herbert Thomas Kalmus and some of his fellow alumni of the Massachusetts Institute of Technology. The name "Technicolor," it turns out, is in honor of MIT!

At first the process was used mostly for short subjects and for color sequences within otherwise black-and-white feature films. With Dr. Kalmus heading up Technicolor, Inc., his wife, Natalie, became the company's Color Director and was responsible for showing producers renting Technicolor equipment how to use it correctly. (Film buffs will remember that Mrs. Kalmus's name appears on the credits of all Technicolor films up until 1949, the year the patent ran out.)

The original Technicolor process was far from perfect. Using two negatives, it resulted in blurred images and in a color range limited to greens and oranges; pure blues and pure yellows were impossible to achieve. By 1931, however, Dr. Kalmus had developed a three-negative Technicolor process that resulted in colors that were practically flawless. The first producer to use the new process was Walt Disney, who began photographing his Silly Symphonies cartoons in advanced Technicolor in 1932.

The first three-strip Technicolor feature film debuted in 1935. The film was *Becky Sharp,* starred Miriam Hopkins, and was produced by two wealthy socialite cousins, John Hay ("Jock") Whitney and Cornelius Vanderbilt ("Sonny") Whitney. The same two gentlemen producers also bought 15 percent of Technicolor, Inc., and while *Becky Sharp* was not a great artistic or commercial success, Technicolor was. In fact, at its peak in the early 1950s, the Romaine Street headquarters had some 2,500 employees working round the clock—and it was here that some of Hollywood's most famous Technicolor films were processed and color corrected.

In 1975, Technicolor moved to North Hollywood and today its former headquarters house casting offices, postproduction facilities, and the film archives of the University of California at Los Angeles (UCLA), whose film department restored the original *Becky Sharp*—the one that started it all.

13. HOLLYGROVE
815 North El Centro Avenue

Formerly known as the Los Angeles Orphans Home Society, this institution dates back to 1880 and has stood on El Centro Avenue since 1911. Surrounded by movie studios and production facilities (Paramount, RKO, Technicolor, Western Costumes), it was here that ten-year-old Norma Jean Baker (Marilyn Monroe) came to live in 1935 after having been bounced around among several foster homes. Crying "I'm not an orphan" as she was taken inside the main building (no longer standing), Norma Jean would spend close to two years here, playing on its sports field, attending the nearby Vine Street School (955 North Vine), occasionally making excursions to downtown Los Angeles (during which she sometimes wore lipstick), plotting at least one escape attempt, and dreaming, perhaps, of a happier life. In 1980, a former "orphan" at the home during the mid-1930s remembered Marilyn in an interview with Lisa Mitchell that appeared in the July issue of *Westways* magazine: "She was a very generous person who would never say no to you if you asked her for something. I remember her sitting quietly at a piano we had there and playing for us. She always reminded me of a doe. A funny thing: In 1962, I got the feeling that I should write to her. Whether she'd remember me or not, I wanted to let her know she had a friend. I did write the letter and a month later, she passed away."

Today, Hollygrove—considerably modernized and relandscaped—provides residential care and treatment for emotionally disturbed boys and girls, ages five through ten.

14. YWCA HOLLYWOOD STUDIO CLUB
1215 Lodi Place

The Hollywood Studio Club was established in 1916 when the YWCA—Mrs. C. B. DeMille and Mary Pickford also lent their support to the project—saw the need to provide a decent place to live for the large numbers of young women who had come to

Former Hollywood Studio Club

Hollywood to work in the movies. Originally located in a former private home at 6129 Carlos Avenue, the first Studio Club housed Zasu Pitts, Carmel Myers, Mae Busch, Janet Gaynor, Marjorie Daw, as well as writer Ayn Rand. But this facility soon proved too small to accommodate the ever-increasing throngs of young hopefuls constantly arriving in Hollywood—and so, after an extensive fund-raising campaign, a new Studio Club was built at Lodi Place. Designed by architect Julia Morgan (her greatest achievement would be William Randolph Hearst's castle, San Simeon), the new building resembled a Renaissance palazzo and featured a trio of graceful arches at the entrance and a beautiful interior courtyard. The Lodi Place Studio Club went on to provide a Hollywood home to everyone from Peg Entwistle (the woman who jumped from the Hollywood Sign to her death in 1932) to Kim Novak, Dorothy Malone, Donna Reed, Nancy Kwan, Rita Moreno, Anne B. Davis, Barbara Eden, Sharon Tate, and Sally Struthers. Its most famous former resident, however, was Marilyn Monroe, who lived in room 334 for a short time in 1948 when she was doing walk-ons as a contract player at Twentieth Century–Fox. In the early 1970s, the club went coed, and by the mid-1970s, it looked as though it was going to close its doors permanently. But in 1977, the YWCA turned it into a training center for the Los Angeles Job Corps program and it is still being used for that purpose.

15. HOLLYWOOD FOREVER CEMETERY
6000 Santa Monica Boulevard

One of the great cemeteries of the world, Hollywood Forever is a dramatic fantasy world that could have been conceived by a Cecil B. DeMille or a D. W. Griffith as a background for an epic film. Inside, there are small Greek, Roman, and Egyptian temples; obelisks and urns, beautiful green lawns, and majestic palm trees. At the same time, Hollywood is everywhere: Paramount Studios—with its water tower soaring into the air—is smack against the cemetery's southern wall. To the north, the Hollywood Sign dominates the Hollywood Hills. No wonder that the insider Hollywood funeral in Robert Altman's *The Player* (1992) took place here. Yet, despite its location in the middle of Hollywood, the Hollywood Cemetery is a delightfully peaceful place and seems strangely set apart from the traffic-clogged city on the other side of its walls. All in all, it seems like an idyllic place for some of the most famous names of early Hollywood to have wound up.

Marion Davies mausoleum, Hollywood Forever Cemetery

The grandest graves are mostly clustered around a lovely little lake on the eastern side of the park. Here, Cecil B. DeMille is
next to his wife, Constance Adam DeMille. A striking double
tomb marks the spot. Across the way, Columbia's Harry Cohn
and his wife, Joan, have the exact same double marble marker as
the DeMilles. Also lakeside are Nelson Eddy, Adolphe Menjou,
Tyrone Power, John Huston, Janet Gaynor, Jayne Mansfield, and
Marion Davies. Miss Davies is buried in a massive white marble
mausoleum inscribed with her family name, Douras. Miss Mansfield, on the other hand, despite her flamboyant public life and
persona, has a simple stone slab that puts her age at twenty-nine,
when she was killed in an auto accident in 1967, though most
records list her as closer to thirty-four.

One of the newer lakeside monuments remembers Hattie Mc-
Daniel ("Aunt Hattie, you are a credit to your craft, your race,
and to your family"), the black actress who won an Academy
Award as best supporting actress for *Gone With the Wind* in
1939. When she died in 1952, however, the then Hollywood
Memorial Cemetery did not admit African Americans (where she
wanted to be buried), so she was laid to rest in downtown L.A.'s

Remembered—but
not buried—at
Hollywood Forever:
1939 Oscar winner
Hattie McDaniel

Rosedale Cemetery, where she was the first of her race to be interred. She is still at Rosedale, but in 1999, she was officially remembered at Forever Hollywood.

The cemetery's biggest star—Rodolfo Guglielmi Valentino (1895–1926)—is inside the Cathedral Mausoleum in crypt 1205 at the extreme southeast end of the building. Even though the famous "Lady in Black" no longer turns up every year on the anniversary of Valentino's death, the flowers on his crypt are always fresh. Peter Finch is directly across the aisle from Valentino. Barbara La Marr, Peter Lorre, and Eleanor Powell are in other alcoves of the same building. Back outside, a stone staircase leads to Douglas Fairbanks's reflecting pool, monument, and final resting place—reportedly paid for by his ex-wife Mary Pickford.

More Hollywood royals are over at the western end of the park in the Abbey of Palms Mausoleum. Here, sisters Norma and Constance Talmadge are together in the Sanctuary of Eternal Love, pioneer producer Jesse Lasky is in the Sanctuary of Light, and director Victor Fleming *(The Wizard of Oz* and *Gone With the Wind)* is in crypt 2081, toward the back of the building.

This cemetery is not all big names, however. There are a lot of everyday folk buried here, too. Surprisingly, many of the less famous monuments in the Hollywood Memorial Park Cemetery bear Armenian names and script. These graves are decorated with tiny vases of flowers, clusters of candles, and various Eastern Orthodox icons. A little-known fact about today's Hollywood is that it has one of the largest concentrations of Armenian Americans in the United States.

Another little-known fact: Hollywood Forever may be the only cemetery in the world to have movie nights! Several times a month in the summer, Cinespia presents outdoor screenings of classic Hollywood films projected against the wall of Valentino's mausoleum. Don't expect zombie films, however.

Hollywood Forever is open from 9 a.m. to 5 p.m. every day and a map indicating who's buried where can be purchased at the flower shop to the right of the main entrance. The cemetery also has guided walking tours every month. For information on these as well as on movie nights, call 323-469-1181 or visit www.forevernetwork.com.

16. RKO STUDIOS SITE
Corner of Gower Street and Melrose Avenue

RKO will always be remembered for classics like the original *King Kong* (1933), the Fred Astaire–Ginger Rogers musicals of the 1930s, and Orson Welles's famous *Citizen Kane* (1941). Before every RKO picture, a huge globe with a radio tower on top of it would flash lightning bolts that spelled out "RKO-Radio Pictures." Today, the former RKO studios, the first to be built in Hollywood exclusively for talking pictures, are part of the Paramount Studios complex but the famous RKO globe, now painted over, can still be distinguished atop the corner of the building at Gower and Melrose.

Some movie fans may also remember RKO's connection with two famous American millionaires who dabbled in the motion picture business. The first was Joseph P. Kennedy—patriarch of *the* Kennedy family—who produced pictures via his FBO (Film Booking Offices of America) organization, which eventually formed part of RKO. Gloria Swanson was Kennedy's leading lady both on and off screen. The second RKO millionaire exec was Howard

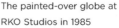

The painted-over globe at RKO Studios in 1985

Hughes; in 1948, Hughes made news when he bought RKO lock, stock, and barrel. In 1957, another RKO sale was in the news. This time the company was going out of the movie business and a former RKO starlet was purchasing the RKO lot for $6 million. The buyer was Lucille Ball, who with her husband, Desi Arnaz, made RKO's Gower Street property part of their Desilu empire. In the mid-sixties, the lot again changed hands when next-door neighbor Paramount took it over and incorporated it into its facilities. Today, Paramount mostly uses the former RKO soundstages for taping television series. *Happy Days* was done here as were *Laverne and Shirley, Mork and Mindy,* and *Taxi.* More recently, *Frasier, Girlfriends, It's All Relative,* and *Becker* have ruled the roost.

As for RKO, the company survives as a small production outfit, co-owned by yet another old-moneyed American millionaire—actress–E.F. Hutton heiress Dina Merrill.

For information on how to attend a taping in the old RKO studio building, call Paramount's ticket information number, 323–956–1777.

17. PARAMOUNT STUDIOS
5451 Marathon Street

In an era when most studios have sold off their back lots and downsized their real estate, Paramount has actually added to its domain to encompass most of the area between Gower Street and Western Avenue north of Melrose Avenue. With its imposing new gates and entryways, this is a very impressive operation indeed. Sadly, the renovations have obscured what was arguably the most beautiful and most famous of all studio entrances, Paramount's ornate Spanish baroque wrought-iron gate at Bronson and Marathon Streets. A classic symbol of Hollywood, the gate was immortalized in *Sunset Boulevard* (1950), when Gloria Swanson, as aging silent movie queen Norma Desmond, returns to her old studio in her great Isotta-Fraschini automobile driven by Erich von Stroheim. For years, it was said that good luck would come to the aspiring performer who hugged the gate and repeated those magic *Sunset Boulevard* words: "I'm ready for my close-up, Mr. DeMille." Now, alas, movie lovers can no longer get near the gate and must be content to admire it from afar.

Paramount Studios gate, as seen in *Sunset Boulevard*

Paramount is the last major studio to be headquartered in Hollywood. Paramount also has the oldest roots of any studio in town—and can trace its origins back to Jesse Lasky, Samuel Goldfish (later Goldwyn), and Cecil B. DeMille, the trio that produced Hollywood's first feature film, *The Squaw Man,* in 1913. Adolph Zukor entered the Paramount picture in 1916 when his Famous Players merged with Lasky's Feature Play Company to form the Famous Players–Lasky Corporation that produced "Paramount" pictures. For over a decade, their studio occupied a hefty chunk of the property formed by Sunset Boulevard, Vine Street, and Selma Avenue. In 1926, Famous Players–Lasky–Paramount made their move to Paramount's current location.

Paramount's great stars of the 1920s included Gloria Swanson, Clara Bow, and Rudolph Valentino. In the early thirties, Claudette Colbert, Miriam Hopkins, Gary Cooper, Maurice Chevalier, and Marlene Dietrich were important names on the Paramount roster—but Mae West was the studio's biggest moneymaker, starring in risqué comedies made from her own screenplays. The late thirties and early forties saw Veronica Lake, Frances Farmer, Fred MacMurray, Ray Milland, Alan Ladd, Betty Hutton, Bing Crosby, Bob Hope, and Dorothy Lamour come to fame in Paramount pictures. The last three are perhaps best remembered for their series of Road pictures.

Cecil B. DeMille was Paramount's most famous director, even though he split from the organization in the mid-twenties to form his own producing organization. After several years operating out of the former Thomas Ince studio in Culver City, DeMille returned to the Paramount lot and made many of his famous epics—*Cleopatra, The Sign of the Cross, Samson and Delilah, The Greatest Show on Earth*—from this base. Other great directors who worked at Paramount were Josef von Sternberg, Ernst Lubitsch, Preston Sturges, and Billy Wilder.

In 1968, now a subsidiary of Gulf & Western, Paramount bought its next-door neighbor, Desilu Studios (formerly the RKO lot), increasing the size of its facilities to some 62 acres. The late sixties and early seventies were heady times for Paramount, especially with the rise of colorful studio executive Robert Evans, who oversaw a number of box office hits—*The Odd Couple* (1968), *Rosemary's Baby* (1968), *Love Story* (1970), *The Godfather* (1972), and *Chinatown* (1974) among them. Evans's fall in the 1980s was as dramatic as his ascent, what with a cocaine bust, the murder of a dodgy business associate (Roy Raiden) in which Evans was a material witness, and the financially and critically disastrous *The Cotton Club* (1984), which he produced with a great deal of his own money. The 2003 documentary *The Kid Stays in the Picture* gives Evans's side of his Hollywood odyssey.

Since 1994, Paramount has been part of the massive media conglomerate Viacom, which also owns MTV, Nickelodeon, Comedy Central, and the CBS network. Paramount's longtime chairperson is Sherry Lansing, one of the few women to rise to this position in Hollywood's male-dominated corporate jungle.

Paramount does not offer tours of its facilities to the general public. There are two ways, however, to experience the studio. One is to attend the taping of a television show on the Paramount lot. For ticket information (tickets are free), call 323-956-1777. The other way to see Paramount is simply to walk around the outside of the studio on Melrose Avenue. And when you see the old entrance, blow a kiss, say the Sunset Boulevard *line, and, who knows, maybe the old magic will still work. You can also visit www.paramount.com.*

18. RALEIGH STUDIOS
650 North Bronson Avenue

With its rustic clapboard office buildings edging Bronson Avenue, the western edge of Raleigh looks more like a ranch than a movie studio. Ironically, back in 1914 when Adolph Zukor's Famous Players made *The Girl from Yesterday* with Mary Pickford here, the place actually was a horse farm. After Famous Players exited the premises, L.A. theater owner William H. Clune purchased the property with money he had made as a producer of D. W. Griffith's *The Birth of a Nation*. Rather than produce films, however, Clune mostly rented out his studio to numerous independent production companies—and indeed kept doing so for close to sixty years. One of the most famous early "tenants" of this important rental lot was Douglas Fairbanks Productions, which did *The Mark of Zorro* and *The Three Musketeers* at Clune's studio in the early 1920s. In the early 1930s, Walt Disney was another famous name who did some work at Clune's—which was then called the Tech-Art Studios. The early thirties also saw Harry "Pop" Sherman produce a number of films on this lot, the best remembered being the *Hopalong Cassidy* series, which he filmed into the

Raleigh Girls: Bette Davis and Joan Crawford on the set of *Whatever Happened to Baby Jane?* at Producers (now Raleigh) Studios

1950s. Famous 1950s TV series done here were *The Cisco Kid, The Life of Riley, Lineup, Gunsmoke*, and *Have Gun, Will Travel*.

In the sixties Clune's was renamed Producers Studios and Robert Aldrich lensed *Whatever Happened to Baby Jane?* here in 1961 with Bette Davis and Joan Crawford. It was also in the sixties that Ronald Reagan hosted *Death Valley Days* at Producers Studios. It was his last professional acting job.

Today, modernized and greatly expanded, Raleigh Studios remains one of Hollywood's most important rental lots. It has been used for such features as the first two *Naked Gun* films (1988 and 1991), *Frankie and Johnny* (1991), *Single White Female* (1992), *Death Becomes Her* (1992), *Showgirls* (1995), *Out to Sea* (1997), *Mouse Hunt* (1997), *The Negotiator* (1998), and *Murder by Numbers* (2002). Raleigh has also provided a base for the TV shows *Boom Town, Whose Line Is It Anyway?*, and the *Gary Shandling Show*.

Meanwhile, Raleigh's new branch studio facility in Manhattan Beach has been even more active on the TV front, as home to *The Practice, Boston Public, CSI: Miami, Cold Case*, and *Ally McBeal*.

Raleigh does not offer a tour of its facilities, but it's possible to have breakfast or lunch at its pleasant and reasonably priced indoor-outdoor Mexican cantina. If you don't spot a star or two, it's at least a chance to see a couple of soundstages and feel the pulse of a working movie lot. Entrance to the cafe is off Melrose Avenue on Van Ness Avenue; a valid photo ID and a security check are required to enter the premises. Also visit www.raleighstudios.com.

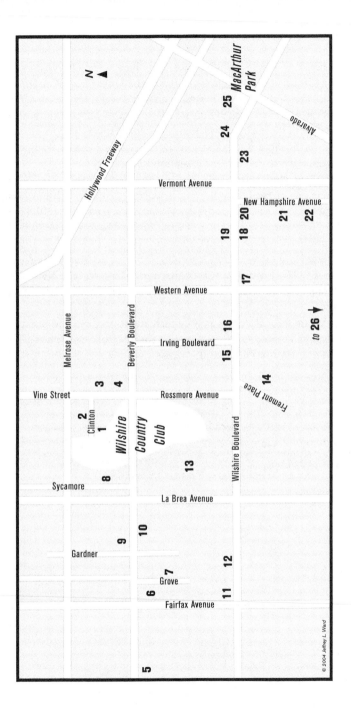

N

MacArthur Park

25

24

23

Alvarado

Hollywood Freeway

Vermont Avenue

New Hampshire Avenue

20 21 22

19

18

17

Western Avenue

to 26

Melrose Avenue

Beverly Boulevard

Irving Boulevard

16

15

Vine Street

3   4

Rossmore Avenue

Fremont Place

14

2

Clinton

1

Wilshire

Country

Club

Wilshire Boulevard

13

8

Sycamore

La Brea Avenue

10

9

Gardner

12

7

Grove

6

11

Fairfax Avenue

5

© 2004 Jeffrey L. Ward

The Wilshire District:
Main Street, L.A.

If the great sprawl of communities that makes up metropolitan Los Angeles can be thought of as having one main street, that street would undoubtedly be Wilshire Boulevard. Named for H. Gaylord Wilshire, a nineteenth-century developer who is said to have been both a millionaire and a Marxist (only in L.A.!), Wilshire Boulevard is a serious commercial thoroughfare for most of its sixteen-mile run from the Pacific Ocean at Santa Monica to downtown Los Angeles. The area known as the "Wilshire District" begins roughly at La Cienega Boulevard and encompasses the neighborhoods on either side of the Boulevard for approximately the next five or six miles to the east. Historically, the westernmost section of the Wilshire District—the one closest to Beverly Hills—has had a large middle-class Jewish population. Beginning at about Highland Avenue, the area starts becoming increasingly Waspy as Wilshire cuts through an old-moneyed enclave of Los Angeles known as Hancock Park. Finally, closer to downtown, the demographics again change and Central Americans, Koreans, Thais, and Filipinos now form the majority. A district in name only, Wilshire encompasses many neighborhoods, ethnic groups, social classes, and lifestyles.

For movie lovers, the Wilshire District and Wilshire Boulevard offer a diverse assortment of sights worth seeing—from the Los Angeles Tennis Club in Hancock Park, one of the few places where the nouveau world of Hollywood rubbed shoulders with the tightly sealed-off society of Old Los Angeles, to a group of grand old apartment houses with fascinating histories of movie-star tenants and sometimes movie-star owners to monumental Art Deco former department stores that were L.A.'s chicest shopping spots during the 1930s and 1940s to the surprising locations where some of Hollywood's greatest films *(Sunset Boulevard, Whatever Happened to Baby Jane?, The Grifters, Mulholland Drive)* and TV series *(Seinfeld, Happy Days, Six Feet Under)* were and are shot.

A car is the best way to see all of the places included in this chapter, although numbers 17 to 25 can easily be done via Metro and combined with many of the sites in downtown L.A. (Chapter 6), which are also Metro-friendly.

1. *HAPPY DAYS* HOUSE
565 North Cahuenga Avenue

For openers, it's not your typical Southern California house—which is no doubt one of the reasons it was chosen to be used as the Cunningham family home in the long-running (1974–1984) TV series *Happy Days*. (The series was set in Milwaukee, Wisconsin.) Another reason for using the house was probably its proximity (a matter of blocks) to Paramount Studios on Melrose Avenue, where the show was taped before a live audience. The series made a megastar of Henry Winkler, who played the leather-jacketed Fonzie, but his post–*Happy Days* career never matched his prime-time success. On the other hand, Ron Howard, who was Richie Cunningham from 1974 to 1980 (and Opie Taylor on *The Andy Griffith Show* from 1960 to 1968), went on to become one of Hollywood's top directors, winning an Academy Award for *A Beautiful Mind* (2001).

Back on Cahuenga Avenue, long before *Happy Days*, Mexican-born Hollywood star, Lupe Velez, lived in this same little Hollywood house in the 1930s. Nearby, at 531 Cahuenga, lived the mother of Lupe's boyfriend at the time—Gary Cooper.

Happy Days house

Miss Velez—who wound up with Johnny "Tarzan" Weissmuller for a husband—is less known for her films than for her news-making suicide in Beverly Hills in 1944. Today the Cunningham/Velez property has been considerably spiffed up, but it is still recognizable.

2. LOS ANGELES TENNIS CLUB
5851 Clinton Street

Beyond the attractive Spanish Colonial clubhouse lie the seventeen courts of the premier tennis club of Southern California. Founded in 1920, the LATC was quickly discovered by the status-conscious stars of early Hollywood who thought it chic to play on the club's courts and attend its matches. Once the club initiated its annual Pacific Southwest Championship tournament in 1927, having a box for the event became *the* thing to do every fall for Charlie Chaplin, Harold Lloyd, Frank Capra, Janet Gaynor, William Powell, Gary Cooper, Joan and Constance Bennett, Clark Gable, and Carole Lombard. One year, Marlene Dietrich dazzled the crowds when she showed up for this tournament dressed in a black-satin tuxedo suit; Jean Harlow

1938 Motion Picture Tournament at the Los Angeles Tennis Club.
Left to right: Frank Shields, Gilbert Roland, Gretl Dupont, Mervin
LeRoy, Josephine Cruickshank, Colly Baiano, Errol Flynn, and umpire
Craufurd Kent

did likewise in white-satin pajamas; Mae West favored furs. Starlets—emulating their better-known colleagues—frequently turned up at matches in full makeup and glamorous attire to be photographed by studio publicity people.

Hollywood's connection with the LATC went beyond show. Many stars who were members of the club took their tennis seriously. One of the best celebrity players was Errol Flynn, who often entered (and sometimes won) LATC tournaments during the 1930s. Other star members were Rudy Vallee, Mickey Rooney, Ozzie Nelson, Charles Farrell, Dinah Shore. These days, Elizabeth Perkins, Patricia *(Everybody Loves Raymond)* Heaton, and Dr. Phil frequently play at LATC. In addition to movie stars, the club has also been home court to an impressive number of major tennis stars—Don Budge, Frank Parker, Jack Kramer, Pancho Gonzales, Alex Olmedo, Stan Smith, Louise Brough, Billie Jean King, and Arthur Ashe.

3. RAVENSWOOD
570 North Rossmore Avenue

Built in the late 1920s, this Art Deco apartment building was where Mae West lived for the half century (1932–1980) she spent in Hollywood. Edging the very conservative old-moneyed area of Los Angeles known as Hancock Park, the Ravenswood would seem an odd place for the controversial Miss West to call home. In fact, her early films were so risqué—even by today's standards—they were one of the reasons that the Catholic Church established its National Legion of Decency censorship board in 1934. It was actually the William Morris office that found Miss West her Ravenswood apartment, thinking that it was convenient—just three blocks from Paramount Studios, where she worked—and would be a good first residence before she found something more permanent in Beverly Hills. Mae, however, chose not to move, even though her films were Paramount's most successful of the early 1930s. Deep down, Brooklyn-born Mae was a city gal and apartment living suited her style. "I'm not a little girl from a little town here to make

Mae West at home at
Ravenswood, mid-1930s

good in a big town," she told all of Hollywood on her arrival in Tinseltown, "I'm a big girl from a big town who's come to make good in a little town."

Living in super-stuffy Hancock Park didn't cramp Miss West's style in the least. The decor of her sprawling sixth-floor apartment is legendary—a fantasy of white, white, and more white with a little gold here and there for accent. According to writer Mitch Tuchman, one of the last journalists to interview Miss West before her death in 1980, every detail of the apartment had been carefully planned to show off its star occupant to her best advantage. At sunset, Miss West's preferred interview time, a champagne-colored light filtered in through the window of the main salon, perfectly framing the chair where Madame Mae held court.

There are many stories that say Mae West owned the Ravenswood. Although Mae had extensive real estate holdings in the L.A. area, it seems, according to various Hollywood old-timers, that Ravenswood was not one of them. Some believe that in the shaky early thirties, financially flush Mae might have helped out the owners of the Ravenswood by holding a mortgage or two on the place, which they paid off when times got better. Mae may have owned the large apartment building across the street from her, however. According to writer Leonard Spigelgass, supposedly Mae didn't like the color of the building her apartment looked out on—so she bought it and immediately had it painted!

Today Ravenswood—still a rental building—remembers its most famous tenant with a framed photo of Miss West in one of the formal salons off the lobby.

4. EL ROYALE APARTMENTS
450 North Rossmore Avenue

Just up the street from Mae West's Rossmore Avenue apartment building, the El Royale was also built in the late 1920s. Among the building's former celebrity tenants are George Raft, Loretta Young, Columbia head man Harry Cohn, comedian Judy Holliday, William Frawley (the actor who played Fred Mertz on *I Love Lucy*), and later President John F. Kennedy—who is said to

El Royale Apartments

have stayed here during the Democratic National Convention in Los Angeles in 1960. More recently, Nicolas Cage joined the ranks of Hollywood Royale-ty, although he has since moved on to a thirty-three-room manor in posh Bel-Air. If the El Royale building looks familiar, it is perhaps because it was once the Denver apartment house that sexual switch-hitter Steven Carrington lived in on the television series *Dynasty*.

5. BEVERLY CENTER
La Cienega Avenue/Beverly Boulevard

Some critics loved it. Others hated this vast futuristic shopping mall with exterior escalators encased in gigantic Plexiglas tubes like Paris's Centre Pompidou art museum, which rose at Beverly Boulevard and La Cienega Avenue in 1981. But despite the mixed reviews, the Beverly Center, with the town's first Hard Rock Cafe as well as one of its first multiplex cinemas, was very much *the* place to hang out in the 1980s. Indeed its popularity and its cutting-edge design may have influenced Paul Mazursky to use the Beverly Center as the quintessential late-twentieth-century shopping mall in his 1991 film *Scenes from a Mall,* which starred Bette Midler and Woody Allen as the quintessentially neurotic late-twentieth-century Southern California couple. The film did not receive mixed reviews, however; it was widely panned. As for the mall, Mazursky cheated a little, shooting a number of scenes on the East Coast in Stamford, Connecticut, at the Stamford Town Center.

Back in L.A., the Beverly Center was also used in another 1991 film, *L.A. Story,* which was written by and starred Steve Martin and which was widely praised. The Beverly Center can also be seen in the 1997 L.A. disaster flick *Volcano,* where it narrowly escaped destruction from the film's runaway lava flow, as well as in numerous episodes of L.A.-lensed TV series and soap operas.

Visit www.beverlycenter.com.

6. CBS TELEVISION CITY
7800 Beverly Boulevard

This sprawling complex at the corner of Fairfax Avenue and Beverly Boulevard is CBS Television's main West Coast base. Built in 1952, it was one of the first studios to be designed solely for television broadcasting—and since that time, news programs, TV series, soaps, and game shows have originated from here. Among the legends: Judy Garland's 1963–1964 TV try, *The Carol Burnett Show, All in the Family, Sonny and Cher, Alice,* and *Newhart.* More recently, *The $25,000 Pyramid, The Bold and the Beautiful, Hollywood Squares, The Price Is Right, The Wayne Brady Show,* and *The Late Late Show with Craig Kilborn* have all been taped here.

To get free tickets for current CBS shows done before a live audience, call 323-575-2624 or visit www.cbs.com.

7. PACIFIC THEATRES AT THE GROVE
189 The Grove Drive

Just when everyone thought the age of the movie palace had come and gone, Pacific Theatres launched its new multiplex at the Grove, an amazing shopping plaza that debuted in 2001 behind the old Farmer's Market. Built to resemble a movie-lot main street—albeit with all the right shops plus an authentic Parisian bistro, an Italian trattoria, and an outrageously opulent Chinese restaurant—the Grove even boasts a computer-controlled dancing fountain and a working vintage L.A. trolley car. But for movie buffs, the most exciting venue here is Pacific Theatres' new fourteen-screen complex. With its enormous Art Deco lobby hung with massive chandeliers, this grand space instantly brings back the allure and glamour of a classic movie palace. Inside the individual theaters, however, everything is state-of-the-art: wall-to-wall curved screens, advanced digital sound, stadium seating, even "love seats," designed for couples.

Visit www.farmersmarketla.com.

8. LE BORGESE APARTMENTS
450 North Sycamore Avenue

In *Mulholland Drive* (2002), David Lynch's weird tale of crime, mistaken identity, amnesia, and murder in today's L.A., two strangers, Betty (Naomi Watts) and Ruby (Laura Elena Harring),

Mulholland Drive prime location: Le Borgese

wind up sharing the same Hollywood apartment. A classic California courtyard complex, with a wrought-iron gate, tropical landscaping, and a gurgling Mediterranean fountain, the building—called Le Borgese in real life—provides an idyllic contrast to the murky goings-on everywhere else in the film. The best touch of all: Lynch's casting former MGM hoofer Ann Miller (1919–2004) in her last film role as Coco, the tough-as-nails building manager.

9. A. B. HEINSBERGEN & CO. BUILDING
7421–7415 Beverly Boulevard

Anthony B. Heinsbergen was one of Los Angeles's most important early muralists and decorative artists. During the 1920s, he lent his talents to the design and decoration of the interiors of some of the city's most lavish movie palaces. Today, among the theaters where his craftsmanship and talent can still be appreciated are the Wiltern on Wilshire Boulevard and the Los Angeles Theater in downtown L.A. Heinsbergen's former office building—erected in the mid-1920s—shows what happens when a designer of fantasy interiors has his way with an exterior. The result here is a medieval marvel of brick, stone, and leaded glass that would be much more at home in the old section of Heidelberg or Ghent than on Beverly Boulevard in Los Angeles. Today, the Heinsbergen building houses a trendy couture shop as well as architects' offices.

10. EL COYOTE RESTAURANT
7312 Beverly Boulevard

Room after room of outrageous Mexican decor—piñatas, gigantic paper flowers, tin lanterns, bright muraled walls—plus waitresses in flouncy South-of-the-Border costumes make a meal at El Coyote a memorable visual, if not culinary, experience. Over the years, the place has lured film-industry people with its own special brand of restaurant show business. These days Gwyneth Paltrow and her set are regulars. In early August 1969, another hot young movie star, her hairdresser, and a couple of friends were reported to have dined at El Coyote before retiring to the star's luxurious home up in the Benedict Canyon section of Beverly Hills for nightcaps. Their Mexican meal may have been their last supper—because later that evening, a crazed group of creatures known as the Manson Family attacked the house and murdered Sharon Tate, her unborn child, and her guests.

Call 323-939-2255.

11. MAY COMPANY DEPARTMENT STORE SITE
6067 Wilshire Boulevard

Before there was Rodeo Drive, there was the Miracle Mile—a long stretch of Wilshire Boulevard between Beverly Hills and Hancock Park where serious L.A. shoppers went to spend their time and their money. Developed in the 1920s, the Miracle Mile became not only an important shopping mecca, but also a showcase of Art Deco commercial architecture. The May Company—with its distinctive gold-and-black "silo" on the corner of Wilshire Boulevard and Fairfax Avenue—was built in 1940 and is an example of a late Deco style that looked to the future rather than to the past.

On January 28, 1966, the May Company was in the news

May Company site

when former superstar Hedy Lamarr was arrested there for allegedly walking off with some $86 worth of May Company merchandise. Eventually acquitted, Miss Lamarr sued the store for $5 million in damages. The suit was later dismissed.

Bette Davis fans may remember the May Company as the department store where their idol, playing washed-up movie star Margaret Elliot, does a brief stint in the lingerie department in the 1952 film *The Star*. Disaster movie fans may register the May Company as one of the city's landmarks that gets destroyed in *Volcano* (1997). Today the venerable department store has been transformed into LACMA West, the new annex of the nearby Los Angeles County Museum of Art.

Visit www.lacma.org.

12. LOS ANGELES COUNTY MUSEUM OF ART
5905 Wilshire Boulevard

Besides its extensive collections of Asian, European, and American art, the L.A. County Museum of Art (LACMA) also has one of the city's most vital film programs. Open to the public, screenings of classic U.S. and foreign films are held year round in the Leo S. Bing Theater. Often a star speaker—Gregory Peck, Hal Roach, Bette Davis, Olivia De Havilland, Catherine Deneuve all appeared here—is part of the program. The museum's film department helped make movie history in 1983 when the late Ron Haver tracked down and reassembled the "missing" twenty-six minutes of the 1954 Judy Garland/James Mason *A Star Is Born*. Movie lovers may also remember LACMA from *L.A. Story* (1991), in which Steve Martin roller-skated through its galleries, and also from Robert Altman's *The Player* (1992), wherein the museum provided the venue for a glamorous industry gala celebrating black-and-white movies. For the event everyone was to wear black and white; Cher, however, in a cameo as herself, wore red.

For information on what's playing at the LACMA, call 323–857–6010 or visit www.lacma.org.

13. *WHATEVER HAPPENED TO BABY JANE?* HOUSE
172 South McCadden Place

Welcome to the house where the former child star Baby Jane Hudson (Bette Davis) did all of those horrible things to her invalid sister Blanche (Joan Crawford) in Robert Aldrich's 1962 Hollywood-gothic classic, *Whatever Happened to Baby Jane?* Note, especially, the wrought-iron driveway gate on the left side of the house—of major plot significance—where Jane ran over Blanche in their car many years earlier. Or did she?

While the McCadden Place house was used for many exterior scenes, most of the film was shot on the nearby lot at Raleigh (then Producers) Studios. At the time, few in Hollywood believed that longtime arch rivals Crawford and Davis would agree to appear in a film together. But the two old pros put their personal animosities aside, knowing that the project—especially at this point in their flagging careers—had "comeback" written all over it. The film was a big hit and earned an Oscar nomination for Bette but not for Joan. Joan got her revenge, however, at the 1963 Academy Awards ceremony, where she had arranged to

Whatever Happened to Baby Jane? house

pick up the Best Actress Oscar for Anne Bancroft, nominated for *The Miracle Worker* and doing a play in New York at the time, should she win. Bancroft did win, and Joan graciously accepted the award that her costar did not win. Bette was *not* amused.

14. FREMONT PLACE
Fremont Place and Wilshire Boulevard

Behind the heavy gates of this ultraprivate Los Angeles community live many of the city's oldest, wealthiest, and Waspiest families. Between 1918 and 1920, Mary Pickford lived here with her mother at 56 Fremont Place. Many years later, black boxer Muhammad Ali moved into a Fremont Place mansion at number 55. Historical footnote: When Nat King Cole bought a home in the nearby Larchmont neighborhood in the late 1940s, property owners banded together and tried to oust the black entertainer. When Muhammad Ali moved into the even more exclusive Fremont Place enclave, no objections were raised.

Lou Rawls and Karen Black have also been Fremont Placers, and in 1977, actor Cliff Robertson was renting a house at number 97 Fremont Place West when he received an IRS form that indicated he had earned $10,000 the previous year from Columbia Pictures. Since Robertson had not worked for the studio in 1976, he looked into the matter further, and ultimately uncovered the forgeries of Columbia executive David Begelman. Thus began the Begelman Affair, one of Hollywood's biggest scandals of the time.

In 1989, Kathleen Turner and Michael Douglas lived at number 119 Fremont Place and did battle with one another in *The War of the Roses.*

15. *SUNSET BOULEVARD* MANSION SITE
Northwest corner, Wilshire and Irving Boulevards

It belonged to a former wife of J. Paul Getty and had not been lived in for several years when Billy Wilder decided to use it as Norma Desmond's mansion in his 1950 film, *Sunset Boulevard.* Actually, the site of the movie mansion was a good six miles from the section of Sunset Boulevard in Beverly Hills where the script said the mansion should be. At the same time, it was a mere ten blocks from Paramount where the film was shot.

It was also, according to Wilder, just the house that he wanted, except for the swimming pool. There wasn't one—and the script, as we all remember, definitely called for one. (The film is narrated by the corpse of William Holden whom we see floating in the swimming pool at the beginning of the film.) The former Mrs. Getty—who had given acting classes on the property—was reportedly pleased at the prospect of having the movie company install a free pool for her. Only thing was, this was a Hollywood pool—which meant that it was for show only and had practically no plumbing. Although it was never used for swimming after the film was shot, the pool that *Sunset Boulevard* built was used in another famous film. The film was *Rebel Without a Cause* (1955), and it was in the bottom of the same pool—now empty—that James Dean, Natalie Wood, and Sal Mineo parodied their parents in a touching scene toward the end of the film.

A few years after *Rebel* was released, the Irving Boulevard house was demolished, the pool filled in. Today, the site is a parking lot for the office building on the corner.

Movie lovers who visit the Sunset Boulevard/Rebel *site should note the impressive Tudor mansion at nearby 605 South Irving. Another former Getty property, this is now the official residence of the mayor of Los Angeles.*

16. LOS ALTOS APARTMENTS
4121 Wilshire Boulevard

Many stories say that William Randolph Hearst built this magnificent Moorish apartment palace that dominates the 4000 block of Wilshire Boulevard. According to the building permit, however, Los Altos was erected by a pair of gentlemen named Luther T. Mayo and Preston S. White. When the place opened in 1925, it made real estate history as the first "own-your-own-apartment" (that is, cooperative) apartment building in Los Angeles. According to some newspaper accounts, Hearst did buy a large apartment in Los Altos for Marion Davies. One account

Los Altos Apartments

says the apartment had ten rooms, six baths, and a screening room. Another puts the Davies suite as a duplex with a mere five bedrooms. A longtime resident of the building, however, doubted if either Marion Davies or Hearst ever lived in the apartment and suggests that it was used mainly for business meetings and receptions. The apartment, number 207, has since been broken up—but the main wing still has massive $100,000 (according to another old-timer) carved doors plus marble floors, vaulted ceilings, and three bathrooms.

A number of other Hollywood names are connected with Los Altos. Silent-screen star Jane Novak (one of many former fiancées of William S. Hart, the Western star who made a habit of becoming engaged to his leading ladies but never marrying them) was a longtime early resident. Clara Bow also lived here, although one resident remembers Miss Bow being in the building in the early thirties and another says she lived on the fifth floor in the late 1940s. Bette Davis is said to have once resided in suite 107; no one is sure just when. By the 1930s, it should be noted, the building was no longer a co-op and had become an apartment hotel that rented suites both on a long- and short-term basis. In the late 1930s, Los Altos is also said to have been June Allyson's first Hollywood address. Later years saw Peter Finch live in the great Wilshire apartment house.

Currently, Los Altos, which is now on the National Register of Historic Places, has a featured role in the TV series *Angel,* as the Hyperion Hotel, where Angel (David Boreanaz) headquarters his Angel's Investigations agency.

17. WILTERN THEATER
3780 Wilshire Boulevard

Designed by G. Albert Lansburgh, the dean of American theater architects (he also did the Warner Theater in Hollywood and the Orpheum in downtown L.A.), the Wiltern ranked with Hollywood's Pantages theater as one of the most impressive Art Deco movie palaces on the West Coast. When the 2,300-seat Wiltern (originally called the Wiltern-Warner) made its debut in 1931, it was to have been the flagship of the Warner Bros. chain and it was quite an opening night. William Powell acted as master of ceremonies and introduced the new theater as well as Warner's

Wiltern Theater marquee

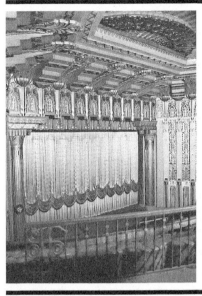

The Wiltern's lavish interior

new film, *Alexander Hamilton,* starring George Arliss. A special wooden "Bridge of Stars" was erected over Wilshire Boulevard (because the city of L.A. refused to block the street), which made celebrity entrances especially glamorous. Speaking of those entrances, Bette Davis once told how Warner Bros., a studio never known for being extravagant, used to bus contract players to premieres, drop them off around the corner from the theater where the same limousine would then take them in small groups round to the front for their official arrival.

Despite its dramatic opening and its extraordinary beauty, the Wiltern was the wrong theater in the wrong place at the wrong time. The Depression was in full swing—even in Hollywood— and the Wiltern was simply too large for the residential neighborhood in which it found itself. Attendance was disappointing, and two years after it had opened, Warner Bros. pulled out and the theater went dark. Later, it reopened as the Wiltern—and was moderately successful from the late 1930s to the late 1950s. The 1960s saw the theater decline steadily in both attendance and maintenance, and by the end of that decade, the Wiltern was reduced to showing kung fu flicks and closed-circuit televised sporting events.

By 1980, the wrecking crews had arrived to demolish not only the theater but the magnificent terra-cotta–tiled, bronze-trimmed office tower (known as the Pellissier Building) that was built around it. Luckily, the preservationists won this one—when, in the nick of time, an enlightened developer bought the Wiltern Theater/Pellissier Building and embarked on an extensive restoration program. Today, the tiled façade of this landmark Art Deco complex gleams once again and the Wiltern Theater has been brought back to life as a performing arts center for plays, musicals, dance, opera, and especially pop and rock concerts. Recent headliners include Dressed to Kill, Peter Frampton, Primus, the Deftones, Seal, Bare Naked Ladies, and Stain. The theater's lobby was used as a Hollywood hotel lobby in the Coen Brothers' 1991 film *Barton Fink*.

To find out what's on at the Wiltern, call 213-380-5005 or visit www.thewiltern.com.

18. AMBASSADOR HOTEL SITE
3400 Wilshire Boulevard

First came the society people—old Los Angeles—who welcomed this luxurious new hotel so ideally situated between downtown Los Angeles and their own grand residences in Hancock Park and Fremont Place. For them, the Ambassador, which opened in 1921, was a wonderful new place to dine, entertain, and throw debutante parties and weddings. There were even, in the early days, horse shows that attracted all the right people held on the hotel's vast grounds.

The Ambassador also attracted, very quickly, movie people. Many, in fact, lived here in large comfortable bungalows that were attached to the hotel. Particularly for actors and actresses who commuted between New York and Los Angeles, a bungalow at the Ambassador often made more sense than renting a house in Los Angeles. And besides, there was room service, the hotel's great pool with its sand "beach," and, best of all, always something to do in the evenings because the Ambassador boasted the most glamorous nightclub in all of Los Angeles: the Cocoanut Grove.

The Grove opened several months after the hotel and was an instant hit. The decor was pure fantasy: a wild interior of palm trees—supposedly leftover set pieces from Rudolph Valentino's film, *The Sheik*—from which stuffed monkey dolls with electrically lit eyes watched over the crowds on the dance floor. The stories of the Grove are endless, and almost every Angeleno has one. There's the time John Barrymore—who lived in an Ambassador bungalow with a pet monkey as a roommate—brought the little beast to the nightclub and let it loose in the palm trees. And Marion Davies—she and William Randolph Hearst had a wing of the Ambassador for close to a year in the early 1920s—once rode a horse through the Ambassador lobby and on into the Grove for a costume party. (Arnold Schwarzenegger did more or less the same thing in the 1994 film *True Lies.*)

The Grove was also where a number of the early Academy Awards ceremonies were held: 1930, 1932, 1934, 1940, and 1943. In those days, Oscar ceremonies were more like parties, and dinner and cocktails were part of the festivities. The 1937 *A*

Lonely landmark: abandoned Ambassador Hotel, 2003

Star Is Born provides a picture of what the Oscars at the Grove were like in a memorable sequence of that film. In the 1954 *A Star Is Born,* the Cocoanut Grove is again used as a location. Only this time James Mason is looking for a late-night date at the nightclub, but is told by the maître d' that the woman he is interested in is "Pasadena," that is, society, that is, hands-off!

Besides Grove stories, there are lots of stories told about about the amorous goings-on that took place inside the Ambassador's bungalows. Once, a very young Tallulah Bankhead—infatuated with a much older John Barrymore—tried to catch the noted actor's attention in the Ambassador dining room by tripping him. It was Miss Bankhead, however, who wound up falling on the floor. Later the same evening, at the urging of her friends and no doubt after many bourbons, Miss Bankhead sneaked into Barrymore's bungalow and hid under his sheets. When Barrymore returned and discovered Tallulah, all he said was: "Another time, Tallu . . . I'm too drunk and you're too awkward." Howard Hughes also lived in an Ambassador bungalow. This was in the late 1920s when he was working on *Hell's Angels* as well as on quite a few young Hollywood beauties. One of the hotel's best-known liaisons took place on-screen, however: The Ambassador was the spot where a young Dustin Hoffman pursued his affair with that notorious older woman Mrs. Robinson (Anne Bancroft) in the 1967 film *The Graduate.*

Valentino is also associated with the Ambassador. It seems that after he had separated from his second wife, Natacha Rambova, Valentino was seeing Ambassador bungalow resident Pola Negri. This was not long before Valentino's death in New York in 1926. When the grief-stricken Miss Negri left her bungalow for the train that was to take her back East to her lover's funeral, she is said to have emerged from the bungalow two times—once for real and a second time so that the photographers could capture every nuance of her performance.

Another superstar with an Ambassador connection was Marilyn Monroe. In 1947, she was a student of Emmaline Snively's Blue Book Modeling Agency, which was located on the Ambassador premises. Later, when she was a star, she would return to the Ambassador and to the Cocoanut Grove often.

Along with all the glamorous goings-on, the Ambassador has had its share of tragic events. One that will always be associated with the hotel is the assassination of Democratic presidential primary candidate Robert F. Kennedy at the Ambassador on June 5, 1968. (The stretch of Wilshire Boulevard outside the Ambassador has been officially renamed the Robert F. Kennedy Memorial Parkway.) Two years later, the Ambassador would also play a supporting role in another great American tragedy: It was here that the jury for the Manson Family trial was sequestered during the trial for some nine months in 1969–1970 before a verdict was reached on the murders of actress Sharon Tate and her friends.

Today, the Ambassador is a sad sight indeed—fenced in, boarded up, and abandoned since 1989. In the 1990s, developer Donald Trump had a plan to revitalize the historic hotel, but this was rejected by city officials, who wanted to turn the property into a trio of public schools. To date, the school scheme is still being debated as the grand old Ambassador rots in the Southern California sunshine.

19. BROWN DERBY PLAZA
3377 Wilshire Boulevard

The Vine Street branch had the glamour and fame, but this little lunch counter in the shape of a hat was the first of what quickly became L.A.'s most famous chain of eateries. The man behind the Brown Derbys (at one time there were four branches) was silent-picture superstar Gloria Swanson's second husband, Herbert K. Somborn; he opened up this Derby in 1926, the same year in which his divorce from Miss Swanson became official. There are many tales of how the Derby got its shape. One says the building was inspired by New York governor Al Smith—a friend of Somborn's—who was wearing a brown derby on a visit to Los Angeles. Another says that Somborn had been challenged by a friend who said: "If you know anything about food, you can sell it out of a hat." Then there are those who see the derby hat as being a symbol of upper-middle-class social acceptability. According to this you-are-where-you-eat theory, what could be classier than dining inside a derby?

Whatever the real reason for the Derby's design, it quickly became a Los Angeles landmark. In 1980, however, the landmark restaurant had closed and was about to be demolished when a

The original Brown Derby

group of concerned citizens intervened and managed to block the demolition. Today, what's left of the grand old hat on Wilshire has been incorporated into a small Korean shopping plaza. Called, appropriately, the Brown Derby Plaza, this two-story mini-mall has the usual liquor store and fast-food restaurants, plus a pool parlor. But way at the back, there's a South Pacific–style bar called Jumak Sheeri, notable mainly for its odd dome-shaped roof—the former hat!

20. THE TALMADGE
3278 Wilshire Boulevard

In the 1980s, a portrait of the great silent screen star, Norma Talmadge, hung above the reception desk and the then manager told a lovely story of the building's beginnings. The year was 1922, and Norma Talmadge and her producer husband Joe Schenck had come to L.A. from New York. It seems that Norma had looked and looked for a place to stay that suited her but couldn't find anything that was right. Whereupon Joe said, "Honey, I'll build you a building." And so he built the Talmadge—out of love. The manager went on to say that Schenck—who never did things small—had plans to erect a duplicate of the Talmadge (shades of the Taj Mahal story) on the other side of Berendo Street with a footbridge connecting the two structures. However, the church that still stands on that corner supposedly refused to sell Schenck the land.

Meanwhile, the building permit mentions neither the name Talmadge nor Schenck but merely says that the Talmadge was built in 1923 by architects Aleck Curlett and Claude Beelman, both important in their field at the time. In fact, it was Beelman who designed the monumental Irving Thalberg Building at MGM Studios in Culver City in the late 1930s. But did he and his partner do the Talmadge for Norma and Schenck? The name of the building would certainly imply that there was a connection between the star and the building, but perhaps the strongest indication of that connection is the 1926 film *Battling Butler,* in which the Talmadge was used as the mansion of the film's rich young hero, played by Buster Keaton. Keaton was not only married to Norma Talmadge's sister Natalie, but his brother-in-law Joe Schenck produced the picture. What better way to save money and keep things all in the family than by using his own building as a location?

Some seventy years later, the writer-director Wachowski brothers, who went on to fame and fortune with the *Matrix* films, used the Talmadge as the Chicago hotel in their film *Bound* (1996). Today, the Talmadge remains a memorable fixture on Wilshire Boulevard. Tall and imposing, with its Beaux Arts entrance angled to the corner, the building has been beautifully maintained and features large luxurious apartments, a grand lobby, lovely gardens, and a patio where glamorous parties were often held in the good old days. But the portrait of Norma is gone from the lobby, and the current manager knows little of the Talmadge's history other than that it was built by a rich businessman for his wife.

21. MARY MILES MINTER MANSION
701 South New Hampshire Avenue

Scandal ended her career rather abruptly in the early 1920s and today few people remember that Mary Miles Minter was one of the silent screen's great beauties and most successful stars.

So successful, in fact, that this was the big brick mansion that the nubile screen siren shared with her domineering stage mother, Charlotte Shelby, at the height of her career.

The scandal that ended the twenty-year-old Minter's brief life at the top began on February 1, 1922, when Miss Minter's director and supposed lover, William Desmond Taylor, was discovered dead in his apartment (now demolished) on Alvarado Street. There were two bullets in his chest—and it definitely wasn't suicide. Since Taylor was also linked romantically with another great star of the day—comedian Mabel Normand—the newspapers and the public went wild. And when it came out that both Miss Minter and Miss Normand had stopped by the dead director's apartment *before* the police on the morning after his murder, the whole affair took on the aura of a real-life Agatha Christie whodunit. Miss Normand's reason for entering the Taylor flat was supposedly to retrieve some letters whose contents she didn't want to be misconstrued. Miss Minter, on the other hand, is said to have been interested in removing some naughty nighties that happened to be monogrammed with the initials

Mary Miles Minter mansion

MMM—although she denied this up until her death in Los Angeles in 1984.

Taylor's most interesting visitor, however, was a mystery man who was reportedly seen leaving the victim's apartment on the night of the murder. More than a little suspicious was the fact that this man, wearing a raincoat, supposedly walked like a woman. Was it a jealous Miss Minter affecting a disguise? Or a jealous Miss Normand? Some speculated that it was neither but rather Miss Minter's mother who was enraged at having discovered Taylor's affair with her daughter. Others say that Mrs. Shelby's anger was really fueled by her own jealousy, because she, too, was under Taylor's romantic spell.

The murderer was never found. But the damage done by all the headlines and hoopla that surrounded William Desmond Taylor's demise was irrevocable. The affair not only ruined Miss Minter's film career, it also had much to do with Mabel Normand's Hollywood downfall as well, since another of the case's revelations showed that Taylor helped supply Normand with the narcotics to which she was addicted. Author Sidney Kirkpatrick, in his 1986 book, *A Cast of Killers,* deals with the Hollywood murder and concurs with the mother-did-it theory. The 1992 film *Forever* also recounts the Mary Miles Minter saga, with Sean Young as Minter, Renée Taylor as mom, and Steve Railsback as Taylor.

Today, Miss Minter and her mother's former mansion is Children's Institute International, a home for unwed mothers.

22. THE SHELLY *(SEINFELD)* APARTMENTS
757 South New Hampshire Avenue

Although most L.A.-based TV series that are supposedly set in New York usually feature establishing shots of actual NYC buildings, the exterior of Seinfeld's frequently seen Manhattan apartment house turns out to be a few blocks south of Wilshire Boulevard near downtown L.A. Called the Shelly, this five-story brick (a little-used building material in earthquake-prone L.A., but standard-issue for NYC) structure with the canopied entrance and distinctive sculpted ornamentation did a pretty convincing job of portraying 129 West Eighty-first Street in

Seinfeld's L.A. address

Manhattan, which was Seinfeld's TV address. Before coming to Hollywood, Jerry Seinfeld once lived at that very address in the Big Apple.

23. SOUTHWEST LAW SCHOOL/BULLOCKS WILSHIRE SITE
3050 Wilshire Boulevard

It's around 1936, we're somewhere in Connecticut, and Marion Kirby (Constance Bennett) is being driven off for a wild weekend at a posh hotel by Cosmo Topper (Roland Young) in the original *Topper* film. The pair (she's a ghost, he isn't) arrive at the elegant Seabreeze Hotel, pull up under its magnificent Art Deco porte cochere, and check in. Soon, Marion's husband (Cary Grant, also a ghost) arrives in hot pursuit—and the Seabreeze is turned upside down by a series of hilarious ectoplasmic exploits.

As it turns out, the glamorous entrance to the Seabreeze was not some art director's fantasy created on the Hal Roach back lot. Instead, a real Los Angeles location was used—the rear entrance of Bullocks Wilshire Department Store. Built in 1929, this masterpiece of Zigzag Moderne architecture is an official historic cultural monument and one of the most beautiful buildings in Los Angeles. An architectural ground-breaker in many ways, Bullocks was one of L.A.'s first large commercial buildings to be designed for shoppers arriving by car. In fact, the rear entrance (facing the parking lot) used in *Topper* is actually the store's main entrance. (In 1942, the film *Tarzan's New York Adventure* did the same trick, this time using the distinctive Bullocks entrance to double for a grand New York City hotel.)

Not seen in *Topper* or *Tarzan's New York Adventure,* but worth a look for anyone visiting the site is the colorful Herman Sacks fresco on the ceiling of the porte cochere. A salute to the *Spirit of Transportation,* the dazzling painting shows early airplanes, dirigibles, ships, and trains. Ironically, no cars are in-

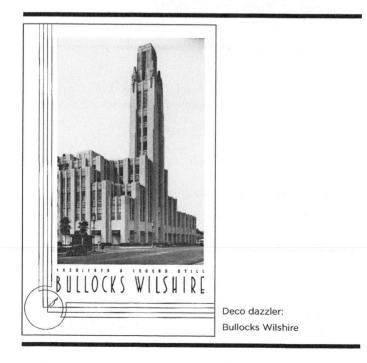

Deco dazzler:
Bullocks Wilshire

cluded. Around at the front of the building, another decorative element worth noting is the stylized relief above the main doorway; it is said to have been the creation of MGM art director Cedric Gibbons. Besides his many movie credits, Gibbons also is known for designing the original Oscar statuette used by the Academy of Motion Picture Arts and Sciences.

Over the years, Bullocks Wilshire has been a favorite 1930s exterior and interior for films, TV movies and series. Its contemporary credits include *Murder, She Wrote, The Agency,* and *Judging Amy* on television, as well as the features *Family Plot* (1976), *Fist of the North Star* (1986), *Bugsy* (1991), *On Deadly Ground* (1994), *The Tie That Binds* (1995), and *Rough Magic* (1997). The film to use this glamorous location most extensively was *Dunston Checks In* (1995), in which Bullocks reprises its *Topper/Tarzan* role as an elegant hotel in this wacky story of an orangutan jewel thief. In fact, the entire production (with the exception of one swimming pool scene) was done here. This was possible because Bullocks went out of business in 1994 and the building's new owners, the Southwest Law School, made the property available to the film company before they set to redoing it as an academic institution. Now that the renovations have been completed, the grand old former department store once again moonlights as a film location. Two recent gigs: the famous Taco Bell commercial with the talking chihuahua and as the nightclub in Martin Scorsese's Howard Hughes biopic *The Aviator* (2004), with Leonardo DiCaprio as Hughes, Cate Blanchett as Katharine Hepburn, Kate Beckinsale as Ava Gardner, and Gwen Stefani as Jean Harlow.

In summer, the Law School's beautiful Art Deco cafe is open to the public and offers movie lovers a chance to see the interior of the magnificent building.

24. BRYSON APARTMENT HOTEL
2701 Wilshire Boulevard

In its glory days, it boasted billiard rooms, music rooms, separate servants' quarters, and a ballroom on the ninth floor. Opened in 1913, the *Los Angeles Times* called it "the finest structure devoted exclusively to apartment-house purposes west

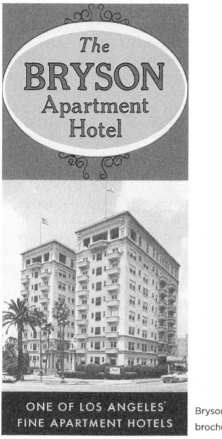

Bryson Apartment Hotel brochure

of New York City." Today, none of the current staff of the Bryson can remember who some of the building's early celebrated tenants were, although no one doubts that there were many. What people do remember is that the building once had a celebrated landlord—Fred MacMurray, who bought the place in the forties and sold it in the seventies.

It was in the forties, too, that Raymond Chandler immortalized the Bryson in his novel, *The Lady in the Lake*. As Detective Philip Marlowe approaches the building, he finds: "a white stucco palace with fretted lanterns in the forecourt and tall date palms. The entrance was in an L, up marble steps, through a Moorish archway, and over a lobby that was too big and a carpet that was too blue. Blue Ali Baba oil jars were dotted around, big enough to keep tigers in."

Hollywood further immortalized the Bryson in Stephen Frears's brilliant 1990 film *The Grifters*. Used as the seedy downtown L.A. hotel that's home to Roy Dillon (John Cusack), both the Bryson's exterior, with its rooftop neon sign and its lion-topped columned entrance, and interior, with its tacky reservation desk and distinctive brass-and-glass cage elevator, are used throughout the film. The hotel was also used as a sleazy location for *Barfly* (1987) and in the opening of P. T. Anderson's edgy 1999 film *Magnolia,* where a man jumps from a high floor but is ultimately killed not by the fall but by a shotgun fired by his mother at his father on a lower floor. The sequence was used to illustrate bizarre coincidences.

Today, despite its literary and cinematic history, the hotel is pretty much the same as it was in the above films, a once-grand building that now caters to a low-budget clientele. But the Bryson still has Hollywood dreams: a sign out front announces its availability as a location.

25. PARK PLAZA HOTEL
607 South Parkview Street

Overlooking Douglas MacArthur Park (the place that inspired the 1960s Richard Harris and the 1970s Donna Summer hit song, "MacArthur Park"), the Park Plaza Hotel was built in the late twenties as an Elks Lodge. Architecture buffs are impressed by the building's monumental concrete façade which bursts forth with gigantic statues at the upper corners. Movie buffs may be interested in knowing that one of the architects, Claude Beelman, designed the nearby Talmadge apartments and the Irving Thalberg Building at MGM Studios. Movie buffs will also be intrigued by the Park Plaza's extraordinary lobby. Dominated by a massive staircase, this grand medieval-looking space has huge chandeliers, a frescoed ceiling, and marble columns, and none of the splendor has been lost on Hollywood location managers and art directors. Among the many movies, TV movies, and TV series that have shot sequences in the Park Plaza's lobby and its equally ornate and versatile ballroom: *New York, New York* (1977), *Blood Feud* (1979), *Stripes* (1981), *Young Doctors in Love* (1982), *Dempsey* (1983), *Dr. Detroit* (1983), *Naked Gun* (1988), *Stargate* (1988), *Wild at Heart* (1990), *The Hunt for Red October* (1990), *Hook* (1991), *Barton Fink* (1991), *Chaplin* (1992), *Final Analysis* (1992), *Reservoir Dogs* (1992), *What's Love Got to Do with It?* (1993), *The Mask* (1994), *Naked Gun 33⅓* (1994), *City of Angels* (1998), *Inspector Gadget* (1999), *Rock Star* (2001), *The Kids* (2004); *Lou Grant, Falcon Crest, Kojak, Family Law, CSI, Alias, Party of Five,* and *Angel.* In addition, it's been seen in many commercials as well as in music videos starring everyone from Pat Benatar to Donna Summer.

Location, location, location:
Park Plaza Hotel

Six Feet Under funeral parlor

26. *SIX FEET UNDER* FUNERAL HOME
2302 West Twenty-fifth Street

The idea of a TV series based on a funeral home was a bit out there—even for cable TV. But in 2000, HBO took a chance on Alan Ball's offbeat concept for a show called *Six Feet Under*, and, well, we all know the rest. Ball, who famously penned the 2000 Academy Award–winning film *American Beauty*, says he set *Six Feet Under* in Los Angeles because "L.A. is the denial of death." For the Fisher and Sons Funeral Home, his location people came up with the perfect property in an eclectic Arts and Crafts–style mansion on a quiet corner in a Filipino neighborhood in South Central L.A. According to Ball, Arrat House, as the place is known, houses the offices of a Filipino historical society.

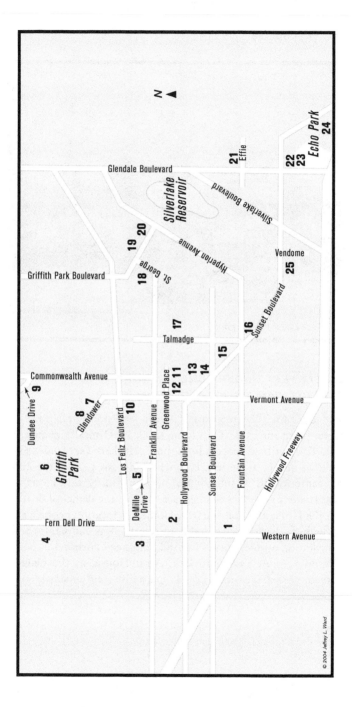

Los Feliz/Silverlake/Echo Park:
The Original "Hollywood"

Los Feliz, Silverlake, and Echo Park are the names of three neighborhoods that lie between Hollywood and downtown Los Angeles. In the earliest days of the movie industry, many of the first
studios were based in these East Hollywood areas, especially
around Silverlake, which was then known as Edendale. Today,
most of these studios are gone but the names of some of their
founders—Mack Sennett, D. W. Griffith, Walt Disney—are a
part of film history. The names of others—William Selig, Sig-
mund Lubin, George K. Spoor—may be remembered by only the
hardest of hard-core silent-movie aficionados.

For the serious film buff, fascinating vestiges of the Silver-
lake/East Hollywood area's once formidable film activity can be
discovered here: the original Vitagraph lot, for example, lives on
as the Prospect Studios; the odd wedge-shaped building, once the
private studio of Mack Sennett comedian Mabel Normand, is
now used to shoot covers for music videos. Other landmarks are
less well preserved: a little sign in a supermarket parking lot and
a photo inside the store are all that mark the site of the first Walt
Disney Studio, the birthplace of Mickey Mouse.

Whereas the studios tended to be clustered in and around Silverlake, Los Feliz—slightly to the north and considerably more

exclusive—was where many early stars and moguls had their homes. Among the neighborhood's legendary residents, Cecil B. DeMille never moved from Los Feliz. Walt Disney, on the other hand, eventually made the switch to Beverly Hills when Los Feliz fell from fashion in the 1940s. Today, however, many of the newer stars—Brad Pitt, Madonna, Kevin Spacey, Leonardo DiCaprio, and Courtney Cox and David Arquette—have rediscovered Los Feliz and are helping to make it trendy, if not chic, once again.

Besides early studios and movie-star houses, Los Feliz, Silverlake, and Echo Park hold even more surprises for the movie lover. Many of these are famous film locations. For example, the extraordinary Frank Lloyd Wright house that has been in many horror and science fiction flicks; the clutch of Victorian houses in Echo Park that has been used to represent everything from Depression-era Australia to today's Aspen, Colorado; the high school that is perhaps Hollywood's most photographed; and the stairs up which Laurel and Hardy tried to deliver a piano in their Academy Award–winning short, *The Music Box*.

Finally, a visit to Los Feliz, Silverlake, and Echo Park—areas that are not on most travelers' itineraries—is a trip into ethnic L.A. In addition to discovering monuments to early filmmaking, movie lovers will come across South American grocery stores, Thai restaurants, Korean shopping centers, Ukrainian bars, and Armenian lunch counters. A whole other Hollywood; call it the real world.

A car is required to best see these neighborhoods. Don't miss a walk or drive around Carroll Avenue. And for a look at the trendy side of Los Feliz, be sure to park and go for a stroll along Hillhurst and Vermont Avenues (between Los Feliz and Hollywood Boulevards), with their cool shops and smart cafes.

1. DELUXE LABORATORIES/FOX STUDIOS SITE
1377 North Serrano Avenue

Before there was a Twentieth Century–Fox, there was a William Fox. His Fox Studios, opened in 1917, once occupied much of the block at the southeast corner of Sunset Boulevard and Western Avenue. Early Fox stars were supervamp Theda Bara, cowboys Buck Jones and Tom Mix, plus Pearl White, Helen Ferguson, Colleen Moore, Jean Arthur, John Gilbert, Hope Hampton, Billie Dove, Janet Gaynor, Dolores Del Rio, and Carole Lombard.

William Fox started out in the picture business in 1904 when, at the age of twenty-five, he sold his cloth processing firm and opened a nickelodeon (price of admission, 5 cents) in a converted storefront in New York City. By 1913, Fox and his partners controlled a large chain of nickelodeons and the need for more films prompted them to start producing their own. In 1915, Fox moved to California, and two years later opened his Sunset/Western studios. It should be noted that while Warner Bros. made history as the studio that introduced talking pictures, Fox immediately met the challenge with its Movietone (sound-on-film) system. Much more sophisticated, it was Fox's sound system that all the studios eventually adopted.

The early thirties were not kind to William Fox or to his studio. In addition to the catastrophic effects of the stock market crash, the studio had serious legal troubles with the U.S. government. By 1935, when the company he founded merged with Joseph Schenck's two-year-old Twentieth Century Films, William Fox was no longer in the picture. Thus, Twentieth Century–Fox was born without Fox. Soon after the merger, the new studio's headquarters were moved to West Los Angeles, which remains their location today.

Today, all that is left of Fox's original Sunset/Western studios is the still-active Deluxe film lab ("Color by Deluxe"). A huge Food 4 Less discount supermarket and parking lot cover the rest of the site.

2. LE TRIANON
1752 North Serrano Avenue

According to numerous legends and at least one real estate brochure, "America's Sweetheart" Mary Pickford not only built Le Trianon in 1928 but had a vast penthouse apartment on the premises that featured "three levels of Old World Charm, hardwood floors, beams, archways, large rooms and more." But real

Le Trianon Apartments

estate brochures have never been noted for their accuracy. The building permit makes no mention of Miss Pickford, and lists the owner as the Chateau Holiday Corporation. A front? Who knows? Since Pickford built, bought, and sold quite a lot of real estate in her time, Le Trianon might well have been a part of her empire. What is sure about Le Trianon's beginnings is the fact that it was designed by a very famous Los Angeles architect of the time, Leland A. Bryant. His most famous creation: the landmark Art Deco Sunset Towers apartment house on Sunset Boulevard. Today, Le Trianon has been beautifully restored and looks just as good as it must have in 1928 when Mary Pickford may or may not have had that fabulous penthouse here.

3. THE AMERICAN FILM INSTITUTE
2021 North Western Avenue

Founded in 1967 "to advance and preserve the art of the moving image," the AFI has its administrative headquarters in Washington, D.C., and its campus (formerly that of Immaculate Heart College) in East Hollywood. Here, aspiring directors, writers, editors, designers, and camera people learn the art and craft of contemporary filmmaking. Among AFI's most successful graduates are directors David Lynch *(Eraserhead, Wild at Heart, Blue Velvet, Twin Peaks,* and *Mulholland Drive)* and Terrence Malick *(Days of Heaven, The Thin Red Line),* screenwriter Tom Rickman *(Coal Miner's Daughter),* and cinematographer Peter Deming *(Mulholland Drive, I ♥ Huckabees).*

Once a year AFI raises its profile considerably when it bestows its Lifetime Achievement Award (televised on the USA cable network) on one of the industry's finest. Recent winners of this prestigious honor have been actors Meryl Streep, Robert De Niro, Tom Hanks, Barbra Streisand, Harrison Ford, Dustin Hoffman and directors Robert Wise, Martin Scorsese, Clint Eastwood, and Steven Spielberg.

Besides its classrooms and production facilities, the AFI campus is also home to the Louis B. Mayer Library. With an extensive collection of film books, periodicals, scripts, transcripts, clippings, and still photographs, this reference/research library is open to AFI students as well as to visiting scholars, researchers, graduate students, and all members of the motion picture and television industry. Call 323–856–7600 or visit www.afi.com.

4. RAMON NOVARRO HOUSE
5699 Valley Oak Drive

Looking like an exotic pre-Columbian temple, this magnificent concrete-and-copper mansion is one of many dramatic Hollywood homes designed by Lloyd Wright, an architect whose significant accomplishments are often overlooked because of the greater fame of his father, Frank Lloyd Wright. Built in 1928, this particular Lloyd Wright landmark once belonged to silent screen superstar Ramon *(Ben Hur)* Novarro. Not content with any ordinary interior for his extraordinary residence, Novarro supposedly had MGM set designer Cedric Gibbons do up the place in black fur and silver. And when Novarro entertained in this marvelous maison, he sometimes insisted that his dinner guests dress for the decor and wear no colors other than black, silver, or white.

Novarro's movie career and his days of living lavishly were all part of the distant past at the time of his death in the late 1960s. By then, the sixty-nine-year-old lifelong bachelor was living—surrounded by the mementos of his glory years—in a ranch-style house on the less fashionable San Fernando Valley side of Laurel Canyon. On Halloween night of 1968, Novarro entertained two male hustlers, brothers who had gotten the former star's phone number from another hustler, at his home. It was nothing new for Novarro, who frequently purchased young male companionship and sex. This time, however, things got out of control and after an alcohol-filled evening, the two brothers turned on their host and savagely murdered him, inflicting a reported twenty-two blows on the frail old man. At the subsequent trial, in the less enlightened and more homophobic 1960s, the defense referred to Novarro as "an old queer," and the brothers, although convicted of first-degree murder, were each let out of prison early, one in six years, the other in nine. Later, actor-turned-novelist Tom Tryon would loosely base the "Willie" story in his 1970s bestseller, *Crowned Heads,* on this grisly and appalling event.

Ramon Novarro's designer house

Silent-screen superstar:
Ramon Novarro

The Novarro/Lloyd Wright House is hard to find. Best way to drive there is to head up Fern Dell Road off Los Feliz just east of Western Avenue. From Fern Dell, turn left onto Black Oak and follow a good map up the hill to Valley Oak.

5. DEMILLE DRIVE
Between Los Feliz Boulevard and Franklin Avenue

Named for none other than old C. B. himself, well-gated DeMille Drive is a twisting private hillside lane between Los Feliz Boulevard and Franklin Avenue. It was here that the pioneer director/producer lived in the same Spanish mansion—number 2000—from 1916 until his death in 1959. Over the years, some of DeMille's neighbors were Charlie Chaplin, who lived next door at 2010 in the late teens, and W. C. Fields, who lived across the street at 2015 in the early forties.

Supposedly, long before DeMille came to Los Feliz, the area was a sacred Indian burial ground said to be inhabited by spirits. In 1942, DeMille's two-year-old grandson—by his daughter Katherine and her then husband, actor Anthony Quinn—drowned in a

At home on DeMille Drive:
director Cecil B. DeMille

pond on Fields's property. Many attributed the child's death to an ancient Indian curse. Until recently, the former Fields house was shared for several decades by comedian Lily Tomlin and her writer-producer partner Jane Wagner. The DeMille house was maintained by the DeMille estate until 1988, when it was sold. Its current owners are restoring the property to its original splendor.

6. GRIFFITH PARK OBSERVATORY
Griffith Park

It's been seen time and again in all sorts of low-budget science-fiction films such as the 1950s-era *When Worlds Collide* and *War of the Colossal Beast*—usually as the laboratory where scientists on Earth are working feverishly to save the planet from alien invaders. But this famous planetarium, built in 1935, also has a number of A pictures to its credit. In 1984, Arnold Schwarzenegger materialized here in the buff as *The Terminator,* and a decade later, in director Carl Franklin's 1995 adaptation of novelist Walter Mosley's evocative thriller *Devil in a Blue Dress,* the Griffith Park Observatory furnishes the eerie backdrop for a scene where detective Easy Rawlins (Denzel Washington) drives the mysterious Daphne (Jennifer Beals) to a suspenseful late-night rendezvous that involves a swap of compromising photos for $30,000.

But no film has ever used this Hollywood Hills landmark as extensively or effectively as *Rebel Without a Cause* (1954). It is here where the students of Dawson High—new kid on campus James Dean is one of them—come on a field trip early on in the film. During the planetarium sky show, Dean's clowning fails to endear him to one group of classmates who later bully him in the parking lot. The scenes at the end of the film are also played against the background of the Griffith Park Observatory and Planetarium. This time, a very frightened Sal Mineo is hiding from the police inside the planetarium. Finally persuaded by Dean to come outside, Sal panics and is shot by one of the law officers. More than just a location, the observatory is used symbolically in the film, suggesting a cold and impersonal higher order of things that seems strangely uninvolved in the affairs of mortals.

James Dean on location at Griffith Park Observatory with *Rebel Without a Cause*

Griffith Park Observatory

The observatory is currently closed down for extensive renovations that will restore the structure as well as upgrade the planetarium and add new exhibit areas, an auditorium, and classrooms. The complex is scheduled to reopen in 2005. Visit www.griffithobs.org.

7. ENNIS-BROWN HOUSE
2607 Glendower Avenue

Of all the fantastic concrete-block residences that Frank Lloyd Wright built in Hollywood during the 1920s, the Ennis-Brown house is the most spectacular. Completed in 1924, the massive Mayan marvel enjoys a prized hillside location and can be seen from many points in the Hollywood flatlands. Possibly because it is so easy to see (and to photograph), the Ennis-Brown house has long fascinated Hollywood art directors and it has wound up in a number of movies. The place is said to have been the inspiration for the mysterious Hungarian castle that was the main location for Universal's horror classic *The Black Cat* (1934), the first picture to pair Boris Karloff and Bela Lugosi. Later, the Ennis-Brown house played the title role in Allied Artists' 1958 *The House on Haunted Hill*. Another of its memorable appearances was as the ultrachic mansion of art director Claude Estee in the 1974 film version of Nathanael West's *The Day of the Locust*. It was also a location for *Terminal Man* in 1974—and in Ridley Scott's *Blade Runner* (1982). Harrison Ford, starring as a twenty-first-century bounty hunter, lived and loved inside this same 1924 Los Angeles landmark building.

Scott returned in 1988 with *Black Rain,* using the Ennis-Brown house for a mob chieftain's lair in Japan, and the early 1990s brought director David Lynch to the Ennis-Brown house, which he used for his weird TV series *Twin Peaks* as well as for a famous Calvin Klein Obsession perfume commercial, which he directed. The 1990s also saw *The Rocketeer* (1990), *Grand Canyon* (1991), *Fallen Angels* (1993), *The Glimmer Man* (1996), *The Replacement Killers* (1997), and *Rush Hour* (1998) shoot here.

On television, the Ennis-Brown house turned up in *Buffy the Vampire Slayer,* as the mansion where the character Angel (David Boreanaz) lived with Spike and Drusilla. And when An-

Frank Lloyd Wright beauty: Ennis-Brown House

At home in the Ennis-Brown house: Harrison Ford in *Blade Runner*

gel got his own spinoff series, *Angel,* several seasons later, he kept his same smart Hollywood Hills address.

The Ennis-Brown House, now administered by the nonprofit Trust for Preservation of Cultural Heritage, runs guided tours several times a week. For information, call 323–660–0607 or visit www.ennisbrownhouse.org.

8. BRAD PITT RESIDENCE
2705 Glendower Avenue

In the last decade, some of Hollywood's coolest people have eschewed Beverly Hills and Brentwood for the much funkier and hipper neighborhoods of Los Feliz and the East Hollywood Hills. Among this in crowd are Madonna, Kevin Spacey, Courtney Cox and David Arquette, Leonardo DiCaprio, Claire Danes, Shannon Elizabeth, Flea, and Brad Pitt, who in his bachelor days called this walled Hills-hugging property with many garages home. These days, however, Pitt and his wife Jennifer Aniston have lavish homes in Beverly Hills and on the outskirts of Santa Barbara.

9. LOVELL HOUSE
4616 Dundee Drive

One of the most memorable locations in director Curtis Hansen's 1997 film noir *L.A. Confidential* was the sleek hillside mansion occupied by Pierce Pagett (David Strathairn). In the film, Pagett operates a prostitution ring that features movie-star lookalikes—Veronica Lake, Lana Turner, Rita Hayworth—but his Hollywood Hills home is the real thing: a 1929 classic of International Style by the noted Bauhaus architect Richard J. Neutra. Today, the house is privately owned and can only be glimpsed from the street; for far better views, rent the movie.

10. LOUISE'S TRATTORIA/BROWN DERBY SITE
4500 Los Feliz Boulevard

The last and least-known of L.A.'s once legendary four Brown Derby restaurants opened in Los Feliz in 1941 and closed in 1959. Today a branch of a popular Italian restaurant chain, Louise's Trattoria, occupies the same space—and remembers its predecessor by featuring its own version of the famous Brown Derby–invented Cobb Salad on the menu. And on the Vermont Avenue side of the property, a hip music club pays further homage to the old Hollywood watering hole by calling itself the Derby.

Over the years, the former Brown Derby has occasionally been used as a location for feature films, including the classic Joan Crawford comeback film, *Mildred Pierce* (1945), plus *Speed* (1994) and *Swingers* (1996).

For reservations at Louise's, call 323-667-0777; for what's on at the Derby, call 323-663-8979.

11. *MELROSE PLACE* APARTMENTS
4616 Greenwood Place

It reigned for seven seasons in the 1990s as one of the decade's prime nighttime soap operas. Based on a group of young people living in a lush Mediterranean courtyard complex in Los Angeles, *Melrose Place* was unique in that most of its residents were not pursuing movie careers. Instead, they worked in advertising,

Melrose Place apartments

health care, physical fitness, hospitality, and social work. The building that anchored their adventures and misadventures was number 4616 Melrose Place. Melrose Place is a chic little off-shoot of Melrose Avenue in West Hollywood, known for its posh interior decorators' offices and showrooms. The building that the series used, however, was actually way across town at 4616 Greenwood Place, a somewhat less chic block-long street, just off Vermont Avenue in East Hollywood. A former real-life resident of 4616 Greenwood Place, which in real life is called El Patio, was writer Raymond Chandler, who lived here in the 1930s.

12. LOS FELIZ THEATER
1822 North Vermont Avenue

It was at this unprepossessing movie theater that well-known L.A. movie house maven Bob Laemmle introduced Tinseltown to foreign films, which he screened here on a regular basis just after World War II. For a long time, the Los Feliz reigned as one of L.A.'s premier "art" houses. But in the early 1990s, the Los Feliz was almost forced to close when Laemmle Theatres was unable to negotiate a new lease with new owners of the theater site. Happily, for movie lovers, this was eventually sorted out and the theater—now a triplex—shows a healthy mix of mainstream U.S. films and offbeat American and foreign fare in what is currently one of L.A.'s trendiest neighborhoods.

For program information, call 323-664-2169.

13. "BABYLON" SITE
4473 Sunset Drive

Here, where the Vista Theater now stands—as well as on much of the land behind it—the great motion picture pioneer, D. W. Griffith, erected one of the greatest movie sets Hollywood has ever known: the towering city of Babylon. The year was 1916, and Griffith built his Babylon for a film originally called *The Mother and the Law,* but which has gone down in film history as *Intolerance.* The film was Griffith's follow-up to (and some say apology for) his immensely popular and racially controversial *The Birth of a Nation.* At the time of its release, *Intolerance* was touted as the most expensive movie ever produced. Despite its

Babylon on Sunset: D. W. Griffith's set for *Intolerance*, 1916

cost, *Intolerance* was not a box-office success and wound up putting Griffith in severe financial straits. For several years after *Intolerance* was released, the massive Babylon set was not torn down and remained a Sunset Boulevard oddity and a tribute to Griffith's creative and financial excesses. In 1919, there was talk of preserving the set as a permanent landmark, but nothing came of it, and the legendary movie-set city of Babylon was eventually swallowed up by a city that was fast becoming equally legendary . . . Hollywood.

Cut to 2001, when a dramatic new shopping-entertainment complex called Hollywood & Highland (see Chapter 1, item 9) debuts on Hollywood Boulevard and re-creates Griffith's Babylon with great elephant-topped columns as its principal stylistic motif. Alas, this noble architectural gesture seems to be lost on the tourists tramping around the new center's spectacular staircases and courtyard, most of whom haven't a clue who D. W. Griffith was. Writing in the *Los Angeles Times,* columnist Paul Brownfield noted in 2004 that "cultural observers said the complex would have been better off modeling the court after a more accessible movie, such as *Meet the Parents.*"

14. VISTA THEATER
4473 Sunset Drive

The pretty oxblood-red Spanish exterior of this little movie house belies the wild 1920s Egyptian decor inside. Originally part of the Lou Bard theater chain, the Vista (then known as the Bard) opened in 1923 with a mixed bill of vaudeville acts and silent movies. One explanation of the theater's schizophrenic architectural personality says that the owners intended to build a totally Spanish-style theater, but decided to go Egyptian in the middle of the theater's construction on hearing of the discovery of Tutankhamen's, or King Tut's, tomb in 1922. For decades an important revival house, the theater, recently restored, now shows first-run films. The theater was used for the 1993 film *True Romance,* as the spot where Christian Slater and Patricia Arquette first meet at a triple bill.

For program information, call 323-660-6639.

15. KCET STUDIOS
4401 Sunset Boulevard

The Cultural Heritage Board of the City of Los Angeles has designated the KCET studio site Historic Cultural Monument No. 198. The oldest continually used studio in the country, the KCET complex was established in 1912 by the Lubin Manufacturing Company, an early film producing organization that was based in Philadelphia. Subsequent occupants were such forgotten silent-picture companies as Essanay (they produced twenty-one Westerns here), Willis and Ingles, and J. D. Hampton. By 1920, matinee idol Charles Ray took over the studio and eventually produced and starred in the ill-fated *The Courtship of Miles Standish* (1924), which bankrupted the actor as well as his production company. Many of the Spanish-style brick buildings that still occupy the KCET lot were built during the Charles Ray reign.

After various other tenants, Monogram Pictures came on the scene in the 1940s. Among the many "B" movies made by Monogram on this site were series such as the *East Side Kids*, the *Cisco Kid,* and *Charlie Chan.* In the 1950s, through a merger, Monogram and its lot became another famous B studio—Allied Artists. Among the memorable Allied Artists films shot and edited here were *The Attack of the 50-Foot Woman* (1958) and the original *Invasion of the Body Snatchers* (1956).

After serving as a rental lot for television productions in the 1960s, the studio was acquired in 1970 by KCET—the Los Angeles Public Broadcasting network. Since that time, KCET has been responsible for producing a number of nationally televised PBS series—including *Hollywood Television Theater, Visions,* Dr. Carl Sagan's *Cosmos,* and most recently *PBS Hollywood Presents,* a series of dramas that have starred Dick Van Dyke, Mary Tyler Moore, Linda Lavin, and Debbie Allen.

KCET organizes group tours of its historic facilities by special arrangement. Besides providing insight into how television shows are produced, the tours also offer a look at the vestiges of KCET's movie-studio days, such the 1933 screening room—a beautiful little theater with white columns, beamed ceiling, bricked walls and floors—that for years was boarded up and used as a storage space until it was "discovered" and restored. For information, call 323-953-5289 or visit www.kcet.org.

16. MACK SENNETT STAGES STUDIO
1215 Bates Street

These days, photo shoots for print ads and record album covers take place inside this little wedge-shaped building with the high-high ceilings. Originally built for making movies back in 1916, this was once the personal studio of Mack Sennett's favorite on- and off-screen comedian, Mabel Normand. At the time, the studio was built entirely of wood and had a canvas-topped roof that could be opened and closed to control the sunlight that lit the sets below. A permanent roof was probably added in the 1920s, at which time the space was taken over by another silent screen great—cowboy star William S. Hart—who also used it for his own production company. In the late 1960s, yet another super-star was linked to this historic site: Barbra Streisand. It was a location for her first film, *Funny Girl*. Since then, Celine Dion, Dolly Parton, Rod Stewart, and Donna Summer have posed for album covers on the same historic stage where Mabel Normand once made silent films.

Still going strong:
Mabel Normand's former studio,
now Mack Sennett Stages

17. THE PROSPECT STUDIOS
4151 Prospect Avenue

Today, the name Vitagraph doesn't ring too many bells, but in the early part of the twentieth century it was a household word. One of the country's most important pioneer movie companies, Vitagraph traces its beginnings back to 1896 when two vaudeville comedians, Albert E. Smith and J. Stuart Blackton, decided to bring a projector and a couple of very short films into their act. When the movies proved more popular than their routines, Smith and Blackton realized that the future lay in the magical new medium of motion pictures—and Vitagraph was born. Based in the Flatbush section of Brooklyn, Smith and Blackton started filming everything from the Spanish American War to Teddy Roosevelt's inauguration. They also developed a powerful distribution system, signed the first actress ever to a movie contract (Florence Turner, the Vitagraph Girl), and like many early film companies, eventually established a California unit.

Vitagraph's first California films were shot in Santa Monica around 1912. In 1915, Al Smith purchased a large tract of land at Prospect Avenue and Talmadge Street in East Hollywood for a grand new studio. The lot became home to silent-era stars such as Anita Stewart, Corinne Griffith, Clara Kimball Young, Antonio Moreno, Bessie Love, Wallace Reid, Dolores Costello, Alla Nazimova, Adolphe Menjou, and Stan Laurel in his pre–Oliver Hardy period. By 1925, however, Vitagraph was having financial difficulties, and an aggressive younger movie company called Warner Bros. not only bought the ailing company but absorbed Vitagraph's stars and the copyrights to all its screenplays. The latter enabled Warner Bros. to remake many of Vitagraph's old hits. Since Warner Bros. had its main studios on Sunset Boulevard and later in Burbank, the former Vitagraph lot was always used by Warners as an annex studio. Nonetheless, all or parts of many important Warner Bros. pictures were shot here from the mid-twenties to the late-forties. Among them: *Trapped in the Snow Country,* starring the most popular box-office star of 1926—Rin-Tin-Tin; *The Jazz Singer* (1927); *The Glorious Betsy* (1928); James Cagney in *Public Enemy* (1931); *The Gold Diggers of 1933* with Ginger Rogers and Joan Blondell; and Errol Flynn in 1935's *Captain Blood.*

Vitagraph Studios, 1924

In 1948, the studio complex was bought and remodeled by the fledgling ABC Television Network. Over the years, as the ABC Television Center, the Prospect lot was used for game shows *(Let's Make a Deal, Family Feud,* the *Dating Game,* the *Newly-wed Game,* and *Password),* variety shows *(American Bandstand* and the *Lawrence Welk Show),* and soap operas, notably the long-running *General Hospital,* which has been based here for years. Recently ABC, now owned by Disney, moved out of the Prospect lot to new headquarters in Burbank. But ABC's local affiliate is still here, as is *General Hospital;* at the same time, Disney is using the historic East Hollywood studio, just as Warner Bros. once did, as an annex for feature-film production.

Movie lovers passing by the studio should check out the new gate, which duplicates the 1920s Vitagraph original. Visit www.abc.com.

18. JOHN MARSHALL HIGH SCHOOL
8939 Tracy Street

The archetypal American high school, this classic of "Collegiate Gothic" architecture has been Dawson High in *Rebel Without a Cause,* Rydell High in *Grease,* and numerous nameless highs in countless television commercials, TV movies, and episodes of series. In reality, John Marshall was built in 1928, has 3,400 students, and narrowly escaped demolition in the early 1970s because it did not meet earthquake code standards. The building has long since been stabilized and saved for future generations of students—and movie companies.

Among the latter have been the two 1980s takeoffs on high-school flicks, *Zapped* and *Zapped Again,* plus *Uncle Buck* (1989), *Wild at Heart* (1990), *The Fisher King* (1991), *Reservoir Dogs* (1992), the original *Buffy the Vampire Slayer* (1992), *The Mask* (1994), the original *Naked Gun* (1994), *Space Jam* (1995), *True Crimes* (1996), and *Better Luck Tomorrow* (2002). TV appearances range from *Mr. Novak* in the 1960s to *Lucas Tanner* and the *A-Team* in the 1970s to *Cheers* and *Tribes* in the 1980s to *Boy Meets World* and *Hang Time* in the 1990s. From 1988 to 1993, John Marshall High had a recurring role as Robert F. Kennedy Junior High in the *Wonder Years,* and lately it's been used as Winslow High School in *Boston Public.* Meanwhile, Los Feliz local Leonardo DiCaprio is a former John Marshall student.

Visit www.lausd.kl2.ca.us/Marshall_HS.

Standard-issue high school:
John Marshall

Fairy-tale apartment
complex, East Hollywood

19. COURTYARD COMPLEX
2900–2912 Griffith Park Boulevard

Legend has it that these enchanting storybook cottages were built by Walt Disney to house studio personnel. Located just around the corner from Disney's original Hyperion Avenue location, this story would seem plausible. City records, however, indicate that the courtyard complex was built by a Lois and Ben Sherwood around 1931. Another theory suggests that while Disney didn't build these little houses, he was influenced by their architecture, especially when he was preparing *Snow White and the Seven Dwarfs*. The Dwarfs' cottage in the film bears a striking resemblance to these Griffith Park Boulevard bungalows.

In David Lynch's creepy 2001 look at Hollywood, *Mulholland Drive*, the director used these fairy-tale cottages to chilling effect as the place where the film's antiheroes Betty (Naomi Watts) and Ruby (Laura Elena Harring) go looking for a mysterious woman named Diana Selwyn. Breaking into number 176 through the window, what they find is not a pretty sight.

20. GELSON'S MARKET/WALT DISNEY STUDIOS SITE
2719 Hyperion Avenue

Once it was a magic kingdom. Today, a supermarket and parking lot stand on the site of the original Walt Disney Studios. Housed in a charming white Spanish Colonial building, Disney's domain was described in the 1930s by reporter Janet Flanner as "the sanest spot in Hollywood . . . remotely located in one of those endless suburban settings of Barcelona bungalows, pink roses and red filling stations that makes Southern California so picturesque. The studio looks like a small municipal kindergarten with green grass for the children to keep off of and, on the roof, a gigantic glorious figure of Mickey to show them the best way. . . . With hysteria the seeming law for movie making, it's a wonder Mickey and Silly Symphonies succeed in this world at all, since the place where they're made is as sensible as a post office" *(Harper's Bazaar,* November 1, 1936).

Disney occupied his Hyperion Avenue quarters from 1926 until moving to the current Disney Studios location in Burbank in 1940. It was during the Hyperion period, however, that Mickey Mouse was born and that Disney's first feature-length film, *Snow*

Disney's Hyperion Avenue studios, 1930

White and the Seven Dwarfs, was produced. Today, a small plaque outside the supermarket and a photo of the original Disney building prominently displayed inside commemorate the magic that once went on here in Silverlake.

21. PS PUBLIC STORAGE/MACK SENNETT STUDIOS SITE
1712 Glendale Boulevard

As the traffic swarms up and down busy Glendale Boulevard, few of the motorists making their way between the Glendale Freeway and downtown L.A. have any idea that the area of Silverlake they're passing through was a lively center of motion picture production back in the early years of the twentieth century. In those days, the neighborhood had the romantic name of Edendale, and Glendale Boulevard was called Allesandro Avenue. The Selig Company was on Allesandro, as were the Pathé West Coast Studio and the Bison Studio. One of the largest and most successful of the Allesandro Avenue movie companies was the Keystone Comedy Company at number 1712. Founded in 1912 as a division of the New York Motion Picture Company, the Keystone studios were headed by the legendary Mack Sennett. It was here that he produced his Keystone Kops and numerous other come-

Silverlake warriors: Mack Sennett's Keystone Kops

dies until 1927 when he moved his headquarters to Studio City in the San Fernando Valley.

In its heyday, the Keystone Comedy Company spread over both sides of Allesandro Avenue and featured stars such as Charlie Chaplin, Gloria Swanson, Roscoe "Fatty" Arbuckle, Buster Keaton, Ben Turpin, Louise Fazenda, Phyllis Haver, Marie Prevost, and Mabel Normand. The studio also featured one of the first enclosed concrete stages ever built. Today, that stage has been restored and stuccoed and transformed into a self-storage facility. Despite the redo, the hulking, high-ceilinged structure, which is set back from the street, still looks like a film studio. A plaque gives the history of the property, now a Historic Cultural Monument.

22. ANGELUS TEMPLE
1100 Glendale Boulevard

She wasn't a movie star—although many said she lived like one, her extravagances supposedly including mansions, money, and men. One thing is certain about evangelist Aimee Semple McPherson: She possessed "star quality" and marketed the commodity as effectively and successfully as any Hollywood personality in history. The clothes were always glamorous, the hair and makeup perfect, and the show—with music, mass baptisms, faith healings—was more spectacular than anything playing at Grauman's Chinese Theater. Thousands came to see and hear Sister Aimee at the great white semicircular temple that she built in 1923 across from Echo Park. With her name blazing in neon on the marquee outside and its huge auditorium within, the place seemed more a theater than a church. "No change," she roared, as the collection plates were passed, "greenbacks only!" Those who couldn't be there in person listened to her over the radio and sent in their contributions. Broadcasting from her own KFSG—the third radio station in Los Angeles and the first in this country's eventual long line of evangelical radio stations—she was one of America's first great radio stars.

Aimee Semple McPherson died (some say of a deliberate drug overdose) in 1944. Her legend and her church continue to this day. A 1980s television movie told her life story and starred Faye Dunaway; Nathanael West based the character Big Sister on

Aimee Semple McPherson's Angelus Temple

Aimee in his *The Day of the Locust*—Geraldine Page played the part in the 1974 film version. The greatest monument to Aimee Semple McPherson's career, however, is the Angelus Temple. Extensively renovated, it still occupies the same site across from Echo Park. If not one of the city's most beautiful houses of worship, it is certainly one of the most dramatic. Like its founder.

For anyone wishing to see the church's interior—which boasts the largest unsupported dome in North America—the doors are sometimes open. Otherwise, check to see when services are scheduled. A small religious bookshop is also on the premises and offers the official version of Sister Aimee's life. Visit www.angelustemple.org.

23. ECHO PARK

Not far from Mack Sennett's old Keystone Studios, this pretty park saw a lot of action back in the antic days of Sennett's Keystone Kops. If somebody landed in the drink at the end of a chase scene or via a mishap aboard a boat, chances are the body of water they wound up in was Echo Park Lake. Edged by tall palm trees and filled with giant water lilies, Echo Park Lake was also the exotic L.A. locale where Jack Nicholson can be spotted aboard a rowboat in an early scene in the 1974 film *Chinatown*. It has also appeared in *True Confessions* (1981), *The Grifters* (1990), *Pulp Fiction* (1994), *L.A. Confidential* (1997). The park and the somewhat seedy surrounding neighborhood star in a low-budget 1988 film about showbiz hopefuls living on the edge in L.A.; the film just happens to be called *Echo Park*. The park, one of the oldest public parks in Los Angeles, was founded in 1891.

Visit www.historicechopark.org

24. CARROLL AVENUE HISTORIC BLOCK
1300 Block

Contrary to what many people think, Los Angeles wasn't always dominated by Craftsman bungalows and dreamy Spanish-style architecture. Once upon a time, in the late 1800s, the city was just as Victorian as the rest of the United States. While little of Victorian L.A. remains today, a notable exception is the hillside near Echo Park in the area known as Angelino Heights. Developed in 1886, Angelino Heights was downtown L.A.'s first suburb and was connected to the city via a cable car that ran along Temple Street. Today, some fifty beautiful Victorian residences and carriage houses—in various states of restoration—still dominate this surprising enclave of another century.

Ready for its close-up:
1330 Carroll Avenue

Besides being listed in the National Register of Historic Places, the 1300 block of Carroll Avenue is also listed in most studio location scouters' notebooks as the place to go for an instant Victorian setting. Feature films, TV movies, and commercials are constantly being shot here. That purple Victorian mansion that a trio of beautiful young San Francisco witches—Pru, Piper, and Phoebe—call home in the series *Charmed* is actually number 1329 Carroll Avenue. The same house was also used in *Sweet Dreams* (1985), *Of Mice and Men* (1992), and *Deuce Bigelow: Male Gigolo* (1999). A few houses down, there's one of the country's most famous haunted houses at number 1345, a scary unpainted number that was the prime location for Michael Jackson's landmark 1980s video "Thriller."

Nothing if not versatile, Carroll Avenue has doubled as 1930s Australia in the famous 1980s miniseries *The Thorn Birds,* in a sequence that was shot in Los Angeles. For the 1977 miniseries, *Aspen,* fake snow was sprayed all over the street to duplicate the chic Colorado ski town. The 1982 TV version of *East of Eden* did up number 1320 Carroll Avenue as Kate and Faye's Bordello; the same house also served as Marjo's rooming house in *Earthquake* (1974) and has appeared in a host of other films: *Nickelodeon* (1976), *Salem's Lot* (1979), *Serial* (1980), *Modern Problems* (1981), *Monster in the Closet* (1987), *Intruders* (1992), *Panther* (1995), *Inherit the Wind* (1999)—and on the small screen in such made-for-TV fare as *The Immigrants* (1978), *Splendor in the Grass* (1981), and the series *Party of Five*.

The 1300 block also has more than one hundred commercials to its credit. Most actors would kill for this résumé.

The Los Angeles Conservancy has tours of Angelino Heights featuring Carroll Avenue several times a month. For information, call 213-623-CITY or visit www.laconservancy.org.

25. *THE MUSIC BOX* STAIRS
932-935 Vendome Street

With the Depression in full swing, there wasn't much to laugh about in America in 1932, but producer/director Hal Roach and the famed comedy duo of Stan Laurel and Oliver Hardy gave

The Music Box, 1932

movie audiences a hilarious lift with a little film called *The Music Box*. The film—in which "the Boys" try to deliver a piano to a house at the top of a long flight of stairs—won Roach an Academy Award as the best short (comedy) subject of 1931–1932. The stairs that Stan and Ollie grappled with are still standing between 932 and 935 Vendome Street, just south of Sunset Boulevard in Silverlake. A little-known fact is that these same stairs were used in an earlier Laurel and Hardy film, *Hats Off*, a 1927 release that had them delivering vacuum cleaners. In the early eighties, the Los Angeles Cultural Heritage Board voted down a proposal to make the *Music Box* stairs an official cultural landmark. They later reconsidered and the site today not only has landmark status but its own street sign.

The Santa Fe Court apartment building next door has its own film history, since it's been used in *Indecent Proposal* (1993), *Nurse Betty* (2000), and *Confessions of a Dangerous Mind* (2002). Not to be outdone by the *Music Box* stairs, the owner of this classic courtyard apartment house has put up his own plaque to document the building's film pedigree.

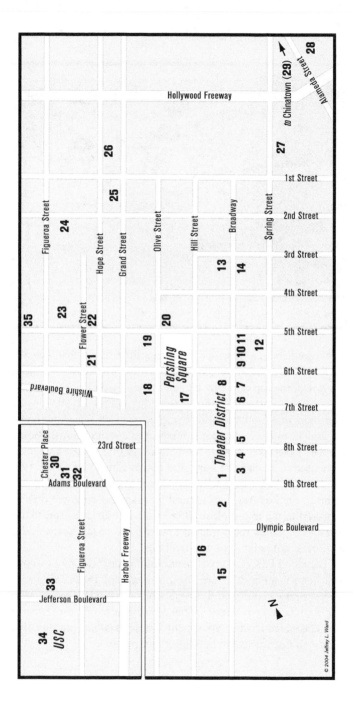

Hollywood Freeway

to Chinatown (29)

Alameda Street

28

27

1st Street

Figueroa Street

24

25

26

Olive Street

Hope Street

Grand Street

Hill Street

Broadway

Spring Street

2nd Street

3rd Street

4th Street

13

14

35

23

Flower Street

22

20

21

19

5th Street

Pershing Square

9 10 11

12

6 7

6th Street

Wilshire Boulevard

18

17

Theater District

8

7th Street

Chester Place

30

31

32

Adams Boulevard

23rd Street

1

3 4 5

8th Street

2

9th Street

Figueroa Street

Harbor Freeway

16

Olympic Boulevard

33

15

Jefferson Boulevard

34

USC

N

© 2004 Jeffrey L. Ward

Downtown Los Angeles: The First L.A.

It started with eleven families back in 1781. Recruited in Mexico as part of Spain's master plan to consolidate its empire and power in California, these early settlers—a band of Mexicans, Africans, and mulattos—named their new town El Pueblo de Nuestra Señora la Reina de los Angeles (Village of Our Lady Queen of the Angels). During its formative years, little of note happened in this small settlement with the long name. In 1826, owing to the revolution in Mexico, Los Angeles became Mexican rather than Spanish—but the change in administration had minimal effect on the town. More influential were the Anglos from the new United States of America. These included trappers, farmers, contractors, and at least one surgeon. Some learned the Spanish language; others didn't. In any event, English soon became the official language of Los Angeles, once California was ceded by Mexico to the United States following the Mexican War in 1848. By 1850, California was a full-fledged state and more and more Americans started moving in. It wasn't until two decades later, however, when transcontinental rail travel became a reality, that L.A.'s boom times really began. In 1870, the town's population numbered 5,000 people; by 1880, it had grown to 11,000; and by 1890, it was close to 100,000.

All this is to say that Los Angeles was a well-established and

Last picture show: Rialto marquee

fully functioning metropolis by the time the movies went West in the early part of the twentieth century. And when those first movie men arrived, they didn't head for Hollywood—most stayed right in downtown L.A. First on the scene was director Francis Boggs, who was with the Chicago-based Selig Polyscope Company of Col. William Selig. After having shot some sequences on the Pacific coast at La Jolla in 1907, Boggs set up a temporary studio on a rooftop at Eighth and South Olive Streets in downtown Los Angeles. About a year later, Boggs established what is considered to be L.A.'s first permanent studio; this time, he used a vacant Chinese laundry, again on Olive Street, and it was here where he shot *The Heart of a Racing Tout* (1909), the first dramatic feature film done entirely in California.

D. W. Griffith arrived in Los Angeles in 1910. Employed at the time by the American Mutoscope and Biograph Company of New York, Griffith worked mostly out of downtown L.A. until 1913, when he left Biograph. As more moviemakers came to Los Angeles, they founded studios in other areas: Silverlake, Santa Monica, Hollywood, Culver City. Nevertheless, for the first ten years of intensive moviemaking in L.A.—roughly from 1910 to

1920—it was downtown that was the nerve center as well as the social center for the new industry.

Downtown hotels were very important to the scheme of things. Not only were these great meeting places for the movie colony, they were often "home," since there was much going back and forth between New York and L.A. in those early days. D. W. Griffith, for example, shot in New York in the summer and fall, and then came West for the winter, staying in the Alexandria Hotel, which still stands at Sixth and Spring Streets, although it has seen better days.

Downtown movie theaters were important, too, for they were the sites of gala movie premieres years before these events happened in Hollywood. In fact, downtown is where the movie palace was born in Los Angeles—and where it flourished. Although these theaters, with a few exceptions, are no longer operating, most are still standing, impressive monuments to another age. For the movie lover, checking out these landmarks can be an exciting archaeological odyssey.

Dangling over downtown L.A.: Harold Lloyd in *Safety Last*, 1923

You don't have to be an archaeologist, however, to see that downtown Los Angeles is currently in the midst of a major renaissance. Not only are large numbers of people moving into the area's new apartments and refurbished loft spaces, the neighborhood now boasts trendy new hotels and restaurants as well as the city's striking new Frank O. Gehry–designed Walt Disney Concert Hall. But for movie lovers, the strongest indication of this new life is the recently opened Los Angeles Center Studios, the first brand-new movie studio to be built anywhere in L.A. in decades. How fitting that the movie business, which began in downtown L.A. almost a century ago, has finally returned to its roots.

Downtown L.A. is best seen on foot. The first fourteen sites in this chapter can be covered in one or two hours. For those wishing a longer walking tour, items 15 through 29 can be added to the itinerary, especially when using the Metro to cut down on some of the walking. A car will be necessary to visit the last five sites.

1. THEATER DISTRICT
South Broadway, between Third and Ninth Streets

By the 1930s, Los Angeles had more theaters than any other metropolitan area in the country—some 1,500 of them to be exact. And nowhere was there a greater concentration of theaters—nickelodeons, movie palaces, vaudeville, and legit houses—than along South Broadway in the middle of downtown Los Angeles. A great surprise was that, as recently as the 1980s, most of these theaters, built between the teens and the thirties, were not only still standing but still operating! These theaters endured, quite simply, because they still drew crowds—and the more lavish the theater, the bigger the take. Of course, back in the 1980s, most of the movies were in Spanish or with Spanish subtitles because by that time South Broadway had evolved into the center of Latino Los Angeles. It was also in the 1980s that Broadway and its theaters were declared a National Historic District.

Today, South Broadway—with its discount stores, jewelry centers, fast-food operations, and vast Mercado Central—is as vibrant as ever. But alas, almost none of the movie houses are showing pictures anymore. Unable to be torn down, thanks to their landmark status, some stand boarded up, whereas others have been recycled into churches, mini-malls, or venues for location shoots and special events. And at least one, the Orpheum, has been totally restored and now reigns as the street's great preservation triumph. But no matter what their current status is, these aging movie palaces still have the power to amaze and are well worth exploring, as is South Broadway.

For an insider look at the South Broadway theater district, the Los Angeles Conservancy offers a two-hour walking tour that takes participants inside some of the historic vaudeville and movie houses; the tour is usually given every Saturday starting at 10 a.m. For reservations and/or information, call 213-623-CITY or visit www.laconservancy.org.

2. UNITED ARTISTS THEATER
933 South Broadway

Mary Pickford and Douglas Fairbanks had just returned from a grand European tour about the time that their production and distribution company—United Artists—was getting into the mo-

United Artists Theater

tion picture theater business. Supposedly, Miss Pickford had been particularly taken with the great cathedrals and castles she had seen on the Continent and insisted that her company's flagship movie palace be just as splendid. Miss Pickford's fantasy was made a reality by the Detroit architect C. Howard Crane, who designed a spectacular theater that was somewhere between a Gothic castle and a great Spanish cathedral. (The theater opened on December 26, 1927, with Miss Pickford and Buddy Rogers—her eventual husband—starring in *My Best Girl.*)

In the lobby of the United Artists, the ceiling is vaulted and frescoed, the gold-edged mirrors enormous, and the banisters fashioned of hand-carved teak. (When the theater opened in 1927, the carpets, specially woven in France, matched the frescoes on the ceiling.) In the house itself, the walls appear to be made of huge stone blocks and the ceiling, embedded with thousands of tiny mirrors, creates a dazzling and magical light show. Two huge murals on either side of the house depict heraldic medieval scenes. The mural on the right, however, is a wonderful spoof: The faces all belong to various members of the board of directors of the United Artists Corporation—including Pickford and Fairbanks.

Today, the United Artists Theater is in remarkably good condition and little has been done in the last half-century to alter the essential splendor of the place. The only bad news for movie lovers is that it no longer shows films. Instead, it is now the Los Angeles University Cathedral Church, featuring evangelist Dr. Gene Scott. Anyone wishing to check out the premises should consider dropping by on Sunday.

3. ORPHEUM THEATER
842 South Broadway

Five magnificent chandeliers light the lobby, designed in 1925 with real and faux marble by G. Albert Landsburgh to re-create the lobby of a European grand hotel. The house itself holds some two thousand spectators and is a spectacle of gold-leafing and stenciling. Two $45,000 (1925 dollars) chandeliers are major decorative elements, along with Gothic arches and great round stained-glass panels under the balcony that are illuminated to provide atmospheric lighting. When it opened in 1925, the Orpheum was the last Orpheum vaudeville theater to be built in Los Angeles. Ironi-

Orpheum Theater marquee

cally, it turned out to be the place where vaudeville held out longer than practically anywhere else in the country. As late as 1950, vaudeville acts were still playing the Orpheum on South Broadway in L.A. In 1994, Bette Midler used the theater as a vaudeville house location for her TV movie version of the Broadway play and 1964 Hollywood film *Gypsy*. The early 1990s also saw *Dead Again* (1991), *Barton Fink* (1991), *The Last Action Hero* (1993), and *Ed Wood* (1994) shoot sequences at the Orpheum.

The theater featured first-run movies with Spanish subtitles up until 2000, when, showing its age, it finally closed down. But today, the Orpheum is one of the great success stories along Broadway, since it was lavishly restored in 2002 and now hosts special events, awards shows, film festivals, and live theatrical productions. The restored Orpehum was also the winner of the coveted Los Angeles Conservancy Preservation Award for 2002.

Visit www.laorpheum.com.

4. TOWER THEATER
802 South Broadway

S. Charles Lee—whose architectural credits include the Max Factor Building in Hollywood and the dazzling Los Angeles Theater down the street on South Broadway—designed the Tower The-

The Tower Theater's
spectacular staircase

ater in 1927. It was the first theater in Los Angeles to be built for talkies and to be "mechanically refrigerated." It was also extraordinarily handsome on the outside since its corner location allowed Lee to design essentially a complete building, rather than just a façade. With the Tower, Lee created a baroque fantasy of tile, sculpted niches, and pseudo-balconies—all dominated by an ornate corner clock tower (which was lowered substantially after the 1971 earthquake). Inside the theater, Lee tried to duplicate, on a small scale, the opulence of the lobby of the Paris Opera using stained glass, sculpted ceilings, and chandeliers. No longer a movie house, today's Tower is the Universal Church, its marquee proclaiming "There is but one Lord—Jesus Christ."

5. GLOBE THEATER
744 South Broadway

Opened in 1913 and originally run by Oliver Morosco (who was later to become a producer in New York and to have a theater named after him off the "other" Broadway), the Globe was one of the first legitimate houses to operate on Broadway in L.A. The Globe also did a stint in the 1930s and 1940s as a newsreel theater. In those pre-television days, it showed—as did many movie houses across the country—newsreels exclusively. At lunch, after work, between jobs, people would pop into this kind of theater to keep up with what was going on in the outside world. Today the Globe, after several decades of featuring movies en Español, houses two commercial establishments: a Mexican dress shop specializing in frocks for First Holy Communions and weddings and a storefront legal firm.

6. CLIFTON'S CAFETERIA
648 South Broadway

A night or an afternoon at the movies on Broadway in the 1930s might also have included a visit to Clifton's Brookdale Cafeteria— not just to eat but to keep the fantasy going. When it opened in 1935, Clifton's tried to create the feeling of being in the great outdoors. Today, the place is still quite an experience. The main dining room has grotto-like walls, a huge forest mural, four tiers of balconies with rough-hewn tables and balustrades, a waterfall that cascades into a burbling brook, plastic plants and flowers, and a

Celebrating cinema: Clifton Cafeteria's terrazzo

full-sized statue of a deer that watches over everything. Only the
self-service cafeteria section at the rear of the restaurant seems considerably modernized. Also the menu has taken a decided Latino
turn, as has the background music. Outside the building, a still-
bright terrazzo sidewalk pictures the attractions—movie studios
are among them—of Southern California. Movie lovers can see the
cafeteria in the 1999 Brad Pitt–Ed Norton film *Fight Club*.

Visit www.cliftonscafeteria.com.

7. PALACE THEATER
630 South Broadway

This theater was designed by G. Albert Landsburgh for the powerful Orpheum vaudeville circuit. Called the Orpheum when it
opened in 1911 as a vaudeville house, it is considered the oldest
surviving Orpheum-built theater in the United States. Renamed
the Palace, the theater showed movies from the 1920s to the
1990s. In 1983, it was used by director John Landis as a location

Downtown splendor:
Palace Theater proscenium

for the Michael Jackson "Thriller" video. Today, the theater is out of business, but movie lovers can still admire its French Renaissance façade and peer through the gates at its deep exterior foyer with gold columns, mirrors, frescoed ceiling, and handsome "island" ticket booth.

8. LOS ANGELES THEATER
615 South Broadway

If Louis XIV had known about motion picture palaces back in the seventeenth century and built one, it most likely would have been the Los Angeles Theater. Impressive on the outside, with a terrazzo sidewalk and a massive columned façade, the Los Angeles is even more dazzling inside. The lobby alone provides a new definition of the word splendor—with glittering chandeliers, monumental mirrors, ornate staircase, fluted columns, and a crystal fountain.

Besides its dizzying decor, the theater offered amenities that gave a new definition to the word luxury. Smokers had their own private lounge with loge seats; infants could be dropped off in a "children's room" where an attendant would watch over them in a cheerful space that was decorated like the inside of a circus tent. There were also soundproof "crying rooms" where parents could see and hear the film and not worry about wailing tots disturbing other patrons. In the basement of this incredible theater, there was even a ballroom where a combo played and patrons could dance or have a bite to eat in the adjacent restaurant while waiting for theater seats. In this same ballroom, a special prism system projected the film being shown upstairs on a small screen. Finally, there were the bathrooms. In the ladies' room, silver combs were handed out to women who could primp as long as they liked before vast marble vanities—and stalls were replaced by private rooms, each done in a different-color marble.

Even the ushers had it easy at the Los Angeles: a special lightboard system in the lobby showed them which seats were unoccupied. To achieve this, every seat of the one-thousand-seat theater was wired!

Designed by S. Charles Lee, the theater was the last great movie palace to be built on Broadway. It opened in 1931 with

Versailles updated:
Los Angeles Theater

Charlie Chaplin's *City Lights*—one of the last great silent films
ever made. One of L.A.'s most glamorous premieres, the gala
event was marred only by the Depression-era breadline down the
street. The Depression, ultimately, was not very kind to the Los
Angeles Theater—for despite its splendor, it went bankrupt very
quickly. One of the main reasons for this was the fact that the
theater was not part of a chain and therefore was limited in the
pictures it could show. Its owner is said to have wound up selling suits at Brooks Brothers.

Up to the 1990s, the Los Angeles Theater showed first-run
movies in English. At the same time, the splendid, if somewhat
threadbare, theater was popular with film companies and was often a location in movies. In *New York, New York* (1977), the
ballroom of the Los Angeles doubled as the lobby of a grand hotel—and the entire opening sequence of Paul Mazursky's *Alex in
Wonderland* (1970), starring Donald Sutherland, was shot at the
Los Angeles. The theater can also be spotted in *W. C. Fields and
Me* (1976) and in the classic Abbott and Costello comedy *Hold
That Ghost* (1941). Today, sadly, the Los Angeles has closed, but

it remains in the film business as a location. Among its splashiest gigs: *Batman Forever* (1995), starring Val Kilmer, Arnold Schwarzenegger's 1999 *End of Days,* and *Man on the Moon* (1999), with Jim Carrey as Andy Kaufman.

9. ARCADE THEATER SITE
534 South Broadway

Look up above the 1910 marquee of the former Arcade Theater and see its original name—Pantages—embossed in the cast-iron façade of the building that houses it. Alexander Pantages, who began his career producing dance-hall shows for gold miners in Alaska, went on to control one of the most important vaudeville circuits in the country. This was his first theater in L.A. The interior—still largely intact—tried to re-create an English music hall and was designed by the firm of Morgan and Walls, which also did the Globe Theater on South Broadway, the El Capitan on Hollywood Boulevard, and the exterior of the Wiltern on Wilshire Boulevard. Today, the Pantages/Arcade houses electronics and jewelry stores.

10. CAMEO THEATER SITE
528 South Broadway

If you ever wondered what a real nickelodeon looked like, this is it. The little Cameo first opened its doors in 1910 as a silent-movie house that charged the whopping sum of a nickel to come inside and see the show. Ironically, most of those first "shows" came from back East since not too many filmmakers had as yet discovered the joys of Southern California. All that would change very quickly. Today, the Cameo, which was still showing films a decade ago, is a cut-rate electronics store.

11. ROXIE THEATER SITE
518 South Broadway

In a district of sumptuous theaters, the Roxie was notable for its lack of opulence. Inaugurated in 1931, it was the last theater to be built on Broadway and its stark Moderne design reflected the austerity of the Depression era. Today, its decaying arcade harbors shops selling wedding gowns, jewelry, and budget-priced clothing.

12. ALEXANDRIA HOTEL
501 South Spring Street

If we are to believe certain of the Alexandria's records, literally everybody who was anybody in early Hollywood stayed in this 1906 hotel at one time or another. Heading one list of former guests—or rather ending it, as the list is in alphabetical order—is the ubiquitous Rudolph Valentino. Then there's Fred Astaire, Theda Bara, the Barrymores, Sarah Bernhardt, Wallace Beery, Humphrey Bogart, Clara Bow, Francis X. Bushman—and that's just the beginning of the alphabet. Ironically, one luminary not on this list is D. W. Griffith, who definitely *did* make the Alex his base during his early L.A. sojourns.

There are many legends associated with the Alexandria in its early days. One holds that cowboy star Tom Mix once rode his horse into the lobby and over the hotel's much touted "million-dollar" Turkish carpet! Another says that Charlie Chaplin often did improvisations in this same lobby. And then there was the time in 1920 when Charlie Chaplin accused Louis B. Mayer of meddling in his divorce from Metro Studios contract player Mildred Harris. Chaplin eventually challenged Mayer to take off his glasses—at which L.B. did just that and solidly decked Chaplin, who wound up in a potted palm. The movie crowd had deserted the Alexandria by the end of the 1920s. By then, the new Biltmore and Ambassador hotels had become the chic spots to stay and play—and Hollywood had a host of smart new hostelries of its own. The worst years for the Alexandria, however, were the 1930s when the Depression all but did the place in, forcing it to close for several years. When it reopened after that, it never regained its former place in the L.A. sun.

It did appear in at least one important Hollywood movie, however—the 1949 film noir *The Reckless Moment,* directed by the classy German-born French metteur en scène Max Ophüls. In the film, the Alexandria is said to have provided the seedy downtown L.A. meeting point for upper-middle-class Newport Beach matron Joan Bennett and the blackmailer-boyfriend of her

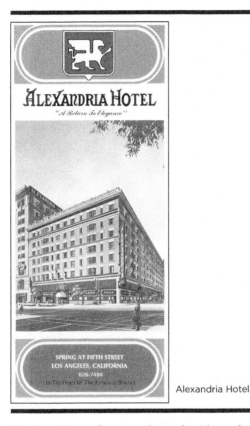

Alexandria Hotel

daughter. Forty-five years later, the Alexandria made an appearance in another dark film, *Seven* (1995), as the kinky serial killer's home. Today, the place is a low-budget hotel that rents rooms by the week. For anyone wishing to catch a feeling of what it was like in its heyday, check out the Palm Court, just off the lobby, where a huge Tiffany stained-glass ceiling still dazzles.

13. MILLION DOLLAR THEATER
307 South Broadway

Five years before the Egyptian Theater premiered in Hollywood and ten years before the Chinese, Sid Grauman created the Million Dollar Theater in downtown L.A. One of the first true motion picture palaces in the country, the Million Dollar opened in

1917 with cowboy actor William S. Hart starring in *The Silent Man*. (While Sid Grauman's name was "above the title" on all of the theaters he managed, Grauman never owned these theaters. He would get someone else to finance and build a house to his specifications and he would, in turn, lease it.)

The Million Dollar Theater is housed within the Million Dollar office building—which is said to have cost as much as its name boasted back in the late teens. Both the entrance to the theater on Broadway and the entrance to the building on Third Street are exuberant expressions of an architectural style known as Churrigueresque—a New World offshoot of Spanish baroque. It is within the auditorium of the 2,200-seat Million Dollar, however, where all hell really breaks loose. Here, the feeling is one of being inside a great South American cathedral: There are numerous niches, statues, and organ-pipe covers that are reproductions of Spanish Colonial altar screens.

Ironically, this first of L.A.'s great picture palaces was the last movie theater in town to still have a live stage show as part of the bill. These featured Mexican and South American headliners (Maria Felix and Dolores Del Rio appeared at the Million Dollar in the seventies) as well as groups. It all came to an end, however, in the late 1980s, when the house, like so many others on Broadway, closed down. In 1991, director Robert Townsend took advantage of the newly dark theater and used it extensively

Million Dollar
Theater, 1926

The Million Dollar Theater's opulent interior

as a location for his film about the rise and fall of a 1960s soul group, *The Five Heartbeats*. The Million Dollar has since been restored and today its marquee announces the theater's availability for private parties and location shoots. Mel Gibson's celebrity photographer–bashing film *Paparazzi* (2004) recently shot at the theater.

14. BRADBURY BUILDING
304 South Broadway

Douglas Sirk used it for the dramatic climax in his 1949 film noir *Shockproof*. That same year Edmond O'Brien met his murderer here in *D.O.A.* It was also Boston Blackie's office in the early 1950s TV series of the same name. It was the sleazy hotel that Jack Lemmon checked into as *Good Neighbor Sam* (1964), Jack Nicholson's office in *Wolf* (1994), Brad Douriff's in *Murder in the First* (1995), Gary Werntz's in *Pay It Forward* (2000), and perhaps most memorably, it was the apartment house that was home to Sabastian, the "genetic designer" in Ridley Scott's 1982 sci-fi classic *Blade Runner*. Those are just a few of the films in which the Bradbury (office) Building has been featured prominently. Perhaps the most unusual building in all of Los Angeles,

Frequently on-screen:
Bradbury Building atrium

it is a dream of pink-marble staircases, wrought-iron balustrades, open elevators that all rise around a light-drenched central atrium. Built in 1893, the Bradbury Building could have been the prototype for all the Grand Hyatt hotels on earth. And as far as movie art directors are concerned, it offers one of the city's most dramatic—and best lit!—interior locations.

The story surrounding the origin of this bizarre and wonderful L.A. landmark—which, surprisingly, looks totally unprepossessing from the outside—could have been the basis for a science-fiction film all its own. It seems that mining millionaire/real estate developer Lewis Bradbury was in ill health and, realizing his days were numbered, wanted his last building to be something truly extraordinary. When the architect assigned to the project failed to come up with a design that pleased Bradbury, the aging millionaire turned to (no one knows just why) one of the architect's assistants. The assistant, thirty-two-year-old George Wyman at first refused Bradbury's offer to design the building. Later, Wyman and his wife supposedly made contact with Wyman's dead brother via a Ouija-type board and received a message that said:

"Take the Bradbury Building. It will make you famous." If instructions from the spirit world weren't enough, Wyman was further inspired by an 1887 science-fiction novel that described a skylit commercial building of the year 2000. The Bradbury Building—which some architects consider one of the most perfectly imagined interior spaces ever devised—was the only building of any importance that Wyman ever designed.

The Bradbury Building is open to the public Monday through Saturday. Recent tenants include the Internal Affairs Division of the Los Angeles Police Department and various architectural design and redevelopment firms. On street level, one of its storefronts, Ross Cutlery, is where O. J. Simpson was alleged to have bought a fifteen-inch knife in a very public 1995 murder trail.

15. *HERALD EXAMINER* BUILDING
1111 South Broadway

Founded in 1903, the *Herald Examiner* was William Randolph Hearst's official Southern California voice up until his death in 1951. In addition to his newspaper empire, Hearst had a strong

Herald Examiner building, 1984

connection to the world of Hollywood through serving as executive producer for most of the pictures made by his movie-star mistress, Marion Davies. The couple was a major force in Hollywood social life during the 1920s and 1930s and together staged some of the town's most lavish parties. Hearst also influenced the Hollywood scene through star gossip columnist, Louella Parsons, who worked for the Hearst organization (and who often was "her master's voice" in her columns) throughout her career. The *Herald Examiner* Building is an extraordinary structure that is classified as an example of the Mission Revival style by students of architecture. Inaugurated in 1912, it is the work of Julia Morgan—the first woman graduate of the prestigious Beaux Arts school in Paris. In addition to its exuberant exterior, Morgan seems to have had a good time with the interior as well. The lobby especially, a lavish space of carved marble columns and arches, hints at the splendors Morgan would create in the 1920s when she was commissioned to design Hearst's famous "castle," San Simeon, in Northern California.

The Hearst Corporation's *Herald Examiner* ceased publication in 1989 and the building stood vacant for a number of years, although it was used extensively in the 1995 film *The Usual Suspects,* as the police station, a restaurant, and for various other interiors. Today, the landmark is being restored as a trendy loft apartment building, set to open in 2006.

16. MAYAN THEATER
1038 South Hill Street

The Mayan has one of the most fantastic façades of any movie house in Los Angeles—perhaps of any movie house in the world. Somewhere between a pre-Columbian temple and a wedding cake iced by a madman, the Mayan's exterior is especially dramatic at night when it is floodlit. The Mayan opened in 1927, not as a movie theater but as a legit house. Anita Loos's *Gentlemen Prefer Blondes* was the premiere attraction. Some twenty years and many incarnations later, the Mayan had become a burlesque house and, according to one source, briefly featured on its stage the woman who would become the most "preferred" blonde of the twentieth century. The woman went by the name of Marilyn

The Mayan Theater's fantastic façade

Marlowe at the Mayan in 1948, writes Richard Lamparski in *Lamparski's Hidden Hollywood* (Simon and Schuster, 1981)—but she was really Marilyn Monroe. The strangest twist in all this is that Marilyn would later star as Lorelei Lee, the heroine of *Gentlemen Prefer Blondes*, in Twentieth Century–Fox's 1953 Hollywood musical version of the Anita Loos classic.

Movie lovers may remember the Mayan as the X-rated cinema where Jack Lemmon hung out in the R-rated film, *Save the Tiger* (1972) and as one of the theaters where Whitney Houston performed in *The Bodyguard* (1992). It was also featured in the "Lust" sequence of the thriller *Seven* (1995), *Father's Day* (1997), and *The Replacement Killers* (1998). On TV, it's often used for commercials and has been a location for the series *Angel*. But today, the Mayan, which hasn't shown films for years, is enjoying great success as a nightclub. Splendidly restored, it's one of downtown L.A.'s hottest spots for lounging and dancing, with top DJs usually at the decks.

Visit www.clubmayan.com.

17. THEATER JEWELRY CENTER/PANTAGES
THEATER SITE
655 South Hill Street

Today, it's a kind of upscale flea market filled with stalls selling jewelry at bargain prices. But a quick look around the inside of this souk-like space reveals that it was once a theater—and a very grand one at that. The gilded ceiling of the lobby is still largely intact, as is the house itself, where the massive proscenium is also gilded and the muraled ceiling is magnificent. Only the modern chandelier is a disappointment.

Back in 1920, this was Alexander Pantages's second vaudeville theater in downtown Los Angeles. Presenting films as well as live acts, the Pantages Theater was housed within the towering, Beaux Arts–style Pantages Downtown Building. It was here that Alexander Pantages had his offices—and in 1929, the Pantages building figured in a sensational scandal when Pantages, who prided himself on his having exclusively female ushers, was arrested for allegedly raping one of them. The public was outraged. The woman who brought suit was just sixteen years old, and Pantages was in his sixties. The jury must have been outraged as well because they found Pantages guilty. When a new trial brought about an acquittal two years later, the aging and physically broken Pantages had already served some of his fifty-year sentence. He died a few months later.

In the meantime, during the period of the Pantages trial, his theater was taken over by Warner Bros., which dropped the vaudeville acts in favor of just showing films. On its last legs in the early seventies, the theater closed down and later had a brief stint as a church, before it began its new life as a specialized shopping mall.

18. OVIATT BUILDING
617 South Olive Street

With mirrored pillars, an illuminated glass ceiling, and silvery Art Deco doors, the spectacular entrance to the Oviatt Building is straight out of a Fred Astaire–Ginger Rogers musical. Although not a set, many movie stars did pass through this glamorous entrance to what was actually the establishment of Alexander & Oviatt—one of the most elegant haberdasheries in all of Los Angeles. Among the major male stars who kept their public images perfectly attired and accessorized here were Clark Gable, John Barrymore, Gary Cooper, and the actor who was considered Hollywood's best-dressed personality for decades—Adolphe Menjou.

James Oviatt—who built the exquisite thirteen-story landmark Oviatt building in 1928—did so with a flourish that matched the most flamboyant of Hollywood's early movie men. Oviatt spared no expense in the design and construction of his dream building. Impressed by a 1925 visit to Paris's famous Exposition Internationale des Arts Décoratifs et Industriels Modernes (the design show that unleashed Art Deco on the world), Oviatt engaged the famed designer and crafter of glass, René Lalique, to create all of the glass panels and lighting fixtures that were used so lavishly in the Oviatt Building. It is said that some thirty tons of Lalique were installed in the original lobby—one of the largest commissions the French artisan ever received.

James Oviatt died in the early seventies and his building—already on the downswing by that time—quickly deteriorated even further after his death. In 1977, however, enlightened developers, who bought the Oviatt Building for a mere $400,000, managed to get it declared an Historic Cultural Monument and proceeded to sink some $5 million into its restoration. Today, the Oviatt's thirteen stories are fully rented, and the original Alexander & Oviatt haberdashery on the first two floors of the building is the home of the glamorous Cicada restaurant. So these days, movie stars dine—rather than shop—in this fabulous Los Angeles landmark.

And sometimes they dine in this lavish Art Deco setting on film, as in *Final Analysis* (1992), *Indecent Proposal* (1993), *Bringing Down the House* (2003), *Bruce Almighty* (2003), and perhaps most memorably in *Pretty Woman* (1991), in a hilarious scene where businessman Richard Gere takes Julia Roberts, whom he's picked up on Hollywood Boulevard a few days earlier, to a fancy business dinner. Despite a prior lesson on dining and silverware etiquette, Julia has a hard time of it. She somehow manages the pâté, but the escargots are another story, as she sends a snail flying across the room, only to be caught by a hyper-efficient waiter.

For reservations, call (213) 488-9488 or visit www.cicadarestaurant.com.

19. MILLENNIUM BILTMORE HOTEL
515 South Olive Street

With almost one thousand guest rooms when it opened in October 1923, the Biltmore was the largest hotel west of Chicago. Designed by architects Shultze and Weaver—who also were responsible for the Biltmore in New York City as well as the Waldorf Astoria—the L.A. Biltmore was instantly the city's grandest hotel, boasting magnificent murals by artist Giovanni Smeraldi, a lavish lobby that duplicated a Spanish palace, and a galleria that was even more spectacular.

Many, many stars have stayed at the Biltmore throughout its history, but the hotel's greatest claim to fame as far as movie history is concerned has to do with a birth that some say occurred in its Crystal Ballroom on May 11, 1927. It was during an elaborate dinner to mark the founding of a new organization called the Academy of Motion Picture Arts and Sciences. Mary Pickford and Douglas Fairbanks were there; so were Louis B. Mayer, King Vidor, Jack Warner, and many more moguls and stars. MGM art director Cedric Gibbons was also there, and during the dinner he is said to have done a rough sketch on a napkin of a little man who would go on to match (and even exceed) the fame of any movie star in history. The little man born that evening was eventually christened Oscar.

As Oscar grew, he visited the Biltmore often—since the hotel was frequently the site of Academy Awards dinners. Oscar's Biltmore years were 1931, 1935, 1936, 1937, 1938, 1939, 1941, and 1942, but he also spent time at the Hollywood Roosevelt and Ambassador hotels during the early part of his career.

In 1969, the Biltmore hotel received a very special award all its own; it was named a Historic Landmark by the Cultural Heritage Board of the City of Los Angeles. Since then many millions have been spent restoring and maintaining this classic hotel,

Old World elegance:
Millennium Biltmore lounge

whose beauty has not been lost on Hollywood art directors. In the last three decades, the hotel has been used as a location for close to 250 feature films, television movies, series episodes, and commercials. It is frequently called on to stand in for grand hotels in other cities—San Francisco in *Vertigo* (1958), New York City in *New York, New York* (1977), Washington, D.C., in *Born Yesterday* (1992), and Chicago in *Grosse Pointe Blank* (1996).

Among its many other film credits are: *Chinatown* (1974), *At Long Last Love* (1975), *The Last Tycoon* (1976), the 1976 remake of *King Kong*, Streisand's 1976 *A Star Is Born, The Other Side of Midnight* (1977), *The Buddy Holly Story* (1977), *The Betsy* (1978), *Airport* (1979), *Altered States* (1980), *True Confessions* (1980), *Foul Play* (1980), *Rocky III* (1981), *Splash* (1983), *Beverly Hills Cop* (1984), *The Fabulous Baker Boys* (1989), *Bugsy* (1991), *True Lies* (1992), *Beverly Hills Cop III* (1992), *Don Juan DeMarco* (1994), *Independence Day* (1995), *Escape from L.A.* (1995), *Primary Colors* (1997), *Fight Club* (1998), *Ocean's Eleven* (2001), *Austin Powers in Goldmember* (2001), *Spider-Man* (2002), *The Italian Job* (2002), and *Bringing Down the House* (2003).

The Biltmore's TV appearances are just as impressive: four

*Cagney & Lacey*s, five *Kojak*s, eleven *Murder, She Wrote*s, nine *West Wing*s (and counting), and many many more. Then there are all the commercials and music videos. Indeed, almost not a day goes by when something's not shooting at the Biltmore.

For reservations, call 213–624–1011 or visit
www.millenniumhotels.com.

20. CLUNE'S AUDITORIUM BUILDING SITE
427 West Fifth Street

Fronting Pershing Square at the northeast corner of Fifth and Olive Streets, the Auditorium Building was the home of the Los Angeles Philharmonic Orchestra for many years until its move to the L.A. County Music Center in 1965. For movie lovers, however, it is the auditorium's pre-Philharmonic history that is of interest. Opened in 1906 and often known as Clune's Theater Beautiful, this was the largest theater of its day in Los Angeles and the place where the public first saw a film that proved just how powerful and emotion-rousing a medium the movies could be. The year was 1915, and the film was D. W. Griffith's controversial (because of its racist overtones) *The Clansman*—which we know today as *The Birth of a Nation*.

Karl Brown, who was an assistant to Griffith's cameraman Billy Bitzer on the picture, wrote of the film's opening at Clune's in his *Adventures with D. W. Griffith* (Farrar, Straus & Giroux, 1973) as follows: "Griffith was given great credit for many things he had not done, while he was given no credit at all for the really enormous advances he had brought to the whole wide world of picture making. The greatest of these was the lifting of the lowly nickelodeon storefront theater, with its tinny honky-tonk piano and its windowless, foul-air smelliness, to the grandeur of a great auditorium with a great orchestra and a great picture that ran three hours and filled an entire evening with thrills and excitement in a setting of opulent luxury such as the great masses of working people had never dreamed possible for them. This sort of thing was for the idle rich who went to the opera to see and be seen. But after that first opening night at Clune's Auditorium in Los Angeles, anybody could be a

Actors dressed as Ku Klux Klansmen outside Clune's Auditorium to promote *Birth of a Nation*, 1915

millionaire for three hours and a Griffith snob for the rest of his life."

If we are to take Brown at his word, D. W. Griffith, *The Birth of a Nation*, and Clune's Auditorium all played a part in paving the way for the development of the great movie palaces that were soon to take over Los Angeles and the rest of the country in the later teens and twenties. (Brown does not mention the politically incorrect promotional gimmick that was used at the *Birth of a Nation* screening. Griffith had actors dressed as hooded Klansmen assembled outside the theater on horseback.)

The old auditorium building was razed in early 1985 to make way for a high-rise, which has yet to rise on the site; today, the historic spot is a parking lot.

21. DOWNTOWN STANDARD HOTEL
550 South Flower Street

Giving the happening hangouts of Hollywood and West Hollywood a run for their money, the new Downtown Standard hotel's roof bar is one of L.A.'s hottest spots for celebrities to party. Here, the likes of Sofia Coppola, Leonardo DiCaprio, Tobey

L.A.'s coolest pool: atop the Downtown Standard Hotel

Maguire, and Nicolas Cage find poolside waterbeds, waitresses dressed as cheerleaders, great DJs, decidedly un-L.A. urban views, and on some nights, classic films screened on the wall of an adjacent skyscraper. The hotel—housed in a mid-century-Moderne former oil company headquarters—was masterminded by hip hotelier Andre Balazs, the force currently behind West Hollywood's legendary Chateau Marmont as well as its also very cool Standard hotel.

Call 213–892–8080 or visit www.standardhotel.com.

22. CITICORP CENTER BUILDING
444 South Flower Street

Opened in 1979 (as the Wells Fargo Building), this forty-eight-story mirror-glass skyscraper is notable for its height and its dramatic palm-treed plaza studded with massive outdoor sculptures by such acclaimed artists as Mark di Suvero, Robert Rauschenberg, and Frank Stella. In 1986, one of the building's most high-profile tenants was the law firm of McKenzie, Brackman, Chaney and Kuzak of *L.A. Law* fame. By 1994, the firm, then known as McKenzie, Brackman, Kelsey, Markowitz and Morales went out

L.A. Law office: Citigroup
Center Building

of business, as the series went off the air. The skyscraper was also
used by director Ridley Scott as background for his 1989 film
Black Rain, which had Michael Douglas tangling with Japan's
notorious Yakuza gangster organization.

23. WESTIN BONAVENTURE HOTEL
404 South Figueroa Street

The architecture of the twenty-first century arrived in downtown
Los Angeles in 1977 with the opening of this dazzling hotel designed by John Portman. A cluster of five thirty-five-story towers, each sheathed in mirrored glass, the 1,474-room Westin
Bonaventure has been frequently seen on both the large and the
small screen—especially when the film or TV show takes place in
the future. *Logan's Run* (1976) and *Buck Rogers in the 25th
Century* (1979) were two of the first science-fiction flicks to take
advantage of the Bonaventure's fantastic façade and futuristic interior of sky-bridges, mirrored fountains, and glass-bubble elevators. A likeness of the hotel also crops up in Ridley Scott's 1982
Blade Runner, as part of the skyline of twenty-first-century L.A.

Sci-fi towers: Westin
Bonaventure Hotel

No longer a newcomer to the downtown cityscape, the Bonaventure is often used in films and television as a backdrop that captures the spirit and look of contemporary L.A. Among the many films in which the hotel has done just that are *Blue Thunder* (1983), *Breathless* (1983), *Ruthless People* (1986), *Rain Man* (1988), *Lethal Weapon 2* (1989), *Final Analysis* (1992), *True Lies* (1994), *Nick of Time* (1995), *Heat* (1995), *Strange Days* (1995), *Forget Paris* (1995), and *My Fellow Americans* (1996). Arguably the film to use the Bonaventure's dramatic interior most effectively is the Wolfgang Peterson–directed Clint Eastwood thriller *In the Line of Fire* (1993), in which a U.S. president is being targeted by a psychopathic sniper (John Malkovich), hiding in one of the Bonaventure's glass towers.

On TV, the hotel has been featured in numerous series: *L.A. Law, Moonlighting, Remington Steele, Wonder Woman, General Hospital,* and *Starsky and Hutch*. The Bonaventure honors its film history with a gallery of posters from many of the features shot on the property. Plaques by the glass elevators also note the films that registered them.

For reservations, call 213-624-1000 or visit www.westin.com.

24. SECOND STREET TUNNEL
Second Street between Hope and Figueroa Streets

Running under what was once one of downtown L.A.'s grandest Victorian neighborhoods—Bunker Hill, which was leveled in the 1960s for a high-rise development—this two-block-long tunnel has frequently provided a dramatic location for action-adventure films. *Blade Runner* (1982), *The Terminator* (1984), *Demolition Man* (1993), *Con Air* (1997), and *City of Angels* (1998) have all featured the tunnel, but its most spectacular appearance is in the Steven Spielberg–produced *Independence Day* (1996), where some three hundred "picture cars" (the term for a vehicle used in a film) employed to create the movie's monumental traffic jam in the wake of a fiery alien attack created a real-life monumental traffic jam (not shown in the film) in downtown L.A.

25. WALT DISNEY CONCERT HALL
West First Street at North Grand Avenue

Bringing new dazzle to the downtown skyline, the assymetrical polished-steel blocks and towers of the Los Angeles Philharmonic's new concert hall is the work of Los Angeles–based superstar architect Frank O. Gehry. The 2,273-seat auditorium

Walt Disney Concert Hall

bears the name of another local hero—the late Walt Disney—thanks to a $50 million gift from the Disney family, who later put in even more millions when the project—just like many major motion pictures—started running over budget. Pop-music fans may recognize the dramatic new structure from Jennifer Lopez's "Jenny from the Block" video, which used it as a location while it was still under construction (the hall opened in October 2003). Given its unusual design and outrageous beauty, the Disney Concert Hall will undoubtedly wind up as background in many more films, TV shows, and videos.

Visit www.wdch.laphil.com/home.cfm.

26. DOROTHY CHANDLER PAVILION
135 North Grand Avenue

The largest of the three monumental marble buildings that make up the Los Angeles Music Center, the 3,250-seat Dorothy Chandler Pavilion was the site of the Academy Awards from 1969 to 1987. It was also home to the Los Angeles Philharmonic until its recent move to the new Walt Disney Concert Hall just across the street. Architect of the Music Center is Welton Becket, the same man who did the landmark Capitol Records Tower in Hollywood.

Visit www.musiccenter.org.

27. CITY HALL
200 North Spring Street

It was the backdrop for all those doomsday press conferences in *The War of the Worlds* (1952). Later, in the same film, it wound up getting zapped by the death rays of invading Martian spaceships. This is also the high-rise that for years served as the *Daily Planet* newspaper building in the long-running 1950s *Superman* television series, and it was also seen in the opening shot of *Dragnet* for ten seasons. At 450 feet in height and twenty-eight stories, City Hall was for many years the tallest building in Los Angeles, indeed the only building allowed to rise above the 150-

Official L.A.: City Hall

foot (usually ten stories) height limit imposed on all other structures between 1905 and 1957.

The venerable public building has had a long and distinguished film career. It has not only been a staple in L.A.-based
films noir—from classics like *D.O.A.* and *Mildred Pierce* to more
recent color homages to the genre such as *The Grifters* and *L.A.
Confidential*—it has done its share of action-adventure gigs as
well: *48 Hours, Another 48 Hours, Internal Affairs,* and *Die
Hard II,* for example. It has also appeared in virtually every
crime series since TV went mainstream in the 1950s: *Kojak, The
Rockford Files, L.A. Law, Cagney & Lacey, Rosie O'Neil,* to
name but a few. And although City Hall usually plays itself, it
has sometimes been used to represent non-L.A. locations—it was
the County Justice Building of Miami in *All the President's Men*
(1976), the Vatican in the 1983 mini-series *The Thorn Birds,* and
the U.S. Capitol in the 1992 Jack Nicholson film *Hoffa.*

In 1994, the City Hall building suffered serious damage in the
Northridge earthquake and was closed down for major repairs
and retrofitting. Today, it is back in business and ready for its
closeup—or long shot—whenever it's needed.

28. UNION STATION
800 North Alameda Street

Completed in 1939, this was the last of the great passenger train terminals ever built in the United States. And a great terminal it is indeed. On the outside, Union Station is a clean-lined Spanish structure that features pleasant patios and gardens as an integral part of its design. Inside, the main arrivals hall is a stunning space with four-story-tall ceilings that are frescoed and crossed with heavy beams. Here, one can easily imagine the glamorous "public" arrivals of movie stars with their secretaries, press agents, and loads of luggage as they alighted from the Super Chief back in the early forties. (Stars who wished anonymity exited the train a stop earlier at Pasadena.) One can imagine, too, the station's hubbub during the years of World War II as cavalcades of Hollywood's most famous personalities went off on War Bond drives—and as hordes of men and women in uniform went off to war.

Given its dimensions and its beauty, it is not surprising that Union Station has been used for countless films and television shows. The sheer scale of the place—perhaps the only interior in

Terminal chic: Union Station

all of Los Angeles that can equal a soundstage in terms of size—
is a cameraman's dream. This is the land of the endless pullback
shot. Perhaps the film that used the terminal most extensively is
a 1950 release that starred William Holden called *Union Station*.
(The film was set in Chicago, however—not Los Angeles!) Other
well-known theatrical and television films that have train station
sequences shot here are *The Hustler* (1961), *The Way We Were*
(1972), *Gable and Lombard* (1975), *The Driver* (1977), *Oh
God, Book II* (1980), *True Confessions* (1982), *The Fabulous
Baker Boys* (1989), *Nick of Time* (1995), and *The Italian Job*
(2003).

Two of the most interesting cinematic uses of the terminal
were in the 1982 films *Dead Men Don't Wear Plaid* and *Blade
Runner*. In the former, thanks to trick photography, Steve Martin is followed through the station by Cary Grant (and then
shares a train compartment with him) via a film clip from Hitchcock's 1941 film noir *Suspicion*. In Ridley Scott's *Blade Runner*,
the terminal represented a police station in twenty-first-century
Los Angeles. Scott is said to have chosen the location because he
liked the immensity of its "Art Deco and neo-Fascist architecture." For the film, the producers built an actual office structure
within the terminal—and inadvertently blocked access to the
ladies' room in the process. It seems that filming needed to be interrupted rather frequently owing to this oversight.

The 1989 film *Bugsy*, which starred Warren Beatty as gangster
Bugsy Siegal, also redid Union Station in a big way, turning one
of its vast terrazzo-floored waiting rooms into the glamorous
train station dining room it once was. Today, although Union
Station may have lost some of its glamour, it is as busy as it was
in its heyday, since it is now a hub of both a newly invigorated
Amtrak and of L.A.'s own burgeoning rapid-transit system. Who
knows, maybe they'll bring back the *Bugsy* dining room?

29. CHINATOWN
1100 North Broadway

L.A.'s original Chinatown, built in the 1870s, was razed in the
early 1930s to make way for Union Station. The current Chinatown subsequently emerged in and around North Broadway and
Alpine Street and today is a thriving Asian commercial center as

John Huston, Jack Nicholson, and Roy Jensen find trouble in *Chinatown*

well as a major tourist attraction. For film companies, parts of Chinatown—with its towering pagodas, tile-roofed shops and restaurants, Fu dogs and Chinese lantern–lit streets—delivered instant Asia as far back as 1937, when the screen version of Pearl Buck's famous novel *The Good Earth* shot a number of scenes here.

Another important Hollywood film to use the neighborhood was—surprise, surprise—Roman Polanski's 1974 *Chinatown,* where it provides the backdrop for the film's harrowing Greek tragedy–like ending. Hardly in the same league, the 1998 Jackie Chan/Chris Tucker martial-arts comedy thriller *Rush Hour* uses Chinatown and its Foo Chow restaurant as a key location for its convoluted story involving the kidnapping of a Chinese diplomat's daughter. Also in 1998, *Lethal Weapon 4* came to Chinatown, with a script that put stars Mel Gibson and Danny Glover up against an Asian crook, played by Hong Kong action star Jet Li, involved in smuggling illegal aliens into L.A. Other features to feature Chinatown have been *City of Industry* (1997), with Harvey Keitel and Timothy Hutton; *The Game*

(1997), with Michael Douglas and Sean Penn; and the TV movies *The Letter,* a 1982 remake of the 1940 Bette Davis vehicle, set in Southeast Asia, and *The Chinatown Murders,* which re-created 1940s L.A.

Constantly used by television, Chinatown has turned up in episodes of everything from *The Rockford Files* in the 1970s to *Hart to Hart* in the 1980s to *Melrose Place* in the 1990s.

Visit www.chinatownla.com.

30. CHESTER PLACE
Off West Adams Boulevard

In the heart of what was one of L.A.'s oldest of old-moneyed areas, Chester Place is a cluster of marvelous mansions built around the turn of the last century. Of these, the most marvelous is the Victorian Gothic château—number 8—that was owned by the Doheny (oil) family for many years. The Doheny main house, with its impressive marble stairs guarded by stone lions, is often

Doheny mansion, Chester Place

used for films and TV shows in which a mysterious mansion figures in the plot. In the 1970s, the TV series *Columbo* was constantly shooting at Chester Place and featuring the former Doheny property. In the 1980s, *Murder, She Wrote* often shot here, whereas these days it's popular with *Alias, JAG, Angel, Party of Five,* and *Providence.*

Often used to represent places other than Southern California, Chester Place and the Doheny mansion have doubled for New York City in *Godfather II* (1974); Boston in the 1981 miniseries *Scruples;* nineteenth-century Boston in the 1976 TV movie *Captains and Kings;* Civil War–era Hambleton, Pennsylvania, in *A Testimony of Two Men* (1977); Providence, Rhode Island, in *Providence;* San Francisco in *Princess Diaries* (2001); and a mythical island off Maine in *Alex and Emma* (2003). In many of these instances, art directors had to "dress" the palm trees to make them fit the landscape. This wasn't necessary, however, in the 1983 made-for-television version of Tennessee Williams's *A Streetcar Named Desire,* which starred Ann-Margret as Blanche DuBois and featured Chester Place as New Orleans's Garden District, nor in Nick Cassavetes's *The Notebook* (2004), set in South Carolina.

Today, Chester Place and many of its buildings—including the Doheny mansion—form the downtown campus of Mount St. Mary's College. When movie companies come to film here, they are allowed to stay just one day so as not to disrupt the college's academic activities to any great extent. Filming is also only permitted on a certain number of days each month. All fees collected from moviemaking here are used to help students needing financial aid.

Mount St. Mary's College recently introduced a program of guided tours of the Doheny mansion. For details, call 213-477-2530 or visit www.msmc.la.edu.

31. THEDA BARA MANSION
649 West Adams Boulevard

From the late nineteenth century and on into the early part of the twentieth, West Adams was one of the most prestigious boulevards in town. Just at the edge of Chester Place, this handsome

Tudor mansion was home to several legendary silent movie celebrities. From 1915 to 1919, super-siren Theda Bara lived here. Billed by the Fox publicity people as the illegitimate daughter of a French artist and an Arabian princess, Miss Bara was actually Theodosia Goodman from Cincinnati! This same house is said later to have been occupied by Roscoe "Fatty" Arbuckle—the comic whose career took a tumble in 1921 when he was implicated in the death of starlet Virginia Rappe. The young woman died after allegedly having been forced to perform some rather unusual sexual acts by Arbuckle in a San Francisco hotel room. Eventually Fatty was acquitted but his career never recovered. Joseph Schenck and Norma Talmadge are other names frequently mentioned as former famous residents of 649 West Adams. Today, the historic mansion is headquarters for the Vincentian Fathers.

32. ST. VINCENT DE PAUL CATHEDRAL
West Adams Boulevard and South Figueroa Street

A magnificent Churrigueresque (Spanish baroque) structure that ranks with some of the great cathedrals of Mexico, St. Vincent's for a long time had a policy that did not permit filming. They granted a dispensation to Arnold Schwarzenegger in 1999, however, and allowed him to use the cathedral extensively in *End of*

Spanish Colonial classic:
St. Vincent de Paul
Cathedral

Days, where the action hero goes one on one with Satan. The cathedral was also featured in a 2001 episode of the TV series *Charmed*, in which the show's sexy white witches fight off an attack by the Prince of Darkness.

33. SHRINE AUDITORIUM
665 West Jefferson Boulevard

When it was built in 1927, it was the world's largest theater and held well over six thousand spectators. (Radio City Music Hall would match it in the next decade.) Designed by famed theater architect G. Albert Landsburgh, the Shrine resembles a gigantic double-domed Middle Eastern mosque on the outside, a massive Moorish palace on the inside.

As far as its movie history goes, ever since King Kong was brought back to civilization and put on display as the Eighth Wonder of the World at the Shrine (doubling as a Broadway theater in the 1933 RKO film), the mammoth auditorium has provided locations for a number of Hollywood classics. In the 1954 *A Star Is Born*, the Shrine is the site of the Night of Stars benefit

Shrine Auditorium

King Kong at the Shrine

at the opening of the film. It's here that Esther Blodgett (Judy Garland) first encounters Norman Maine (James Mason). Then, at the end of the same picture, Esther—now superstar Vicki Lester as well as Norman Maine's tragic widow—returns to the Shrine and utters her triumphant "This is . . . Mrs. Norman Maine" line as the camera slowly pulls back to reveal tiny Judy alone on the great stage.

Also used in *The Turning Point* (1977) and *Foul Play* (1978), the Shrine was much in the news in 1984 when Michael Jackson was singed and taken to the hospital when a pyrotechnic effect went astray while filming a Pepsi Cola commercial here. The commercial aired nonetheless a few months later on the same Grammy Awards show (telecast from the Shrine) that saw Jackson win a record number of Grammys.

Speaking of awards shows, the Shrine hosted the Oscars seven times between 1988 and 2001, before the event moved to its new headquarters at the Kodak Theatre on Hollywood Boulevard in 2002. The 1994 film *Naked Gun 33⅓* features an Academy Awards at the Shrine sequence. Today, even with the Academy

Awards gone, the Shrine is still L.A.'s top awards-show site, with the Emmys, the Screen Actors Guild Awards, the MTV Movie Awards, the American Music Awards, and the ALMA (Latin Music Awards) all done here. The theater also hosted the 2000 Democratic Party convention.

Visit www.usc.edu/dept/CCR/theme/shrine.html.

34. THE UNIVERSITY OF SOUTHERN CALIFORNIA
West Jefferson Boulevard/Hoover Boulevard

Founded in 1879, this impressive institution, which now has a student population of more than thirty thousand, has been an important force in the American cinema since 1929, when it established its School of Cinema (now Cinema and Television) and became the first university in the country to award a B.A. in film. Among the faculty in its initial years were some of the industry's most important figures: director D.W. Griffith, actor-producer Douglas Fairbanks, mogul Darryl Zanuck, and studio wunderkind Irving Thalberg.

Over the years, USC has turned out some of the country's top filmmakers—starting with George Lucas, for whom several campus buildings are named. Other star alumni include: directors Ron Howard, James Ivory, John Singleton; producers Brian Grazier *(A Beautiful Mind)*, John Wells *(The West Wing)*, and David Wolper; cinematographer Conrad Hall; and film critic Peter Rainer. Indeed the School of Cinema and Television can boast of having had at least one of its graduates nominated for an Academy Award every year (except two) since 1965.

For movie lovers who wish to visit the vast USC campus, the university gives free orientation tours. The campus can also be seen in *The Graduate* (1967), where it stood in for Berkeley and Dustin Hoffman was an undergraduate, and in *Young Frankenstein* (1974), where Gene Wilder as the title character was a professor.

For walking-tour information, call 213–740–6605; and visit www.usc.edu.

Celebrating *Terminator 3*: L.A. Center Studios

35. LOS ANGELES CENTER STUDIOS
1201 West Fifth Street

The first full-service movie studio to open in downtown L.A. since the 1920s, this sleek modern rental lot has six enormous soundstages and the latest in technical equipment. Among the features that have availed themselves of its high-tech facilities since its 1999 opening have been *Mission Impossible 2, Charlie's Angels, Charlie's Angels 2, Numbers, The Planet of the Apes, The Sum of All Fears, Vanilla Sky, Panic Room, Terminator 3, Legally Blonde 2, Me Again, Anchorman,* and *Out of Time.*

Visit www.lacenterstudios.com.

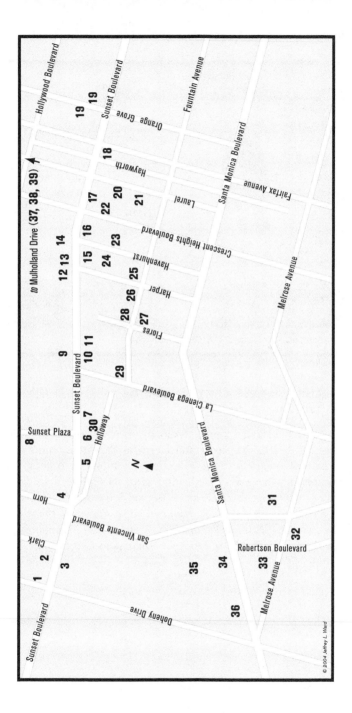

West Hollywood: Border Town

One of the most enduring images of Hollywood at its most glamorous is that of the beautiful starlet, dripping in fur, exiting a limo with her handsome escort, and entering a glittering nightclub along the Sunset Strip. In the 1930s and 1940s especially, the Strip was the center of Hollywood's smartest nights on the town, and its clubs and casinos—the Trocadero, Mocambo, Ciro's, the Clover Club, the Colony Club—were household names throughout the nation.

Why was so much of Hollywood's nighttime excitement centered around the Sunset Strip in West Hollywood? One of the reasons was the area's unusual status in the administrative scheme of Los Angeles. Originally called Sherman, West Hollywood was one of the few communities in Los Angeles County that voted against being annexed to the City of Los Angeles. At the same time, unlike Beverly Hills and Santa Monica—which stayed independent, incorporated cities—most of West Hollywood remained administered by the County of Los Angeles. With just the county and not the city watching over things, some say, all sorts of questionable places—gambling casinos and bordellos among them—thrived in parts of West Hollywood, whereas they would have had a much rougher go of it within the

City of L.A. The Sunset Strip was also a preferred address for many of Hollywood's showbiz agents because county tax laws made collecting a commission more lucrative here than practically anywhere else.

Today, the Sunset Strip remains one of West Hollywood's greatest attractions for the movie lover. The clubs with the famous names are gone now, but many live on as restaurants, cabarets, and bars with new names, new owners. The Strip is also home to one of Hollywood's most famous hotels—the Chateau Marmont—as well as to a number of hip new hostelries, making it one of the coolest places to stay in L.A.

West Hollywood is more than just the Strip. The area also showcases some of L.A.'s most unusual architecture. A block south of Sunset, Fountain Avenue—with its incredible concentration of turreted French Norman apartment houses built in the 1920s—stuns the eye as some crazy kind of twentieth-century château country. The fact that a number of movie people lived in many of these apartment buildings—as well as in the Spanish haciendas, the Moorish palaces, the Art Deco towers that are on and off Fountain—make the area even more intriguing.

Today, West Hollywood is also interesting from a sociological point of view. In the 1970s, the area became a preferred address for L.A.'s gay population, since it was out of reach of the City of L.A.'s then notoriously homophobic Los Angeles Police Department. In the mid-1980s, the residents—which included not only gays and lesbians but a large number of the elderly as well as an influx of Russian immigrants—voted to incorporate as an independent city within the County of Los Angeles. Known for its liberal leanings and tolerance of alternative lifestyles, the City of West Hollywood now boasts, among its many assets, one of the country's most vibrant gay and lesbian scenes, centered largely along Santa Monica Boulevard between La Cienega and San Vicente Boulevards, with bookshops, clothing boutiques, fitness centers, restaurants, cafes, and nightclubs. It may be a far cry from that glamorous image of the starlet getting out of the limousine in front of the Trocadero . . . but the beat still goes on in West Hollywood. Only the drummer is different.

Many of West Hollywood's sights are best seen on foot. The serious sightseer might wish to spend a good two to three hours

covering items 9 through 29, which take in the best of the Sunset
Strip as well as the glamorous apartments on Fountain Avenue
and its side streets. Melrose Avenue is another area of West
Hollywood that makes for interesting walking, although its
attractions are more for shoppers than for movie lovers. Finally,
items 37, 38, and 39 form a separate driving tour through Laurel
Canyon and the Hollywood Hills. Technically not part of West
Hollywood, Laurel Canyon and Mulholland Drive are included in
this chapter because of their proximity to the area.

1. RAINBOW BAR & GRILL
9015 Sunset Boulevard

Once upon a time, this was an Italian restaurant known as the
Villa Nova. The site of at least two notable romantic encounters,
the Villa Nova saw Vincente Minnelli propose to Judy Garland
in 1945 and also provided the location for the 1953 blind date
that paired Joe DiMaggio with Marilyn Monroe. In those days,
the lighting was low and the music soft. These days, Rainbow
Bar & Grill caters to "those who wanna rock 'n'roll all night and
party every day."

Call 310–278–4232 or visit www.rainbowbarandgrill.com.

2. THE ROXY
9009 Sunset Boulevard

One of L.A.'s top live-music venues, these days the Roxy hosts
the likes of Jane's Addiction, Sonic Youth, Southern Komfort,
Hellish Hounds, Tsunami, the Girlz Garage Tour, and Antigone
Rising. In the 1970s and 1980s, the names that played here were
more mainstream: the Bee Gees, Billy Joel, the Pointer Sisters,
Frank Zappa, Bruce Springsteen, Bette Midler, Chuck Berry,
Waylon Jennings, Linda Ronstadt. In the 1940s, however, according a Hollywood old-timer, the same building housed the
poshest grocery store in town. Called the West Side Market, this
was where many of Hollywood's top stars did their marketing—
and where the regulars were somehow able always to get the
choicest cuts of beef, the richest cream and butter, and the best
of whatever else was being rationed during the days of World

War II. It was, in effect, a wide-open black market that billed customers by the month and even delivered!

Call 310–276–2222.

3. THE VIPER ROOM
8852–8860 Sunset Boulevard

Called "the most consistently hip club in town" by the *Los Angeles Times,* this unprepossessing black boîte—with a liquor store in the middle—at the corner of Clark and Sunset boasts actor Johnny Depp as one of its star backers. Among the many name groups and solo artists who have played here are Courtney Love, Oasis, Billy Idol, Sheryl Crow, the Cult, Stone Temple Pilots, and Billy Corgan of Smashing Pumpkins. Often the biggest names—Bruce Springsteen, for example—appear unannounced. Often, too, the audience members are more famous than the performers on stage: Tom Hanks, Rita Wilson, Drew Barrymore, Rosanna Arquette, Cameron Diaz, Alicia Silverstone, Sean Penn, and of course, owner Johnny Depp, who has a booth permanently reserved for him and his entourage.

In the last decade, the Viper Room has frequently found itself in the headlines. In 1996, there was an incident where a photographer was roughed up by Mick Jagger's bodyguard after taking a photo of the rock star embracing Uma Thurman (a lawsuit followed). It was also here that Motley Cru's Tommy Lee shoved a photographer trying to video him and his then wife Pamela Anderson Lee in 1996. (Lee wound up getting twenty-four months probation and two hundred hours of community service.)

But the incident that will ensure the Viper Room's place in Hollywood history is the tragic event that happened here on Halloween night of 1993, when up-and-coming actor River Phoenix collapsed on the sidewalk outside the club and died, supposedly of a drug overdose. Poised for the big time, Phoenix *(The Mosquito Coast, Running on Empty, My Own Private Idaho)* was dead at the age of twenty-three. For the world, the tragedy was one of those reality checks that point out the fragile nature of success—especially in Tinseltown.

Call 310–358–1880 or visit www.viperroom.com.

4. SPAGO SITE
8795 Sunset Boulevard

Looking up at this boxy building, currently sporting a restau-rant-for-lease sign, across from Tower Records on Sunset Strip, it's hard to imagine that it was once one of L.A.'s most glam-orous places to dine. For this was the original Spago, the restau-rant that made Austrian chef Wolfgang Puck one of the biggest stars in Hollywood with its open kitchen, wood-burning pizza oven, and paper-covered tables. In fact the place was so popular with the right people that in the mid-1980s, super-agent Irving "Swifty" Lazar transferred his chic little Academy Awards night bash from the Bistro in Beverly Hills to this hip West Hollywood hangout. The party was so exclusive that many Hollywood heavyweights skipped the actual Academy Awards ceremony en-tirely and watched the show on television along with Swifty and his wife, Mary, at Spago. But once the Oscars had been handed out and the telecast was over, all of the A-list presenters, winners, and losers turned up at Spago to nibble on pizza and ogle one an-other and all those shiny statuettes. When Lazar died in 1994, the private party to be reckoned with became the one hosted by *Vanity Fair* magazine, which is currently held at another West Hollywood in-spot, Morton's. Glamour, yes—but most insiders say there will never be another Oscar night party to match Swifty's. Meanwhile, the West Hollywood Spago closed in 2001, but lives on as a tony (no more paper tablecloths) joint in Beverly Hills. It, too, is a far cry from the good old days on Sunset Strip.

5. LE DOME
8720 Sunset Boulevard

A very elegant restaurant now occupies this handsome little neo-classical building that was erected in 1934 as the studio of interior decorator William Haines. Haines, a former MGM boy-next-door, was also a homosexual who did little to hide his lifestyle. When Louella Parsons started dropping hints about Haines's off-screen activities in her columns, this was too much for his boss, Louis B. Mayer. Supposedly Mayer told Haines to choose between his boyfriend and his MGM contract. Haines chose the former and wound up becoming one of the town's top decorators. One of his

Don Loper salon, 1946—now Le Dome restaurant

biggest star clients was MGM colleague Joan Crawford. Besides doing and redoing her Brentwood home many times, Haines also did her New York apartment. Other Hollywood people who lived in Haines-decorated mansions included Constance Bennett, Jack Warner, and William Goetz. Of his career change, Haines once had this to say: "I've never been divorced from show business . . . many of my friends are my clients. I feel part of them. I'm still an actor who's hanging some curtains."

After Haines moved from his Sunset Strip studio in the 1940s, the premises were later taken over by Hollywood dress designer Don Loper. *I Love Lucy* fans may remember the episode where Lucy—sporting a bad California sunburn—appears in a Don Loper celebrity-wives fashion show wearing a tweed suit.

For reservations, call 310-659-6919.

6. TROCADERO STEPS
8610 Sunset Boulevard

Three steps at the southeast corner of Sunset Boulevard and Sunset Plaza are all that remain of the Trocadero Cafe. The Troc—along with Mocambo and Ciro's—was one of the Sunset Strip's great nightclubs of the 1930s and 1940s. It was opened in 1934

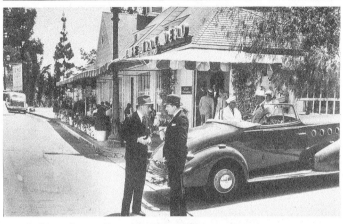

Hot boîte on Sunset: Trocadero Cafe, 1937

by W. R. Wilkerson, publisher of the *Hollywood Reporter*—the film colony's trade paper/gossip sheet. When David O. Selznick needed a glamorous nightspot for a sequence in his 1937 *A Star Is Born,* he set it at the Troc. And when Selznick and Jock Whitney needed a place to celebrate the opening of *Gone With the Wind,* the Troc was again recruited. During its heyday, practically every star in Hollywood walked up its three steps at one time or another. There were even rumors of a secret gambling parlor downstairs, but most people who remember the Troc don't recall any gambling on the property. What they do recall is good food, good drinks, good entertainment (Nat King Cole had his own "room" here) . . . and they remember glamour. In 1946, after a change of ownership, the Troc closed down.

7. *77 SUNSET STRIP* SITE
8524 Sunset Boulevard

A low-rise 1990s office and theater building now occupies the southern 8500 block of Sunset Boulevard. Before that, however, a half-timbered restaurant stood here. In the late 1950s and early 1960s the place was Dino's Lodge and its owner was Dean Martin. Its greatest claim to fame came not from its celebrated owner but from its weekly appearance on the popular television series

Roger Smith, Efrem
Zimbalist Jr., and Edd
Byrnes at *77 Sunset
Strip*

77 Sunset Strip. It was here—under Dino's porte cochere—that
teen idol Edd "Kookie" Byrnes parked cars, combed his locks,
and occasionally helped costars Roger Smith and Efrem Zimbalist Jr. solve a case.

8. JUDY GARLAND/VINCENTE MINNELLI HOUSE
8850 Evanview Drive

North of Sunset Strip, Sunset Plaza Drive winds its way, often
very very steeply, up the West Hollywood Hills. A sharp left
leads to Evanview Drive, where in the 1940s, the long Moderne
mansion with the tiny windows at number 8850 was home to
one of Hollywood's golden couples—director Vincente Minnelli
and his frequent star performer and wife, Judy Garland. The
clean lines and cutting-edge design of the house obviously suited
Minnelli, a former art director. Inside their stylish abode,
however, things were often considerably less smooth, what
with Judy's tantrums, insomnia, and substance-abuse problems.

Fights were frequent, which would sometimes send Judy running down the street to seek solace from her neighbors, actress Sylvia Sidney and her husband, Carlton Alsop. It was on Evanview, too, where Judy is said to have discovered her husband in bed not with another woman, but a man. There were good times, too, especially with the birth of Liza in 1946. But these were few and far between. In June 1950, after several years of bad health, breakdowns, sanitariums, therapy, and studio suspensions, Judy was fired once and for all by her longtime studio, MGM. Three days later she made what was perhaps her most publicized suicide attempt, when she slashed her throat with a broken glass in the Evanview bathroom. Her wounds were decidedly superficial. By Christmas of the same year, the Minnelli-Garland marriage finally came to an end, as did their life on Evanview. But Judy's life and career were far from over. The following year, she had a new man, Sid Luft, and she was about to wow the world with a whole new side of her prodigious talent—as a concert performer.

9. THE COMEDY STORE/CIRO'S SITE
8433 Sunset Boulevard

Written on its outside walls are the names of the comics who have played here in the last three decades. Topping the list is Johnny Carson. One of the most vital comedy-workshop clubs in Los Angeles, the Comedy Store showcases established comedians who come to try out new material, as well as unknowns waiting to be discovered. Among the more successful in the latter category have been Robin Williams, John Ritter, Richard Pryor, David Letterman, Howie Mandell, Gabe Kaplan, Chris Rock, Jay Mohr, Judy Tenuta, and Bill Maher.

While the Comedy Store makes entertainment history at 8433 Sunset Boulevard, another club that once flourished at this address will hold even greater interest for movie lovers. The name of the spot was Ciro's and it was founded in 1939 by the *Hollywood Reporter*'s publisher, W. R. Wilkerson. Ciro's really hit its stride in the mid-1940s when a man named Herman Hover took it over and started to spend big money on publicity and promotion. Suddenly, Ciro's was the place to see and be seen and—above all—to be photographed! It is said that contract players

Ciro's, 1957

were sent to Ciro's on dates arranged by their studio's publicity departments. Once their pictures were taken, and it was established that they had indeed been there, these same "couples" would quickly slip out the back door and go their separate ways.

But Ciro's wasn't just for show. This truly was a place where the top stars of Hollywood could always be found both in the audience and on stage. Mae West performed here with her musclemen, Dean Martin and Jerry Lewis were often on the bill, and classy stripper Lili St. Cyr caused a minor scandal at Ciro's when her act was closed down by the police for lewdness.

The drama at Ciro's wasn't always limited to the stage. Johnny "Tarzan" Weissmuller reportedly dumped a table of food onto the lap of his soon-to-be ex, Lupe "Mexican Spitfire" Velez, in one of the club's better known public brawls. Bar fights were not uncommon either—but there was a house rule that permitted only three fights per customer. After that, even the most regular of regulars would be permanently eighty-sixed. Ciro's final drama took place in 1957 when the Internal Revenue Service claimed that Hover owed the government an enormous sum of money for not collecting a 20 percent entertainment charge on private parties. Despite the fact that the courts later ruled that Hover didn't owe the original sum, Ciro's and its owner had gone bankrupt.

Call 323–656–6225 or visit www.thecomedystore.com.

10. MONDRIAN HOTEL
8440 Sunset Boulevard

If chefs—such as Wolfgang Puck and Michael McCarty—were Hollywood's newest superstars in the 1980s, hoteliers could arguably claim the same status in the 1990s. And no star hotelier was bigger or brighter than Ian Schrager, who along with French designer Philippe Starck is often credited as the father of the "design hotel." In New York, Schrager (with then business partner, the late Steve Rubell) scored big with the cutting-edge Royalton in 1989; in Miami, he reinvented the beach hotel with the Delano in 1992; and in Hollywood, he took over a tired Sunset Strip high-rise and made it the hottest property in town. Called Mondrian, Schrager's Hollywood debut stunned Tinseltown with the thirty-foot-tall mahogany door sculpture that greeted guests at the entrance, the artist-designed furniture in the lobby, the video installations in the elevators, and the ultracool pool patio set with Moroccan lanterns and mega-mattresses. For the bar, Schrager brought in Randee Gerber (who would go on to marry supermodel Cindy Crawford) to make Mondrian's Sky Bar a favorite of le tout young Hollywood, including Leonardo DiCaprio, Drew Barrymore, Cameron Diaz, Courtney Love, and Jewel (whom action star Jean-Claude Van Damme reportedly met and fell for here). None of the above names have any trouble getting on the bar's famously exclusive guest list, whereas noncelebrity, non–hotel guests do. Today, Mondrian has a lot of hip new competition, and Schrager has had financial problems with some of his other properties, but his Sunset Strip hot spot remains a hit.

For reservations, call 323–650–8999 or visit
www.mondrianhotel.com.

11. ARGYLE HOTEL/SUNSET TOWER SITE
8358 Sunset Boulevard

Now a luxury hotel, this distinctive fourteen-story Sunset Boulevard tower has the same kind of streamlined glamour as the sleek Deco sets of 1930s black-and-white Hollywood films. Erected as a posh apartment house between 1929 and 1931, the Sunset Tower, as it was called at the time, was known for its many rich and famous tenants. Of these, Howard Hughes was perhaps the richest and most famous. Supposedly, in addition to his own apartment, the eccentric millionaire kept a couple of extra pads in the building for his lady friends. Other big-name tenants were Billie Burke, John Wayne, Paulette Goddard, Carole Landis, Zasu Pitts, Joe Schenck, Preston Sturges, Lloyd Pantages (son of theater magnate Alexander Pantages), and gangster Bugsy Siegel (who, reportedly, was asked to leave).

Movie lovers can see the striking Sunset Tower building in the 1944 RKO release *Murder, My Sweet,* which was that studio's second film version of the Raymond Chandler novel, *Farewell, My Lovely.* (The first was *The Falcon Takes Over,* which

Sunset Tower, now the
Argyle Hotel, seen here
prerestoration in 1984

was made in 1941 after Chandler had signed one of the worst contracts in history: RKO got practically unlimited rights to *Farewell, My Lovely* for a mere $2,000.) In *Murder, My Sweet,* Dick Powell as detective Philip Marlowe is taken to a lavish Sunset Tower suite, where, after being shown the beautiful view ("On clear days, Mr. Marlowe, you can see the ships in the harbor at San Pedro"), he is beaten up and held captive.

Some fifty years later, Robert Altman used the building (which narrowly escaped demolition in the 1980s before being restored and reborn as a hotel) as a location for a very funny sequence in *The Player* (1992), his insider take on the movie business. In the scene, producer Griffin Mill (Tim Robbins) is taking a meeting with a pair of screenwriters at the hotel (called the St. James Club at the time, but now the Argyle). In a veritable tour of the lavish Art Deco property (and a tour de force of cameo casting), Robbins bumps into Malcolm McDowell in the lobby and Andie MacDowell in the bar, where they schmooze about Roddy McDowall, before he finally arrives at the pool for the screenwriters' pitch.

Other films to capitalize on the Sunset Strip's most striking silhouette, listed on the National Register of Historic Places, have been *Wayne's World 2* (1993), *Get Shorty* (1995), *Strange Days* (1995), *A Night at the Roxbury* (1998), *Freaky Friday 2* (2003), and the 2000 *Brady Bunch* TV movie, *Growing Up Brady.*

Call 323-654-7100 or visit www.argylehotel.com.

12. CABO CANTINA
8301 Sunset Boulevard

In the 1960s, America started getting into health foods in a big way, and California, true to its countercultural image, led the revolution. In L.A., a prime purveyor of whole-grain goodies and soy protein delicacies was a funky Sunset Strip restaurant called the Source, where at one point the waitstaff dressed in long white robes. By the late 1970s, the health-food thing had pretty much waned on the East Coast, but was still going strong in Southern California. It was then that Woody Allen called on the Source as a quintessential L.A. locale for what many critics argue is his greatest film, *Annie Hall* (1977). In a pivotal scene in the film, writer Alvie Singer (Allen), over a lunch of alfalfa sprouts and mashed "glute," tries to convince his actress girl-friend Annie Hall (Diane Keaton), who abandoned both him and New York for Hollywood, to come home and marry him. Alvie is unsuccessful on both counts, but later the encounter turns up in a play he's written back in New York. Meanwhile, the former Source has moved with the times and changing culinary fashions: it is now a Mexican cantina, serving wicked margaritas and cheese enchiladas with not an alfalfa sprout in sight.

13. MIYAGI'S/PLAYERS CLUB SITE
8225 Sunset Boulevard

In the 1940s, the multitalented Preston Sturges—writer and di-rector of witty little Paramount comedies like *The Great Mc-Ginty* (1940), *Sullivan's Travels* (1941), *The Lady Eve* (1941), *The Palm Beach Story* (1942), and *The Miracle of Morgan's Creek* (1943)—opened a restaurant on the Sunset Strip. A highly sophisticated spot, Sturges's Players Club was a second home for many of the literary types—Robert Benchley, Dorothy Parker, George S. Kaufman, F. Scott Fitzgerald—who were holed up across the street in the Garden of Allah or in the Chateau Mar-

Players Club, 1940

mont next door. Very much an East Coast meets West Coast kind of place, the Players Club was popular with millionaires and their sons from Boston, New York, Philadelphia, and Chicago who hung out here in order to meet some of the prettiest starlets in Hollywood. The Players Club was also known for its drinks—the best and most potent in town. Sturges—who liked a good drink himself—wouldn't have had it any other way. Over the years, the former Players Club, with its prime Sunset Strip location, has been all manner of clubs and cafes. Its latest incarnation is as a Japanese restaurant-nightclub.

14. CHATEAU MARMONT
8221 Sunset Boulevard

A living legend—a vintage Hollywood hotel that's still luring celebrity guests. They come to this fabulous French château on Sunset Boulevard for its luxury, its privacy, and above all, its history. Opened in 1929, the Chateau was described as "the newest and most luxurious apartment house in Los Angeles," despite the fact that Sunset Boulevard was a dirt road at the time. The Chateau Marmont had forty-three apartments back then—and each came decorated with expensive European and Asian furnishings.

One of the Chateau's star long-term residents was Jean Harlow, who at age twenty-two was already on her third husband, Hal Rosson. Harlow shared suite 33 with Rosson for a year. When Billy Wilder came to Hollywood from Europe in 1934, the Chateau—now a hotel—was his first Hollywood base. His room had a Murphy bed and cost $75 a month. Wilder later used it as the model for the apartment that Fred MacMurray lived in in *Double Indemnity*. Heading the Chateau's frequent-guest category was Howard Hughes, who favored a penthouse suite that had a great view of the pool below. Hughes is reported to have often stood at his window, binoculars in hand, checking out the ladies down at the pool. Garbo also frequented the Chateau Marmont in her post-Hollywood period—checking in, as was always her custom, under the name of Harriet Brown. Garbo/Marmont stories abound and have her doing such things as making vegetable stews for breakfast, sleeping in the hotel lobby to escape the noise of a party near her room, and reporting that the Chateau Marmont was the only hotel in America where birds came and

Old Hollywood survivor:
Chateau Marmont

sang on her windowsill. Marilyn Monroe is said to have stayed here, too. After she had abandoned Hollywood for New York and the Actors Studio, she supposedly holed up at the Marmont on her return to Tinseltown in 1956 to star in *Bus Stop*. And, of course, there was John Belushi—whose drug death in a Chateau Marmont bungalow (number 2) made lurid headlines in March 1982.

Despite this tragedy, the Chateau remains one of Hollywood's hippest addresses—especially after savvy hotelier Andre Balazs took over the place in the early 1990s and redid it with the help of such heavyweights as designer Stephen Sprouse, architect Alison Spear, and artist/filmmaker Julian Schnabel. Balazs also gave the hotel a glamorous new restaurant area as well as Bar Marmont, which the *Los Angeles Times* calls "the sharpest bar in Hollywood."

Among the Chateau's big-name fans these days are actors Robert De Niro (who lived for two years in the penthouse), Whoopi Goldberg, Richard Gere, Keanu Reeves, Ethan Hawke, Sofia Coppola, Matt Dillon, Christopher Walken, Andie Mac-Dowell, Dennis Hopper, Bud Cort, Diane Keaton, Jill Clayburgh, Dustin Hoffman; directors John Waters and Tim Burton; photographers Bruce Weber and Annie Leibovitz; and writers Jay McInerney and Dominick Dunne. They all find staying and/or playing at this faux French château on Sunset Strip the closest thing to living out their Old Hollywood fantasies.

For reservations and information, call 323–656–1010 or visit www.chateaumarmont.com.

15. DUDLEY DO-RIGHT'S EMPORIUM/JAY WARD PRODUCTIONS
8200 Sunset Boulevard

Dedicated to a gang of cartoon characters—Bullwinkle, Rocky the Flying Squirrel, Natasha, Boris, Dudley Do-Right, and company—who conquered America on television in the 1960s, this little store specializes in all sorts of kitschy souvenirs of the Bullwinkle era. Behind the shop lies the headquarters of Jay Ward Productions, the company behind the cartoon, which has recently been involved in unleashing a restored version of the old gang on DVD. The late Jay Ward and cartoonist Alex Anderson are also credited with the first made-for-TV cartoon series, *Crusader Rabbit,* which debuted in 1949.

A few steps down the block (at 8218 Sunset Boulevard), diehard Bullwinkle fans will find a giant statue of their hero in front of Jay Ward's former base, which is now an operation called Hollywood Hounds, offering "canine coiffure and doggie daycare—where every dog is a star."

16. GARDEN OF ALLAH SITE
8150 Sunset Boulevard

You name them—Bogie and Bacall, F. Scott Fitzgerald and Sheilah Graham, John Barrymore, Errol Flynn, Clara Bow, Tallulah Bankhead, Marlene Dietrich—they all either stayed or played here, or both. Alas, a tacky strip mall and a Washington Mutual Bank now stand where the fabled Garden of Allah once sprawled across the southwest corner of Sunset and Crescent Heights Boulevards. A cluster of twenty-five low Spanish bungalows built around a main house that belonged to silent-screen ac-

West Hollywood legend: Garden of Allah, 1946

tress Alla Nazimova, the Garden of Allah was opened as a hotel by Nazimova in the late twenties.

Besides being popular with the top stars of the day, the place was also a haven for the literati who flocked to Hollywood in the 1930s. Robert Benchley, Dorothy Parker, George S. Kaufman, F. Scott Fitzgerald all helped earn the Garden of Allah its reputation as the Algonquin Round Table West. Round Table East member Alexander Woollcott referred to the place as "the kind of village you might look for down the rabbit-hole." The Garden of Allah was also known for the hard drinking that went on—in its bar and bungalows as well as around its pool. Robert Benchley, upon falling into the pool (built in the shape of the Black Sea—a tribute to Nazimova's Russian background), is credited with the famous line: "Get me out of these clothes and into a dry martini."

By the time the 1940s rolled around, the Garden of Allah had started losing some of its appeal—many of the personalities who had made it famous had moved on in their careers and no longer hung out here. By the 1950s, the place was rapidly deteriorating, and the hookers had moved in. In 1959, it all came to an end when the nostalgic Old Hollywood compound was razed for the bank that now stands on the former Nazimova property. Instead of sparking massive protests (as would be the case today), the demolition of the Garden of Allah was heralded with a festive farewell party. A thousand guests turned up—many of whom were celebrities dressed up like the celebrities of the 1930s who had given the Garden of Allah its name. Today, even the scale model, which for many years stood under a glass bubble at the back of the bank, is gone.

17. SCHWAB'S SITE
8024 Sunset Boulevard

Forced to close in late 1983 because of financial difficulties, Hollywood's most famous drugstore was torn down a few years later to make way for a mall. Many of the regulars at the old Schwab's—especially the breakfast bunch—resided at the neighboring Garden of Allah or Chateau Marmont. And since the latter had no room service in the old days, Schwab's often provided this vital amenity for Chateau guests who preferred neither eating out nor cooking in. Although most of the world now knows that Lana Turner was not discovered at Schwab's, we repeat it here one more time—just for the record. Recently a new Schwab's opened in the new Sunset & Vine development (see Chapter 2, item 10).

The drugstore's last days: Schwab's, 1984

18. DIRECTORS GUILD OF AMERICA
7920 Sunset Boulevard

This arresting round glass-and-brown-marble structure has since 1994 been the headquarters of the labor union representing film directors. Currently the Directors Guild of America has some 12,700 active members. Besides looking out for the rights, contracts, and pensions of its members, the DGA started a program in 1948 to honor its own, "free from prejudices and unhampered by outside influences." (The current high-pressure lobbying now so much a part of the Academy Awards comes to mind.)

The winner of the first Annual Award for Directorial Excellence was Joseph Mankiewicz for his *A Letter to Three Wives.* Today the DGA Awards include not only features but TV, documentaries, commercials, student films, and a Lifetime Achievement Award. In most instances, a DGA Award for best director of a feature means an Oscar as well. Indeed there have been only six instances in the awards' fifty-years-plus history when that hasn't been the case. Among the biggest upsets were in 1972, when Francis Ford Coppola won a DGA Award for *The Godfather* but lost out to Bob Fosse and *Cabaret* in the Oscar stakes, and in 1985, when though Steven Spielberg won the DGA for *The Color Purple,* Sydney Pollack won the Academy Award for *Out of Africa.*

Visit www.dga.org.

19. *HALLOWEEN* HOUSES
1530 and 1537 Orange Grove Drive

Supposedly it all takes place in the small Midwestern town of Haddonfield, Illinois, but when John Carpenter made his landmark slasher film *Halloween,* for a mere $300,000 back in 1978, there was obviously no money to go on location. So *Halloween* found the Midwest in Hollywood—on a quiet, tree-lined street of mostly clapboard houses, with tidy front lawns, just north of Sunset Boulevard. Although the street is called Orange Grove Drive, there's hardly a citrus tree in sight, but a careful viewing of the original film does reveal a palm tree every now and then. Two houses on Orange Grove were used extensively in the film:

Babysitter hell: Jamie Lee Curtis outside *Halloween* house

number 1537 was the "haunted" house and number 1530 is where Jamie Lee Curtis (in her first screen role) had the babysitting job from hell. As a moneymaker, *Halloween* was sheer heaven, however: the ultra-low-budget feature raked in over $50 million and spawned a slew of equally profitable sequels with higher budgets and no palm trees.

20. F. SCOTT FITZGERALD APARTMENT
1403 North Laurel Avenue

F. Scott Fitzgerald spent the last years of his life in Hollywood and the last months of his life in number 6 at the rear of this West Hollywood apartment house that was inspired architecturally by the châteaux of Normandy, France. It was here that Fitzgerald—his health having failed him after many years of hard drinking—worked on a film script, some short stories for *Esquire,* and his Hollywood novel, *The Last Tycoon.* Among his neighbors in the building was a B-picture beauty named Lucille Ball, who was living with her soon-to-be-husband, a Cuban bandleader-singer-actor named Desi Arnaz. More important, as far as Fitzgerald was concerned, was the fact that his own lady friend, columnist Sheilah Graham, lived a block away at 1443 North Hayworth.

In her book, *Beloved Infidel* (Holt, Rinehart and Winston, 1959), Graham speaks idyllically of their days as neighbors/ lovers in West Hollywood: "To economize, we shared the same maid, each paying half of her salary. We dined at each other's apartment on alternate nights: one night she cooked his dinner and I was his guest, the next, she cooked mine and he was my guest. Again, like a married couple, we went shopping at night in the supermarkets on Sunset Boulevard, or spent an hour in Schwab's drugstore, five minutes away, browsing among the magazines and ending our visit sipping chocolate malted milks at the ice-cream counter." Indeed Graham describes the summer of 1940 as their happiest time together. For one thing, Fitzgerald hadn't touched alcohol for a year. Still, it all came to an end very quickly. Fitzgerald succumbed to a heart attack a few days before Christmas of that same year. He was forty-four years old. He never finished *The Last Tycoon*, although it was published posthumously and made into a movie in the 1970s.

F. Scott Fitzgerald's West Hollywood home

Courtyard cool: Villa d'Este

21. VILLA D'ESTE
1355 North Laurel Avenue

One of the most beautiful courtyard apartment complexes in all of Los Angeles, the Villa d'Este was where Dean Jones and Carol Lynley lived in the 1963 Columbia film, *Under the Yum Yum Tree*. Erected in 1928, this haunting Mediterranean building is the work of the brothers F. Pierpont and Walter S. Davis and has seduced many Hollywood celebrities over the years with its tiled fountains, its jungly courtyards, and its peace and quiet. No wonder the exotic silent screen beauty Pola Negri felt at home here. And rumor has it that the great producer/director of historical epic films—C. B. DeMille—also kept an apartment at the Villa d'Este for his "private" purposes. Today, the building is beautifully maintained and remains one of West Hollywood's poshest addresses.

22. THE GRANVILLE/THE VOLTAIRE
1424 North Crescent Heights Boulevard

Originally known as the Voltaire, this marvelously maintained "château" was once owned by the Skouras family (the late Spyros Skouras was the Twentieth Century–Fox studio executive held largely responsible for the debacle known as *Cleopatra* in the early 1960s). Besides Skouras, other Hollywood names connected with the Voltaire are Ann Sothern, Jack Lord, Arthur Treacher, and Janet Gaynor—all of whom were former tenants.

In late 1954, Marilyn Monroe had separated from Joe DiMaggio and was about to abandon Hollywood and her Twentieth Century–Fox contract for a new life on the East Coast. At the time, her lawyers suggested she lie low and out of reach of Fox's lawyers until the moment she was ready to get on the plane. She followed their advice and suddenly newspaper headlines started asking: "Where Is Marilyn?" Marilyn, it turned out, was staying with a friend of hers at the Voltaire—the building that belonged to the family of one of the heads of the studio she was quitting!

In the 1980s, the Voltaire was turned into a luxury hotel and rechristened the Granville. It's currently a condominium building.

The grand Granville

Bette Davis's last address: Colonial House

23. COLONIAL HOUSE
1416 North Havenhurst Drive

On the National Register of Historic Places, this staid bit of Britain in otherwise architecturally exotic West Hollywood was once home to Carole Lombard and her first husband, William Powell. The famous couple resided here from 1931 to 1933. Lombard—who went on to marry Clark Gable—was in her early twenties during her Colonial House years. On the other hand, another screen legend, the indomitable Bette Davis, made Colonial House her last Hollywood home, occupying the penthouse apartment on the sixth floor up until her death in 1989. When La Davis put up a set of unauthorized pink-and-white awnings, the co-op board supposedly balked, but the awnings were never removed.

Toward the end of her life, despite being weakened and emaciated from strokes and cancer, trouper Davis nonetheless refused to be an invalid and did her best to call up her star power whenever given the chance. The results were sometimes disastrous, such as her appearance on the 1988 Academy Awards telecast when she couldn't read the TelePrompTer and had to be escorted unceremoniously offstage. But in September 1989, she traveled against doctors' orders to San Sebastian in Spain to receive a lifetime achievement award from that city's famous film festival. Decked out in the latest Patrick Kelly–designed gown and hat and chain-smoking to the end, the frail star stood before an adoring audience on a glittering opera house stage and took in their wild applause and standing ovations one last time. A few hours later, she slipped into a coma and was flown to the American Hospital in Paris, where she died at age eighty-one.

After Davis's death, Jodie Foster, another no-nonsense Hollywood lady, reportedly purchased Bette's penthouse. Meanwhile, the building's most famous fictional resident was Budd Schulberg's Sammy Glick, the success-obsessed title character of Schulberg's 1941 Hollywood novel, *What Makes Sammy Run?* In the book, Schulberg describes Sammy's Colonial House apartment as "one of the smallest in the building and even that must have been way beyond his means . . . but he wrote off only part of the expense to shelter, the rest to prestige." In 2004, Ben Stiller was slated to produce, direct, and star in a film version of *What Makes Sammy Run?*

24. VILLA ANDALUSIA
1471–1475 North Havenhurst Drive

Arthur and Nina Zwebell designed this enchanting Spanish/ Moorish masterpiece in 1926. Not visible from the street are the apartment building's various patios—one with an elevated swimming pool, another with an elegant tiled fountain and magnificent exterior fireplace. The apartments themselves have beamed ceilings, tiled floors and staircases. Clara Bow lived here—as did Katy Jurado, Jean Hagen, Cesar Romero, Teresa Wright, Jack Weston, Marlon Brando Sr. (Marlon's father), Anna Kashfi (Marlon's former wife), John Ireland, and Claire Bloom. This is 1920s Hollywood architecture at its best.

25. VILLA PRIMAVERA
1300–1308 North Harper Avenue

Yet another creation of the architectural efforts of Arthur and Nina Zwebell, the Villa Primavera has the look of a Mexican hacienda and enjoys one of the most expansive front lawns of any apartment building in West Hollywood. One of the reasons for this lavish use of land may have been that Villa Primavera dates back to 1923, which makes it one of the area's first buildings. The interiors of the apartments in the complex are just as appealing as the exterior—all face a central courtyard and have fireplaces, beamed ceilings, wonderful little niches and secret spaces. Former residents insisted that James Dean had a pad here—and went on to tell of the bizarre sexual behavior (bondage) that supposedly went on in the closet of his apartment. Katharine Hepburn is said to have been another former tenant. The 1950 film *In a Lonely Place,* starring Humphrey Bogart and Gloria Grahame, used the Villa Primavera as the Beverly Patio apartments, where Bogart and Grahame were more than just neighbors.

For a look at yet another 1920s Zwebell masterpiece, the Patio del Moro Apartments is just around the corner at 8229 Fountain Avenue. The fantasy behind this design is all-out North African—and the building not only has a spectacular front gate, which unfortunately these days is locked, that would be very much at home in Marrakech, but a miniature mosque tower in back as well. Actress Joyce Van Patten once lived at El Moro.

26. ROMANY VILLA
1301–1309 North Harper Avenue

Design for living: In 1930, Marlene Dietrich, newly arrived in Hollywood, takes an apartment in the same building (Romany Villa) as her discoverer, director, and mentor, Josef von Sternberg (the exact nature of their personal relationship was—and still is—the subject of much speculation). Von Sternberg, estranged from his wife, Riza, at the time, is torn between the two women. Practically as soon as Marlene arrives on the scene, von Sternberg wires Riza in New York to come to California. Riza comes, moves into Joe's apartment—and the sparks start flying! Marlene, hating Hollywood and suffering from a very bad case of homesickness (remember, she has left a husband and daughter back in Germany), threatens to return home. Von Sternberg, with a big professional investment in seeing Marlene succeed in Hollywood, spends hours in her apartment every evening trying to calm down the temperamental star. Riza is not amused—and eventually asks her husband why he doesn't marry Marlene. To this, von Sternberg is quoted as replying: "I'd as soon share a telephone booth with a frightened cobra." No matter. Riza returns to New York, files for divorce . . . and later sues Marlene for alienation of her husband's affections as well as for libel because of something Marlene reputedly has said about her in a magazine interview. The press has a field day, but eventually Riza dropped her suits against Marlene and polite letters were exchanged between the two Teutons. So it went . . . and, according to an old Hollywood friend of Riza von Sternberg, some of it started right here at the Romany Villa.

Some eighteen years later, a locally born movie actress, Marilyn Monroe, shared a Romany Villa flat with her acting teacher Natasha Lytess. At the time, Marilyn was very much involved with agent Johnny Hyde, who was both her lover and the man credited with molding her early film career. When Hyde died suddenly of a heart attack, Marilyn was devastated and is said to have taken an overdose of sleeping pills at the Romany Villa, the first of many suicide tries by the troubled star.

In the 1960s, Zsa Zsa Gabor lived for a year in this same building—during one of her brief periods between husbands—after a fire had gutted her Beverly Hills manse. Charlie Chaplin is rumored to have been one of Romany Villa's original owners.

Romany Villa

Villa Celia

27. VILLA CELIA
8320–8328 Fountain Avenue

One of Fountain Avenue's loveliest châteaux, Villa Celia is said to be a copy—on a smaller scale—of Château Azay-le-Rideau in France's Loire Valley. It's therefore fitting that famous French actress Michèle Morgan once lived in this 1928 West Hollywood castle. Al Pacino had an apartment at Villa Celia during the filming of the 1983 remake of *Scarface*.

28. LORETTA YOUNG VILLA
8313 Fountain Avenue

For many years, Loretta Young owned the modern villa that stands semisecluded behind these high Fountain Avenue walls. In the 1960s, Joan Crawford often stayed in a small apartment on the premises. In the 1970s, former Warner Bros. glamour girl Alexis Smith and her husband, Craig ("Peter Gunn") Stevens, bought and managed the property.

El Palacio queen:
Dorothy Dandridge

29. EL PALACIO APARTMENTS
8491–8499 Fountain Avenue

Dorothy Dandridge was ahead of her time—a talented, beautiful African American actress whose career was curtailed by the racism that was still a powerful force in Hollywood in the 1950s. To be sure, she did score a couple of prime roles, notably as the lead in *Carmen Jones,* which got her an Academy Award nomination in 1954, and as Bess in *Porgy and Bess* (1959). But, ultimately, there just weren't that many leading parts for women of color back then (there are still precious few today), and Dandridge never made another film after 1960, although she worked as a nightclub singer. Plagued by bad investments, bad career choices, as well as by alcohol and drug problems, she was found dead in 1965 in her apartment in this beautiful Spanish Baroque building on the edge of West Hollywood's châteaux country. Cause of death: an overdose of barbiturates. Halle Berry, the first African American to win a best actress Oscar *(Monster's Ball,* 2002), played Miss Dandridge in the 1999 biopic *Introducing Dorothy Dandridge.*

30. SAL MINEO APARTMENT
8563 Holloway Drive

Just up the road from the elegant châteaux apartment houses of
Fountain Avenue, Holloway Drive is decidedly less glamorous
architecturally. Indeed the most distinguishing features of the
long line of stucco buildings on the north side of the street are
the garage doors. It was in one of these garages that thirty-seven-
year-old actor Sal Mineo was murdered in 1976. Although he
had starred in *The Gene Krupa Story* (1960) and received an
Academy Award nomination for *Exodus* that same year, Mineo,
whose homosexuality was well known in Hollywood, never
managed to achieve a bankable film career. The early 1970s saw
his profile rise as a stage actor, however, especially with his powerful performance in Miguel Piñero's raw and raunchy prison
play *Short Eyes,* which he played both in New York and on the
road. At the time of his death—which was officially listed as an
armed robbery but which insiders felt was at the hands of a male
hustler Mineo had tried to bring home—the actor was in re-
hearsal for a play.

Mineo's most famous role was as the sensitive teenager in
Rebel Without a Cause, and his death was the third in what has
become known as the *Rebel Without a Cause* curse. Mysteri-
ously, four of the principal actors from the 1955 film died premature and in most instances violent deaths: James Dean in a car
crash in 1955, Nick Adams of an unexplained drug overdose in
1968, Mineo murdered in 1976, and Natalie Wood in a freak
boating accident in 1981.

31. PACIFIC DESIGN CENTER
8687 Melrose Avenue

One—actually two—of West Hollywood's most impressive
sights, this pair of monumental glass buildings, one blue, the
other green, house interior decorators' offices, design firms, and
some 130 showrooms of furniture, fabrics, and home furnishings. A branch of the Los Angeles County Museum of Art and a
movie theater are also part of the complex. Designed by the
architect Cesar Pelli, the first Design Center building—called

Center Blue, but better known by its nickname, the Blue Whale—was completed in 1975. Producer Dino de Laurentiis wasted no time in featuring L.A.'s new architectural wonder in his 1976 film *Lipstick,* which starred another striking mid-1970s phenomenon, model Margaux Hemingway. *Lipstick* showed off the Blue Whale's crisscrossing escalators and glassy galleria roof, but not Miss Hemingway's acting talents. Her younger sister Mariel, who played Margaux's younger sister in the film, fared much better and went on to have a laudable film career. Margaux, alas, was not so fortunate and took her own life in 1996.

The second Design Center building—Center Green—opened in 1988. It, along with its elder sibling, was featured in another unremarkable film, *Demolition Man* (1993), a sci-fi comedy thriller, set in L.A. circa 2036. The film starred Sylvester Stallone, a very young Sandra Bullock, and classy British actor the late Sir Nigel Hawthorne, who reportedly was not impressed by Mr. Stallone's acting technique, feeling he spent more time working out in his on-set gym than on his character.

Plans call for Center Red, the final phase of the Pacific Design Center, to go up at some time as yet to be determined. Hopefully, a better film role awaits it.

32. MORTON'S
8764 Melrose Avenue

The creation of restaurateur Peter Morton, best known as the genius behind the Hard Rock Cafe concept and chain, this West Hollywood hot spot has been a major watering hole for industry big shots for several decades, both here and at its original location on the other side of Robertson Boulevard. On any given night, you might find Johnny Carson, Steven Spielberg, or Kevin Costner here. But the ultimate evening to be at Morton's these days is on Academy Awards night, when *Vanity Fair* magazine's editor-in-chief Graydon Carter hosts what is now considered to be the most prestigious Oscar party in town and the successor to the late agent Irving "Swifty" Lazar's Spago bashes, which came to end in 1994 with Lazar's death. Still, there are differences in the two events: Lazar's was very much an insider affair, with most of the press kept carefully on the other side of the velvet ropes. The *Vanity Fair* party, however, staged by a New York–based media company (Condé Nast Publications) no less, is designed to hype film, stars, and the magazine's own annual Hollywood issue. And even if you are one of the zillions who haven't been able to get on the guest list, you can read all about it, complete with scores of photos, a month or so later in the magazine. The *Vanity Fair* party winds up in the supermarket tabloids even earlier—with scoops on everything from the latest Courtney Love freak-out to Julia Roberts's hitting the men's room to avoid the queue at the ladies' to the elaborate measures involved in keeping recently estranged star partners from potentially embarrassing close encounters.

For reservations, call 310–276–5205.

33. THE FACTORY
652 North Lapeer Street

A former sheet-metal factory in West Hollywood was the unlikely setting for a movie-star nightclub—but the year was 1967 and anything could happen back in those crazy days of the late sixties. Known as the Factory, this cavernous private play-place had various bars, a pool room, dance floor, big dining room, small dining room, even an art gallery. The Factory also had names like Sammy Davis Jr. and Peter Lawford on its board of directors—and all of their Rat Pack chums were members. Originally announced at $1,200 a year, the club's annual membership fee quickly dropped to $500—and it was rumored that many good-looking ladies got in for free.

Despite the hype and the supposed exclusivity, the Factory was a bomb. When it proved difficult to fill this vast space with famous faces, the management dropped all pretention and let literally anybody in. By the beginning of the 1970s, it was all over. A few years later, however, the Factory was reborn as Studio One. A sign of the times, Studio One was a gigantic predominantly gay disco that rivaled New York City's Studio 54 and attracted a fair share of straight celebrities to its dance floor and laser shows. Today, Studio One—which includes the main disco as well as the smaller UltraSuede dance club and various bars and lounges all housed within this former West Hollywood factory building—has been renamed the Factory and appears to be going strong.

For information, call 310-659-4551.

34. MARGO LEAVIN GALLERY/NORMA TALMADGE STUDIO SITE
812 North Robertson Boulevard

If you look carefully at the rear of this sleek, white, seemingly modern building that houses one of L.A.'s top art galleries, you can make out the outline of a barnlike peaked roof that has been stuccoed over. Everyone says that this was once a movie studio owned by Norma Talmadge and that some of the surrounding neighborhood's lovely clapboard bungalows were dressing rooms. While there seems little in the way of hard-core evidence to back up this legend, the fact that one of the little streets in this charming West Hollywood neighborhood is called Norma Place would indicate a Norma Talmadge connection.

Whatever its beginnings (the original permit seems to have been lost), from the mid-1950s to the 1990s, the then wooden building was the studio of the late set/costume designer Tony Duquette and boasted one of Hollywood's most theatrical interiors—a magical world of exotic artifacts and one-of-a-kind set pieces that were a far cry from the art gallery's current minimalist austerity.

35. DOROTHY PARKER HOUSE
8983 Norma Place

From 1957 to 1963, writer/great American wit Dorothy Parker lived in this small white West Hollywood house with her writer husband, Alan Campbell. The two—who lived off and on in Hollywood for several decades—collaborated on screenplays. Their most famous collaboration was the script for the 1937 *A Star Is Born,* which resulted in an Oscar nomination for the pair. Campbell died on Norma Place in 1963. Parker died a recluse in New York City in 1967. Of Hollywood, Parker once said: "The only 'ism' Hollywood believes in is plagiarism."

A quarter of a century after Parker's death, the Alan

Rudolph–directed film *Mrs. Parker and the Vicious Circle* documented the tempestuous and tormented life of the great lady of American literature and screenwriting. Starring as Parker was Jennifer Jason Leigh, who, ironically, had lived just a few doors away from the Parker-Campbell West Hollywood cottage at 8955 Norma Place.

36. DAN TANA'S RESTAURANT
9071 Santa Monica Boulevard

Sadly, many of Old Hollywood's most famous watering holes—like Chasen's, Romanoff's, and the Brown Derbys—have bitten the dust. Happily, Dan Tana's steak house is keeping the spirit of these classic haunts alive. Run by Yugoslav immigrant and former actor, Dan Tana (né Dobrivoie Tanaskovic), the restaurant that bears his American name is an island of old-fashioned style—red-and-white tablecloths, wood-paneled walls, leather booths—that offers a comforting escape from the aggressive minimalism and high-decibel acoustics that characterize so many of L.A.'s currently trendy dine spots. Tana also takes care of his celebrity regulars in a hands-on, old-fashioned way, working the tables, the bar, and keeping the press and paparazzi at bay. Among his biggest fans early on were legends such as Fred Astaire, Cary Grant, John Wayne, and John Belushi, who is said to have placed a dinner order here just before he died of a drug overdose at the nearby Chateau Marmont. These days, you're likely to find Cameron Diaz, George Clooney, Leonardo DiCaprio, Nicole Kidman, James Woods, Dabney Coleman, and Shaquille O'Neal dining here. Don't reach for your camera, however: the taking of photos is strictly forbidden. Cell phones are also frowned upon.

For reservations, call 310-275-9444.

37. LAUREL CANYON/HOUDINI RUINS
2398 Laurel Canyon Boulevard

South of Sunset Boulevard, Laurel Avenue is a sedate West Hollywood street of pretty apartment buildings and private homes. Just north of Sunset, Laurel Avenue goes through a distinct transformation. It changes its name for one thing—to Laurel Canyon Boulevard—and becomes a road rather than a street as it starts winding up into the Santa Monica Mountains. The architecture changes, too. The hillside-clutching houses and bungalows of Laurel Canyon and its numerous narrow twisting side roads have a decidedly rustic look to them. The whole feeling is one of being in the great outdoors—rather than the middle of the second-largest city in the United States. Laurel Canyon was never glamorous: it was real. It was not a place of great wealth or ostentation. In the sixties, hippies thrived here. As for the movie colony, those film folk who have lived here traditionally tended to be screenwriters rather than screen stars.

Of course the neighborhood has changed what with L.A.'s booming property market and with Laurel Canyon former shacks now going for megabucks. Still, when director-writer Lisa Cholodenko's film about a free-spirited record-producer L.A. mom (played by Frances McDormand) came out in 2002, it was set in and titled not Coldwater, not Benedict, not Nichols (all names of other famous L.A. canyons) but *Laurel Canyon.* The real estate prices and demographics may have changed but the offbeat legacy remains.

One of the most unusual sites in Laurel Canyon is what's left of the once great Italianate estate of magician Harry Houdini. It can be seen off to the right at the intersection of Laurel Canyon Boulevard and Lookout Mountain Avenue. Besides being a magician and escape artist, Houdini had a very brief career as a movie star in the late teens and early twenties. His silent screen epics were fast-action adventure yarns that featured sensational stunts and dramatic escapes. Today all that is visible of his Hollywood home is a set of elaborate stone steps and balustrades, once crumbling and overgrown, but which a new owner seems to have restored. Or perhaps the ghost of Houdini, said to haunt the estate, had something to do with the recent spruce-up?

38. MULHOLLAND DRIVE/UNIVERSAL CITY OVERLOOK
Mulholland Drive at Torreyson Place

Like Laurel Canyon, Mulholland Drive has iconic status in Los Angeles. This twisting, often breathtaking corniche that skirts the ridge of the Santa Monica Mountains—a range that effec-

Errol Flynn's Mulholland Drive hideaway

tively bisects the metropolitan area of L.A.—has always had a powerful air of mystery, danger, wildness. Up here coyotes and mountain lions roam the canyons. No wonder director-writer David Lynch chose Mulholland Drive to symbolize the primal danger lurking beneath the civilized veneer of Los Angeles in his 2001 film that could have no other title than that of the tortuous roadway itself.

No wonder, too, that Mulholland Drive seems to attract edgy, slightly dangerous Hollywood males—Jack Nicholson, Warren Beatty, bad-boy rocker Tommy Lee, Keenan Ivory Wayans—all of whom live or have lived up here in this special slice of L.A. Perhaps the most dangerous of all was longtime Mulholland Drive resident Errol Flynn, whose former estate can be glimpsed from the Universal City Overlook observation point at the junction of Mulholland Drive and Torreyson Place. These days, little more than the slate roof of Flynn's Mulholland house is visible, but behind the thick foliage that now protects the property, which Flynn built in 1942, all sorts of wild and wicked escapades took place—especially in the bedrooms, which Flynn equipped with one-way mirrored ceilings, so that both participants and spectators could have full views of whatever went on in bed.

The most spectacular views from the Universal City Overlook are not up into the mountains but down into the San Fernando Valley. For movie lovers, a stop here is a chance to see most of the great studios that blanket the Valley: Universal, Warner Bros., Disney, and the former Republic (now CBS). If you're con-

fused as to which is which, a laminated plaque identifies everything. Elsewhere, there are displays featuring photos of the same
scene in 1915–1916, 1936, and the early 1960s.

Besides offbeat residents, Mulholland Drive also boasts some
pretty eccentric architecture. None more so than Chemosphere,
the strange flying-saucer-shaped home that shoots up from a
great fat pedestal embedded in the hillside off to the right of the
former Flynn property. Designed in 1960 by John Lautner, this
bit of space age architecture, which can also be seen from the
Universal City Overlook, has been used as a location for many
TV series and TV movies. And on the feature front, director
Brian De Palma used the house extensively in *Body Double*, his
1984 homage to various Hitchcock films, notably *Rear Window*.
In the film, Chemosphere has a "very special feature," which
turns out to be a perfect view through a telescope of a very seductive and exhibitionistic neighbor. In *Charlie's Angels* (2000),
the evil Eric Knox lives in this same hexagonal oddity, where Angel Drew Barrymore almost spends the night but winds up making a dramatic exit out of one of its wraparound windows.

*For more great views, drive east from Torreyson and stop at
Runyon Canyon Park at 2300 Mulholland Drive. A quick walk up to
the top of the hill puts all of downtown Hollywood at your feet.
Then drive a little farther east and stop at the observation deck at
Mulholland Drive and Sunny Cove for an unusual look at the rear of
the Hollywood Bowl and a straight-on view of the Hollywood Sign.*

39. FRANKLIN CANYON PARK
Mulholland Drive/Coldwater Canyon Drive

Another of L.A.'s secret preserves of great natural beauty,
Franklin Canyon Park sits high in the Santa Monica Mountains
between Beverly Hills and the San Fernando Valley community
of Studio City. With thick forests of redwood, pine, and cedar
trees surrounding a shimmering mountain lake, this is a great
place for a hike, a run, or a picnic. It's usually delightfully crowd-
free—except for the occasional party of location scouts or perhaps an actual film crew, because this is one of L.A.'s most popular off-studio locations.

Franklin Canyon has been used extensively for filmmaking

Filmed in Franklin Canyon:
It Happened One Night with
Clark Gable and Claudette Colbert

since the 1930s. When Clark Gable carried Claudette Colbert piggyback across that "stream" in 1934's multiple-Oscar-winning *It Happened One Night,* the body of water was actually Franklin Canyon's Heavenly Pond. Two years later, when Nelson Eddy and Jeanette MacDonald sang of their love to each other in the middle of the Canadian Rockies in *Rose Marie,* the forests were Franklin Canyon's.

Over the years, Franklin Canyon has proved an especially popular backdrop for horror, sci-fi, and otherwise scary films and mini-series: *The Blob* (1958), *Tales from the Crypt* (1972), *A Nightmare on Elm Street* (1985), *Twin Peaks* (1990), and *Silence of the Lambs* (1991) all have sequences shot here. The Canyon has also been used at one time or another by virtually every L.A.-based TV series—*Picket Fences, Thirtysomething, Doogie Houser, M.D., Quantum Leap, Hunter, Baywatch,* and *JAG*—as well as in numerous commercials for Budweiser, Anacin, and Jeep Cherokee. It has even been featured on at least one record album cover, Simon and Garfunkel's classic 1964 *Sounds of Silence* LP.

Franklin Canyon Park can be reached from West Hollywood or Hollywood by driving west on Mulholland Drive to Coldwater Canyon Drive and then turning left onto Franklin Canyon Drive to the Park. It's also possible to get here from Beverly Hills by driving north up Beverly Drive and continuing onto Franklin Canyon Drive. Once at the Park, visitors can pick up a free movie list and map at the Nature Center. The park also offers a guided movie hike once a month. Call 310–858–7272 (extension 131) for details or visit www.LAMountains.com.

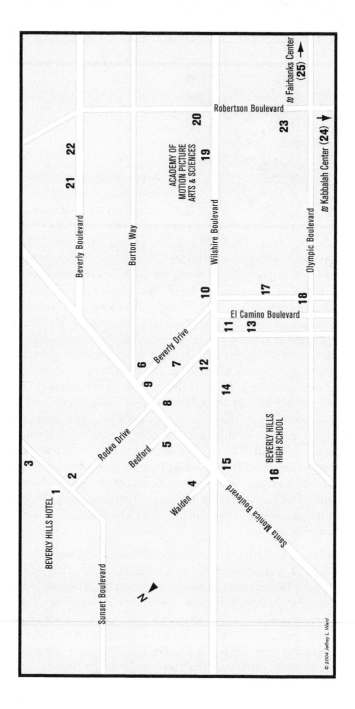

BEVERLY HILLS HOTEL 1

3

2

Sunset Boulevard

Rodeo Drive

Bedford

Walden

5

4

8

9

6

Beverly Drive

7

12

15

16 BEVERLY HILLS
HIGH SCHOOL

14

Santa Monica Boulevard

10

11

13

El Camino Boulevard

17

18

Wilshire Boulevard

Olympic Boulevard

ACADEMY OF
MOTION PICTURE
ARTS & SCIENCES

19

20

Robertson Boulevard

23

to Fairbanks Center
(25)

to Kabbalah Center (24)

Burton Way

Beverly Boulevard

21

22

N

© 2004 Jeffrey L. Ward

Beverly Hills:
Hollywood's Golden Ghetto

It's been called the most fabulous six square miles on earth. It's the land of Rodeo Drive, movie-star houses, extraordinary wealth and fame—and if the streets aren't paved with gold, they are constantly filled with the most expensive automobiles in the world. In Beverly Hills, Rolls-Royces, Mercedeses, Porsches, and Maseratis truly are the rule rather than the exception.

Beverly Hills got off to a slow start. Originally a Spanish land grant called Rodeo de las Aguas (the gathering of the waters), the area that today comprises Beverly Hills saw several owners and a number of development schemes during the nineteenth century—from wheat fields to oil fields to a plan to establish a town for German immigrants. All of these schemes met with failure, however, and by the end of the century, Rodeo de las Aguas was known for its lima bean fields, if it was known at all.

At the beginning of the twentieth century, a group of wealthy businessmen were again convinced that there was oil under Rodeo de las Aguas. Headed by Burton E. Green, the new Amalgamated Oil Company acquired the bean fields and started drilling. Alas, no oil was found—supposedly because the equipment used to tap it couldn't drill deep enough. On the other hand, an equally important—and valuable—discovery was made:

water. And so the Amalgamated Oil Company segued into the real estate business under the banner of the Rodeo Land and Water Company.

The new development company officially founded Beverly Hills in 1907. (It is said that Beverly Hills was named after Beverly Farms in Massachusetts, either because Burton Green had visited the place and liked it or because he had read of President William Howard Taft's visit there.) Despite its classy "Eastern" name, for a while it looked as if Beverly Hills was also headed for failure. By 1910, there were only a handful of houses in what was to have been Burton Green's dream city of lush parks, tree-edged boulevards, and handsome homes.

Seeing how poorly things were moving, Green and company next decided to erect a grand hotel to promote their beautiful Beverly Hills, and in 1912, the Beverly Hills Hotel was opened. The hotel helped somewhat, but by 1920, the population of Beverly Hills was a mere 700. It took Douglas Fairbanks and Mary Pickford to really put Beverly Hills on the map—which is exactly what the movie-star newlyweds did when they set up housekeeping at Pickfair in 1920. From then on, Pickfair came to symbolize all of the fantasy, magic, and luxury of the film world for millions of movie fans. Pickfair also started a trend within the movie colony—as stars and moguls began to buy land in Beverly Hills and build their own fantasy realms.

It is no surprise, therefore, that the top sights in Beverly Hills remain its movie-star mansions. The movie community did more than build homes here, however. Many took an active part in the city's affairs and influenced its history. The main reason that Beverly Hills remains an independent city and was never annexed by Los Angeles was the campaign led by some of the major names in the motion picture industry in the early 1920s. Several years later, the town would even have a film celebrity as its honorary mayor. More than just a bedroom community for Hollywood, in many ways and for many people, Beverly Hills *is* Hollywood.

This chapter covers the basic attractions of Beverly Hills of interest to movie lovers; the following chapter deals with the city's legendary movie-star houses. Items 5 through 15 in this chapter—

all on or near Beverly Hills' famous Rodeo Drive—can be seen on foot. To see the other sites mentioned here, a driving tour is suggested.

1. BEVERLY HILLS HOTEL
9461 Sunset Boulevard

This great pink palace, a classic example of the architectural style called Mission Revival, is one of the oldest hotels in Los Angeles. When it opened in 1912, there was literally nothing but bean fields and empty lots surrounding it. That was the problem, indeed the reason why the hotel was built in the first place—because the newly launched real-estate development of Beverly Hills wasn't doing so well. Few people were even looking at, much less buying, the lots that Burton Green's Rodeo Land and Water Company were selling. But with a hotel, where people could come and see the wonders of Beverly Hills firsthand, all that would change. At least that was the idea—and to make sure that the Beverly Hills Hotel would be a hit, Green and company managed to hire Mrs. Margaret Anderson away from the popular Hollywood Hotel to come and manage the new Beverly Hills.

The Beverly Hills Hotel

When many members of the movie colony, led by Mary Pickford and Douglas Fairbanks, started moving to Beverly Hills in the 1920s, the Beverly Hills Hotel immediately felt their impact. Besides becoming a social center for film folk, the hotel often took care of their progeny, with special showings of movies just for kids and their nannies as well as with a private children's dining room.

In the 1930s, in fact, that same little dining room became one of the hotel's most famous public rooms—the Polo Lounge. Hollywood was passionate about polo back in those days, and the Beverly Hills Hotel was where the Sunday chukkers crowd often wound up after the matches. Darryl Zanuck, Will Rogers, and producer Walter Wanger were among the town's top polo enthusiasts—and were part of the group who gave the Polo Lounge its name. Always a popular place, during the 1960s and 1970s, the Polo Lounge succeeded the Brown Derby in Hollywood as the top spot in town to be paged while having lunch or cocktails. Booths came equipped with telephones in the center and the tables all had jacks, which was quite a big deal in those pre–cell phone days. Eventually most of the pages were more for show than anything else—but that didn't diminish the cachet of the Polo Lounge. Today, the phones are still there and the pagings go on, albeit much less frequently than in the hotel's heyday.

Through the years, the Beverly Hills has had its share of movie-star guests—and movie-star scandals. Marilyn Monroe and Yves Montand made gossip columns during the filming of *Let's Make Love* when both took their film's title literally in a Beverly Hills Hotel bungalow. John F. Kennedy is also said occasionally to have checked into a bungalow at the Beverly Hills—without Jackie. The hotel's biggest bungalow booster, however, is Elizabeth Taylor, who spent a record-breaking six out of eight honeymoons in various Beverly Hills Hotel cottages.

Besides star guests, the Beverly Hills Hotel at one time had a group of illustrious local owners. That was back in the early 1940s when a private consortium purchased the hotel from the Bank of America. Among the names involved in this transaction were Irene Dunne, Loretta Young, and Harry Warner. The hotel's current owner is also a celebrity: the Sultan of Brunei, one of the richest men in the world, who has controlled the property since

Marlene Dietrich at the Beverly Hills Hotel's Polo Lounge in the 1930s

1987. In 1992, he closed down the whole hotel for a total makeover that took two and a half years and did its best to honor the spirit of the original.

The Beverly Hills has appeared in many films, its pool and cabanas often representing Hollywood living at its lushest. Much of the opening of *Designing Woman* (1957) with Lauren Bacall and Gregory Peck takes place poolside at the Beverly Hills. The 1937 *A Star Is Born* also features this famous pool patio. The Polo Lounge has also figured as a Hollywood location in many a Hollywood flick—*Valley of the Dolls* (1967), *The Way We Were* (1973), and *Shampoo* (1975) to name a few. Then there's Neil Simon's *California Suite* (1977), in which the entire action of the film takes place at the Beverly Hills Hotel. Based on his play of the same name, the film version actually shot only one sequence on location at the Beverly Hills—a scene in which Jane Fonda is on the terrace of her room. Since, at that point, the hotel no longer permitted filming in its public areas, the rest of the hotel—from its classic porte cochere to its pool, lobby, and the Polo

Lounge—was carefully studied by art directors and set designers and then duplicated at the Warner Bros. Studios in Burbank. Today, the no-filming rule still applies.

Call 310–276–2251 or visit www.thebeverlyhillshotel.com.

2. WILL ROGERS MEMORIAL PARK
Sunset Boulevard at Cañon Drive

Just across Sunset from the Beverly Hills Hotel, a pretty little park takes over the triangle of land bounded by Cañon Drive, Beverly Drive, and Sunset Boulevard. A peaceful enclave of green lawns, glorious gardens, and tall palm trees, this was once called Sunset Park and is the oldest municipal park in Beverly Hills. In 1952, it was renamed in honor of not only one of Beverly Hills' most famous citizens, but also its first honorary mayor: humorist Will Rogers. Of his job as mayor, he once said that his main official duty was directing folks to Pickfair, the fabulous estate

Mayor of Beverly Hills:
Will Rogers

of Hollywood's royal couple of the 1920s, Mary Pickford and Douglas Fairbanks.

3. GREYSTONE PARK AND MANSION
905 Loma Vista Drive

If you feel you've seen this great Gothic mansion before, you have—countless times on both the big and small screen. On TV, it's done all the usual series: *Dynasty, Falcon Crest, Knot's Landing, Dark Shadows,* and more recently *Gilmore Girls, Snitch,* and *Boom Town.* Its more notable feature film appearances include such classics as *Forever Amber* (1947), with Linda Darnell and Cornel Wilde; *Dead Ringer* (1964), starring Bette Davis at the height of her horror-film period; the 1964 Jerry Lewis comedy *The Disorderly Orderly;* and *The Loved One,* the 1965 Tony Richardson–directed film version of Evelyn Waugh's novel of the same name. In the film, which satirized the funeral customs of Southern California, both Greystone's mansion and its grounds were used to represent Whispering Glades, the Forest Lawn–like cemetery around which much of the plot revolved.

Since then, Greystone has appeared in many many more features. Among them are *Ghostbusters* (1984), *All of Me* (1984), *The Witches of Eastwick* (1987), *The Fabulous Baker Boys* (1989), *Guilty by Suspicion* (1991), *The Marrying Man* (1991), *Memoirs of an Invisible Man* (1992), *Death Becomes Her* (1992), *The Bodyguard* (1992), *Indecent Proposal* (1993), *Nixon* (1995), *The Phantom* (1996), *Air Force One* (1997), *Mercury Rising* (1998), *Hanging Up* (2000), *Rock Star* (2000), *X-Men* (2000), *Simone* (2000), *Batman and Robin* (2001), *Town and Country* (2001), *America's Sweethearts* (2001), *Spider-Man* (2001), *Austin Powers in Goldmember* (2001), and *Charlie's Angels 2* (2003).

Greystone was originally the name of the huge 400-acre Beverly Hills ranch of the Edward L. Doheny (oil and later real estate) family. Doheny built the magnificent fifty-five-room stone mansion in the late twenties for his only son, E. L. Doheny Jr. Three weeks after the younger Doheny moved into Greystone with his wife and five children, both he and his male secretary were found dead in Doheny's bedroom. The official version of the story says that the secretary shot Doheny and then himself when Doheny refused to give him a raise. Another version of the events suggests that Doheny and his secretary were lovers . . . and that it was Doheny who fired both shots, possibly because he feared that their affair was about to be discovered by his family.

No matter what really happened in 1928 in Doheny's bedroom, Greystone remains one of Beverly Hills' most impressive estates—and unlike its counterparts, this is one great property that is open to the public. That's because the City of Beverly Hills bought Greystone and eighteen of its original 400 acres in the mid-1960s. (Most of the rest of the acreage has been used for the ultra-exclusive development called Trousdale Estates, former residents of which include Richard Nixon and Elvis Presley.) In 1971, Greystone's grounds were made a public park, while the main house served as the headquarters for the American Film Institute's film school. After the AFI moved to East Hollywood in 1983, the City of Beverly Hills restored the mansion to its original condition, which made it even more desirable for location shoots.

Greystone Park is open from 10 a.m. to 5 p.m. daily. The mansion is not open to the public, however.

Movie-star mansion: Greystone

Beverly Hills bizarre: Witch's House

4. WITCH'S HOUSE
516 Walden Drive

This is easily Beverly Hills's most bizarre house—a fairy-tale cottage where everything from peaked roofs to leaded windows is wonderfully askew. One almost expects to see the late Margaret Hamilton wandering about the front lawn in full *Wizard of Oz* witch's drag. Just who was responsible for all of this whimsy right in the middle of Beverly Hills? The answer: a movie studio several miles to the south over in Culver City. The crazy cottage was originally built as the offices for Irwin C. Willat Productions and was moved to Beverly Hills in the early 1930s when the studio went out of business. Although it has been a private residence ever since, the house may be familiar to movie lovers from its appearance in MGM's *The Loved One* (1965), in which it was used as the Hollywood abode of the character played by Sir John Gielgud. It can also be seen in Amy Heckerling's 1995 comic look at Beverly Hills bratdom, *Clueless,* and in Roger Corman's 1957 low-budget horror film *The Undead.*

5. CHURCH OF THE GOOD SHEPHERD
505 North Bedford Drive

If you're Catholic and live in Beverly Hills, this is your church. Famous former and current parishioners include Desi Arnaz, Charles Boyer, Rosemary Clooney, Gary Cooper, Jeanne Crain, Irene Dunne, Jimmy Durante, Peter Finch, José Ferrer, Eva Gabor, Jack Haley, Alfred Hitchcock, Gene Kelly, Dean Martin, Ann Miller, Carmen Miranda, Bob Newhart, Maureen O'Sullivan, Rosalind Russell, Danny Thomas, Jane Wyman, Loretta Young, and Rudolph Valentino.

In May 1950, an eighteen-year-old Elizabeth Taylor was married at the Church of the Good Shepherd to Mr. Conrad Nicholson ("Nicky") Hilton Jr. It was a fairy-tale wedding that would not be matched until Grace Kelly married Prince Rainier in Monaco some six years later. For Elizabeth's wedding, MGM insisted on having designer Helen Rose do the "costumes." Also, the opening of Elizabeth's new film, *The Father of the Bride,* was deliberately scheduled for the month after her real wedding so as to get the maximum benefit of the publicity. According to Kitty Kelley in *Elizabeth Taylor: The Last Star* (Simon & Schuster, 1981), Elizabeth delighted the guests at the ceremony with one of the most dramatic and longest post-vows kisses in the church's history. And when the ceremony was over, while scores of photographers were recording it all for the world to see, Elizabeth was heard to say to her mother: "Oh, Mother, Nicky and I are one now—forever and ever." It was Miss Taylor's first "forever" and this one lasted about three months. Another Good Shepherd marriage that didn't last was that of Rod Stewart and supermodel Rachel Hunter.

Besides marriages, Good Shepherd has seen some pretty spectacular Hollywood funerals in its time. The biggest was undoubtedly for Rudolph Valentino in 1926, although Frank Sinatra's in 1998 came close to matching it with virtually every living Hollywood legend in attendance and a few thousand fans outside. Carmen Miranda, Gary Cooper, Jimmy Durante, Peter Finch, Alfred Hitchcock, Rosalind Russell, Vincente Minnelli, Danny Thomas, Rita Hayworth, and Eva Gabor had Good Shepherd send-offs as well. One of the best-known Good Shepherd funerals, however, was staged—it was that of Norman

Church of the Good Shepherd

Maine (James Mason) in the 1954 *A Star Is Born*. In one of the film's most wrenching and frightening sequences, Vicki Lester (Judy Garland) collapses when she is set upon by reporters and fans as she is leaving the church; she barely makes it into the waiting limousine.

The Church of the Good Shepherd—dedicated in 1925—is the oldest church in Beverly Hills.

6. PACIFIC CENTER GROUP/MCA SITE
7370 Little Santa Monica Boulevard

MCA—the Music Corporation of America—was founded as a band-booking agency in 1925 by Dr. Jules Stein, an ophthalmologist who decided early in his career that show business was more fun (and more profitable) than medicine. By the late 1930s, MCA had grown to become one of Hollywood's most important talent agencies—and when it came time for MCA to build new headquarters, Dr. Stein wanted something that wouldn't look like an office building. Translating Stein's dream into reality was the work of distinguished African American L.A. architect, Paul R. Williams, who came up with this graceful neo-Georgian structure that still turns heads in Beverly Hills.

Music Corporation of America's former headquarters

There are many myths surrounding the building. One says that the sweeping double staircase in the main lobby was used in *Gone With the Wind,* which is definitely not true. Another is that the Tuscan colonnade in the plaza at the rear of the original MCA building was salvaged from Ocean House, the great Santa Monica estate (144 rooms!) of William Randolph Hearst and Marion Davies, most of which was demolished in 1956. This, it turns out, may well be true—since, according to several former and current MCA officials, Dr. Stein bought many treasures at Ocean House's predemolition auction.

As for MCA, the company grew and grew and in the 1950s became less involved in representing talent and heavily involved in television production, eventually moving to Universal City where it took over Universal Studios and became MCA-Universal. In the 1990s, the whole operation was bought by the massive European media conglomerate Vivendi, which, in 2003, sold its MCA-Universal division to NBC as part of the ongoing corporate game of movie studio musical chairs. The sedate original MCA headquarters in Beverly Hills is now an office complex.

7. RODEO DRIVE

The residential part of this famous Beverly Hills street—north of Santa Monica Boulevard—once had a bridle path in the middle; it has long since been landscaped with grass and palmettos. Besides horses, at least one very famous jogger used the bridle path, according to director Billy Wilder, who remembers often seeing Greta Garbo running along Rodeo in the mid-1930s.

Garbo did more than jog on Rodeo. She—along with her good friend, health-food activist Gaylord Hauser—wound up buying a nice hunk of the commercial part of it south of Santa Monica Boulevard. Since the area has become one of the most expensive shopping streets (and pieces of real estate) on earth, Garbo was able to spend her post-Hollywood life doing what she liked best—being left alone—right up to her death in 1990.

With its embarrassment of glittering shops and glamorous designer outposts, Rodeo Drive has appeared in many films, usually as a symbol of capitalism at its most seductive. In *Pretty Woman* (1990), for example, Richard Gere takes his one-week-stand Julia Roberts on a memorable shopping spree along Rodeo Drive, whereas in Brian De Palma's 1984 *Body Double,* the porn actress played by Melanie Griffith goes shoplifting along the same street. Rodeo Drive also shows up in the features *Down and Out in Beverly Hills* (1986), *Indecent Proposal* (1993), *Clueless* (1995), *Romy and Michelle's High School Reunion* (1997), *Parent Trap* (1998), *A Civil Action* (1998), *Bowfinger* (1999), and *The Muse* (1999). Needless to say it was a frequent location for the Aaron Spelling series *Beverly Hills 90210.*

8. ARTISTS AND WRITERS BUILDING
9507 Little Santa Monica Boulevard

Will Rogers was one of the forces behind this little building, which went up in 1921 to provide creative artists with workspace in Beverly Hills. Since then, the Artists and Writers Building has been a fashionable, if somewhat inconvenient (for years the place had no hot water or air conditioning) address for Hollywood writers, producers, and directors. Among its most famous tenants have been director Billy Wilder, actor-producer Jack Nicholson, game-show maven Chuck Barris, science-fiction writer Ray Bradbury, and actor-director Bill Bixby.

9. THE MUSEUM OF TELEVISION AND RADIO
465 North Beverly Drive

Concerned about the sad state of preservation of America's radio and television heritage, CBS honcho William S. Paley founded the Museum of Broadcasting in New York in 1975. This unique facility not only set to collecting masses of vintage radio and TV programs, it also enabled scholars and the public to see and/or hear them in its cool little private booths. In 1997, the museum, renamed the Museum of Television and Radio, opened a West Coast branch in this striking white Richard Meier–designed building in Beverly Hills. MT&R currently has a computerized catalogue of some 120,000 radio and TV shows and commercials, which can be accessed by scholars and fans. In addition, the museum has daily screenings and rebroadcasts from its collection. These might be anything from a long-lost TV show such as the landmark 1954 drama *Twelve Angry Men* to rare radio coverage of a historical event such as the Lindbergh baby kidnapping trial in 1935.

The MT&R is open Wednesdays to Sundays from 12 noon to 5 p.m. Call 310-786-1000 for further information or visit www.mtr.org.

10. BEVERLY THEATER SITE
206 North Beverly Drive

With its huge dome and soaring minarets, this Islamic Moderne folly began its life as the Beverly Theater when it opened in 1925. The first real movie palace to be built in the City of Beverly Hills, the Beverly meant that all of the film people who had moved there in the 1920s could now go to the movies in style without driving five miles to Hollywood or ten to downtown Los Angeles. Today,

Beverly Theater, 1925

after many decades as an Israeli bank—only in Beverly Hills—the exotic Islamic-style building has been turned into offices.

11. REGENT BEVERLY WILSHIRE HOTEL
9500 Wilshire Boulevard

When Elvis Presley was starting to indulge his star power during his early Hollywood days, he kept a suite here—and kept security guards on their toes, what with all of the comings and goings of ladies of the evening. And when Liz Taylor had conquered Richard Burton in *Cleopatra* and returned to Hollywood with him, she continued to shock the world when she and Burton shared the Presidential Suite of the Beverly Wilshire—even though both were married to other mates at the time. Warren Beatty didn't just stay here—he lived in a Beverly Wilshire penthouse suite for over a decade and considered the hotel "the only place to live in L.A." (But that was before he met Annette Bening and finally turned family man at age fifty-three.) Steve McQueen lived here, too, right before he took off for Mexico and the Laetrile treatments that did not cure the cancer that had taken over his body. The staff remembers McQueen as very kind, gentle: He gave away all his plants to the maids before his departure.

Two of the most famous celebrities to stay here did so on film. They were Richard Gere and Julia Roberts, whose weeklong liaison in *Pretty Woman* (1990) mostly took place in the Beverly Wilshire's lavish top-floor Presidential Suite. The hotel has also hosted Eddie Murphy in *Beverly Hills Cop* (1984); Robert Redford, Demi Moore, and Woody Harrelson in *Indecent Proposal* (1993); Warren Beatty (return visit) in *Bulworth* (1998); and Nicolas Cage and Téa Leoni in *The Family Man* (2000). The hotel's grand ballroom is also frequently filmed, most recently in *Intolerable Cruelty* (2003), in a scene where divorce attorney George Clooney is addressing a convention, supposedly in Las Vegas, of the National Organization of Matrimonial Attorneys.

The hotel—which over the years has welcomed royalty, presidents, the highest of high society—dates back to 1928, when its serious nine-story Beaux Arts façade confirmed the fact that Bev-

Richard Gere and Julia Roberts check into the Beverly Wilshire Hotel in *Pretty Woman*

Regent Beverly Wilshire Hotel

erly Hills had truly arrived as a city. Whereas the Beverly Hills Hotel was built (in 1912) to lure visitors to what was then just a real estate developer's fantasy, the Beverly Wilshire was erected because that fantasy had become a reality that exceeded everyone's wildest expectations. Taken over by Four Seasons Hotels in the late 1980s, the hotel was thoroughly restored and renamed the Regent Beverly Wilshire. Today, it remains one of L.A.'s most prestigious addresses.

Call 310–275–5200 or visit www.regenthotels.com.

12. THE GRILL ON THE ALLEY
9560 Dayton Way

This fashionable steak house, wedged on an odd triangular block between Wilshire Boulevard and Rodeo Drive, is the unofficial commissary for the nearby William Morris Agency. Here, deals are discussed over $20 chicken pot pies, $28.50 crab cakes, and $30-plus steaks. This, after all, is Beverly Hills.

For reservations, call 310–276–0615 or visit www.thegrill.com.

13. WILLIAM MORRIS AGENCY
151 and 150 El Camino Drive

Did you hear the one about the actor who murdered his wife? With the law closing in on him, he went to his most trusted friend and asked what he should do to disappear. His friend's answer: "Sign with William Morris." The largest (get the joke now?), oldest (it was started in 1898 by a vaudeville booking agent named William Morris), and perhaps most famous talent agency in the world, William Morris has had as much influence on the history of Hollywood as any studio. Over the years, the William Morris Agency has controlled the careers of megastars like Mae West, Al Jolson, Spencer Tracy, Katharine Hepburn, James Cagney, Judy Garland, Rita Hayworth, Frank Sinatra, Steve McQueen, Bill Cosby—and collected 10 percent of their and many others' considerable earnings.

It was a William Morris agent, Johnny Hyde, who would get a legend known as Marilyn Monroe off the ground. Generally credited for molding her career, Hyde landed Marilyn roles in *The Asphalt Jungle* and *All About Eve* and negotiated the Fox contract that put her on the map. It was both a professional and a personal relationship—and "Johnny Hyde's girl" was with him in Palm Springs when he suffered the heart attack that ended his life in 1950. Marilyn also had a room in Hyde's Beverly Hills home—which she was forced by Hyde's family to vacate immediately after his death.

In those days, William Morris was located on Cañon Drive. The company moved to its present location in 1954, and built the matching structure across the street in the 1980s. With offices in four other cities (New York, Nashville, London, and—with an eye to the burgeoning Latino market—Miami), William Morris, from its black-glass Beverly Hills headquarters, looks after the careers of such heavyweights as Catherine Zeta-Jones, Russell Crowe, Kevin Spacey, Reese Witherspoon, Queen Latifah, and director Ridley Scott.

Visit www.wma.com.

14. SAKS FIFTH AVENUE
9600 Wilshire Boulevard

It was here on December 12, 2001, in this smart Beverly Hills branch of the venerable New York City department store that a beautiful young movie star, Winona Ryder, who to the outside world seemed to have it all, wanted just a little bit more: $5,560.40 worth of designer tops, handbags, and scarves, in fact, which she attempted to take out of the store without paying. Although she later told the court that she took the goods as part of her research for an upcoming role, she was nonetheless convicted of grand theft and sentenced to three years probation, 480 hours of community service, and given a $10,000 fine. The incident did not seem to harm Miss Ryder's popularity with the industry or her fans. Indeed, some cynics argued that, if anything, the exposure may have provided just the boost her career, which had somewhat leveled off at the time, needed. The publicity didn't seem to hurt Saks either—reportedly the store had a very good quarter just after the incident.

15. CREATIVE ARTISTS AGENCY
9830 Wilshire Boulevard

In 1975 four young men made Hollywood history when they exited the prestigious William Morris and opened a brand-new talent agency called Creative Artists Agency (CAA). Brash, aggressive, and above all terminally energetic, the quartet was headed by twenty-nine-year-old Michael S. Ovitz, who quickly became known as the toughest guy in town as he raided both his former agency and rival ICM (International Creative Management), taking their star actors, writers, and directors.

The new agency flourished and, to cement their success, Ovitz and company eventually engaged none other than the internationally renowned architect I. M. Pei to build a headquarters befitting their power and status. The result was this handsome three-story circular black glass and white marble structure at the corner of Wilshire Boulevard and Little Santa Monica Avenue. Dedicated in 1989, the building, which sports an art-filled atrium and a one-hundred-seat screening theater, has won several architectural awards.

I. M. Pei's Creative Artists Agency building

In 1995, some six years after the ribbon cutting for its new offices, Ovitz again stunned the industry by leaving the company he had founded to become president of the equally high-flying Walt Disney Company, headed by his buddy Michael Eisner. The two mega-egos quickly found themselves on a collision course, however, and after a mere fourteen months on the job, Ovitz was fired—but with a reported $100-million-plus parachute. Not one to retire to the South of France, Ovitz again was in the news in 1999, when he formed yet another new artists management agency, called Artists Management Group. He started off with a bang, luring $20-million-a-movie Robin Williams away from CAA. Ovitz's new operation was no repeat of his CAA success, however. He had made too many enemies in too high places, and there were now too many other young Mike Ovitzes out there. In 2002, Robin Williams not only returned to CAA, but CAA wound up absorbing Ovitz's new company, a move that effectively stripped Ovitz of power. The whole Ovitz saga is the stuff of Greek tragedy—and old-fashioned Hollywood movies.

Visit www.caa.com.

16. BEVERLY HILLS HIGH SCHOOL
255 South Lasky Drive

It's one of the top high schools in the USA. It has its own drama department, its own cable TV channel, and a gym where the floor opens up to reveal a swimming pool—which was famously featured in Frank Capra's 1946 Christmas classic *It's a Wonderful Life*. If that isn't enough, it even has its own oil wells, which have been helping to keep school taxes low ever since 1927 when Beverly Hills High School was established. In 2003, these famous oil wells landed the company operating them in court in a suit that cited air-quality violations. The company was fined $10,000 and forced to install a $60,000 pollution monitoring system. The law firm behind the suit was that of the real-life Erin Brockovich, immortalized by Julia Roberts in the 2000 film that won her an Academy Award.

Of the thousands of children of the movieland elite that Beverly Hills High has educated, some have gone on to fame and fortune on their own—from Desi Arnaz Jr. to Shaun and Patrick Cassidy, Rob Reiner, Carrie Fisher, Joanna Gleason (Monty Hall's daughter), Angelina Jolie, and Marlo Thomas. Other former Beverly Hills students that have done pretty well for themselves are Betty White, Richard Chamberlain, June Haver, Rhonda Fleming, Joel Grey, Richard Dreyfuss, Bonnie Franklin, Burt (Batman's Robin) Ward, Nicolas Cage, Lenny Kravitz, David Schwimmer, media mogul Barry Diller, ballerina Maria Tallchief, tennis star Louise Brough, and writer Nora Ephron.

In 1994 Beverly Hills High became a celebrity in its own right when it served as the inspiration for the Aaron Spelling series *Beverly Hills 90210*. Called West Beverly Hills High in the series, the school used as a location was not the real Beverly Hills High, which has strict guidelines that limit the time and hours of any filming done on campus. Instead, the exteriors were done at Torrance High, south of Los Angeles International Airport in the community of Torrance.

Visit http://bhhs.beverlyhills.K12.ca.us/home.html.

Beverly Hills lovebirds:
Hepburn and Tracy

17. HEPBURN-TRACY HIDEAWAY
328 South Beverly Drive

Although there has been much speculation as to the exact nature of their relationship, Katharine Hepburn and Spencer Tracy shared an intimate partnership for almost three decades in Hollywood. They never officially lived together, but early in their friendship, they spent a lot of time in a small flat that Tracy had rented in downtown Beverly Hills. In her book *Me* (Knopf, 1991), Hepburn describes the place as "a terrible little apartment . . . down an alley off the actual drive. Trying to make it attractive was really not possible. In desperation we had Erik Bolin—French furniture maker—make some wooden valances for the curtains." The apartment, on the second story, at the back of a small courtyard building, is now an office.

18. MONUMENT TO THE STARS
Beverly Drive and Olympic Boulevard

Water played an important role in the early lives of most of the communities in the Los Angeles basin. In many instances, it simply came down to the fact that the city of Los Angeles controlled the main water supplies—which meant that many communities had the option of being annexed by L.A. or dying of thirst. Hollywood, for example, voted to become part of Los Angeles in 1910 for just this reason.

When the company that furnished Beverly Hills with its water claimed that it could no longer provide adequate amounts of the stuff in the early 1920s, the question of annexation became a hotly debated issue. The rallying cry for the pro-annexation forces was "Annexation or Stagnation." The anti-annexation group was led by eight of filmdom's most illustrious citizens: Mary Pickford, Douglas Fairbanks, Will Rogers, Conrad Nagel, Tom Mix, Harold Lloyd, Rudolph Valentino, and director Fred *(Ben Hur)* Niblo. The issue came to vote in April 1923—and the star-led faction won 507 to 337. To this day, Beverly Hills is a totally independent community within the County of Los Angeles.

In 1959, a monument was erected in honor of the eight luminaries who had helped save Beverly Hills from Los Angeles. Topped by a huge metal sculpture depicting a spiraling piece of movie film, the Monument to the Stars shows each of the actors in the group wearing a costume from one of his or her famous films.

Monument to the Stars

19. ACADEMY OF MOTION PICTURE ARTS AND SCIENCES
8949 Wilshire Boulevard

It was founded in 1927 by Mary Pickford, Douglas Fairbanks, Louis B. Mayer, and a crowd of other film notables—all of whom felt that the image of the motion picture industry and of motion pictures needed upgrading. (Many sources say that Mr. Mayer's real motive in establishing the Academy was to use it as a means of keeping unions out of the motion picture business.) Besides handing out Oscars, the Academy is involved in such diverse activities as film preservation, lecture and seminar programs, and the development and encouragement of new talent through scholarships and grants. Since 1975 its main center of operations has been this seven-story mirrored-glass office building on Wilshire Boulevard. In 1991, however, the Academy moved its library to a new facility, now called the Fairbanks Center, in another part of Beverly Hills (see item 25), and in 2002, it transferred its archives to the new Pickford Center in Hollywood (see Chapter 2). Movie lovers might wish to check out the grand

Academy of Motion Picture Arts and Sciences

lobby and fourth-floor galleries of the Wilshire Boulevard building, which frequently feature exhibits that usually focus on the
work of an Academy Award winner. In addition to exhibitions,
the Academy also has a series of screenings, open to the public,
in its beautiful Samuel Goldwyn Theater.

*For details on exhibitions and screenings, call 310–247–3000 or
visit www.oscars.org.*

20. *CHARLIE'S ANGELS* OFFICE
189 North Robertson Boulevard

It debuted in 1976 and quickly became one of television's
highest-rated series, thanks not to its scripts but to the sex appeal
of its three leading ladies: Kate Jackson, Jaclyn Smith, and
Farrah Fawcett-Majors, whose signature shag haircut is still a
popular style at shopping-mall salons all across America. The
premise of the show had three beautiful young female detectives
working for a mysterious, never seen boss named Charlie
Townsend (actor John Forsythe provided the voice) at Townsend
Investigations. The pretty little brick building that served as the
Townsend headquarters in the series still stands at the corner of
North Robertson Boulevard and Clifton Way in Beverly Hills. It
is currently a showroom for the upscale European household ap-
pliance firm Miele.

Charlie's Angels ran for five seasons. Miss Fawcett-Majors
(who dropped the Majors after her divorce from actor Lee Majors in the late 1970s) left the show after just one season for a
film career that never fully materialized. Shelley Hack and later
Cheryl Ladd played the role in subsequent seasons. *Charlie's Angels* had its own brush with the big screen when it was resur-
rected as an action-adventure feature in 2001, starring Drew
Barrymore, Cameron Diaz, and Lucy Liu, which quickly gave
rise to a sequel. Townsend Investigations, which looked very
much like the old TV location but was actually a set, bit the dust
toward the end of the first flick, when it was blown up by the evil
Knox Technology gang.

Bristol Farms Market—formerly Chasen's restaurant

21. BRISTOL FARMS MARKET/CHASEN'S SITE
9039 Beverly Boulevard

It was Ronald Reagan's favorite restaurant. The chili was legendary and may have been the most expensive on earth, but that didn't stop Elizabeth Taylor from having buckets of it shipped to her while on location in Rome with *Cleopatra*. A big favorite with the who's who of Old Hollywood, Chasen's counted the Jimmy Stewarts, the Gregory Pecks, Buddy and Beverly Rogers, and the Frank Sinatras among its regulars. Founded by Dave Chasen in 1936—with $3,500 borrowed from his friend, *New Yorker* editor Harold Ross—Chasen's got off to a great start and everything was going smoothly until World War II intervened and Dave was served with a draft notice. With no one qualified to run Chasen's in his absence, his wife, Maude, persuaded him to show her the ropes. She not only ran the place during the war but also after her husband's death in 1973 and right up to its closing in 1995. Today, Chasen's distinctive white neo-Colonial building is still in the food business, but as an upscale supermarket. And for Liz Taylor and other fans of Chasen's chili, the good news is that you can still order it, thanks to the Internet.

Visit www.chasenschili.com.

22. INTERNATIONAL CREATIVE MANAGEMENT
   BUILDING
   8899 Beverly Boulevard

Created in 1974 through the merger of two sizable talent agencies (International Famous and Creative Management Associates), International Creative Management, aka ICM, quickly became William Morris's leading competitor. Things changed a year later, however, when Michael S. Ovitz and three other William Morris agents formed an ultra-agressive new agency called Creative Artists Agency (CAA). ICM is still a major player, however, representing such talents as Richard Gere, Denzel Washington, Michelle Pfeiffer, Mel Gibson, Christopher Walken, and hot newcomers Orlando Bloom and Evan Rachel Wood. The agency had a major shock in 2003 when three of its top-grossing female stars—Julia Roberts, Cameron Diaz, and Lucy Liu—bolted the agency and moved over to CAA.

Speaking of moneymakers, Barbra Streisand, back in 1981, then one of ICM's leading stars, clashed with its top agent, Sue Mengers (whose rise from secretary to million-dollar flesh ped-

International Creative Management building

dler is the stuff of Jackie Collins novels). What seems to have happened is that Streisand agreed to do a role in Mengers's director husband's first U.S. film, *All Night Long*. For her services—which she considered a personal favor to help Mengers and mate—Streisand would receive $4 million plus 15 percent of the profits. Everything was fine until it came time to pay Barbra. Before handing over Babs's check, Sue took out her customary 10 percent commission, that is, $400,000. When Streisand saw what Mengers had done, she got angry because she had lent her name and talents to the project only as a favor. Mengers wound up giving back the $400,000 to Streisand; Streisand wound up firing Mengers. But the two ultimately patched things up, and Mengers was a guest at Streisand's 1998 Malibu wedding to actor James Brolin.

Visit www.icmtalent.com.

23. JANE FONDA'S WORKOUT SITE
369 South Robertson Boulevard

It started here. Before the book, before the record, before the videotape, before the millons of dollars, there was this little gym in the heart of the design/interior decorator area of Beverly Hills where Jane Fonda started out in the exercise business and changed the way America worked out. Eventually it came out that more than exercise was involved in forming Fonda's fabulous figure, when she admitted to suffering from bulimia. Today, in her sixties, Fonda still keeps fit but admits she is no longer obsessed with having the perfect body. The low-rise brick building that housed her original studio is now offices.

24. KABBALAH CENTER
1062 South Robertson Boulevard

In the 1980s it was Scientology; in the 1990s, Buddhism was big; and now that we're in the new millennium, the hottest religion in Hollywood is the Kabbalah. A new-age version of a mystical medieval offshoot of Judaism, Kabbalah has attracted Madonna and her husband Guy Ritchie, Demi Moore, Ashton Kutcher,

Madonna of the Kabbalah

Kirk Douglas, Britney Spears, and Barbra Streisand. The main L.A. base of operations is this Spanish-style building in Beverly Hills. Since medieval Spain was a great center of the Kabbalah, the architecture is appropriate.

25. FAIRBANKS CENTER FOR MOTION PICTURE STUDY
333 South La Cienega Boulevard

In 1991, the Academy of Motion Picture Arts and Sciences moved its award-winning Margaret Herrick Library to handsome new quarters in a landmark 1927 Spanish Colonial Revival building. Looking like a great cathedral, the building was, in fact, the former Beverly Hills Waterworks, which had been abandoned since 1976 and was slated for demolition. Extensively and ingeniously restored, the building—named for pioneer movie actor-producer as well as the Academy's first president Douglas Fairbanks—houses one of the country's finest research centers specializing in the history of the development of the motion pic-

Hollywood treasure trove: Fairbanks Center for Motion Picture Study

ture. Among its treasures are extensive collections of clippings, periodicals, photographs—plus production files on more than 82,000 films and biography files on some 73,000 filmmakers and stars. Among its special collections are the personal papers, scripts, stills, and scrapbooks of Mary Pickford, Alfred Hitchcock, John Huston, George Cukor, Hedda Hopper, Louella Parsons, and Mack Sennett. The center is open to students, researchers, and the public by appointment.

Call 310–247–3000 or visit www.oscars.org/facilities/fairbanks.html.

Beverly Hills: Star Houses

The movie-star residences of Beverly Hills have long been among the top tourist attractions of Los Angeles. For those coming to Hollywood in hopes of seeing glamour, money, fame, and fantasy—Beverly Hills is one part of town that lives up to everybody's expectations of what a movie capital should be.

To list all the houses in Beverly Hills that have had star own-

Movie-star map salesmen, 1936

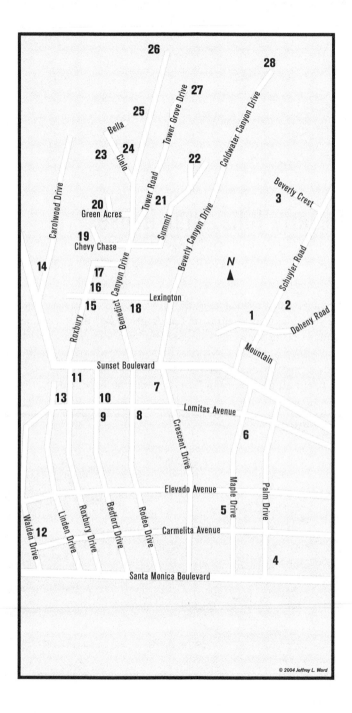

ers or renters would be impossible. For one thing, movie people are not known for their stability as far as where they live is concerned and they often stay in a house for just a few years, sometimes just a few months—depending on the vagaries of career, finances, and domestic situations. Another problem with Beverly Hills houses as far as sightseeing is concerned is that many of these legendary places are not visible from the street. Needless to say, their occupants—already in the public eye—would choose homes that offer as much privacy as possible.

The houses included here have been selected first of all because the majority can be seen from the street, and second because all have played some part in the history and legends of Hollywood. These are the best of Beverly Hills—the classics.

When touring these or any other of the private residences and properties mentioned in this book, movie lovers should take the utmost care to respect the privacy of their occupants. For convenience, items 1 through 4 from the previous Beverly Hills chapter can be added to the itinerary that follows.

1. *THE OSBORNES* HOUSE
513 Doheny Road

Of the many bizarre "reality" television shows that blanketed the airways in the early twenty-first century, the dysfunctional family life of an aging British rock star and his obscenity-spewing wife, set in a posh Spanish mansion in Beverly Hills, seemed a long shot at best. But the success of *The Osbornes* has proved the oddsmakers way wrong. The Beverly Hills mansion, which serves as the Osbornes' reality TV studio and real-life living quarters, now sports a massive electronic gate to keep away gawkers. So fans will have to settle for the best views of the property on television, not in person. But that's why they call it reality *TV*.

2. ELIZABETH TAYLOR HOUSE
1330 Schuyler Road

Elizabeth Taylor shared this big beautiful Spanish mansion with her third husband, Mike Todd. This is where Taylor was living in 1958 when Todd's private plane, *Lucky Liz,* went down over

New Mexico, killing Todd and the three others aboard. Liz had planned to be aboard, too, but had stayed home nursing a cold. As the world knows, Eddie Fisher helped her through the difficult days that followed.

3. ROCK HUDSON HOUSE
9402 Beverly Crest Drive

In the 1970s, this macho movie star's Sunday-afternoon pool parties were notorious for bringing together some of the best-looking young people in Hollywood. The crowd was mostly male, however. Indeed the amazing thing was that the movie star, Rock Hudson, somehow managed to live an exclusively gay off-screen life, yet keep the straight public pretty much in the dark about his sexual orientation. Ironically, the closeted actor's death from AIDS in 1985 helped bring much-needed attention to the deadly epidemic and his coming out in his posthumously published autobiography, *Rock Hudson: His Story* (with Sarah Davidson, Morrow, 1986), helped the gay rights cause as well. The former Hudson home, high in the hills off Schuyler Road, was often on television in 1985, as news crews hovered on the street outside, awaiting the dying actor's latest health bulletin. The house has since been torn down and replaced.

4. MARILYN MONROE HOUSE
508 North Palm Drive

Portrait of a marriage: It was April 1954 when Marilyn Monroe and her husband of three months, Joe DiMaggio, moved into this Elizabethan cottage just north of busy Santa Monica Boulevard in the flats of Beverly Hills. They had tried living with Joe's family up in San Francisco—but that hadn't really worked out. Besides, Marilyn now had to be in Hollywood to do *There's No Business Like Show Business*. While the setting appears blissful enough, the marriage was not. The quarrels had already begun, as had Marilyn's taste for Champagne—at all hours of the day. Things came to a head in September, when Marilyn flew to New York City to do location shooting for *The Seven Year Itch*. Joe followed. There was the famous sequence shot on Lexington Av-

Marilyn Monroe and Joe DiMaggio's Beverly Hills rental

enue: Marilyn—in white halter dress with panties to match—shows a bit too much of the latter, for take after take. For DiMaggio, it was much too much, and he quickly returned to L.A. The marriage was over. When he moved out of the Elizabethan cottage shortly thereafter, photographers and reporters were there en masse to document his exit. By November, Marilyn had moved out, too—and 508 North Palm Drive was ready for another set of tenants, another story.

5. LOUELLA PARSONS HOUSE
619 North Maple Drive

She was feared, hated, fawned over. She was one of the most powerful women in Hollywood—and this unpretentious stuccoed Spanish villa was her home base from the 1930s until the mid-1960s when failing health necessitated moving her to the first of a series of nursing homes where she would spend her last days as a lonely, senile old lady.

George Burns and Gracie Allen house

6. GEORGE BURNS AND GRACIE ALLEN HOUSE
720 North Maple Drive

If it looks familiar, perhaps it's because a duplicate was used in the famous husband-and-wife comedy team's TV series in the 1950s. After his beloved Gracie died in 1964, Burns, who had a whole new career as a movie star in the *Oh, God!* films of the 1970s and 1980s, continued living here for a number of years. He died just days short of his one-hundredth birthday in 1996.

7. VINCENTE MINNELLI HOUSE
812 North Crescent Drive

Standing across Sunset Boulevard from the Beverly Hills Hotel, this stately Mediterranean mansion was Vincente Minnelli's home for most of his post–Judy Garland years. According to the terms of the Minnelli-Garland divorce in the early fifties, little Liza was to spend six months of each year with her father and six with her mother. Among the many things Princess Liza enjoyed when in residence at her poppa's palazzo was a backyard playhouse specially decorated for her by artist Tony Duquette. She also had a closet full of costumes from famous films—*Gone With the Wind, The King and I, An American in Paris*—all in little-girl sizes. According to Candice Bergen in her autobiography, *Knock Wood* (Linden

Press/Simon & Schuster, 1984): "I remember always asking to go to Liza's to play dress-up because in her closet hung little girls' dreams." It wasn't all a dream, however. Liza once said of her early years bouncing around Beverly Hills between parents and stepparents: "It was a childhood to be reckoned with."

Fast-forward to 2002. Shortly after Liza's lavish but short-lived marriage to producer David Gest, the Minnelli family home was all over the tabloids, when Vincente Minnelli's ninety-four-year-old widow Lee accused Liza of "elderly abuse" for trying to evict her from the property, which belonged to Liza. Liza's stepmother went so far as to sue her, claiming that not only was Liza selling the house out from under her, but that she had cut off the electricity and fired the staff. But after all the brouhaha, a phone call from Liza to the old woman, promising her a Beverly Hills condo, supposedly set things right. "I didn't want to sue her because I love her," Lee said after dropping her suit. "She's my daughter."

8. LUPE VELEZ HOUSE
732 North Rodeo Drive

Casa Felicitas ("happy house" in Spanish) was definitely the wrong name for this Bev Hills hacienda where actress Lupe Velez resided in the 1940s. For it was here that the Mexican-born screen star—former lover of Gary Cooper, John Gilbert, and Randolph Scott; former wife of Johnny "Tarzan" Weissmuller—carried out one of Hollywood's most bizarre suicides. After dinner with a few close friends, Lupe retired to her glamorous bedroom—in which she had placed masses of flowers and lighted candles—and she proceeded to take an overdose of sleeping pills. While Louella Parsons reported on the dignity of Lupe's demise, Kenneth Anger tells the story differently in his book, *Hollywood Babylon* (Straight Arrow Books, 1975). According to Anger, Lupe's maid discovered her dead mistress—not in her satin bed, but in the bathroom. Evidently the pills had made her violently ill and sent her off to the bathroom vomiting. Here, she stumbled, landed headfirst in the toilet bowl, and met death by drowning—not Seconals. Whatever really happened, Lupe was dead at the age of thirty-six. At the time, she was supposedly carrying the child of a man who had refused to marry her.

Scandal site: Lana Turner's North Bedford Drive mansion

9. LANA TURNER HOUSE
730 North Bedford Drive

It was one of the biggest stories of 1958—and it happened here. On April 5, Lana Turner's daughter, Cheryl Crane, stabbed Turner's lover, Johnny Stompanato, to death while Lana and Johnny were embroiled in an argument in which Stompanato threatened Turner's life. The media had a field day with the revelations regarding Lana's love life that the trial brought out into the open. At the time, too, many speculated that Turner had actually stabbed Stompanato and had gotten her teenaged daughter to take the rap and a decidedly lesser sentence so as not to tarnish her movie career. The rumor persisted for decades until Ms. Crane put the story to rest in her autobiography, *Detour* (Michael Joseph, 1988), where she asserts that she did indeed do the stabbing.

10. *DOWN AND OUT IN BEVERLY HILLS* HOUSE
802 North Bedford Drive

Paul Mazursky's 1986 comedy *Down and Out in Beverly Hills* saw Nick Nolte as a homeless bum unsuccessfully try to commit suicide in the swimming pool of a posh Beverly Hills estate and then stay on to insinuate himself into the lives of the nouveau-riche owners played by Bette Midler and Richard Dreyfuss. The

Down and Out in Beverly Hills house

Beverly Hills house where it all took place is this standard-issue Spanish mansion on an easy-to-photograph corner at Bedford Drive and Lomitas Avenue.

11. MARLENE DIETRICH HOUSE
822 North Roxbury Drive

During the 1930s, glamorous Marlene Dietrich lived in this attractive Art Deco mansion. A decade later, Rita Hayworth and her third husband, Aly Kahn, resided here as well.

Marlene Dietrich's Art Deco digs

12. *BEVERLY HILLS COP II* HOUSE
614 North Walden Drive

In the original *Beverly Hills Cop* (1984), Eddie Murphy played Axel Foley, a cop from Detroit who came to Beverly Hills to track down the man who had killed his best friend. In that first film, Murphy encountered a great deal of resentment and resistance from the locals on the Beverly Hills police force. By the time of the sequel (1987), Murphy is now buddy-buddy with Beverly Hills' finest. He also goes native this time out, squatting in this unpretentious little house in the 'hood. In the film, the house was undergoing renovations and Murphy commandeers it by pretending to be a building inspector.

13. BUGSY SIEGEL HOUSE
810 North Linden Drive

Actually this grand Spanish mansion was being rented by his actress girlfriend Virginia Hill, when gangster Benjamin (he hated to be called "Bugsy") Siegel was offed by rival mobsters in 1947. The shotgun blasts came through the living-room windows, bringing about a violent end to an American life of epic proportions. Siegel, a man of impeccable manners and excellent taste, went from minor mob figure to visionary, when he helped put the little desert community of Las Vegas, Nevada, on the map with his Flamingo Hotel and Casino project. But the old days and old enemies were hard to

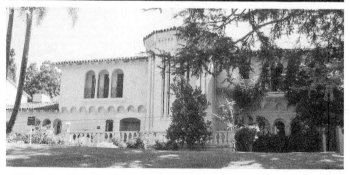

Bugsy Siegel's final address

escape, and ultimately they did him in at the height of his main-stream success. Actor Warren Beatty portrayed Siegel in the 1990 film *Bugsy,* which Beatty also directed and which starred Annette Bening as Virginia Hill. It was during the filming that then fifty-two-year-old Beatty gave up his decades-long status as Holly-wood's most eligible but least available bachelor, when he and Bening fell in love, married, and started a family. The last scene in the film vividly depicts the grisly shooting that rocked normally staid Beverly Hills on this very spot over a half century ago.

14. CAROLWOOD CANYON
North Carolwood Drive

Of all the elegant drives in Beverly Hills, perhaps none can claim as many A-list celebrities per square foot as Carolwood Drive, a won-derfully secluded and woodsy road that gently climbs for about a half mile just north of Sunset Boulevard. Indeed, at one time, not so very long ago, Carolwood boasted the following residents: Burt Reynolds, all hedged in at 245; George Harrison, in the big Span-ish mansion next door at 265; Barbra Streisand, who made 301 her home away from Malibu for several decades; Frank Sinatra, who had the enormous spread at 320; Walt Disney, behind the big gate at 355; Gregory Peck, behind another gate, bordered by magnificent gardens at 375; and Rod Stewart, in a big villa next door at 391. Imagine the block association meetings.

Jimmy Stewart house

15. JIMMY STEWART HOUSE
918 North Roxbury Drive

Stewart not only owned the house, but also the corner lot next door where gentleman Jim grew his own vegetables. Stewart lived at what may have been the last working farm in Beverly Hills up until his death in 1997.

16. LUCILLE BALL HOUSE
1000 North Roxbury Drive

In 1955, at the height of their *I Love Lucy* fame, Lucille Ball fell in love with this expansive two-story colonial house in Beverly Hills and wound up paying $85,000 for it. Desi was too busy with their burgeoning production company to go house-hunting with her but had no reservations about the house other than that it meant their moving from the ranch they had lived in for a decade in the distant San Fernando Valley community of Chatsworth. Arnaz would move out in 1960, when TV's golden couple divorced. A year later, Miss Ball's second husband, comedian Gary Morton, moved in, and she and Morton resided here until her death at age seventy-eight in 1989.

The last few years were not happy ones for the former

Lucille Ball's longtime home

Queen of Comedy. In failing health and devastated by the disastrous reaction to her ill-fated sitcom comeback attempt in 1986, *Life With Lucy*, which was canceled after a mere eight episodes, Ball spent most of her time holed up in her Beverly Hills house playing backgammon, watching and critiquing videos of her old shows, and drinking a bit too much. Despite her problems, she turned up looking great for one final TV appearance, along with her longtime friend and colleague Bob Hope, to introduce a segment at the 1989 Academy Awards ceremony. It was the old Lucy. A month later, she died following heart surgery.

17. JACK BENNY HOUSE
1002 North Roxbury Drive

Like Burns and Allen's Beverly Hills home, Jack Benny's was sometimes seen on his television shows in the 1950s and 1960s. Born Benjamin Kubelsky, Benny got his start doing comedy sketches with his violin while in the U.S. Navy. He went on to conquer radio and television with his tightwad persona, his pregnant pauses, his never-changing age of thirty-nine, and often his trusty violin. In later years, he was a big hit on the

Jack Benny's TV and real-life home

lecture circuit, resurrecting his old violin shtick. Benny died in 1974; two decades later the violin reportedly sold for some $84,000 at auction. The tightwad was probably rolling over in his grave.

18. MARION DAVIES HOUSE
1700 Lexington Road

In the mid-1920s, William Randolph Hearst bought this beautiful mansion for his mistress, Marion Davies. Just to keep everything on the up and up—on paper anyway—the house was bought in the name of Marion's mother, Rose, who also lived there. Because Marion loved to entertain lavishly, a ballroom was immediately added to the house; according to Hollywood legend, this was accomplished in a week's time with carpenters and craftsmen working around the clock. According to the late silent-screen actress Eleanor Boardman, it was here that she married director King Vidor in 1926. It was to have been a double wedding, the other couple being John Gilbert and Greta Garbo; Garbo, however, chose not to attend. Gilbert thus proceeded to get very drunk—until, finally, Louis B. Mayer pulled him aside and counseled him just to sleep with Garbo and not to bother about marrying her. This further incensed Gilbert, who lunged at Mayer and knocked him out. It was a bad move—because after the episode, Mayer supposedly did everything in his power to muck up Gilbert's career—including, according to many sources, tampering with Gilbert's voice in his first talkie. Gilbert died in 1936. He was forty-one, a hopeless alcoholic and has-been.

19. GRETA GARBO HOUSE
1027 Chevy Chase Drive

Garbo had many L.A. addresses during her Hollywood days. She lived in this hedge-hidden Beverly Hills bungalow for about a year, from 1929 to 1930—sharing it with a chow chow, four cats, a parrot, and a Swedish couple who were her staff. Supposedly, Garbo liked the pool—but not the neighbors who kept looking into her garden.

Harold Lloyd's Green Acres estate

20. HAROLD LLOYD HOUSE
1740 Green Acres Place

One of Beverly Hills' greatest estates, Harold Lloyd's Green Acres was built in 1928 and was home to the famous comedian from that year until his death in 1971. Today, the forty-four-room (not counting twenty-six bathrooms!) property is on the National Register of Historic Places and has been considerably altered by subsequent owners. In the 1980s TV series *Dynasty,* Green Acres was used as the royal palace of Moldavia. The property can also be seen as the Hollywood studio executive's mansion in *The Godfather* (1972), where the exec winds up with a dead horse's head in his bed . . . and as part of Roman World in the Michael Crichton sci-fi thriller *Westworld* (1973).

21. CHARLIE CHAPLIN HOUSE
1085 Summit Drive

One of Chaplin's numerous L.A. addresses, this was the only house he built from the ground up. And not well, according to some accounts that say Chaplin tried to save money by employing studio carpenters as construction workers. Supposedly he had so many problems with the place owing to its shoddy construction that it was dubbed Break-away House by his friends. The former Chaplin house, which can only be glimpsed through the driveway, later belonged to actor George Hamilton.

22. PICKFAIR
1143 Summit Drive

The most famous Beverly Hills mansion of them all. This is where Douglas Fairbanks and Mary Pickford reigned as king and queen of Hollywood from 1920 up to their divorce in 1936. In Pickfair's grandest days—the 1920s—an invitation to this fairy-tale realm was no less important than an invitation to the White House. At Pickfair, Doug and Mary received the world— kings, queens, dukes, duchesses, and international socialities, as well as the cream of Hollywood. And because Pickford and Fairbanks were two of the first big stars to desert Hollywood and downtown Los Angeles to live in Beverly Hills, they were directly responsible for popularizing the place and for luring other movie-industry residents.

After her divorce from Fairbanks, Pickford continued to live at Pickfair with her last husband, Charles "Buddy" Rogers. In-

Fairest of them all: Pickfair

Douglas Fairbanks and Mary Pickford canoeing at Pickfair, 1921

creasingly reclusive in her later decades, Miss Pickford died at Pickfair in 1979 at the age of eighty-five. Rogers ultimately sold the estate to sports entrepreneur Jerry Buss, who then sold it to diminuitive singer Pia Zadora and her Israeli millionaire businessman husband, Meshulam Riklis, who shocked the neighborhood by tearing down the historic forty-two-room residence and building an even bigger one. Today Zadora, divorced from both Riklis and another husband whom she married in 1995, still lives at the former Pickfair, where the only vestiges of the Pickford-Fairbanks era are the cherub statues atop its gateposts.

23. SHARON TATE HOUSE
10050 Cielo Drive

As one goes farther up into the hills of Beverly Hills, the land seems lonelier, wilder. It was here—at practically the end of Benedict Canyon—that one of the most horrible events in Hollywood's history took place in the late 1960s. From the road, only the gate of the former rented estate of actress Sharon Tate and her husband, director Roman Polanski, is visible. Still, this is somehow haunting enough when one remembers that the

Manson Family made their way up the then ungated driveway one evening in the summer of 1969 and savagely murdered Sharon Tate, her unborn baby; Abigail Folger (of the "Mountain Grown" coffee family) and her boyfriend, Voytek Frykowski; super-stud hairdresser Jay Sebring; and Steve Parent, a teenager who was visiting the property's caretaker.

24. VALENTINO STABLES
10051 Cielo Drive

Across from the former Tate/Polanski driveway, this private residence was created from the former stables of Rudolph Valentino's fabulous Falcon Lair estate. Falcon Lair is farther up in the hills.

25. FALCON LAIR
1436 Bella Drive

If the former Sharon Tate/Roman Polanski property seems a bit off the beaten track, Falcon Lair is positively isolated. But total isolation was exactly what Rudolph Valentino required when he

Rudolph Valentino's
Falcon Lair

moved to this Benedict Canyon mansion in 1925. At the height of his popularity, Valentino wanted to get as far away from his adoring—and often annoying—fans as possible. Falcon Lair, named for his film *The Hooded Falcon,* was to have been Valentino's dream house, "as near to ideality as you can find in a place," he wrote to a fan magazine at the time. As for the decor, Valentino furnished his dream house with classic movie-star extravagance, and mixed Middle Eastern furniture, precious Renaissance art objects, Oriental carpets, Medieval tapestries, weapons, and armor.

Like so many Hollywood dreams, Falcon Lair never lived up to its owner's idyllic expectations. For one thing, by the time he moved in during 1925, his marriage to his second wife, Natacha Rambova, had broken up. For another, the pains in his stomach were becoming more frequent and more debilitating—a forewarning of the ulcer that would kill him the following year on August 23, 1926.

After Valentino's death, Falcon Lair passed through various owners and eventually became one of the many residences of the reclusive tobacco heiress Doris Duke. Duke spent the last three years of her life here in the early 1990s, ill and in the care of a manipulative alcoholic Irish butler named Bernard Lafferty. Like a character in a 1940s film, Lafferty not only got the millionairess to change her will, leaving the bulk of her fortune to him, but he was also suspected of playing a role in her death in 1993 from the cumulative effects of too much morphine. Lafferty's windfall was short-lived however, since Duke's lawyers stepped in and got him to relinquish his claim on the estate. As for the murder accusations, they were declared unfounded by the Los Angeles District Attorney's office in 1996, the same year that Lafferty died.

Though little can be seen of the main house from the road, a visit to Falcon Lair is interesting nonetheless—especially when one considers what the trip must have been like in the 1920s when Valentino piloted one of his glamorous touring cars up what must have been a very dusty canyon road at the time. Visitors to Falcon Lair should note the words "Falcon Lair," still visible above the pillars of the main gate.

26. GEORGE REEVES HOUSE
1579 Benedict Canyon Drive

He made an auspicious screen debut in 1939 in the biggest picture in Hollywood history, *Gone With the Wind,* but his career never really took off until 1951, when he starred in the popular kids TV series *Superman.* The show was canceled six years later and Reeves found himself, at age forty-three, virtually unemployable, because he was considered too identified with his television character. The only work he was able to find was as a professional wrestler, dressed in his old Man of Steel drag. In 1959, having had enough of Superman and Hollywood, Reeves shot himself in the head in this pretty Benedict Canyon clapboard cottage.

27. HEIDI FLEISS HOUSE
1270 Tower Grover Drive

For about fifteen minutes, she was one of the most powerful people in Hollywood, operating one of the classiest call-girl networks in town. When she got in trouble with the law in 1993, all of L.A. anxiously awaited the revelations of her little black book of clients. In the state and federal trails that followed, Charlie Sheen—who racked up a $53,000 bill for Fleiss's services—seemed to be the only big name to come out of the proceedings as one of her regular customers. Fleiss's conviction by the State of California on three counts of pandering was later overturned; she did, however, serve thirty-seven months in federal prison for tax evasion and money laundering.

In 2003, Fleiss was in court again—this time as the plaintiff, having charged her actor boyfriend Tom Sizemore *(Saving Private Ryan* and *Black Hawk Down)* of beating and threatening her. The actor was convicted on seven of the sixteen counts of domestic violence lodged against him and sentenced to six months in jail. That same year, Fleiss also made a deal with Paramount to turn her story into a movie with the working title *Pay the Girl.* Before the project got off the ground, however, HBO came out in 2004 with *Call Me: The Rise and Fall of Heidi Fleiss,* with Jamie-Lynn DiScala as Fleiss. Fleiss was not pleased.

"I'm big-time," she told *Star* magazine. "I'm not a made-for-TV movie. I'm big-screen, baby."

In her heyday, Fleiss's base of operations was way way up in the hills on Tower Grove, where little can be seen of the property from the road, which, given the nature of her business, probably made sense.

28. CHARLTON HESTON HOUSE
2859 Coldwater Canyon Drive

High up Coldwater Canyon, actor and recent National Rifle Association president Charlton Heston's hilltop compound is appropriately lofty for a man who is perhaps best known for playing Moses in C. B. DeMille's 1956 version of *The Ten Commandments*. Movie lovers got an insider look at Heston's heavily gated aerie when activist director Michael Moore did an on-the-spot interview here with the anti-gun-control advocate for his 2003 Academy Award–winning documentary *Bowling for Columbine*. Initially affable, Heston becomes increasingly rattled as Moore puts him on the spot about his views. Heston terminates the interview abruptly and sends Moore packing. Welcome to Beverly Hills.

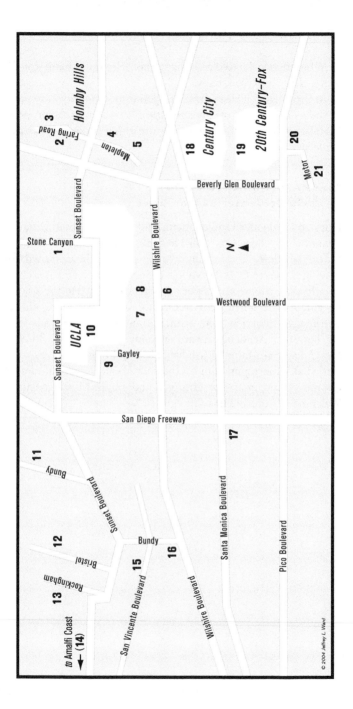

The Fashionable Westside: Between Beverly Hills and Santa Monica

When Angelenos today speak of "the Westside," they can mean any of a group of wealthy communities that lie between Beverly Hills and Santa Monica. Bel-Air, the Holmby Hills, Westwood,

Brentwood's dearest
mommie: Joan Crawford

Brentwood, Century City, and the Cheviott Hills are all posh Westside enclaves—and harbor a number of sites relevant to the movie history of Los Angeles. Of these, the most important Westside attraction may well be the Twentieth Century–Fox Studios, where the 1890s New York Street set built in the late sixties for *Hello, Dolly!* still stands just beyond the main gate. Other Westside stops range from one of the world's most luxurious and secluded celebrity hideaway hotels to a television mogul's 123-room Holmby Hills "manor" to Joan Crawford's *Mommie Dearest* digs in Brentwood to James Dean's frat house at UCLA to the secret cemetery where Marilyn Monroe and a number of other stars are laid to rest.

Almost every site mentioned in this chapter will involve a car. The one exception: Westwood Village (items 6 through 10), which is an easy and agreeable area to stroll.

1. BEL-AIR HOTEL
701 Stone Canyon Road

L.A.'s ultimate hideaway—a fantasy realm of romantic Spanish bungalows, exotic foliage, quiet courtyards, gurgling fountains, and a serene lake that has swans gliding across it. Since the 1940s, some of the greatest names of Hollywood have sought seclusion in this dream world. Names like Garbo, Dietrich, Gable, Peck, Grant, Grace Kelly. Howard Hughes carried on so much business in the hotel's wood-paneled bar that it became known as his unofficial office. Today, the Bel-Air still lures the rich and the celebrated—often when they're ducking the press. Tom Cruise, for example, hid out in a cushy Bel-Air bungalow in late 2001 and early 2002, when his ten-year marriage to Nicole Kidman was coming undone and his romance with Spanish actress Penelope Cruz was heating up.

The Bel-Air was not always a hotel. Its main building, long since remodeled, was originally the sales office of the real estate company of oil millionaire Alfonso Bell. It was Bell who developed the ultra-exclusive gated community of Bel-Air on what was his former ranch. In those days, the 1920s, Bel-Air did not sell lots to movie people, nor to minority groups such as Jews,

Superstar hideway:
Bel-Air Hotel

African Americans, or Asians. Things "opened up" after the Depression, however, when a few movie people, some of them Jewish, managed to make it to the inside of Bel-Air's great wrought-iron gates. By the 1940s, anybody who could afford to live in Bel-Air did. It was also in the 1940s when the Bel-Air real estate office and grounds were converted to the movie-set hotel that today makes every guest feel like a star.

Call 310–472–1211 or visit www.hotelbelair.com.

2. CLAUDETTE COLBERT HOUSE
615 North Faring Road

No one can fault the late Claudette Colbert's taste. Her longtime L.A. home was this attractive Holmby Hills Colonial mansion designed by the noted architect, Lloyd Wright, son of Frank Lloyd Wright. Besides being beautiful, the home must have been very convenient for Miss Colbert's husband, Dr. Joel Pressman, who was a leading surgeon at the nearby UCLA Medical Center. Pressman died in 1968—whereas Colbert, who died in 1993, spent the last decades of her life in a handsome plantation house on the Caribbean island of Barbados.

Class act: Claudette Colbert's Holmby Hills home

3. HARVARD-WESTLAKE SCHOOL
700 North Faring Road

One of the poshest private girls' schools in town: Candy Bergen, Jill Schary, Shirley Temple, Vicki Milland all went here. Former May Queen Bergen remembers it as the kind of place where "dirty saddle shoes were a misdemeanor and a pair of loafers could get you sent home." Insiders also say that, for many years, Westlake had a "quiet quota" system that set the school's Wasp-Jewish ratio in order to keep the former group in the majority. Jill Robinson, writer daughter of Dore Schary, remembers trying to get into Westlake at various times and always being rejected. But when her father made Hollywood headlines in 1951 by succeeding Louis B. Mayer as top man at MGM, a place at the school seems miraculously to have turned up for her.

Since 1991, the school, which merged with the nearby Harvard School for Boys, has been a coeducational institution.

Visit www.harvardwestlake.com.

Holmby Hills royalty: Lauren Bacall and Humphrey Bogart

4. BOGEY AND BACALL HOUSE
232 South Mapleton Drive

Gable and Lombard, Lucy and Desi, Mary and Doug, Liz and Dick—sometimes it takes two people to make a Hollywood legend. And of all of Hollywood's couples, none was more famous than Bogey and Bacall. In fact, the 1982 popular song "Key Largo" paid tribute to the legendary duo with the lyrics: "We had it all—just like Bogey and Bacall."

They met on *To Have and Have Not* in 1944. She was nineteen; it was her first picture. He was twenty-five years older, had been a big name for some time. It was the kind of on-screen chemistry that directors and studio heads dream of. They went on to make three more films together: *The Big Sleep* (1946), *Dark Passage* (1947), and *Key Largo* (1948). Off-screen, the chemistry was just as potent. They married in 1945—and from 1946 until 1957 lived in this handsome Holmby Hills home and raised two children.

Here, too, Bogey and Bacall played vital roles in a sociological phenomenon of mid-fifties Hollywood known as the Holmby Hills "Rat Pack." Frank Sinatra was president of the group, Judy

Garland (she and her husband Sid Luft lived just up the street from the Bogarts at 144 South Mapleton) was vice president, Bacall was den mother, literary agent Irving "Swifty" Lazar was treasurer, and Bogey was the rat in charge of public relations. Other members included Peter Lawford, Sammy Davis Jr., David Niven, Mike Romanoff, Noël Coward, and Dean Martin. Together, they drank, hit all the glamour spots on the Sunset Strip, drank, and didn't give a damn about Hedda, Louella, or any other columnist in town. What did it mean to be a "rat"? To PR man Bogart, in an interview with writer Ezra Goodman, it meant "staying up late and drinking lots of booze. We're against squares and being bored and for lots of fun . . . we don't care who likes us as long as we like each other. We like each other very much."

Beautiful house, beautiful children, great careers, great friends, great marriage. Bogey and Bacall did indeed "have it all"—until Bogart's painful death from cancer took it all away in 1957. Alone, Bacall went on to become a Broadway actress, and people remember Bogart as a tough guy in the movies. But together, they are the stuff that myths and great movies are made of.

Boys in the 'hood: Rat Packers Peter Lawford, Dean Martin, Sammy Davis Jr., and Frank Sinatra

Aaron Spelling's 123-room mansion

5. AARON SPELLING MANOR
594 South Mapleton Drive

Even by Hollywood standards, this is one of the most grandiose monuments to one man's ego since William Randolph Hearst erected his palatial San Simeon retreat in northern California in the 1920s. In 1983, flush from his long string of hit TV series—which, at the time, included *The Love Boat, Fantasy Island, Charlie's Angels,* and *Dynasty*—producer Aaron Spelling purchased Bing Crosby's old Holmby Hills estate, tore it down, and set to building the largest single-family home ever erected in California. The Manor, as it is known, has a total of 123 rooms, including a bowling alley, gym, and several screening rooms. What Spelling does with all this space is anybody's guess, but since the producer is famously fearful of flying (he charters private train cars when he needs to cross the country and will only travel overseas by ship), perhaps he simply feels there's no place like home.

But even $48-million mansions are not immune to such mundane problems as leaky roofs. In fact, in 1996, the Spellings sued their roofer for $5 million for just that. They lost the suit, however, since it came out that the couple had chosen a cheap ($750,000) sheet-metal roof over the pricier lead-coated copper number that would have afforded them with more protection. You get what you pay for, even when you're paying three-quarters of a million dollars.

6. PIERCE BROTHERS WESTWOOD MEMORIAL PARK
1218 Glendon Avenue

Her body lay unclaimed at the L.A. County Morgue until Joe DiMaggio got into the act and took over the funeral arrangements. It was a small ceremony—DiMaggio had invited only a handful of people—and it took place in the chapel of a little Westwood cemetery that's hidden behind a high-rise, a bank, and a parking lot off busy Wilshire Boulevard. Despite its secluded location, Marilyn Monroe's loyal fans to this day stream to her aboveground crypt, which lies just beyond the Sanctuary of Tranquility. Alas, even in death, it seems that Marilyn (1926–1962) missed out on the peace she so desperately sought. For some twenty years, DiMaggio, the actress's second husband, sent roses to her grave several times a week, but thanks to her many admirers, Marilyn never lacks for floral tributes. Some pilgrims even leave lipstick prints on her cold marble vault. Others sit quietly on the small stone bench opposite her crypt, which was dedicated on the thirtieth anniversary of her death on August 5, 1992.

Marilyn is one of many major Hollywood legends buried in this tiny cemetery. Not far from her tomb, Monroe's former studio boss at Twentieth Century–Fox, Darryl Francis Zanuck (1902–1979), is buried next to his wife Virginia in the grassy center section of the cemetery. The famous Twentieth Century–Fox logo—blazing klieg lights on either side—has been incorporated into the inscription on Zanuck's marble marker. And Monroe's *Some Like It Hot* director Billy Wilder and her co-star Jack Lemmon are just across the lawn in the Rose Garden, near the cemetery office. Meanwhile, over in the Sanctuary of Love, Marilyn's last co-star, Dean Martin, of the ill-fated *Something's Gotta Give,* which she never completed, is laid to rest.

Other star names and graves to look for here—all easy to find, since the cemetery is so small—are Burt Lancaster, Carroll O'Connor, Walter Matthau, Fanny Brice, Peggy Lee, Natalie

Marilyn Monroe's crypt at Pierce Brothers Westwood Memorial Park

Wood, Donna Reed, Eva Gabor, Eve Arden, Jim Backus, Mel Torme, Roy Orbison, producer Ross Hunter, director John Cassavetes, agent Irving "Swifty" Lazar and his wife Mary, and perhaps most surprising of all, writer *(In Cold Blood* and *Breakfast at Tiffany's* were two of his books that were turned into famous films) Truman Capote. Capote, who spent most of his life in New York, died in L.A. in 1984, while staying with Johnny Carson's ex-wife Joanne. But Capote's East Coast friends insist that despite the large vault that bears his name at the Westwood cemetery, his ashes are not in L.A., a city which he supposedly loathed, but were dispersed in 1996, along with those of his longtime partner Jack Dunphy, in the nature preserve that bears both of their names near Bridgehampton, Long Island, New York.

The entrance to Pierce Brothers Westwood Memorial Park and Mortuary is a half block south of Wilshire Boulevard, just east of Glendon Avenue. The cemetery is open from 8 a.m. to 6:30 p.m. daily.

7. FOX VILLAGE THEATER
961 Broxton Avenue, Westwood

It now belongs to the Mann theater chain, but it still goes by its old name—Fox—both on the marquee and atop the tall Spanish Colonial tower that crowns this handsome Westwood movie palace. The theater's Spanish design is no accident, since Westwood Village was built in the 1920s as a master-planned commercial center. Part of the plan required that all of Westwood Village's buildings—from banks to shops to gas stations—conform to a Spanish Colonial architectural theme. The Fox theater, which opened in 1931, fits right in. Besides its striking columned tower, this beautifully maintained first-run movie house is notable for its four-sided neon-lit marquee, its spacious forecourt, and its tiled ticket booth. Inside, the Spanish fantasy continues with vaulted ceilings, flamboyant murals, brightly tiled water fountains. One of the most glamorous of Westwood's movie houses, the Village theater is frequently the scene of studio premieres.

Visit www.manntheatres.com.

Fox Village theater, Westwood

Mann's Bruin Theater, Westwood

8. MANN'S BRUIN THEATER
923 Broxton Avenue, Westwood

The work of star theater designer S. Charles Lee, the Bruin opened in late 1937. By this time, other architectural styles—such as this sleek example of late-1930s Moderne—had begun to deviate from Westwood Village's Spanish Colonial master plan. The Bruin's semicircular neon marquee is original, but inside the theater, the marvelous murals that glowed in the dark have been painted over.

Visit www.manntheatres.com.

9. SIGMA NU
601 Gayley Avenue

When eighteen-year-old James Dean left Fairmont, Indiana, for Los Angeles in June of 1949, he planned to enroll in UCLA's theater arts program that fall. Besides his passion for acting, another reason Dean chose to attend college in Los Angeles was because his father lived there. Indeed, Dean had once lived there, too—since his father and mother had moved from the Midwest to L.A. when Jimmy was five years old. But when his mother died of cancer three years later, he was shipped off to Iowa, where he was raised by an aunt and uncle and by his paternal grandparents.

When Dean arrived back in Los Angeles in 1949, it was the first time he had been there since his mother's death. The plan was for Jimmy to live with his father and stepmother while he attended UCLA. But Dean's dad had other plans. Since he was living in Santa Monica, it made much more sense for his son to attend Santa Monica City College. Also, theater was out of the question. So, James Dean spent his freshman year of college at SMCC—as a physical education major.

The following fall, however, Jimmy managed to realize his dream and he registered at UCLA—in theater arts. He also moved out of his father's home and into the Sigma Nu fraternity house on Gayley Avenue. Dean's fraternity days proved to be short-lived. According to his biographer, David Dalton, in *James Dean: The Mutant King* (St. Martin's Press, 1974), Dean's fraternity brothers razzed him about his theatrical activities one time too often and he retaliated by punching one of them out. The end of the story: The movies' most famous "Rebel" was expelled from his fraternity.

Dean's academic career was practically as brief as his fraternity experience. He dropped out of UCLA and, after doing a couple of bit parts in movies, he left Los Angeles for New York in the fall of 1951. There, he was determined to become an actor—for real. The move paid off: When he returned to Hollywood a mere three years later, it would be to star in *East of Eden*. But once again, it would be another abortive Southern California stay—because after just a year and a half and two more pictures *(Rebel Without a Cause* and *Giant)*, it would all come to an end.

Or would it? Speaking at Jimmy's funeral back in Fairmont, Indiana, the Reverend Xen Harvey put it this way: "The career of James Dean has not ended. It has just begun. And remember, God himself is directing the production." A half century later, the career, the production, the legend of James Dean go on—and on.

10. UNIVERSITY OF CALIFORNIA AT LOS ANGELES
Gayley and Le Conte Avenues

The Los Angeles campus of the University of California was established in Westwood in 1929. One of the state's most prestigious institutions of higher education, UCLA has a student body of over thirty thousand. The university also has an especially strong motion picture/television curriculum which draws upon the talents and facilities that its proximity to "Hollywood" offers. UCLA has in turn contributed an impressive number of major talents to the Hollywood scene: actress Carol Burnett, director Francis Ford Coppola, screenwriters Colin *(Harold and Maude)* Higgins, Robert *(Chinatown)* Towne, and actor-writer-director Ben Stiller are all former UCLA film school students.

The vast campus is also used occasionally as a location, especially for television shows. Secret agent Sydney Bristow (Jennifer Garner) studied at UCLA during the first seasons of the series *Alias.* So did vampire slayer Buffy Summers (Sarah Michelle Gellar), after she graduated from Sunnydale High, and Julia Roberts as Erin Brockovich in the 2000 film of the same name. A few decades earlier, the popular 1970s series *Medical Center* used UCLA's towering Center for Health Sciences as its location.

In the real world, UCLA's Film Archives is strongly involved in the preservation of early motion pictures. For years it has been transferring silent films from their original—and fast decomposing—nitrate film onto safety film. Important UCLA preservation projects also include saving the 1954 Humphrey Bogart–Ava Gardner saga *The Barefoot Contessa,* the 1955 Robert Mitchum thriller *The Night of the Hunter,* and the painstaking restoration of the first commercial feature film shot in three-strip Technicolor, *Becky Sharp* (1935).

The university's Television Archives, in conjunction with the Academy of Motion Picture Arts and Sciences, is a major force in the preservation of television artifacts and programs, an especially important endeavor given the fact that historians are finding that videotape has a relatively short shelf life. The archive—with some 23,000 programs—is open to the public, and appointments can be made to screen specific shows.

Both the TV and Film Archives at UCLA have screenings of classic

and contemporary, well- and little-known movies and television
shows at the University's James Bridges Theater, practically every
day. Sometimes, an artist who contributed to the work being
presented is on hand to speak and answer questions. For schedule
information, call 310–206–FILM or visit www.ucla.edu.

11. MOUNT ST. MARY'S COLLEGE
12001 Chalon Road

When Hollywood needs to go abroad, it often heads no farther
than to the beautiful Chalon Campus of Mount St. Mary's College. Encompassing 56 acres high up in the hills behind Brentwood, this glorious enclave of lavish lawns, gardens, and
tile-roofed buildings (the first was built in 1929–30), has long
provided magnificent Mediterranean settings for films, TV
shows, and commercials. For example, the 1960s TV series, *Mission Impossible,* with many episodes that took place overseas,
frequently shot at Mount St. Mary's, turning the campus into
France and Spain, as well as various fictional Eastern European
countries.

Besides the beauty of the architecture and foliage of Mount St.
Mary's, another reason that film companies like to shoot here is
because its high-up location assures some of L.A.'s best available,
smog-free light. The light factor is especially important when
filming commericals, since companies want to show off their
product to its best advantage. Car companies, especially, often
use the courtyard of Mount St. Mary's, with its arches and
colonnades, as a background for TV commercials as well as for
print ads. Near the courtyard, another often-photographed locale: Mount St. Mary's chapel. It was the site of Jane Wyman's
trip to the altar in a 1984 episode of *Falcon Crest,* and also wit-
nessed Ali MacGraw's and Jan-Michael Vincent's on-screen nup-
tials in the 1983 miniseries *The Winds of War.* For anyone who
missed the weddings, they may have seen the campus play a decidedly different role in Mel Brooks's 1977 film, *High Anxiety.*
In the Brooks spoof of various Alfred Hitchcock flicks, Mount
St. Mary's doubled for the Psycho-Neurological Institute for the
Very Very Nervous. The campus has more recently appeared in

the 2001 thriller *The Glass House* as well as in episodes of the
TV series *Monk* and *The O.C.*

*The Mount St. Mary's campus is not a tourist attraction and it
offers no parking for visitors who are not expected. The college
has a policy that allows filmmakers only one day of shooting on
the premises so as to disrupt campus life as little as possible. All
monies collected from shooting fees go toward helping students
needing financial aid; visit www.msmc.la.edu.*

12. JOAN CRAWFORD HOUSE
426 North Bristol Avenue

This sprawling but unprepossessing Brentwood mansion was the
scene of Miss Crawford's often turbulent domestic life for some
three decades. It started quietly enough in 1929 when she moved
into the house with her first husband, Douglas Fairbanks Jr. He
was twenty, she was supposedly twenty as well, although her real
age was closer to twenty-five. Many suspected Joan's motives in
marrying Doug Jr., feeling that she was trying to marry up—and
into the glamorous world of Doug's dad and stepmother at Pick-

Casa Crawford, Brentwood

fair. If that was the case, Joan's plan backfired because it was a long time before she even got an invitation, much less was socially accepted by the lord and lady of Pickfair.

Nonetheless, Joan tried hard at playing the role of the Perfect Wife. No matter that it was she who had paid for their Brentwood base (Fairbanks was in debt at the time of their marriage), she appeared to adore her young husband and was photographed gazing up worshipfully at his bust on the fireplace. It was all very cozy and cutesy: She called him Dodie, he called her Jodie, they called their house El JoDo, à la Pickfair. A few years later, the name-calling was no longer so romantic. Dodie moved out, Jodie redecorated, and Jodie and Dodie officially called it quits in 1934.

Joan remained queen of Castle Crawford through two more husbands (Franchot Tone and Philip Terry), many more remodelings, and four adopted children. One of those children, Christina, would go on to describe in chilling detail La Crawford in a new role, that of "Mommie Dearest," raising her Brentwood brood. The house used in the film version of *Mommie Dearest* bore little resemblance to the real thing. Crawford sold her Brentwood place in 1959 after she had been widowed by her fourth husband, Pepsi Cola executive Alfred Steele, with whom she had lived in New York. Far from leaving her a rich widow, Steele died with quite a few bills outstanding—which was one of the reasons why Joan bailed out of Brentwood. MGM musical star Donald O'Connor and his family were subsequent residents of 426 North Bristol.

13. SHIRLEY TEMPLE HOUSE
231 North Rockingham Road

Shirley Temple was born in Santa Monica in 1928. Her father worked for a bank and they lived in a modest little house. A mere seven years later, little Shirley had already made close to twenty films, been awarded a special Academy Award, and been signed to a $4,000 a week contract that, with bonuses, made her the highest paid child in the world. At the same time, her great success enabled her family to move into this beautiful, vaguely French farmhouse in exclusive Brentwood. Here, Shirley had her own "doll house," which was actually a full-sized guest house where the little tot kept her huge doll collection and where she had her own soda fountain. Later, when her child-star days were over, a seventeen-year-old Shirley Temple moved into her "doll house" with her new husband, actor John Agar, before he went off to World War II. They were divorced several years and one daughter (whom David O. Selznick instantly tried to put under contract!) later.

In 1950, Miss Temple went on to marry Charles Black of the Northern California/Pacific Gas and Electric Company Blacks. Despite the fact that Black was dropped from the Social Register for marrying an actress, the union worked. Shirley Temple Black's grown-up accomplishments are also impressive. These include hosting several television series, a stint as an interior decorator, and most notably, holding the posts of U.S. Representative to the United Nations, U.S. Ambassador to Ghana and later Czechoslovakia, and U.S. Chief of Protocol.

Back on Rockingham Road, about a block from the former Temple residence, football player-turned-actor/spokesperson Orenthal J. (O.J.) Simpson lived at number 360. He was residing here in 1994, when his estranged wife Nicole Brown Simpson was murdered in her nearby Brentwood condo. O.J. sold his Brentwood mansion in the late 1990s to help pay the legal fees

Shirley Temple house, Brentwood

of his two trials—the criminal one which acquitted him of the murder, while the civil trial found him guilty. The subsequent owner of the former Simpson property tore down O.J.'s house and erected another. Simpson has since moved to Florida.

14. THE AMALFI COAST
Pacific Palisades/off Sunset Boulevard

One of Italy's chicest resort areas is the spectacular mountain-backed Amalfi Coast south of Naples, which includes the lovely towns of Positano, Amalfi, and Sorrento as well as the glamorous island of Capri. Not to be outdone, L.A.'s exclusive Pacific Palisades community has its own version of the Amalfi Coast stretching for several blocks off the western end of Sunset Boulevard not far from the Pacific Ocean. Here, ultraluxurious homes and estates can be found on streets with names like Amalfi Drive, Sorrento Drive, Corsica Drive, and Capri Avenue. Here, too, some of Hollywood's top names reside or have resided: Steven Spielberg and Sylvester Stallone on the 1500 block of Amalfi Drive; Tom Cruise and Nicole Kidman, and later just Ms. Kidman, nearby on the 1500 block of Sorrento Drive; Tom Hanks and Rita Wilson on the 900 block of Corsica Drive; Goldie Hawn and Kurt Russell on the less fashionable south-of-Sunset 700 block of Amalfi Drive.

Historically, L.A.'s Amalfi Coast has also attracted Hollywood intellectuals, many of them European, such as the German writer Thomas Mann and his actress wife Louise Rainer (who won an Academy Award for *The Good Earth* in 1938); *Brave New World* British author Aldous Huxley, who wrote screenplays in Hollywood in the 1930s and 1940s; and novelist Vicki Baum, who penned *Grand Hotel*—all of whom lived on Amalfi Drive.

Whereas most of Hollywood's movie-star maps have exact addresses for some of the above names, few of these properties have visible street numbers and all are seriously fenced, hedged, and guarded.

15. MARILYN MONROE HOUSE
12305 Fifth Helena Drive

This was where it all came to an end on August 5, 1962. Marilyn had been living in this one-story villa at the end of a cul-de-sac off Helena Drive in Brentwood for about six months. Urged by her psychiatrist to "put down roots," she had found the house and bought it—all by herself. She had liked the house and took a trip to Mexico to look for furnishings and fabrics. She especially liked the garden, where she often played with her poodle, Maf. But the house, the garden, the dog just weren't enough to compensate for the many areas of her life that were not going well, not working out. For one thing, she had been fired from *Something's Gotta Give*, the film she had been working on with Dean Martin. For another, she was supposedly involved with a very public figure who was also a very married man. Finally, she was ill—both physically and emotionally. The drugs helped somewhat, got her through the bad days, and worse nights. But the drugs weren't the answer either—and in the end, one of them, Nembutal, was what "officially" did her in. But, in truth, the end had been a long time in coming.

As for her final house, it has had numerous owners in the forty-plus years since her death. Nonetheless, fans continue to send letters and gifts to the house at 12305 Fifth Helena Drive.

16. NICOLE BROWN SIMPSON RESIDENCE
879 South Bundy Drive

In Hollywood, horrific events have a way of occurring against deceptively beautiful backdrops. A case in point is the heinous crime that was committed on the night of June 16, 1994, in the lovely front yard of this pretty Mediterranean-style condominium in upscale Brentwood. For it was here that the former wife of O. J. Simpson was brutally butchered along with her actor-waiter friend Ron Goldman. The slow-motion car chase, the trail, the dirt, the hysteria, and the characters (Brian "Kato" Kaelin, Marcia Clark, Mark Fuhrman, Johnnie Cochran, Barry Scheck, Lance Ito, et al.) that followed riveted America for a good two years after the event. As the world knows, Simpson was acquitted of the murder in the criminal trial but found guilty of murdering Nicole Brown Simpson and Ron Goldman in the subsequent civil suit. Meanwhile Ms. Simpson's old condo has since been sold, remodeled, relandscaped, even renumbered (it used to be 875 South Bundy)—because in L.A., prime Westside real estate is prime Westside real estate, despite what may have happened there.

17. NUART THEATER
11272 Santa Monica Boulevard

This famous L.A. revival house emphasizes foreign, offbeat, and experimental films. Midnight screenings on Fridays often feature new prints of the cult and the camp: *Beyond the Valley of the Dolls, Harold and Maude, Valley Girl, The Last American Virgin, Ed Wood.* Saturdays, the midnight slot is usually reserved for *The Rocky Horror Picture Show.*

For program information, call 310–281–8223 or visit www.landmarktheaters.com.

18. CENTURY CITY

Part of it was Chicago, another part was Algiers, still another harbored a South Seas lagoon. It was one of Hollywood's greatest back lots—but in 1961, Twentieth Century–Fox was practically bankrupt from the production delays and massive costs of its then uncompleted *Cleopatra.* Realizing at the time that its real estate was worth more than its movies, Fox sold off a huge chunk of its back lot to the Aluminum Company of America for the development of a massive complex of offices, shops, condos, theaters, and restaurants that is now known as Century City.

Ironically, Century City quickly reverted to its former back-lot status when film and television production companies discovered that its state-of-the-art architecture was wonderfully photogenic and easily could be made to look like practically any thoroughly modern metropolis in America. Century City's walkways, landscaped plazas, and high-rises have been seen in hundreds of series and television movies. Its distinctive twin triangular towers, espe-

Trouble in Century City: *Conquest of the Planet of the Apes*

cially, frequently represent high-profile office buildings. In the TV series *Remington Steele,* the towers turned up every week, and in *Moonlighting,* they housed the office where Cybill Shepherd and Bruce Willis worked as detectives. Willis also found himself in Century City for his action-adventure outing in *Die Hard* (1988), where he fought terrorists who had taken over the complex's Fox Tower, called Nakatomi Tower in the film. Century City also furnished L.A. locations for *The Man Who Loved Women* (1983) and *Against All Odds* (1984). But in the 1977 film about the world of professional dance, *The Turning Point,* Century City's former ABC Entertainment Center doubled as New York City's Lincoln Center. And in at least two films and one TV series, Century City has played cities of the future: in *Conquest of the Planet of the Apes* (1972) it provided the concrete jungle where human workers were pitted against slave apes; in *Demolition Man* (1993), it represented Los Angeles, circa 2036; and in the 2004 series *Century City,* the compound furnishes the "near future" setting for a law firm that handles "difficult cases."

Although known for its Twentieth Century–Fox connections, Century City's newest landmark is the thirty-five-story MGM Tower at 10250 Constellation Boulevard, where Metro-Goldwyn-Mayer, which no longer has its own studio, occupies some seventeen floors of the building.

19. TWENTIETH CENTURY–FOX STUDIOS
10202 West Pico Boulevard

Although, like most studios, Twentieth Century–Fox is off-limits to casual visitors, intrepid movie lovers can still get a peek, from the studio's main entrance off Pico Boulevard, at what's left of the New York City set that was created for *Hello, Dolly!* in the late 1960s. Granted, the set—built to three-quarter scale since the camera makes everything look larger than life—has seen better days; but like D. W. Griffith's great Babylon set for *Intolerance,* which stood on Sunset Boulevard for several years back in the teens, Fox's New York City is a landmark that celebrates the essential magical nature of filmmaking. In addition to being a landmark, the *Hello, Dolly!* street is still used as a set, and occasionally turns up on a television show—especially when the script calls for a dilapidated inner-city neighborhood.

The history of the Twentieth Century–Fox lot goes back to William Fox, who bought the land along Pico Boulevard in 1925. At the time, his Fox Film Corporation, based at Sunset Boulevard and Western Avenue in Hollywood, needed additional shooting space for the Tom Mix Westerns that were the studio's mainstays. (Today, Tom Mix's barn is still on the lot and is used as an office.) A decade later, when financial difficulties had pushed Fox out of the company and prompted the Fox Film Corporation to merge with Joseph Schenck and Darryl Zanuck's two-year-old Twentieth Century Pictures, the new Twentieth Century–Fox organization decided to make Fox's Pico Boulevard property its headquarters. Eventually, Darryl Zanuck became the new studio's chief and remained a major mogul at Twentieth Century–Fox on and off up until the early 1970s.

Twentieth Century–Fox's biggest moneymaker in its early years was Shirley Temple, whose pictures provided the studio with a strong financial base. Today, Miss Temple's back-lot cot-

Star cottage: Shirley Temple's Twentieth Century–Fox bungalow

tage is the studio hospital and the studio commissary still has a private dining room named after the top tot star. Other top Twentieth Century–Fox stars in the late 1930s were Tyrone Power, Alice Faye, Carmen Miranda, Don Ameche, Will Rogers, Janet Gaynor, and Sonja Henie. Later, Betty Grable, Anne Baxter, Jennifer Jones, Victor Mature, Gregory Peck, and Marilyn Monroe would join the Fox fold.

Among the greatest Twentieth Century–Fox pictures made on the Pico property were *Cavalcade* (Fox's executive office building—with balconies that resemble a ship's—were used in this shipboard film), *The Story of Alexander Graham Bell, In Old Chicago, The Grapes of Wrath, How Green Was My Valley, The Song of Bernadette, State Fair, Forever Amber, Gentleman's Agreement, All About Eve, The Robe* (in which Fox introduced CinemaScope), *How to Marry a Millionaire, The King and I,* and *Hello, Dolly!*

The present Fox lot, however, is only a shadow of its former self. In 1961, the studio was again in financial trouble—especially with the massive costs that *Cleopatra* was running up—and much of the original back lot was sold to the Alcoa Corporation for the Century City complex. In 1981, oil tycoon

Marvin Davis purchased the studio, and sold it four years later to Australian media mogul Rupert Murdoch, whose News Corporation still counts Twentieth Century–Fox among its prime assets. Since the Murdoch reign, Fox has had some of its greatest successes in the blockbuster genre, with films such as the *Die Hard* trio (1988, 1990, 1995), *Independence Day* (1996), and the surprise hit and Oscar winner of 1998, *Titanic*. Among the studio's greatest all-time hits are the *Star Wars* films.

Besides peeking at the Hello, Dolly! *set, movie lovers should also check out the studio's western wall, where, at Tennessee Avenue, the original main gate is now an auxiliary entrance. At Orton Avenue, the building with the cupola was former studio head Darryl F. Zanuck's office; it is said that the room within the cupola was where his "casting couch" was located. The best way to see the studio, however, is to attend a taping of a television show on the premises. To find out what's taping at Fox and to book tickets, contact Audiences Unlimited at 818–753–3483.*

20. HILLCREST COUNTRY CLUB
10000 West Pico Boulevard

Many people are under the impression that this famous country club—just south of Twentieth Century–Fox Studios—was founded by Jewish movie folk like Al Jolson, Jack Benny, George Burns, and George Jessel because they couldn't get into the Wasp-only Los Angeles, Wilshire, and Bel-Air country clubs. False. The actual fact of the matter is that Hillcrest was founded in 1921—not by movie people, but rather by Jewish businessmen, lawyers, and doctors who couldn't get into the aforementioned Wasp-only clubs. Later the movie moguls and movie stars also joined—including not only all the above names but eventually a couple of pretty well known Gentiles as well, the most famous of the latter: Frank Sinatra. Besides famous members, Hillcrest is renowned for its food, which is said to be better than any restaurant in Los Angeles.

21. *BIG BUSINESS* HOUSE
10281 Dunleer Drive

In one of Laurel and Hardy's last silent films—*Big Business* (1929)—the boys are selling Christmas trees. When the owner of this house on Dunleer Drive destroys their sample tree, Stan and Ollie retaliate by destroying the man's house. According to an interview given by Hal Roach that appears in Kevin Brownlow's *Hollywood: The Pioneers* (Alfred A. Knopf, 1979), the *Big Business* crew started shooting the film at the wrong house! Its owners were away at the time—but returned just as their place was being devastated by Laurel and Hardy. On witnessing the sight, they, too, were devastated.

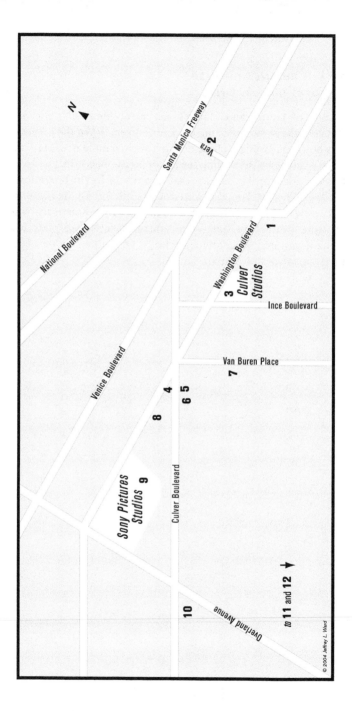

N

Santa Monica Freeway

Vera **2**

National Boulevard

Washington Boulevard

1

3 *Culver Studios*

Ince Boulevard

Venice Boulevard

Van Buren Place

7

4

5
6

8

Sony Pictures Studios **9**

Culver Boulevard

10

Overland Avenue

to **11** *and* **12**

© 2004 Jeffrey L. Ward

Culver City:
"The Heart of Screenland"

A splashing fountain and gleaming stainless-steel sculpture in the shape of a loop of motion picture film proclaim Culver City "The Heart of Screenland" over at the corner of Overland Avenue and Culver Boulevard. A plaque at the base of this monumental piece of public art goes on to say: "Dedicated by the Citizens of Culver City—the Motion Picture Capital of the World."

Culver City? What are they talking about? What's going on here? Actually, quite a bit went on here—especially in the 1930s and 1940s when, at one time, this little middle-class Los Angeles community, about six miles southwest of Hollywood, produced over half of the movies made in America. This dramatic statistic was largely owing to the presence of Metro-Goldwyn-Mayer, which was Culver City's single greatest employer. But Culver City's film fame wasn't just because of MGM. Hal Roach, David O. Selznick, as well as a number of smaller Culver City studios enabled city officials to adopt the slogan: "Culver City—Where Hollywood Movies Are Made." For some civic boosters, slogans weren't enough, they wanted nothing less than to change Culver City's name. The name they chose? "Hollywood"!

Unlike many areas of Los Angeles, the movies didn't "come"

Child of MGM:
Judy Garland, ca. 1936

to Culver City, they were brought there. The man responsible for this was the town's developer, Harry H. Culver, who as early as 1915 saw the potential of the movie industry and went about enticing studios to set up shop in his new real estate development. First on the scene was the Kalem Motion Picture Company, which later was known as Essanay. They didn't stay long, but the highly successful producer/director Thomas Ince did. In fact, it was Ince who built the studio that eventually became MGM. It was also Ince who built another historic studio that wound up being home to such greats as Cecil B. DeMille, David O. Selznick, RKO, and even Lucille Ball and Desi Arnaz's Desilu Productions.

Today, both of Ince's former studios are not only still standing, they are still turning out films. The Hal Roach Studios, however, have been torn down, although die-hard Laurel and Hardy fans will find many locations used in both their silent and sound Hal Roach comedies in downtown Culver City. Indeed, for film buffs of all stripes, if you haven't seen Culver City, you haven't really seen Hollywood.

The sites of downtown Culver City—from numbers 3 to 10—can be seen easily on a walking tour of about forty-five minutes to an hour. Good news for movie lovers is that Sony Pictures, which now owns the historic MGM lot, has a tour, which is highly recommended (see item 9).

1. CULVER CITY MAZDA/HAL ROACH STUDIO SITE
West Washington Boulevard at National Boulevard

At the southwest corner of Washington and National Boulevards, there's a postage-stamp-sized park with a picnic table, two benches, and a simple marker that bears the following inscription: "Site of the Hal Roach Studios . . . Laugh Factory to the World . . . 1919–1963." And that it was—for it was here that Roach produced (and often directed) early Harold Lloyd films, the *Our Gang* comedies, the Laurel and Hardy series, and the *Topper* films. Besides all of Roach's funny fare, he sometimes did serious films such as *Captain Fury* (1939), *Of Mice and Men* (1939), and a great number of propaganda movies during World

Culver City Kids: Hal Roach's *Our Gang*

War II. Called "Fort Roach" during the war years, the studio boasted Lieutenant (later Captain) Ronald Reagan as its leading leading man. Proving how times have changed since World War II, today, behind the little park, the area where Roach's studios stood has been taken over by Culver City Mazda.

2. *A PERFECT DAY* HOUSE
3120 Vera Avenue

It was anything but *A Perfect Day* in this Laurel and Hardy classic that saw the boys trying to set off on a picnic only to have one disaster after another keep them from ever getting anywhere. The house in front of which most of the action of the film takes place—a cozy Cotswolds-like cottage with bulging roof—has changed little since *A Perfect Day* was released in 1929. Laurel and Hardy fans may also recognize the house next door (3116 Vera) and the house across the street (3115 Vera)—both of which also appear in *A Perfect Day*.

Laurel and Hardy in *A Perfect Day*, 1929

Selznick International Studios, 1935

3. THE CULVER STUDIOS
9336 West Washington Boulevard

Remember that shot of the white mansion with the elegant columns that preceded every David O. Selznick film in the late 1930s and early 1940s? It wasn't Tara—although many assumed that it was, since Selznick's most famous production was *Gone With the Wind*. The mansion was actually the main office building of Selznick International Studios. Selznick set up his own company in Culver City in 1936 after having been a vice president and producer at nearby MGM. One of Selznick's principal backers in this venture was millionaire playboy John Hay "Jock" Whitney, who served as chairman of the board of Selznick International.

Selznick produced an impressive group of motion picture classics from his Culver City base. *Little Lord Fauntleroy* (1936), *The Garden of Allah* (1936), *A Star Is Born* (1937), *Nothing Sacred* (1937), *The Prisoner of Zenda* (1937), *Intermezzo* (1939), and *Rebecca* (1940) were all filmed here—as was much of *Gone With the Wind* (1939). In fact, the hills directly behind the studio are those seen in the sequence where Scarlett and Melanie flee Atlanta.

It was not Selznick, however, who built the great white mansion that became the trademark for his films. The building and the studio were actually founded back in 1919 by the pioneer director-producer Thomas Ince, who had his greatest early success with a string of Westerns that starred William S. Hart. Among the famous Ince films done on his Culver City lot were *The Typhoon* (1920) with Sessue Hayakawa and *Human Wreckage* (1924), which was inspired by silent superstar Wallace Reid's fatal bout with drug addiction and which starred the late actor's wife, Dorothy Davenport.

After Ince's untimely death in 1924 aboard William Randolph Hearst's yacht (see Chapter 2, item 21), the studio he built had a series of occupants before Selznick arrived. One of those interim tenants was Cecil B. DeMille, who had broken away from Paramount in 1925 to form his own company, which he set up on the former Ince lot. It was here that DeMille lensed his classic story of the life of Christ, *King of Kings,* in 1926–27.

After DeMille returned to Paramount in the late 1920s, Pathé—which via mergers became RKO-Pathé—took over. Some of RKO's greatest pictures were shot at this little Culver City stu-

Made in Culver City:
Gone With the Wind

dio: *What Price Hollywood?* (1932), *King Kong* (1933), *Becky Sharpe* (1935), *Top Hat* (1935). And, when Selznick burned Atlanta for *Gone With the Wind,* part of what he set aflame was the old jungle set from RKO's *King Kong*!

It should be noted that even during the Selznick era, RKO continued to shoot films such as *Citizen Kane* (1941) at Culver City, since Selznick only leased the studios from RKO. Thus, when Selznick International disbanded in 1943, the lot was still part of RKO and remained so until 1957 when Lucille Ball and Desi Arnaz acquired it for their mushrooming Desilu empire. When that empire was dissolved in the late 1960s, the Culver City studio became for the next two decades a rental lot known as Laird International Studios. (Steven Spielberg shot much of *E.T.* at Laird in 1981.)

In 1991, Sony Pictures, which had aquired the former MGM studios a few blocks away, also took over the historic Selznick/RKO lot and renamed it simply the Culver Studios. In 2004, the studio changed hands once again, when Sony sold it to a private investment group for $125 million. But no matter who owns the place, that wonderful columned mansion still stands for all the world to see, a timeless symbol of all the famous films that have been shot on the premises.

Visit www.theculverstudios.com.

4. THE CULVER HOTEL
9400 Culver Boulevard

According to Judy, "They got smashed every night and the police had to pick them up in butterfly nets." She may have exaggerated a bit—but when 124 Munchkins hit Culver City in 1938, the small L.A. community had its hands full. Most stayed at the Culver Hotel where, according to one story, a policeman was needed on every floor to break up their wild sex orgies. According to other stories, their raucous behavior was not limited to their hotel. Evidently one of them caused quite a disturbance at MGM when he bit a guard in the leg. Others were said to carry knives—and several of the women supposedly propositioned *The Wizard of Oz* stagehands on various occasions. In her book, *The Making of the Wizard of Oz* (Alfred A. Knopf, 1977), Aljean

Culver City Hotel guests: the Munchkins, here with Judy Garland, in *The Wizard of Oz*

Harmetz concludes that while some of the stories about film-dom's most famous little people (they ranged in height between two feet, three inches and four feet, eight inches) may have been true, many rank among Hollywood's tallest tales.

What *is* true is that many of the Munchkins not only stayed at the Culver Hotel in 1938 when they were shooting *The Wizard of Oz,* but again in 1997, when those still around had a reunion. Today, the hotel, which was restored in 1998, remembers the Munchkins with all sorts of *Oz* and MGM photos and memorabilia in its street-front windows. The distinctive wedge-shaped building may also look familiar to classic movie lovers since it's been used as a location for various *Our Gang* comedies and Laurel and Hardy flicks. More recently, it featured in Arnold Schwarzenegger's *The Last Action Hero* (1993) as well as in episodes of *Judging Amy* and *7th Heaven* on TV.

Call 310–838–7963 or visit www.culverhotel.com.

Twenty-first-century Deco: Pacific Theatres Culver Stadium 12

5. PACIFIC THEATRES CULVER STADIUM 12
9500 Culver Boulevard

Another of the Pacific Theatres chain's attempts to revive classic movie palace architecture, this neo-Deco multiplex opened in spring of 2003 in a newly pedestrianized section of downtown Culver City. The new Pacific Theatre has twelve curved wall-to-wall screens, digital sound, stadium seating, and twenty-four-hour electronic ticketing.

Visit www.pacifictheatres.com.

6. DESILU MURAL
Irving Street and Culver Boulevard

This colorful mural depicts Lucy and Ricky Ricardo in their 1955 Pontiac convertible on their *I Love Lucy* journey to California. It pays homage to the fact that Lucille Ball and Desi Ar-

Celebrating Desilu: Culver City mural

naz's Desilu Studios had a Culver City presence from 1957 to 1967, when they controlled the former RKO/David O. Selznick studios. The muralist is listed as François Bardol.

7. HOTEL WASHINGTON
3927 Van Buren Place

"What a dump!" The line forever belongs to her arch rival, Bette Davis, but it aptly describes Joan Crawford's first L.A. digs. Just a couple of blocks from MGM, where she was making $75 a week, the hotel saw Joan (née Lucille Fay Le Sueur) check in in early 1925. Today, the Washington is a welfare hotel.

8. KIRK DOUGLAS THEATER
9820 West Washington Boulevard

With its gigantic billboard-like façade, the Culver Theater was typical of post–World War II movie house design. It was also the pride of Culver City and frequently the site of MGM previews and screenings. Split up into three theaters in the 1970s, the Culver was also an example of how movie theater owners dealt with the challenges presented by television, cable, and home video. Today, the Culver has been made one again as part of an $11-million restoration that has just turned it into the Kirk Douglas Theater. Although it will be used for special events, including films, it will primarily function as the new venue for the live productions of L.A.'s prestigious Center Theater Group. Mr. Douglas and his wife, Anne, contributed $2.5 million toward the project.

Call 213-628-2772 or visit www.taperahmanson.com.

9. SONY PICTURES STUDIOS/FORMERLY MGM
10202 West Washington Boulevard

"More stars than there are in the heavens." That's what MGM claimed during its glory years in the 1930s and 1940s. And, in fact, the claim wasn't so far-fetched—since this was the studio that employed Judy Garland, Mickey Rooney, Clark Gable, Jean Harlow, John Gilbert, Greta Garbo, Marion Davies, Joan Crawford, Norma Shearer, Greer Garson, Myrna Loy, Spencer Tracy, Katharine Hepburn, and Elizabeth Taylor—to mention but a few. Name a legend, and chances are, he or she was under contract at MGM. Indeed, if Hollywood had had no studio other than Metro-Goldwyn-Mayer, the town still would have been the movie capital of the world.

MGM had more than just superstars. It also had some of the finest technical people in the business—set designers, costumers, special-effects men. It counted among its great directors George Sidney, George Cukor, King Vidor, Sidney Franklin, Victor Fleming, Clarence Brown, W. S. Van Dyke II, Stanley Donen, and Vincente Minnelli. In some ways, even more important than its directors were MGM producers. Early on, for example, one of the most vital forces at the studio was Irving Thalberg, who was its first head of production. Working in this capacity from 1924 up to his premature death in 1936, Thalberg was responsible for the string of successful films—including *Ben Hur, Flesh and the Devil, Anna Christie, The Big Parade, Grand Hotel, David Copperfield*—that quickly made the studio's name and fame.

Classic MGM: Esther Williams in *Million Dollar Mermaid*

Another important force at MGM was Arthur Freed, whose "Freed Unit" produced most of those lavish musicals that have come to be synonymous with the letters MGM. Freed's top productions: *The Wizard of Oz* (in association with Mervyn LeRoy), *Babes in Arms, Strike Up the Band, Babes on Broadway, Girl Crazy, Meet Me in St. Louis, The Pirate, The Harvey Girls, Easter Parade, Singin' in the Rain, Show Boat, An American in Paris*, and *The Band Wagon*.

Finally, the biggest name of all at MGM was the infamous Louis B. Mayer. For almost thirty years he ruled his studio and Hollywood with an iron hand—and was respected, feared, often hated, and rarely loved. But in 1951, he fell from power. Nonetheless, a frequently told story about his funeral in 1957 says that the reason it was so crowded was because everybody wanted to make sure he was really gone.

A former junk dealer, Mayer got into the picture business in 1907 when he bought a movie house in Massachusetts. He

quickly acquired more theaters, and before he knew it he owned
a chain. By 1918, Mayer was in Los Angeles making his own
movies under the banner of Louis B. Mayer Pictures. MGM
came about in 1924 through a three-way merger that brought together Mayer's company, Samuel Goldwyn's studio, and Metro
Pictures. It was decided at that time that Goldwyn's lot in Culver City would be Metro-Goldwyn-Mayer's headquarters. Originally built for Thomas Ince's division of Triangle Pictures in
1915, the MGM property grew along with the new studio's success. Indeed, in its heyday—from the 1930s to the 1950s—the
MGM Culver City property encompassed 183 acres. Some of it
had massive offices like the Irving Thalberg Building (visible
from the street at the junction of Madison Avenue and Culver
Boulevard). Erected in the late 1930s in honor of Thalberg—
who died in 1936 at the age of thirty-seven—this impressive
WPA-Moderne structure looks as if it would be more at home in
Washington, D.C., than in Southern California. Indeed, architecturally it is much more a tribute to Louis B. Mayer's ego than to
Thalberg's creative genius.

Most of the old MGM's acreage was taken up by its back lots,

MGM's original main gate

which depicted European villages, American small towns, Manhattan tenements, Parisian back streets and grand boulevards. But in 1969 the studio, under new ownership, took a cue from Twentieth Century–Fox and decided to sell off its back lots to real estate developers. Gone went the Andy Hardy street, the huge artificial lake used for *Mutiny on the Bounty* (1935) and *Showboat* (1951), and the sets of *Meet Me in St. Louis* (1944) and *Raintree County* (1957). One of the new developments on the old MGM back lot called itself the Raintree Apartment and Condominium Complex. All in all, MGM went from 183 acres to 30 acres in this real estate deal.

The closing decades of the twentieth century saw the power of Leo the Lion's roar continually diminish, as MGM's history became one of mergers, corporate takeovers, and complicated financial maneuverings. One of the biggest blows to the company was Ted Turner's buyout in 1986, a deal which saw him keep much of MGM's priceless film library but sell off the company's other assets to various companies. This included its historic Culver City lot, which was purchased by Lorimar Telepictures and subsequently in 1991 by Sony Pictures, its current owner. Meanwhile, a company called Metro-Goldwyn-Mayer continues to produce films, but it now has a Century City address and no studio facilities. These days, too, the name MGM is attached to casino hotels, as in the MGM Grand, and theme parks. But no matter where MGM finds itself in the corporate jungle of twenty-first-century America, as long as there are movies, there will always be the mythical MGM—a magical land where Mickey and Judy sang and danced, where Greta Garbo was the most ravishing creature on earth, and where almost all endings were happy ones. The old lot may be called Sony and the old company may have been sliced up and scattered, but the great MGM movies are as big and lavish as they ever were.

For movie lovers, the good news is that Sony Pictures now offers a guided walking tour of its historic Culver City facilities. This is a wonderful way to see not only a working movie studio, but also many of the office buildings and soundstages of the MGM era. These include the Thalberg Building; the old Writers Building, where L. B. Mayer was constantly terrorizing his contract screenwriters; historic soundstages; and the original ornately columned main gate (also visible from the street on Washington Boulevard). Tour participants also get to see prop and scene shops as well as the sets of current films and TV shows, such as The Guardian, The King of Queens, Wheel of Fortune, *and* Jeopardy. *The two-hour tour currently costs $24 and must be booked in advance. Children under 12 are not allowed. Call 323-520-TOUR.*

Another way to see the Sony Pictures/MGM facility from the inside is to attend a taping of a TV show there. Call Audiences Unlimited at 818-753-3483 for details or visit www.sony-pictures.com.

10. FILM STRIP U.S.A.
Culver Boulevard at Overland Avenue

The most exuberant tribute to Culver City's vital role in the film history of Los Angeles, this stainless-steel fountain/sculpture was erected in 1981 in front of the Veterans Memorial Building, across the street from the housing development that used to be an MGM back lot. Natalie Krol is the sculptor.

Film Strip U.S.A. sculpture

Holy Cross Cemetery Grotto

11. HOLY CROSS CEMETERY
5835 West Slauson Avenue

This enormous grassy hillside looking out on MGM off to the north is the final resting place of some of Hollywood's most famous stars of the Roman Catholic faith. Of these, one of the brightest was Rosalind *(Auntie Mame)* Russell, whose grave is marked by a large white cross in section M. *Maltese Falcon* star Mary Astor is not far off, in the section marked N, whereas in the mausoleum higher up on the hill are Fred MacMurray, James Broderick, John Candy, Ray Bolger, Joan Davis, Spike Jones, Mario Lanza, Carol Burnett's producer and former husband Joe Hamilton, and choreographer Hermes Pan.

Another great concentration of names at Holy Cross can be found around the cemetery's artificial, but very pretty, Grotto to the left of the main entrance. Here lie Zasu Pitts, Jack Haley, Jack Haley Jr., Bela Lugosi, Jimmy Durante, Charles Boyer, Bonita Granville, Macdonald Carey, Jackie Coogan, Audrey Meadows, Edmond O'Brien, and Pat O'Brien. Here, too, a haunting reminder of the Manson Family's madness: the grave of

Rosalind Russell memorial, Holy Cross Cemetery

Sharon Tate Polanski (1943–1969) and that of her unborn child, Paul Richard Polanski.

Two of the biggest stars around the Grotto are Rita Hayworth (1918–1987), where a fresh rose always graces her gravestone, up near an angel to the right of the Grotto, and Harry Lillis "Bing" Crosby (1904–1977), who is buried alongside his first wife, Wilma W. Crosby (1911–1952), better known as the singer Dixie Lee. A few markers down from the Crosbys is the cemetery's most bizarre grave site. The marker reads: "Carmel Gene Gallegos . . . Going Bing's Way . . . A Road to Jesus." Only one year—1924— is inscribed on the marker. According to a Holy Cross caretaker, it seems that this Crosby fan, on hearing of his idol's death, re- served his own plot as close to Bing's as possible. Columnist Louella Parsons (1881–1972), who is just across the driveway by a small tree, would have had a lot of fun with this one. Louella, by the way, had a varied religious background: She was born Jew- ish, raised Episcopalian, and became a convert to Catholicism.

Hours are 8 a.m. to 5 p.m. daily. The cemetery office will provide visitors with a celebrity list and a map.

12. HILLSIDE MEMORIAL PARK CEMETERY
6001 Centinela Avenue

About a mile north of the Los Angeles International Airport, a big white-marble building atop a smooth green hillside instantly catches the eye of anyone driving along the San Diego Freeway. Below the building, a round monument with tall columns looks like a modern version of an ancient Greek temple and has water cascading down in front of it. The hill is called Mt. Scholum, the large white building is a mausoleum, and the little "temple" is the grave of the great entertainer, Al Jolson. The first actor ever to "talk" in a feature-length commercial motion picture, Jolson changed the course of film history with the words "You ain't heard nothin' yet," which he uttered in *The Jazz Singer* in 1927. Needless to say, he was right—because the success of the film meant that movies would never be silent again. A small statue of Jolson behind his tomb shows the entertainer kneeling with arms outstretched—just as he used to do when singing "Mammy."

A number of Jolson's cronies are also laid to rest in this vast Jewish cemetery. Up in the big white mausoleum, Jack Benny's

Al Jolson memorial, Hillside Memorial Park Cemetery

large black-marble crypt is center stage in the alcove at the end of the Hall of Graciousness. Here, the perennially thirty-nine-year-old comedian is remembered as: "Beloved husband, father and grandfather . . . A Gentle Man . . . 1894–1974." Eddie Cantor and his wife, Ida, are to the left of Mr. Benny—and George Jessel, "The Toastmaster General of America," is outside in the mausoleum's central courtyard.

The mausoleum's Memorial Court is where TV star Michael Landon, who succumbed to cancer in 1991, is laid to rest. In that same courtyard is David *(The Fugitive)* Janssen's wall crypt. Janssen, who died of a heart attack in 1980, was barely fifty at the time. Back inside the mausoleum (on the second floor, directly above Messrs. Benny and Jessel), another star who exited before his time: Ira Grossel—who died in 1961 of complications following surgery at the age of forty-two. Movie lovers will remember this handsome matinee idol better by his screen name—Jeff Chandler.

Television lovers will also want to visit the pavilion known as the Courts of the Book, where they will find Dinah Shore, *Night Court* matron Selma Diamond, and Lorne Greene of *Bonanza.* And they will also want to stop by Acacia Gardens to pay their respects to Mr. Television himself, Milton Berle (1908–2002), who has a simple wall crypt with the inscription "Loving husband, adored father, beloved 'grandpa Milton'—you filled our lives with laughter and love."

Hillside Memorial Park and Mortuary is open daily from 8 a.m. to 5 p.m., except Saturdays and Jewish religious holidays. The office will provide visitors with a detailed celebrity list and a map. Visit www.hillsidememorial.com.

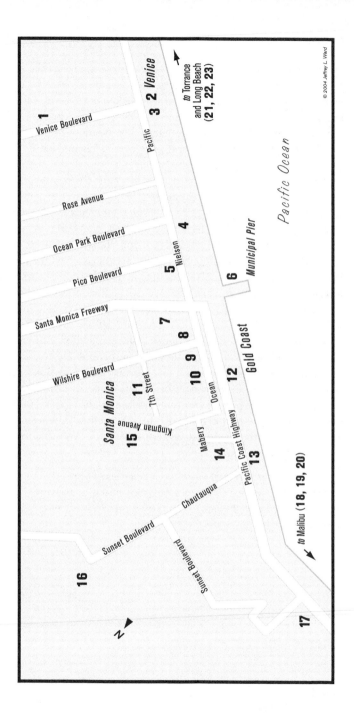

1

Venice Boulevard

3 2 *Venice*

Pacific

to Torrance
and Long Beach
(**21, 22, 23**)

Rose Avenue

Ocean Park Boulevard

4

Nielson

Pico Boulevard

5

Santa Monica Freeway

7

8

Municipal Pier

6

Pacific Ocean

9

Wilshire Boulevard

10

Ocean

12

Gold Coast

Santa Monica

11

7th Street

Kingman Avenue

15

Mabery

14

Pacific Coast Highway

13

to Malibu (**18, 19, 20**)

Chautauqua

Sunset Boulevard

Sunset Boulevard

16

N

17

© 2004 Jeffrey L. Ward

Venice/Santa Monica/Malibu/ Long Beach: Hollywood by the Sea

There are some people who look on all of L.A. as one big beach town. Although this is a vast oversimplification, the proximity of the Pacific Ocean has had much to do with the mystique and ultimate appeal of America's second-largest city. If we are to believe the history books, it was that same Pacific Ocean that attracted the first film crew to the area back in 1907. The crew was headed by director Francis Boggs, who was working for the Chicago-based Selig Polyscope Company, and they are thought to have used the cliff-backed coast of La Jolla as a location for some especially dramatic ocean footage for an early version of *The Count of Monte Cristo*. Liking the territory, the Selig company eventually set up permanent quarters in downtown Los Angeles and later in Silver-lake—but it was the ocean that brought them to Southern California in the first place.

That same ocean attracted other early filmmakers. Mack Sennett was one of them and he often used the beaches of Santa Monica and Venice as locations for his fabled Mack Sennett "Bathing Beauty" films. And then there was producer/director Thomas Ince, who thought he had found the perfect place for

Gloria Swanson and Mack Sennett Bathing Beauties, 1916

shooting Westerns on a large tract of land, which he called "Inceville," where Sunset Boulevard meets the Pacific. Vitagraph was another important film company that had its first studio in Santa Monica. There was one serious problem with these seaside studios . . . the weather. During certain parts of the year, the Southern California coast experiences foggy foggy mornings—which were especially bothersome to silent film companies that depended on the sun as their principal source of light. Eventually, all the movie companies moved inland.

But while the film factories headed east, their stars, directors, and producers often looked west—back toward that big beautiful ocean. Instead of working by the sea, they would live alongside it—at least in the summer and on weekends. By the middle of the 1920s, many of Hollywood's leading lights had built "cottages" (some had as many as fifty rooms) along what soon came to be known as Santa Monica's Gold Coast.

Today, a number of these extraordinary homes are still standing and are among the many delights awaiting the movie lover who visits Santa Monica. Other treats in Santa Monica—as well as in the communities of Venice and Long Beach to the south and Malibu to the north—are Greta Garbo's first and longest Los Angeles residence, the site of one of Hollywood's most baffling unsolved murders, a funky amusement pier where the stars once played and where many famous films have been made, and the ultimate movie-star colony, where a fabled estate that once belonged to one of its most famous residents—Barbra Streisand—is now open to the public.

A car is a must for covering the sites in this chapter, although there are numerous places to park and walk. Among the best strolling areas are the Santa Monica Pier, the Gold Coast houses, downtown Venice, and Malibu Creek State Park, a former movie ranch where films like How Green Was My Valley, M*A*S*H, *and* Pleasantville *were shot. Please note: Proceed with caution along the Pacific Coast Highway. Look—only after you've arrived at your destination. This is especially true if you are the driver.*

1. VENICE HIGH SCHOOL
13000 Venice Boulevard

Until the spring of 2003, a stylized sculpture that depicted three dancing figures stood in front of the Art Deco main building of Venice High School. One represented the Physical, another the Mental, and the third the Spiritual. A then–art instructor at the school named H. F. Winebrenner designed the statues in the 1920s, using students as his models. A football player was called on to pose for the Physical, a pretty girl with a high academic average modeled for the Mental, and another lovely young woman—with an especially lithe body—inspired the Spiritual. The identities of the first two student models are anybody's guess. Miss Spiritual is another story. Her name was Myrna Williams, and she was said to have been embarrassed about the statue and asked that her participation be kept secret. Somehow or other, the cat got out of the bag—especially once Miss Williams changed her last name and started making pictures at MGM. Today, movie lovers can catch Myrna Loy as the sophisticated Nora Charles in the classic *The Thin Man* films, which are often shown on television, but owing to extreme deterioration, her image as a dancing teenager in front of her former alma mater in

Venice, California, has been relegated to the school's basement until funds are available for restoration. Donations, anyone?

Besides boasting Myrna Loy as a famous former student, Venice High made a name for itself in the opening sequence of *Grease* (1978), and has also appeared in *American History X* (1998), *Charlie's Angels* (2000), and *Matchstick Men* (2003). The school was also used extensively for Britney Spears's "Baby One More Time" video as well as in the MTV spoof of the same.

Visit www.venicehigh.net.

2. VENICE

It was an outlandish undertaking—even for Southern California. Convinced that the gentle climate and dramatic topography of Los Angeles would give rise to the ultimate flowering of American culture, a wealthy cigarette manufacturer and real estate baron named Abbot Kinney decided to get the jump on the coming renaissance by building his own version of Venice, Italy, just

Death in Venice: Charlton Heston in *Touch of Evil*, 1958

south of Santa Monica. With plenty of cash to back up his dream, Kinney began hiring architects and engineers around the turn of the century to create a canal system as well as a master plan of buildings with extravagant Venetian colonnaded façades. On July 4, 1905, the fantasy city celebrated its grand opening.

It was fun for a while—what with gondolas and gondoliers plying the canals; exotic hotels, pavilions, and bath houses; and a 1,600-foot pier for fishing and strolling. But the cultural renaissance of Kinney's dreams never materialized, and Venice quickly became little more than a glorified seaside amusement park.

Today, little is left of Kinney's Venice—just enough to make seeing the city an intriguing archaeological experience. The best examples of the city's neo-Italianate architecture are the arcaded buildings along Windward and Pacific Avenues, and while most of the canals were declared health hazards and filled in in the late 1920s, a few remain—along with their charming arched bridges— at Carroll, Linnie, Sherman, and Howland.

In its early days, Venice, with its flamboyant architecture and beautiful beach, quickly became a popular location for silent movies. Two of the first producers to film here were Thomas Ince and Mack Sennett. Sennett often used the beach for his famous "Bathing Beauties"; he also shot his 1914 Keystone Production, *Kid Auto Races,* in Venice; the film was Charlie Chaplin's second movie—and the first in which he was seen wearing the mustache and baggy trousers and carrying the cane that would eventually become his trademarks.

Chaplin not only filmed in Venice he also relaxed here—and is said to have stayed at the Waldorf Hotel, which is still standing and is now an apartment building at the corner of Westminster and Speedway. The grander St. Marks Hotel was also popular with movie folk, and Rudolph Valentino and Douglas Fairbanks both supposedly stayed there. Today, only a portion of its colonnade remains at the corner of Windward and Ocean Front Walk.

Known as a place for fun and play, Venice brought out stars in search of good times and often turned them into children. Marion Davies, one of Hollywood's wealthiest women, loved the pier, the hamburgers and hot dogs, the Ferris wheel, and once rode the roller coaster until seven in the morning! Charlie Chaplin was nuts over the bumper cars. In 1935, Carole Lombard, who like

Miss Davies was always up for a good time, took over the entire Venice Pier and hosted one of Hollywood's most famous parties. Le tout Hollywood came to the affair, rode all the rides, played all the arcade games, and let down their hair. A famous photograph from this party shows Paramount Pretties Marlene Dietrich and Claudette Colbert zipping down a slide together.

In the mid-1950s, Dietrich returned to Venice to play the role of a sheriff's former mistress in Orson Welles's haunting film, *Touch of Evil*. By this time, Venice was practically at its lowest point—and Welles capitalized on its seedy state and crumbling arcaded buildings to portray the sleazy Tex-Mex border town in which his film took place. Another 1950s film which used Venice extensively was a very low-budget Roger Corman horror flick called *Bucket of Blood* which captures the town during its beatnik days of the late 1950s. It was during this era that a coffeehouse called the Gashouse drew the leading poets, comics, and musicians of the counterculture before less-enlightened locals managed to get the place shut down in 1960.

Marlene Dietrich and Claudette Colbert have fun on the Venice Pier at Carole Lombard's 1935 bash

By the 1970s, however, Venice was on the upswing. Artists, especially, had discovered its great beach, its fantasy architecture, and, above all, its low rents—and this influx of new talent brought new life and a new look to the place. The most striking additions were the huge murals that began appearing on buildings all over town. In an odd way, Venice had come full circle: it was, at last, the prime site of a cultural renaissance in Los Angeles. Kinney's dream, at last, had come true. One of the first films to take advantage of Venice's "new" dazzle was the 1983 remake of *Breathless,* with Richard Gere, which beautifully showed off the city, its murals, and its restored buildings. Another was *L.A. Story* (1991), where a free-spirited young woman named SanDeE* (Sarah Jessica Parker) lived in an outrageously muraled apartment building in downtown Venice. Perhaps not to be outdone, Cameron Diaz had a very cool canalside pad in *Charlie's Angels* (2000).

And speaking of Venice residents, Julia Roberts, Dennis Hopper, and über-architect Frank O. Gehry have all lived here in real life.

3. GOLD'S GYM SITE
1006 South Pacific Avenue

The sign painted atop the front of this squat white building has faded, but is still recognizable as Gold's Gym. Founded by Joe Gold in 1960, this little fitness facility was made world-famous in the 1975 film *Pumping Iron,* which also brought a certain Austrian bodybuilder named Arnold Schwarzenegger into the limelight. Gold's was also the scene of a Mr. America contest in 1977 at which Mae West—eighty-five at the time—handed out the trophies. Indeed, Muscle Beach, Jane Fonda, and Gold's Gym have all been responsible for helping to make Venice and neighboring Santa Monica the unofficial "Fitness Capital of the U.S.A."

In 1981, the original Gold's moved to its current Venice location at 360 Hampton Drive. It also branched out big-time—and now has some 650 locations worldwide. As for the bodybuilder with the long name and the funny accent, well, we all know what happened to him.

4. JANE FONDA HOUSE
152 Wadsworth Avenue

This block of restored Victorian houses between Barnard Way and Neilson Way would be worth seeing—even if Jane Fonda hadn't lived here in the 1970s with her husband, California State Assemblyman Tom Hayden. The ultra-unpretentious Fonda/Hayden house showed the world (and Hayden's liberal constituents) that Jane and Tom were just another California couple. Their once-a-year block-party beer-busts further added to the image. After divorcing Hayden in 1990, Fonda opted for a much grander lifestyle with her next husband, billionaire media mogul Ted Turner. The Turners divorced in 2001 and Ms. Fonda's most recent incarnation is as a newly committed Christian and philanthropist. A college (Vassar) dropout, she recently donated $12.5 million to the Harvard School of Education to found a center on gender and education studies.

5. SANTA MONICA CIVIC AUDITORIUM
1855 Main Street

This is where the Academy Awards were presented and televised from 1960 to 1968. Built in 1958, the auditorium—with its huge

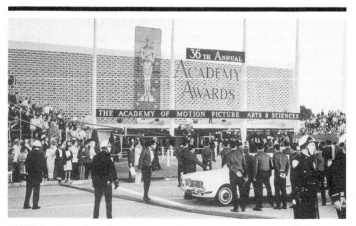

1963 Academy Awards ceremony at the Santa Monica Civic Auditorium

stage, vast dressing room areas, and state-of-the-art electronic equipment—was the best place in town to accommodate an awards ceremony that had become one of the most widely watched television shows in the world. An extra added attraction of the Santa Monica Civic Auditorium—today considered a fine example of mid-century Moderne architecture—was its sweeping driveway, which made it ideal for focusing on star-car arrivals.

6. SANTA MONICA PIER
Foot of Colorado Avenue

Natalie Wood's crazy mother (Ruth Gordon) told fortunes here in *Inside Daisy Clover* (1964). Barbra Streisand and Omar Sharif strolled along it (it was doubling as Brooklyn's Coney Island) in *Funny Girl* (1968). Jane Fonda and Michael Sarrazin marathon-danced their way to oblivion on it in *They Shoot Horses, Don't They?* (1969). Paul Newman operated its carousel (as well as an illegal gambling operation) in *The Sting* (1973). John Ritter, Suzanne Somers, and Joyce DeWitt rode its bumper cars in the opening credits for the TV series *Three's Company,* and Judge Reinhold drove off of it in *Ruthless People* (1986). These are but a few of the many screen appearances that the Santa Monica Pier has logged over the years. Others include *Son of Kong,* the 1933 sequel to the original *King Kong*; *Quicksand* (1950); *The Glenn Miller Story* (1954); *Cannonball* (1976); *Victim of Love* (1991); *Forrest Gump* (1994); *Beverly Hills Cop III* (1994); *Clean Slate* (1994); *The Net* (1995); *Species* (1995); *The Majestic* (2001); and *A Coat of Snow* (2004). The pier has also appeared in countless TV series—nothing like a little carnival/boardwalk ambience to perk up an otherwise lackluster script.

One of Santa Monica's oldest and most famous attractions, the pier has been around since the early part of the last century. Also one of Santa Monica's most glorious survivors, the pier has withstood both storms and developers—and is now on the National Register of Historic Places. Its vintage merry-go-round (built in 1922) is one of the best-preserved all-wooden carousels in the United States and boasts fifty-six handsome hand-carved horses, each one unique. The pier also boasts the world's first solar-powered Ferris wheel and a dizzying new overwater roller coaster. More than a National Historic Landmark, the pier is a symbol of the simple seashore resort that Santa Monica once was.

Visit www.santamonicapier.org.

7. VITAGRAPH STUDIO SITE
1438 Second Street

This pretty little brick building is thought to be the oldest extant building in Santa Monica. Dating back to 1873, it started out as a saloon, later served as a city hall, Salvation Army office, political headquarters, and an art gallery. For movie lovers, its most interesting incarnation was around 1912 when the building was part of the offices of the Vitagraph film company, which also occupied a larger building (now gone) next door. Based in New York, Vitagraph came to Santa Monica as early as 1911 to do location shooting, and remained there until 1915 when it made East Hollywood its permanent base. In 1925, Vitagraph was absorbed by Warner Bros.

Vitagraph Studios, 1914

Marcus Welby, M.D. hospital

8. CALIFORNIA BANK AND TRUST BUILDING
100 Wilshire Boulevard at Ocean Avenue

Television viewers may recall this twenty-two-story Ocean Avenue high-rise as Hope Memorial Hospital on the highly popular 1970s series *Marcus Welby, M.D.* Set in Santa Monica, the series starred Robert Young as Dr. Welby and a young James Brolin as his assistant Dr. Steven Kiley. Another familiar sight in the same series was Pacific Palisades Park, just across Ocean Avenue, which provided the photogenic Santa Monica locale where Dr. Welby had countless "meaningful" talks with Kiley and other younger doctors working with him.

9. FAIRMONT MIRAMAR HOTEL
101 Wilshire Boulevard

In the spring of 1925, Louis B. Mayer went off to Europe to scout foreign talent for the newly formed Metro-Goldwyn-Mayer studio. In Berlin, Mayer's prime objective was to put director Mauritz Stiller under contract with MGM. Stiller, however, played hard to get and insisted that he would only come to

Bungalows at the Fairmont Miramar Hotel

America if Mayer also gave a contract to his protégée, a twenty-year-old Swedish actress named Greta Garbo. Mayer was not impressed with the pudgy Miss Garbo, but reluctantly met Stiller's terms and the Stiller/Garbo team arrived in California in September of the same year.

The studio rented a Santa Monica house with a pool for Stiller. Garbo was put up in a suite at Santa Monica's Miramar Hotel. Garbo's Santa Monica life was a simple one: She worked at the studio, took walks on the beach, and often visited her friend Stiller, where she enjoyed swimming in his pool. She lived at the Miramar longer than at practically any other address in Los Angeles, almost three years. A lot happened during those years. For one thing, the actress whom Mayer had not wanted to sign became the studio's greatest star. For another thing, in classic *A Star Is Born* fashion, Stiller's career instantly went downward and after bitter clashes with Mayer, he wound up never completing a film at MGM. His luck wasn't much better during the brief stint at Paramount that followed. In 1927, Stiller returned to Europe a broken man. A Hollywood casualty, he died a year later. Garbo wept . . . and soon left the Miramar for her own house with a pool in Beverly Hills.

Today's Miramar is quite different from the hotel that Garbo knew. In her day, it consisted of an 1889 mansion (the former home of Santa Monica cofounder, Nevada senator, and silver tycoon John P. Jones) and the six-story brick building erected in 1924 that housed her suite. (Happily, for Garbo fans, the one part of the hotel that hasn't changed dramatically since her residence is the wing where she stayed.) In the late 1930s, the hotel lost the Jones mansion, and in 1959, it gained a modern ten-story tower. It also gained a new pool area which can be seen in the Bermuda sequence of *That Touch of Mink* (1962) with Cary Grant and Doris Day. Today, thirty-two cushy bungalows surround the pool. British actor Anthony Hopkins, before he moved to California and became an American citizen, favored one of the most lavish of these digs when in L.A. to shoot or loop (rerecord) dialogue on films such as *JFK, Nixon,* and *Silence of the Lambs.* In 2002, a group of British actresses, headed by Helen Mirren, descended on the Miramar to shoot a scene for Disney's *Calendar Girls*—which tells the story of some middle-class English women who became media stars through a hospital fund-raising calendar in which they appear nude. In the film, the gals are in L.A. to do *The Tonight Show with Jay Leno*—and they check in at the Miramar. Since then it's also been used as a location for *Along Came Polly* (2004) with Ben Stiller and Jennifer Aniston.

Call 310-576-7777 or visit www.fairmont.com/santamonica/.

10. THE GEORGIAN HOTEL
1415 Ocean Avenue

With its big front porch and sleek Art Deco façade, this eight-story hotel, built in the early 1930s, is a dead ringer for a hotel on Ocean Avenue in Miami's South Beach. It's no wonder then that in Barry Sonnenfeld's 1995 film *Get Shorty,* the Georgian doubled for, of all things, a hotel in Miami. In director Don Roos's 1998 comedy, *The Opposite of Sex,* the Georgian provides a haven for Lisa Kudrow and Martin Donovan, who've

Georgian Hotel

come to L.A. to track down Donovan's half sister Christina Ricci, who's run off with his boyfriend Ivan Sergei. The Georgian has also put up a number of celebrities in its time—from legends like Charlie Chaplin, Clark Gable, and Carole Lombard, and gangsters Bugsy Siegel and Al Capone to present-day stars like Matt LeBlanc, Robert Downey Jr., Tim Robbins, Al Pacino, Jean-Claude Van Damme, Claire Danes, Nicolas Cage, and Matthew Perry. The Georgian can also be spotted in the feature *Bongwater* (1998) and in episodes of *Girls Behaving Badly, Real World, Karen Sisco,* the Discovery Channel's *The Bermen & Bermen Show,* and VH-1's *Where Are They Now?*

Call 310–395–9945 or visit www.georgianhotel.com.

11. ST. MONICA'S CHURCH
715 California Avenue

It swept the 1944 Academy Awards, winning Best Picture as well as Oscars for its star, Bing Crosby; its costar, Barry Fitzgerald; its writer and director, Leo McCarey; and one of its songs, "Swinging on a Star," by James Van Heusen and Johnny Burke. The film was *Going My Way,* and although it was set in New York City, the two priests who are said to have inspired McCarey's screenplay were based in Santa Monica at this Mission Revival–style church on the corner of Seventh Street and California Avenue. The older priest (the Barry Fitzgerald character) was Monsignor Nicholas Conneally, who served as rector of St. Monica's from 1923 to 1949. The younger man (played by Bing Crosby) was Father John Siebert; he eventually became monsignor.

12. THE GOLD COAST

Today, Malibu is the place that has Hollywood's most desirable beach property as far as movie folk are concerned. But in the 1920s and 1930s, Santa Monica was where the stars all flocked and built lavish houses on the beach by the Pacific Ocean. Called the Gold Coast, the area along the Pacific Coast Highway directly below Palisades Park and roughly between the Santa Monica Pier and Marguerita Street still has many of the original star homes of Santa Monica's most glamorous days.

Hard to miss is Cary Grant's former Gold Coast mansion. A half-timbered number with a bright orange tiled roof, it stands alone between two parking lots at 1038 Pacific Coast Highway (aka Ocean Front Road and Palisades Beach Road). For a while during the 1930s, Grant shared the place with fellow bachelor, Randolph Scott. The studios were reportedly less than thrilled with this living arrangement. At the time the notoriously penny-pinching Grant explained the situation to *Modern Screen* magazine in terms of economics: "Here we are living as we want to as bachelors with a nice home at a comparatively small cost. If we got married, we would have to put up a front. Women—particularly Hollywood women—expect that." What Grant failed to mention was that, even though he made more money than Scott,

William Randolph Hearst and Marion Davies's 118-room Ocean House

he allowed his housemate to pay most of the bills. Prior to Grant, the house had belonged to Norma Talmadge and her producer husband, Joe Schenck.

A good half mile farther north (at approximately where the pedestrian walkway joins the Palisades Park with the street and beach below), 707 Pacific Coast Highway is another handsome neo-Elizabethan house. It was here where MGM's second-in-command, production head Irving Thalberg, lived with his wife, MGM star Norma Shearer. The couple was married in 1927, and built their beach house in 1931.

MGM's number-one man, Louis B. Mayer, had his Santa Monica palazzo not far from the Thalberg/Shearer property at 625 Pacific Coast Highway. Mayer employed his studio's top art director, Cedric Gibbons, to decorate the neoclassic Mediterranean villa. Equipped with a soundproof projection booth, Mayer's living room was frequently used to preview the latest MGM picture, the movie screen rising dramatically up from the living room floor. It is said that one of the first screenings of *Gone With the Wind* took place here. Some years later, another MGM name—actor Peter Lawford—owned the former Mayer villa and lived there with his then wife, Patricia Kennedy. JFK and RFK were frequent guests at the Lawfords, and it is rumored that one or the other (or both) of these Kennedy gentlemen romanced Marilyn Monroe here in the early 1960s.

A few doors away, Harry Warner of Warner Bros. lived lavishly at 605 and 607—which together formed one large residence. Before Warner, pioneer producer and a founder of Paramount Pictures, Jesse Lasky, built the original house at 607 as an addition to his large home (now gone) at 609.

Jesse Lasky's former partner, Samuel Goldwyn, built the mansion with the three garages at 602. Later, the same house was occupied by producer/director Mervyn *(The Wizard of Oz)* LeRoy as well as by the Academy Award–winning writer and director of *Going My Way,* Leo McCarey.

Twentieth Century–Fox was represented on the Gold Coast at 546—which was where the studio's longtime head, Darryl Zanuck, spent his beach time. Meanwhile, William Goetz, who was an important producer at Fox as well as Louis B. Mayer's son-in-law, was steps away from the Zanuck house at 522. The Goetz house was designed by architect Wallace Neff,

Beach buddies: Cary Grant and Randolph Scott at their Santa Monica beach house in the 1930s

Mae West's former beach house, today

who also designed Douglas Fairbanks and Mary Pickford's Pickfair.

An even bigger name in architecture was responsible for designing Mae West's streamlined home at 514. The architect was Richard Neutra, one of America's most important and innovative "modern" architects. Mae didn't even like the beach, indeed feared even the smallest amount of direct sunlight lest it flaw her alabaster skin. Still, she spent a fair amount of time at her seaside digs, since her companion of the last twenty-five years of her life, muscleman Paul Novak, preferred the beach to Miss West's opulent Hollywood apartment at Ravenswood. Unfortunately, a recent redo of Mae's former property has taken away much of its original architectural integrity.

Next door to Mae's place, writer Anita *(Gentlemen Prefer Blondes)* Loos once lived in another attractive Moderne manse, 506, with her writer/producer husband, John Emerson. A bit farther down the beach, Harold Lloyd and his family had the Colonial "cottage" at 443.

Last, but most assuredly not least, comes the great white hulk at 415, which has sat vacant since suffering considerable damage in the 1994 Northridge earthquake. Formerly a beach club and briefly a community center for the City of Santa Monica, which now owns the property, this is all that is left of the Gold Coast's grandest estate. Originally a 118-room compound of Georgian buildings called Ocean House, it all belonged to Marion Davies and William Randolph Hearst. Designed around 1926 by Julia Morgan, the Hearst/Davies headquarters consisted of a three-story main house, three guest houses, servants quarters, tennis courts, and swimming pools (one spanned by a Venetian marble footbridge). Just as Hearst had done at his "ranch" at San Simeon, he imported whole rooms from fabulous European villas to be reassembled at Ocean House. For parties—which sometimes had guest lists in the thousands!—Miss Davies would bring together the orchestras of several of L.A.'s top hotels, install carousels, and constantly create ingenious costume themes. Hollywood has never seen anything like the entertaining that went on here, before or since. When Hearst and Davies finally sold Ocean House (even Marion had come to call it a "white elephant" by that time) in the 1940s, the great estate went for a mere $600,000. Besides its initial cost in the millions of dollars, Marion said that she had spent another $7 million on the place during the fifteen or so years she had actively used it. After its sale, Ocean House became a beach club, later a hotel, until most of it was demolished in the mid-1950s. Today, there are plans to tear down even more of the estate, while the Santa Monica City Council debates the future of what was once the grandest beach house ever built in California.

There are several ways to see the Gold Coast. The most satisfying way is to do it on foot, which allows movie lovers to look at many of the mansions from both the street and the beach. Naturally, the occupants should never be disturbed! Another way to see some of these same houses is from Palisades Park, which overlooks the Gold Coast from the cliffs above.

13. WILL ROGERS STATE BEACH
Pacific Coast Highway at Chautauqua

Named for the famous humorist Will Rogers, this public Santa Monica beach has been a longtime favorite sun spot for the gay community. In 1989, Will Rogers received another kind of notoriety when it became the principal beach used in the TV series *Baywatch,* which featured some of Hollywood's hottest hunks (David Hasselhoff, for example) and sexiest babes (Pamela Anderson). The series spent almost a decade in Southern California, before heading to Hawaii in 1999—and an eventual long life on the syndication circuit. Back at Will Rogers, TV lovers will find the lifeguard tower and rescue boat used in the series, and on the still popular gay section of the beach, plenty of *Baywatch*-quality male eye candy.

14. SALKA VIERTEL HOUSE
165 Mabery Road

She collaborated on the screenplays of a number of Garbo's 1930s films, including *Queen Christina, Anna Karenina,* and *Conquest.* She also was one of Garbo's few close Hollywood friends—and the friendship lasted until her death in Switzerland in 1978. Her name was Salka Viertel, and in the 1930s and 1940s, she and her husband, director Berthold Viertel, had this pretty little place on a beautiful street leading down to the Pacific in an area known as the Santa Monica Canyon. This part of Santa Monica, with its ocean views and lush vegetation, has long been a favorite of English and European expatriates, many of whom once gathered at the Viertel house on a regular basis. Besides Garbo, those who frequented the Viertels were Bertolt Brecht, Igor Stravinsky, Thomas Mann, Aldous Huxley, and Christopher Isherwood.

In his book, *Tales from the Hollywood Raj* (Viking Press, 1984), Sheridan Morley quotes from the diary of a British actress on holiday in Hollywood in the 1930s. Of a dinner party at the Viertels', the actress had this to say: " 'Please do not dress up,' warned my hostess, 'and do not tell anyone you have been invited. Greta loathes meeting strangers and might not come.' . . .

She appeared at the door, witch's hat tilted over her forehead, and because the famous dark glasses were missing I saw her eyes boring into mine. Salka rushed forward crying, 'Greta, darling.' But Greta darling turned on her flat heels and vanished into the darkness with her hostess in hot pursuit. Shamelessly we bent our ears to catch a few words of the low-voiced altercation in the garden. Presently footsteps were heard but Mrs. Viertel reappeared alone and, pointing an accusing finger at me, said, 'You stupid girl, it's all your fault. I told you to stay on the couch where Greta would not be able to see you.' "

15. CEDRIC GIBBONS HOUSE
757 Kingman Avenue

MGM art director Cedric Gibbons—the man said to have sketched the original Oscar statuette for the Academy of Motion Picture Arts and Sciences—codesigned this stunning Art Deco residence in the Santa Monica Canyon with architect Douglas Honnold. Gibbons, who garnered eleven Oscars between 1929 and 1956, lived here in the 1930s with his Mexican movie-star wife Delores Del Rio. The house can be seen in all its Art Deco glory in the 1998 film noir *Twilight,* where it serves as Susan Sarandon and dying husband Gene Hackman's digs. In the film, Paul Newman is an aging detective who lives over the garage on the property.

16. WILL ROGERS STATE HISTORIC PARK
14253 Sunset Boulevard

The 187-acre Pacific Palisades estate of Will Rogers offers a glimpse of Hollywood at its most genteel. This is where the most civilized of picture people came on weekends to ride horses and to play polo on Rogers's 300-by-900-foot polo field. Old Hollywood's leading polo people were Leslie Howard, Jack Warner, Spencer Tracy, Darryl Zanuck, Walter Wanger, Robert Montgomery, Hal Roach, Walt Disney, Leo Carrillo, director Fred Niblo, pioneer cinematographer Clarence Brown, and, naturally, Will Rogers.

A former rodeo performer and later a Ziegfeld comedy star,

Legendary MGM art director Cedric Gibbons's Santa Monica showplace

Rogers came to Hollywood in 1919 to work for Samuel Gold-wyn. At first, the "Cowboy Philosopher" had only moderate success in silent films, but once the great American humorist got on the radio and into the talkies, his career soared. Rogers, an important figure in early Beverly Hills, bought his Pacific Palisades "ranch" in 1922 as a country place. In 1928, he moved there permanently with his wife and three children. He died eight years later at the age of fifty-five in the same plane crash that killed his famous globe-circling aviator friend, Wiley Post. Upon the death of Rogers's wife in 1944, the property became a state park.

The Will Rogers State Historic Park is open daily (except Thanksgiving, Christmas, and New Year's Day) from 8 a.m. to 5 p.m. It has hiking trails, picnic areas, and tours of Rogers's perfectly preserved thirty-one-room ranch house, which is filled with mementos of his career. Besides the fact that this beautiful house and property are open to the public, another tribute to Will Rogers is the polo that is still played here on weekends. Admission to the park and the polo matches is free, although there is a parking fee as well as a charge for the house tour. Visit www.parks.ca.gov.

17. THELMA TODD'S BEACH SIDEWALK CAFE SITE
17575 Pacific Coast Highway

Hollywood whodunit: About three miles north of Santa Monica's Gold Coast, a funky Spanish building edges the east side of the Pacific Coast Highway. Back in the mid-1930s, the building housed Thelma Todd's Beach Sidewalk Cafe, a racy roadhouse that was co-owned by a well-known movie comedian named Thelma Todd. Thirty years old, Miss Todd played wisecracking blondes opposite the Marx Brothers in *Monkey Business* (1931) and *Horse Feathers* (1932), appeared with Harry Langdon as well as Laurel and Hardy in several films, and starred in a series of comedies that paired her with Zasu Pitts and later Patsy Kelly.

So much for the bio. On the night of December 14, 1935, Miss Todd was guest of honor at a glamorous Hollywood party at the Trocadero nightclub. The party was hosted by comedian Stanley Lupino, father of actress Ida Lupino, who was also one of the guests. According to newspaper accounts at the time, Miss Todd was driven back to her home—it was located just above her restaurant—at around 4:20 a.m. on Sunday morning. The chauffeur supposedly dropped his passenger off in front of the restaurant and left her to negotiate the steps to her house on her own.

On Monday morning, the Ice Cream Blonde was discovered by her maid in her garage. She was still wearing her gown of Saturday evening, her diamonds, and her fur coat. She was seated at the driver's seat of her Lincoln Phaeton touring car—and she was dead. Although her face was streaked with blood, the coroner's report listed carbon monoxide poisoning as the cause of death. It was also decided that the bizarre demise of Thelma Todd was an accident.

To this day, Hollywood thinks otherwise. There were just too many unanswered questions, too many inconsistencies. For one thing, police ascertained that Miss Todd died at around 5:00 a.m. on Sunday morning. Yet, there were witnesses who claimed to have seen her driving her Lincoln on Sunday afternoon in the company of a "dark" gentleman companion. Another friend of Miss Todd's went on record as having spoken with her on the phone on that same Sunday afternoon; this same woman went on to say that she had invited Miss Todd to a party, which she had agreed to attend.

What really happened? One theory pins the blame for Miss Todd's death on the Mafia, who were said to have wanted to install an illicit gambling operation upstairs at Thelma's restaurant. When Miss Todd didn't play ball with the mob, they snuffed her out. A more widely believed explanation of the Todd case lists the prime suspect in this great unsolved mystery as Miss Todd's manager, business partner, and supposed lover. The man's name was Roland West and he had, among other things, made a living in Hollywood directing thrillers. Was Thelma Todd's murder his ultimate achievement? The 1991 TV movie *White Hot: The Mysterious Murder of Thelma Todd,* which starred Loni Anderson as Todd and Lawrence Pressman as West, came to that conclusion.

In recent years, the building that once housed Thelma Todd's Beach Sidewalk Cafe has been used as a center for the production of religious films of the Paulist religious order. Most recently, it was sporting a "for sale" sign.

18. MALIBU

In 1981, producer/director Blake Edwards took the ultimate of satirical looks at the oddities and excesses of what was then called "New Hollywood" in the film *S.O.B.* A sign of the times was that virtually none of *S.O.B.* took place in Hollywood—or even in Beverly Hills. Instead, almost all the action was centered in and around Malibu. About ten miles north of Santa Monica along the Pacific Coast Highway, this beach-edging town, officially a city since 1991, has some twenty-seven miles of coastline and some 27,800 residents. It also has far and away the greatest concentration of movie celebrities of any area of greater Los Angeles—or of the world, for that matter. Malibu residents include literally anybody who is anybody in today's motion picture/television/recording industries. The old-timers were the late Jack Lemmon, Walt Disney, Julie Andrews and Blake Edwards, Johnny Carson, Dick Clark, Farrah Fawcett, Ryan O'Neal, Larry Hagman, Goldie Hawn, Shirley MacLaine, Aaron Spelling, Robert Redford, Steven Spielberg, Bruce Willis and Demi

Moore (before they split), Cher, Barbra Streisand—all of whom once called, or still call, Malibu home, for either all or part of the year. Newer residents are Charlize Theron, John Cusack, Michael Eisner, and Courtney Cox.

The cost of even the simplest tear-down house is rarely under $2 million, and it's not unheard of for a place to go for over $25 million. Indeed, a recent sale on Encinal Bluffs topped $35 million, as billionaires buy out millionaries! Many people rent—and some pay between $20,000 and as much as $100,000 *a month* for the privilege of living in a Malibu maison. But nobody who lives here complains—not even about the fact that Malibu still has no sewer system. Besides the beach and the rugged mountains just behind it, the lures of Malibu are clean air, privacy, informality, and that heady feeling of knowing that you're living in just about the best place in the world (except perhaps during the occasional monsoon rains, when the Pacific Coast Highway gets flooded and the cliffs come tumbling down . . . and in extreme dry periods, when the hills are frequently aflame).

For sightseers, Malibu can be an elusive place, since so many of its beaches and star compounds are private. If this stellar community has a center, it might be the area known as the Colony. At the junction of the Pacific Coast Highway and Webb Way (just before the Malibu Canyon Road), the Colony is an ultraexclusive enclave of beach houses guarded by gates, barrier reefs, and a large security force. Intrepid movie lovers can drive by the backs of some of the Colony's houses along Malibu Road. The house with six garages was formerly Jack Warner's. Bing Crosby once lived at 1 Malibu Colony—as did Robert Redford and Bob Newhart. The Colony Crowd also includes Sting, Tom Hanks, Ted Danson, John McEnroe, and Olivia Newton-John.

If you're a serious celebrity spotter, the shopping center on the "public" side of the Colony gates is probably the best place to see some stars, especially at Wolfgang Puck's Granita restaurant, where Martin Scorsese, Ryan O'Neal, Diana Ross, Barbra Streisand, James Brolin, or David Geffen could well be dining at a nearby table. The Malibu Country Mart, on the other side of the Pacific Coast Highway, has more local hangouts, the smartest of which is currently the supercool Japanese restaurant Nobu, where some of Malibu's biggest names frequently turn up.

Malibu is not just the Colony. It includes private and semiprivate (depending on the tides) clusters of beach properties both to the south (at La Costa and Carbon beaches) and to the north. These days, it seems, the farther one ventures north, the choicer the address. Especially fashionable now are Paradise Cove, Point Dume, Broad Beach, Encinal Bluffs. Many of the poshest Malibu pads of all are not by the beaches, but rather in the canyons. The longtime Queen of the Canyons was Barbra Streisand, whose sizable tract in Ramirez Canyon is now a park (see item 19). Other famous canyon dwellers have been Kelsey Grammer, Stacy Keach, and Jack Nicholson—who is said to have once owned a good half of Decker Canyon off Yerba Buena Road almost at the Ventura County line. Then there's Brad Pitt and Jennifer Aniston, whose $11 million oceanfront retreat is so fashionably far north it's on the outskirts of Santa Barbara! Indeed, Santa Barbara may be the new Malibu. In addition to the Pitt-Anistons, Rob Lowe, Julia Louis-Dreyfus, and Oprah Winfrey all have bases there. Still, they're not the first Hollywood celebrities to have had that idea—the Ronald Reagans had a Santa Barbara ranch for years, which in the 1980s was immortalized as the Western White House.

19. RAMIREZ CANYON PARK
5750 Ramirez Canyon Road

Her intent was to create an "uplifting spiritual retreat," and between 1974 and 1993 Barbra Streisand transformed 22.5 acres of pristine Malibu canyon land into her own personal Eden, which she called the Ranch. Turning many of the property's simple existing buildings into showpieces of architecture and interior design, Streisand, for example, completely covered a modest stucco structure with old and aged wood to create the Barn, a three-bedroom home with a thirty-foot peaked ceiling that became the nouveau Arts and Crafts living quarters she shared with her then-partner hairdresser-turned-producer Jon Peters.

After doing up the Barn, Streisand converted a former stables into the Peach House, a Mediterranean villa, more pink than peach, which sported a guest apartment and a large living/screening room. The pièce de résistance of the Ranch, however, was

Streisand's Art Deco house, which the famously fastidious diva spent five years making perfect—right down to the tile floors that matched the design of the rugs that covered them and the two color-coordinated automobiles permanently parked in the driveway: a silver Rolls-Royce and a burgundy vintage Dodge roadster with rumble seat. Streisand originally planned to live in her Deco dream house, which was featured as a cover story in a 1993 edition of *Architectural Digest,* but after finding it a bit cold, she moved back to the Barn.

In the mid-1980s, when the original edition of this book was published, getting even a peek at Streisand's legendary canyon compound was virtually impossible, as this was one of Hollywood's most secluded and private of properties, hidden down back roads and camouflaged by thick foliage. The only giveaway that this was the Streisand Ranch was the handsome, electronically controlled Art Nouveau gate.

In the early 1990s, however, Ms. Streisand put the property on the market, supposedly for $19.5 million. According to Malibu realtors, she was not able to get anywhere near that, so she wound up donating the entire property (for an estimated $15

Barbra Streisand's Art Deco dream house

million in tax relief) to the Santa Monica Mountains Conservancy as a park. Today, the great news for movie lovers and Streisand fans is that Ramirez Canyon Park, as the Ranch is now called, offers a weekly tour of the superstar's former domain. This includes going inside four of the estate's five houses and a walk around most of the truly glorious grounds, where Streisand planted some one thousand trees and went so far as to reroute a stream so that she could hear the water. One of the outdoor highlights of the tour is the Meadow, a natural amphitheater backed by a terraced hillside of fruit trees, where in 1986 Barbra Streisand gave her first full-length concert in twenty years, the famous "One Voice" fund-raiser for the Democratic Party, which was captured by HBO.

The price of the Ramirez Canyon tour—currently $35—is expensive, but it's money well spent for a two-and-a-half-hour insider look at how one of the world's greatest stars once lived. Or, as writer Stephen Drucker, in a 2002 article on the Streisand property in *Travel + Leisure* magazine, put it: "If you want to know somebody famous, don't read *People* or *The National Enquirer*; look at her home. The furniture never lies."

The Ramirez Canyon Park tour is currently offered every Wednesday, from 1 to 3:30 p.m. It must be booked well ahead, for although it's not publicized, word has gotten out. For information and reservations, call 310–589–2850 or write Ramirez Canyon Park, 5750 Ramirez Canyon Road, Malibu CA 20365. In addition to the tours, the former Streisand Ranch can be booked for private parties, weddings, and other special functions. Visit www.LAMountains.com.

20. MALIBU CREEK STATE PARK
Las Virgenes Road

In 1940, director John Ford was all set to lens Richard Llewellyn's best-selling novel, *How Green Was My Valley*, for Twentieth Century–Fox. All Ford needed was a coal mining town in Wales. Needless to say, this was in the days when going on location overseas was practically unheard of—not to mention the fact that World War II was in full swing in Europe. So, in-

M*A*S*H set at Malibu Creek State Park

stead of going to Wales, Ford and Fox created a Welsh village in the Los Virgenes Canyon behind Malibu. The land used at the time belonged to a very exclusive mountaineering/country club called the Crags Mountain Club. In 1942, Fox again used the canyon for *My Friend Flicka;* and by 1946, the studio had bought some 2,300 acres of the property from the club and renamed it the Century Ranch.

The area making up the former Century Ranch is one of the most beautiful of Southern California and has been used over the last forty years by Fox as well as by other studios to depict the Old West, the jungles of Africa and Asia, foreign countries, alien planets. Some of the best-known Fox films that have been partially shot at the Century Ranch are *Viva Zapata* (1952), *The Rains of Ranchipur* (1955), *Love Is a Many-Splendored Thing* (1955), *Love Me Tender* (1959), *The Sand Pebbles* (1966), *Doctor Dolittle* (1967), *Planet of the Apes* (1968), *Beneath the Planet of the Apes* (1969), *Butch Cassidy and the Sundance Kid* (1969), *Tora! Tora! Tora!* (1970), *M*A*S*H* (1970), *Battle for the Planet of the Apes* (1973), *The Towering Inferno* (1974).

Non-Fox films done at the Ranch include: *Mr. Blandings Builds His Dream House* (RKO, 1948), *Ma and Pa Kettle* (Universal-International, 1949), *How the West Was Won* (MGM, 1962), *Finian's Rainbow* (Warner Seven Arts, 1970), and numerous MGM *Tarzans*.

Television has also used the ranch extensively—with *Daniel Boone, Custer, Lancer, Adventures in Paradise,* and the long-running TV version of *M*A*S*H* among the many series that have shot sequences here.

Although the Century Ranch became a State Park in 1974 (Twentieth Century–Fox sold it to the State of California that year for $4.8 million), the land is still frequently used for filming—especially for TV: *The X-Files, Cold Case, Diagnosis Murder, The Pretender, Buffy the Vampire Slayer,* and *Six Feet Under.* Recent features include *Murder by Numbers* (2000), *The Scorpion King* (2002), *Windtalkers* (2002), and *Pleasantville* (1998), for which director Gary Ross constructed the perfect 1950s American small town on the park's parking lot for his funny yet biting examination of the country's media-fueled values.

Mr. Blandings's dream house, Malibu Creek State Park

The *Pleasantville* set is gone, but for movie lovers, there are many interesting vestiges of the park's cinematic past to see first-hand. These include the house that portrayed Cary Grant and Myrna Loy's ideal Connecticut country place in the 1948 *Mr. Blandings Builds His Dream House* (it was built as a "real" house for a studio exec and is now a park headquarters sitting above the Camping Center near the park's entrance); the Rock Pool—veteran of many a jungle and Western adventure; the Visitor Center—which has a display of *M*A*S*H* memorabilia as well as photos of famous films and television shows shot at the Century Ranch; the Reagan Picnic Area—named after the famous American couple who once owned the property; and *M*A*S*H*'s Korean/Southern Californian hills.

Malibu Creek State Park is open daily from 8 a.m. to sunset. The area is vast: the Visitor Center with its M*A*S*H exhibit is almost a mile from the gatehouse parking lot; the Rock Pool is 1.1 miles from the same spot; the M*A*S*H hills, 2.5 miles; and the Reagan Picnic Area, 3.5 miles. To really enjoy Malibu Creek State Park, movie lovers should wear sturdy shoes, bring a picnic, and buy the map that is for sale at the main gate.

When coming from Malibu, the easiest way to reach Malibu Creek State Park is to turn right off the Pacific Coast Highway at Malibu Canyon Road, head north for about five miles until the road merges with Las Virgenes Road. The park entrance is another half-mile to the north. The ranch can also be reached from the San Fernando Valley by taking the Ventura Freeway to the Las Virgenes Road exit, then heading south along Las Virgenes. A visit to the park can also be combined with another great movie locale, the nearby Paramount Ranch (see Chapter 13, item 24).

Visit www.parks.ca.gov.

21. TORRANCE HIGH SCHOOL
2200 West Carson Street

Northwest of Los Angeles International Airport, Torrance is one of those faceless Southern California communities of middle-class tract houses that few tourists have ever heard of, much less visited. Its biggest claim to fame is the sprawling Del Almo

Shopping Mall, which is hardly reason to make a detour. TV addicts might consider one, however, to check out Torrance High School, which thanks to its relative obscurity and generic American high-school architecture makes an ideal and uncomplicated location. No wonder the Spelling people cast Torrance in the role of West Beverly Hills High for their series *Beverly Hills 90210*, since the real Beverly Hills High had too many restrictions regarding filming on campus. In 1997, Torrance was again a TV star, this time as Sunnydale High School in the creepy-campy *Buffy the Vampire Slayer* series.

Visit www.torrancehigh.com.

22. COWBOY COUNTRY BAR
3321 South Street, Long Beach

Ridley Scott's 1991 buddy/road movie *Thelma and Louise* broke new ground by making the buddies two women (Geena Davis and Susan Sarandon) on the run for shooting a would-be rapist

Thelma and Louise cowboy:
Brad Pitt

Thelma and Louise trouble spot: Cowboy Country Bar, Long Beach

(Timothy Carhart) in the parking lot of a country and western bar. The bar and parking lot where it all took place was this barn of a club with a location manager's dream of a huge parking lot in a small mall in Long Beach. Besides boosting the bankability of Davis and especially Sarandon, the film is also notable for launching the career of a handsome young actor whose performance as an ingenuous cowboy–con man had "movie star" written all over it. The actor: Brad Pitt.

Visit www.cowboycountry.mu.

23. THE *QUEEN MARY*
1126 Queen's Highway

Built in 1936, the great Cunard liner the *Queen Mary* ruled the North Atlantic—both as a posh passenger ship and, during World War II, as a very important troop transport—for almost thirty years. Cunard withdrew the great but no longer profitable ship from service in the 1960s to make way for its more modern and fuel-efficient *Queen Elizabeth 2*. For a while, the *Queen Mary*'s future was up for grabs. To the surprise of many skeptics, the City of Long Beach purchased what was considered a white elephant and turned it into a hotel, conference center, and tourist attraction. Happily for Hollywood, the *Queen Mary*'s new permanent location gave the studios a full-fledged ocean liner to use whenever the script called for one. Since 1967, the proud fixture in Long Beach Harbor has appeared in several hundred films, TV shows, and commercials. Among the more notable have been *Mame* (1974), *Farewell, My Lovely* (1975), *W. C. Fields and Me* (1976), *Goliath Awaits* (1981), *The Natural* (1984), *Treacherous Crossing* (1992), *Chaplin* (1992), *Batman Forever* (1995), *The Cable Guy* (1996), *L.A. Confidential* (1997), and *Pearl Harbor* (2001).

And long before the *QM1* was removed from active service as an ocean liner, it (or a movie-set version) appeared in films such as *Dodsworth* (1936), *Foreign Correspondent* (1940), and *Meet*

Queen Mary, Long Beach

Danny Wilson (1952), which starred Frank Sinatra and Shelley Winters, who, ironically, would be nominated for an Academy Award some twenty years later for her role in another film that used the *Queen Mary* as a location—*The Poseidon Adventure.*

In 2004, Cunard launched the *Queen Mary 2,* the largest, longest, tallest, widest, and most expensive oceangoing vessel ever built. So far though, the *QM2* hasn't been used for any films—but stay tuned.

Visit www.queenmary.com.

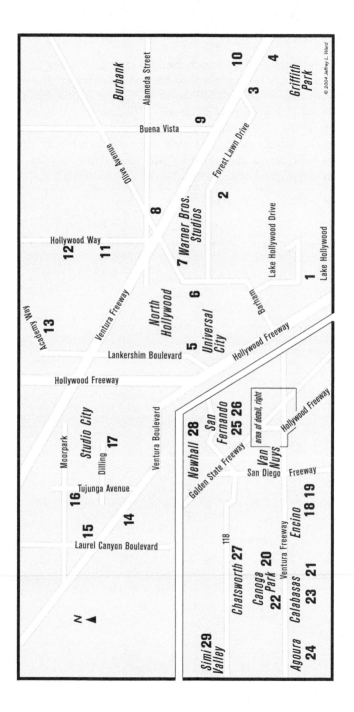

San Fernando Valley: The Big Spread

There is Los Angeles . . . and there is the Valley. The latter, roughly speaking, is everything on the other side of the Santa Monica Mountains and Hollywood Hills—that is, the seemingly endless sprawl of mostly middle-class communities characterized by tract houses, shopping centers, right-wing politics, "Valley Girls," and—surprise—movie studios. In fact, what with Disney, Universal, Warner Bros., DreamWorks SKG, CBS, and NBC Television all based in San Fernando Valley towns, the Valley is today responsible for more moviemaking and television production than any other area of Los Angeles.

The first moviemaker to see the potential of this vast and, at the time, sparsely populated stretch of countryside was Carl Laemmle, the founder of Universal. Laemmle came to California from New York in 1912 and first operated out of Hollywood. When success enabled him to build the studio of his dreams, he found the perfect location for it on the other side of the Hollywood Hills in the township of Lankershim. There, in 1914, he turned a 230-acre chicken ranch into the legendary Universal City. First National was another early film company to cross over the Hollywood Hills and into the Valley when it built a big studio in Burbank in 1918. Warner Bros. eventually bought out

First National and the same Burbank lot has been Warner Bros. headquarters ever since.

As Los Angeles prospered in the 1920s and its population and real estate values soared, the Valley—which was developed several decades later than Los Angeles proper—became an extremely attractive "Hollywood" alternative for many studios. When Mark Sennett outgrew his Silverlake facilities in the late 1920s, for example, he didn't look for another lot in crowded Silverlake or Hollywood but instead headed for the wide-open spaces of Studio City. A decade later, Walt Disney followed suit and moved from Silverlake to Burbank. At the same time, a number of Hollywood studios established and maintained annexes in the Valley; these were called "ranches" and, appropriately, were often used for the production of Western films. Not to be outdone, stars and moguls purchased Valley ranches, too, and horsey weekends in the country became the rage.

Today, not only the studios but some of the movie ranches in the San Fernando Valley are still going strong. Of particular interest to the movie lover is the fact that two of the greatest studios—Universal and Warner Bros.—offer tours to the public, as does NBC's television complex. Besides studios, the Valley has other fascinating and sometimes offbeat connections to movie history. A few of them: the ranch that a great silent star willed to his community as a public park; the housing development that once was Clark Gable's estate; the battlefield of *The Birth of a Nation;* a museum dedicated to a certain movie star who became president of the United States; and the final resting place of everyone from Bette Davis to Fred Astaire and Ginger Rogers to Bob Hope.

Figure on a good half day for the Warner Bros. VIP Tour and as much as a full day for the Universal Tour and all the other attractions included in the price of admission, so movie lovers will have to budget the rest of their Valley sightseeing accordingly. The William S. Hart Park, the Ronald Reagan Presidential Library and Museum, and the Oakwood Memorial Park and Cemetery are all quite far afield, which should also be taken into account when planning your itinerary.

1. LAKE HOLLYWOOD

One of the biggest surprises in the Hollywood Hills, Lake Hollywood is the name of the reservoir formed by the Mulholland Dam, which was built in 1925. The dam is named—as is the Hollywood Hills' main East-West roadway—for William Mulholland, the head of the Los Angeles Water Department in the early part of the twentieth century and the man who engineered the aqueduct that brought water to Los Angeles and to the San Fernando Valley from some 233 miles away in the Owens Valley. The story of how certain unscrupulous speculators tricked the farmers of the Owens Valley into giving up their water rights so that real estate fat cats in L.A. could get rich is one of the ugliest in the history of Los Angeles.

The 1974 Academy Award–winning film *Chinatown* takes on this very subject and fictionalizes the corrupt games that developers played with government officials in order to bring water to their real estate. Although fiction, it is interesting to note that in this grizzly Roman Polanski–directed film, the character of the Los Angeles water commissioner is named Hollis Mulwray—and you don't have to be Agatha Christie to figure what *Chinatown*'s writer, Robert Towne, may have been getting at.

Chinatown even uses Lake Hollywood as a location. Early on in the picture, the aforementioned Hollis Mulwray is found dead along the shores of the lake the real William Mulholland helped create. The same location also provides drama for another 1974 movie, *Earthquake*. In this Universal disaster epic, the Mulholland Dam cracks open, spilling millions of gallons of water down into a city that's already having a pretty rough go of things.

The irony of it all is that despite its turbulent history—both in real life and in the movies—Lake Hollywood is an extremely beautiful spot where locals can be found jogging around its fenced-in shores. One of the easiest ways to reach the lake is to take Lake Hollywood Drive off of Barham Boulevard on the north (Burbank) side of the Hollywood Hills. Beyond the lake, Canyon Lake Drive leads to some of the best views of the Hollywood Sign as well as of a fabulous former home of Madonna, a great Moorish fortress with red-and-yellow striped walls that can be seen dominating the hillside off to the right.

2. FOREST LAWN MEMORIAL PARK HOLLYWOOD HILLS
6300 Forest Lawn Drive, Burbank

Smaller and not as well known as its over-the-top cousin in Glendale, the Hollywood Hills branch of this famous Southern California funeral institution celebrates America. Here, visitors will find full-sized replicas of such historic U.S. places of worship as Boston's Old North Church and Henry Wadsworth Longfellow's Church of the Hills meetinghouse in New England as well as a monster mosaic combining twenty-five famous paintings depicting major events in the country's early history.

This cemetery also celebrates Hollywood with a significant number of stars and industry VIPs interred here. The current headliner is Bette Davis, whose large tomb off to the left at the entrance to the Court of Remembrance is hard to miss. Inscribed on her tombstone: "She did it the hard way." Her mother, Ruth Favor Davis, and sister, Barbara Davis Berry, are buried here as well, but with decidedly lower billing.

Bette Davis memorial,
Forest Lawn Memorial Park

Vying with Davis for the largest memorial in the Court of Remembrance is that of (Wladzio Valentin) Liberace, the campy pianist who did the outrageous wardrobe thing long before Elton John. Born in 1919, Liberace, who never publicly owned up to his homosexuality, died of AIDS in 1987.

One big star who made a brief Forest Lawn appearance in the Court of Remembrance was Lucille Ball, whose ashes were interred here in 1989, but removed in 2000, and taken to the Hunt-Ball family plot in her hometown of Jamestown, New York, as part of the city's ongoing tribute to—and marketing of—its most famous native daughter.

In addition to all the film people buried here—others include Buster Keaton, Charles Laughton, Stan Laurel, Ernie Kovaks, George Raft, Freddie Prinze, the Nelsons (Ozzie, Harriet, and Ricky), *James Bond* producer Albert R. Broccoli, and *Woody Woodpecker* creator Walter Lantz—the hillside on which Forest Lawn rests has special significance in the history of the American cinema. For it was here that in 1914, D. W. Griffith shot most of the battle sequences for his own epic look at the country, *The*

Replica of Boston's Old North Church: Forest Lawn Memorial Park

Birth of a Nation. Veteran cameraman Karl Brown, in his *Adventures with D. W. Griffith* (Farrar, Straus & Giroux, 1973) was there for the filming and describes the location as "ideal . . . photographically. A sort of ridge of high ground curved around the rim of a gently descending slope of clear ground that ran down to where the dry-as-dust riverbed of the Los Angeles River lay baking in the sun. There were little clumps of trees clustered on both sides of this open area, with small hills rounding up here and there in the background to provide splendid locations for artillerymen to rake the field with grape and canister, the two favorite close-range charges of the Civil War cannoneers."

Today, even when viewed from the road, the hillside looks just as Brown described it.

Forest Lawn Hollywood is open from 8 a.m. to 5 p.m. daily. A map—with no star names—can be requested at the entrance. Depending on who's on duty, you may or may not be able to get further directions. The groundskeepers are usually helpful, however. Visit www.forestlawn.com.

D. W. Griffith directing real Civil War veterans in *Birth of a Nation* battle scene, 1914

Bette Davis's Glendale home

3. BETTE DAVIS PICNIC GROUND
Riverside Drive at Victory Boulevard, Burbank

At the northeast end of L.A.'s vast Griffith Park lies a lovely little picnic grounds with tables shaded by California oak trees
along the edge of the (usually dry) Los Angeles River. At the border of Burbank and Glendale, this is a convenient spot for a
sightseeing break or perhaps a BYO fast-food lunch. The fact
that the picnic area bears Bette Davis's name is not thanks to a
generous bequest to Griffith Park in her will. Park officials report
it's simply because they knew that Davis once had a house
nearby in Glendale and that she frequently rode horses stabled at
the park's adjacent Equestrian Center.

4. MUSEUM OF THE AMERICAN WEST
4700 Western Heritage Way, Griffith Park

Although he is best known as a movie cowboy, Gene Autry
(1907–1998) was one of Hollywood's consummate renaissance
men: film star, TV and radio personality, singer, songwriter
("Here Comes Santa Claus" and "Rudolph the Red Nosed Rein-

deer" were among his three-hundred-plus popular tunes), and media mogul, with an empire that encompassed television and radio stations, film production companies, and at one point, the California Angels baseball team.

Born in Texas, Autry had a genuine love for the West, and his dream was to share that love and his appreciation of the region's history with the world. To that end, he gave some $54 million to establish the Autry Museum of Western Heritage, which opened in Griffith Park in 1988. Now regarded as one of the country's premier institutions involved in preserving and interpreting the traditions of the U.S. West, the Autry Museum has an impressive collection of art and artifacts that include Frederic Remington sculptures, Albert Bierstadt paintings, Native American ceramics, Spanish colonial armor, and much much more, what with a recent merger with L.A.'s esteemed Southwest Museum whereby the two institutions now share each other's treasures as well as a new name: the Museum of the American West.

Frequent special exhibitions focus on a particular aspect of the West and its history, such as the Gold Rush, African American cowboys, Jewish cowboys, and celluloid Western icons. Appropriately, the museum has a section documenting the media career of its famous founder. Rounding out the attractions are film showings and a series of summer concerts in the open-air plaza.

For information on museum programs and exhibitions, call 323-667-2000 or visit www.autry-museum.org.

5. UNIVERSAL STUDIOS
100 Universal City Plaza, Universal City

All over Southern California, huge billboards, TV and radio commercials, and newspaper and magazine ads proclaim the Universal Studios Tour. More than a tourist attraction, the Universal Tour has become a Hollywood institution—since for almost forty years, it has been one of the few recognized places in town where the glamour and excitement of moviemaking have been packaged for public consumption. Whereas all (with the exception of two) of the other major studios do their best to keep

Universal Studios gate, 2004

the public on the other side of their walls and gates, Universal welcomes the world with open arms and cash registers (current price of admission for anyone over four feet tall: $49.75!). The tour makes the studio millions of dollars, and taking a cue from its rival Disneyland, Universal has opened similar movie-studio theme parks in Orlando, Florida, and Osaka, Japan.

Serious movie buffs may find the Universal Tour too commercial—but if one overlooks the fluff, it can be amusing and informative. Riding with 175 other people in a Super Tram, one not only gets a close-up look at the largest back lot left in Los Angeles but is also treated to a whole series of crowd-pleasing "extras," most of them based on Universal blockbusters. These range from a frightening encounter with the dinosaurs of *Jurassic Park* to narrowly escaping a *WaterWorld* tidal wave to a bit of *Back to the Future* time-traveling. The newest attraction is a "multisensory" *Shrek* film in 4-D. In addition to these adventures, the tour visits special effects stages to unlock some of the secrets of *Jurassic Park, Gladiator,* and *The Mummy.*

After the tour is over, there's still more for the intrepid sight-seer to experience at Universal—what with all the live-action shows being performed nonstop by actors, stuntpeople, trained animals, ghoulish monsters, and magicians. One of the newest of these is "Spider-Man Rocks," a rock 'n' roll show inspired by the comic-book-character–turned–movie hero. On a quieter note, *I Love Lucy* fans will want to visit the Lucy Museum, housed in the former studio bungalow of Lucille Ball, who spent most of her post-Desilu years based on the Universal lot.

Today's wildly successful Universal Studios Tour began in 1963 when studio management decided to boost business at the commissary by allowing a tour company to drive tourists around the lower back lot and then drop them off at the commissary for lunch. The following year, the tour debuted in earnest. However, the tradition of allowing the public on the Universal lot actually goes back all the way to 1915. At that time, Universal's founder, Carl Laemmle, had just turned a 230-acre chicken ranch into his studio. Besides making movies, the enterprising Mr. Laemmle made even more money by letting the locals sit in bleachers he had set up around some of the outdoor stages. Here, for 25 cents

Universal Studios Tour, 1975

a head, anyone could watch directors of the day putting actors through their paces.

Extremely popular back in those days were Universal's Westerns, which together with adventure reels comprised much of the studio's early product. The top stars in Universal's early years were Hoot Gibson, Mae Murray, Laura LaPlante, and Priscilla Dean. Directors included Erich von Stroheim, John Ford, and William Wyler (Laemmle's nephew). Universal was the studio where Irving Thalberg worked before moving over to MGM and where Columbia's Harry Cohn had his first job in the film business.

An early Universal standby was the "woman's picture." Master of these early-thirties tearjerkers was director John Stahl. His most famous films—*Back Street* (1932), *Imitation of Life* (1934), and *Magnificent Obsession* (1935)—would all be remade at Universal by producer Ross Hunter, often with director Douglas Sirk, in the fifties and sixties.

Universal's biggest contribution to the history of cinema, however, may well be its perfection of the great American horror film. One of Universal's first big successes with this genre had Lon Chaney scaring the wits out of the world in *The Phantom of the Opera* (1925). Later, Bela *"Dracula"* Lugosi and Boris *"Frankenstein"* Karloff would join the studio's fright brigade. And with the release of *Van Helsing* (2004), featuring both Dracula and Frankenstein's monster, Universal is embarking on a drive to bring many of its old monsters back to the screen for contemporary audiences.

Back in the mid-1930s, however, even Boris and Bela were unable to bail the studio out of some serious financial difficulties—and it would be a teenager named Deanna Durbin who saved Universal from bankruptcy with a string of light, low-budget musicals. More help came in the 1940s with the comedies of Bud Abbott and Lou Costello, the Arabian Nights romances of Jon Hall and Maria Montez, Basil Rathbone's *Sherlock Holmes* series, the *Ma and Pa Kettle*s, and Donald O'Connor's numerous films pairing him with Francis the Talking Mule.

By the end of the 1950s, however, Universal (now called Universal-International after a merger in 1946 with International Pictures) was again in financial trouble. It was saved this time by

A Harry Carey Western being shot at Universal in 1916

MCA—the talent agency that had become a very successful producer of television series. Needing more space for its television subsidiary, Revue Productions, MCA bought the Universal lot in 1959 and acquired the whole studio several years later. Since then, Universal has been one of Hollywood's greatest success stories, and that success is largely owing to its extensive involvement in television. In fact, so much filming went on at Universal in the 1960s and 1970s that this was the only studio in town that functioned like the traditional movie studio of Hollywood's grand days of the 1930s and 1940s. Until 1978, for example— long after all the other studios had dropped them—Universal still had a vital talent-development system that gave promising young actors and actresses the traditional seven-year contracts of Old Hollywood. Among the television stars that grew up and out of the Universal contract system are Sharon Gless, James Brolin, Katharine Ross, Gary Collins, Susan Saint James, and Lee Majors.

Besides television, Universal also remained strong in the feature-film department. Among its great successes in the last decades have been all of Alfred Hitchcock's later films (the *Psy-*

cho house is one of the tour's top sights), *To Kill a Mockingbird, The Sting* (its Chicago street is another back-lot attraction), *Earthquake, Animal House,* and Steven Spielberg's super-hits *Jaws* and *E.T.*

The studio has not been immune to the takeovers and mergers that have characterized late-twentieth-century Hollywood. Its most recent owner was the European media conglomerate Vivendi, but in mid-2004, the studio was acquired by NBC in a $14 billion deal, and its official name was changed to NBC Universal. No matter who owns the studio, of all its successes, the greatest of all may well be that $49.75-a-pop tour.

The Universal Studios Tour operates every day—except Thanksgiving and Christmas. Price: $49.75; $39.75 for those under 48 inches tall. For information and tickets, call 800-UNIVERSAL or visit www.universalstudios.com. For tickets to television shows taped before live audiences at Universal, call 818-753-3470. Visit http://themeparks.universalstudios.com.

6. THE SMOKE HOUSE
4420 Lakeside Drive, Burbank

Lying in the shadow of the towering walls of Warner Bros. Studios just across Olive Avenue, this California-Tudor roadhouse has served as the aforementioned studios' unofficial commissary since 1946. Besides all the showbiz buzz—especially at lunchtime—the Smoke House is also famous for its garlic bread and its beef. Try the Steak Sinatra—named for guess-who's favorite entrée—pieces of filet sautéed with tomatoes, onions, and bell peppers.

Call 818-845-3731 or visit www.smokehouserestaurant.net.

7. WARNER BROS. STUDIOS
4000 Warner Boulevard, Burbank

One of Hollywood's best-kept secrets is the Warner Bros. Studios VIP Tour—which, unlike other studios' VIP tours, is open to the public. The tour is expensive (currently $35), serious, and limited

First National Studios in the 1920s

to no more than twelve people, none of whom may be less than eight years old. For movie lovers, however, this tour is a must because it offers the rare opportunity to see the workings of one of Hollywood's most historic studios up close.

The history of the Warner Bros. Studios began in 1918 when the lot was built by First National—an important early film company that featured the talents of Norma Talmadge, Constance Talmadge, Corinne Griffith, Anita Stewart, Hedda Hopper, Charles Chaplin, Buster Keaton, Pola Negri, Colleen Moore, Richard Barthelmess, Jackie Coogan, Barbara La Marr, Mary Astor, Alla Nazimova, Ronald Colman, and Mickey McGuire (later Rooney).

In 1927, after Warner Bros. had revolutionized the motion picture industry with the sound success of *The Jazz Singer,* they took over First National and spent millions redoing the studio's Burbank lot for talkies. Thus, from the late 1920s up until the present, the history of the lot is largely the history of Warner Bros. In the 1930s, Warner Bros. was known for gangster films, serious social dramas, Busby Berkeley's black-and-white musicals, and Paul Muni's biography (Emile Zola, Louis Pasteur) pictures. The studio was also known for being able to turn out pictures of great technical polish on extremely tight budgets. Queen of the lot was Bette Davis, who in 1936 became embroiled in a history-making legal battle with the studio when she refused to do roles the studio demanded she play. Although Miss Davis lost in court, she ultimately won the respect of the brothers Warner and continued to be the studio's top star. Other big names at Warner Bros. in the 1930s were Humphrey Bogart, James Cagney, Edward G. Robinson, Errol Flynn, Joan Blondell, Ann Sheridan, Olivia de Havilland, Dick Powell, and Marion Davies (whose fourteen-room MGM "bungalow" was moved from Culver City to Burbank when she changed studios in the mid-thirties).

In the forties, Ida Lupino, Paul Henreid, Ronald Reagan, John Garfield, Peter Lorre, Sydney Greenstreet, and Alexis Smith all became firmly entrenched in the Warner Bros. pantheon. It was also at Warners that Joan Crawford made her post-MGM "comeback" pictures, the most notable of these being *Mildred Pierce,* for which she won an Oscar in 1945. The late forties and early fifties was the era of the Doris Day Technicolor musical at the studio, and the mid-fifties saw James Dean achieve screen immortality with just three films *(East of Eden, Rebel Without a Cause,* and *Giant),* all done at Warner Bros.

One of the great pleasures of the Warner Bros. VIP Tour is the chance to see the lot on which so many memorable Warner Bros. pictures were filmed. "French Street," for example, will bring back memories of the Paris flashbacks in *Casablanca.* More déjà vu at "Brownstone Street"—setting for innumerable gangster films in the thirties and forties as well as home to Murphy Brown's Washington, D.C., residence in the TV series of the same name and Dr. Mark Greene's Chicago apartment in *ER.* On Hennesy Street, which was built in 1982 for the film *Annie,* the 1920s-style New York tenements have been used for *Spider-Man, Minority Report, Bugsy, Dick Tracy,* and as Gotham City in three *Batman* films. Midwest Street, complete with a small white church and matching courthouse, was River City, Iowa, for *The Music Man* and has been seen in *Rebel Without a Cause, Bonnie and Clyde, The Shootist* and in the TV shows *The Waltons, The Dukes of Hazzard, Growing Pains, Sisters, ER,* and *Gilmore Girls.* And practically all of the Warner lot was used to represent the Oliver Niles Studios in the 1954 Judy Garland–James Mason film *A Star Is Born.*

The VIP tour also visits some of Warners' historic sound-stages, such as Stage 16, where *Casablanca, Rebel Without a*

Cause, The Treasure of Sierra Madre, Ocean's 11, My Fair Lady, Camelot, and the three *Batman* films were shot. On Stage 23, there's the Oval Office used on *The West Wing,* whereas Stage 11 has the *ER* examination rooms. Besides seeing the sights, the VIP Tour goes—whenever possible—onto "live" soundstages where films or TV shows are being shot. If any "scoring" is being done at the time of the tour, the participants will be taken into a soundproof control room to witness how technicians match the music of a live orchestra (on the other side of the glassed-in room) to a film sequence that is projected over the heads of the musicians. It's a fascinating process—and one that outsiders are rarely permitted to see.

Today, Warner Bros. is part of the Time-Warner media empire.

The Warner Bros. Studios VIP Tour is given at regular intervals Monday through Friday. The current cost is $35 per person—and no children under eight years old are permitted. Reservations are necessary and should be made several weeks in advance, although last-minute openings occasionally occur. Call 818–972–TOUR. For tickets to attend tapings of Warner Bros. television shows—such as The Drew Carey Show, The George Lopez Show, Everybody Loves Raymond—*call 818–753–3470 or visit www.studio-tour.com.*

8. NBC TELEVISION STUDIOS
3000 West Alameda Avenue, Burbank

Welcome to "Beautiful Downtown Burbank!" Fans of *Rowan & Martin's Laugh-In* will remember that this expression put both Burbank and its NBC TV studios on the map back in the late 1960s. In addition to the *Laugh-In* connection, audiences may also know of NBC's Burbank base through its longtime association with *The Tonight Show.*

Designed to let the public experience its studios firsthand, NBC offers a seventy-minute walking tour of its facilities. Billed as a "totally unstaged tour of a giant broadcasting complex," this walk around NBC covers dressing rooms, set construction and wardrobe departments, newsrooms, plus visits to the *Days of Our Lives* set and the tiny studio used for *The Tonight Show.*

In 2004, NBC acquired Universal's movie, television, and theme park operations (owned at the time by the French media conglomerate Vivendi) in a deal estimated at $14 billion. The company has been renamed NBC Universal.

The tour is offered daily at regular intervals, usually between 9 a.m. and 3 p.m., weekdays; cost $7.50 for adults, $4.00 for children, $6.75 for seniors. For tickets to television shows originating from the NBC Burbank Studios, the ticket counter at NBC is open daily. Tickets for The Tonight Show *are available only on the day of the show and are distributed on a first-come first-served basis—so it is essential to be at the booth early. For further information, call 818-840-3537.*

9. THE WALT DISNEY COMPANY
500 South Buena Vista, Burbank

Mickey and the gang moved from Walt's small headquarters on Hyperion Avenue in Silverlake to this big Burbank studio in 1940. Mickey, however, had nothing to do with the move. Blame it all on *Snow White*—for it was the tremendous success of this first-ever feature-length animated film that enabled the Disney Brothers (Walt was the artist, Roy the businessman) to greatly expand their operations.

The new Burbank studios were designed with artists in mind: Most rooms had windows that would admit only north light, and since drawing and sketching were such sedentary activities, there were Ping-Pong tables, horseshoes, and a volleyball court so that the Disney artists could exercise during breaks. According to Los Angeles artist and former Disney employee Tony Duquette, "All the best artists in town worked for Disney—especially during the Depression—because it was the one place where an artist could get paid for being an artist." It wasn't all idyllic, however, for in 1941, Disney animators went on strike, protesting the studio's authoritarian rule. A number of this group eventually resigned and went on to form a new company called United Productions of America.

Despite its labor problems at the beginning of the decade, Disney continued to flourish during the forties, with hits like

Dumbo, Bambi, and *Song of the South.* Disney also became involved in nonanimated film projects and went on to produce such classic family fare as *Treasure Island, 20,000 Leagues Under the Sea, Old Yeller, Swiss Family Robinson, The Shaggy Dog* series, and *Mary Poppins.* When he died in 1966, Walt Disney had won more Academy Awards than any other individual in the history of the motion picture industry. His record number of twenty-six Oscars still stands.

The years following Walt Disney's death were difficult ones for the studio. Racked by internal power struggles and weakened by lackluster releases, Disney found itself a prime target for a hostile corporate takeover in 1984. To make a long story short, the Disney board of directors managed to fight off a takeover by notorious corporate raider Saul Steinberg in the final hour, but realized that big changes were necessary for the studio to survive.

One of the biggest of these was bringing in former Paramount president Michael Eisner as chairman and CEO of the company. Quickly, under Eisner's direction, Disney's fortunes and profile started to rise. In addition to focusing on producing adult pic-

Disney Studios gate, Burbank

tures on modest budgets through its Touchstone division—
Down and Out in Beverly Hills (1986), *Pretty Woman* (1990),
and *Sister Act* (1992), for example—Eisner took Disney back to
its roots and ultimate strength: the animated feature film. Often
using the latest in computer technology (a development that
has begun to spell the demise of the traditional two-dimensional
animation artist), the studio started churning out some of its
most successful animated movies ever: *Beauty and the Beast*
(1991) and *The Lion King* (1994, 1998) and *Toy Story* (1995,
1999—with Pixar Animation Studios). Not only that, Disney
found gold on Broadway by turning some of these animated successes into hit legit musicals—starting with *Beauty and the Beast*
and most notably with *The Lion King,* with companies playing
all over the world.

In 2003–2004, however, Eisner's fortunes were reversed when
the Disney board as well as its stockholders began doubting his
leadership as well as his huge bonuses at a time when the company was experiencing another slump. In March 2004, the situation came to a head and Eisner was voted out of his position as
chairman of the board, although he remained CEO of the company. Six months later, he announced that he would not stay on
as chief executive past 2006.

No matter what the future holds for the demoted executive,
Eisner's legacy can be seen back in Burbank at the Disney studios, where at the height of his power he called on the talents of
classy architect Robert A. M. Stern to design dramatic new
buildings for company's old headquarters. The most impressive
of these is the Feature Animation Building, where gigantic statues of the Seven Dwarfs hold up the neoclassical roof as if it were
an ancient Greek temple. Not open to the public—don't even
think about crossing through the handsome gate with the stylized palm trees on Alameda Avenue to take a photo!—the studio
and the spectacular Feature Animation Building can easily be
seen from the street. For a far closer encounter with the Disney
magic, however, head down to Anaheim, some forty freeway
minutes south, where the original Disneyland remains one of
Southern California's top attractions.

Visit http://disney.go.com/studiooperations/index.html.

10. DREAMWORKS SKG STUDIOS
1000 Flower Street, Glendale

Founded in 1994 by a triumvirate of Hollywood heavyweights—
Steven Spielberg, Jeffrey Katzenberg, and David Geffen—this
relatively young studio has focused mainly on Speilberg-directed
and/or produced features and Katzenberg-managed animated
fare. (Geffen takes care of the business side of things.) Thus far
some of DreamWorks SKG's biggest hits have been *Saving Private Ryan* (1998), *Catch Me If You Can* (2002), and *Minority
Report* (2002), whereas the *Shrek* series has proved a gold mine
for the animation division. This reportedly has not thrilled Disney's Michael Eisner, with whom Katzenberg, after a ten-year
stint as head of production at Disney, had a much publicized
falling-out when he bolted the studio to cofound the rival
DreamWorks SKG. An austere, neo–Mission-style complex, built
on the Burbank-Glendale border on land that was once the Glendale Airport, is the studio's stylish headquarters. And in case
you're wondering what the SKG stands for, think Spielberg,
Katzenberg, and Geffen.

Visit www.dreamworks.com.

11. WARNER BROS. STUDIOS RANCH
3701 West Oak Street, Burbank

For back-lot voyeurs, a walk around the high fence of this little-
known movie ranch in the middle of a Burbank residential area
will reveal such delights as a dilapidated train that's a veteran of
numerous Western films, the tower of the Old North Church set
from *1776* (1972), and the unglamorous backs of all sorts of
movie-set façades. Acquired by Harry Cohn's Columbia Studios
in the late 1920s, the Columbia Ranch (as it was known up to
the 1970s) was where the exterior sequences of many Columbia
pictures—*Mr. Deeds Goes to Town* (1936), *You Can't Take It
with You* (1938), *Mr. Smith Goes to Washington* (1939), and
The Three Stooges series—were shot. It was here, too, where the
plane-crash sequence of Frank Capra's *Lost Horizon* (1937) was
lensed. Stanley Kramer's *High Noon* (1952) was also done here.

The ranch was especially important to Columbia in the 1950s when it came to be used heavily for television production. Columbia was the first of the major studios to meet the challenge of television head-on. Whereas some studios tried to fight the new medium by not permitting their films to be sold to TV and, in some instances, not even allowing a television set to appear as a prop in their films—Columbia formed its Screen Gems division in 1949 with the expressed purpose of turning out product for the small screen. Some of the most famous TV series shot here were *Bewitched, The Partridge Family,* and *Leave It to Beaver*—all of which used the ranch's all-American suburban housing tract, surrounding a tree-filled park and swimming pool.

Warner Bros. purchased the Ranch in 1972 and has continued to use it for TV—the *Friends* fountain is on the lot—and for features. Again, that suburban street set is extremely popular and versatile, serving as Connecticut for *The Witches of Eastwick* (1987), Los Angeles for the *Lethal Weapon* films (1987–1998), and Anywhere U.S.A. for the street on which the famously dysfunctional Burnham family (Kevin Spacey, Annette Bening, and Thora Birch) lived in the 1999 Oscar-winning film *American Beauty.*

12. BOB HOPE AIRPORT
2627 Hollywood Way, Burbank

The former Burbank-Glendale-Pasadena Airport was renamed in 2004 in honor of longtime Valley resident Bob Hope, who not only kept his private jet there, but who was reportedly always a little jealous of the fact that John Wayne had an airport named after him down in Orange County.

Inaugurated in 1930, the Burbank Airport was L.A.'s major commercial air terminal up until 1947. It was then that most passenger carriers started using the larger Los Angeles Municipal Airport in Inglewood, which became today's Los Angeles International Airport.

But back to Burbank: First known as the United Air Terminal, this was the airport that all the chic and daring "prop-people" of the 1930s flew in and out of. Although highly fashionable in those days, plane travel—especially the transcontinental flights

Valley boy: Bob Hope

that most movie people made—was extremely rigorous. In 1932, for example, TWA's coast-to-coast routing went as follows: At 9:30 a.m., passengers would leave New York City aboard an eleven-passenger Ford Trimotor that stopped at Philadelphia, Harrisburg, Pittsburgh, Columbus, and Indianapolis, before reaching Kansas City, where everyone got off the plane and spent the night. Next morning, the intrepid passengers reboarded their little plane (no in-flight meals, and blankets provided warmth) and continued on to Los Angeles via Amarillo, Albuquerque, and Winslow (Arizona), arriving at Burbank at 9:53 p.m. The trip wasn't cheap, either: A one-way ticket cost $288 in 1932— which in today's dollars would be in the neighborhood of several thousand. But compared to three nights on the train, many felt flying was worth the expense and the hardship.

It was also in the 1930s that millionaire movie producer/aviator Howard Hughes used the Burbank Airport as a base for some of his considerable aeronautical experiments and exploits. Besides designing and redesigning aircraft at Burbank, Hughes set at least two world speed records flying out of the terminal. In 1936, he piloted a Northrup Gamma from Burbank to Newark, New Jersey, in a record nine hours and twenty-seven minutes. A year later, he again broke the transcontinental speed record—flying a plane of his own design called an "H1"—with a time of seven hours and twenty-eight minutes. (Leonardo DiCaprio plays Hughes in the 2004 film *The Aviator.*)

And then there was *Casablanca*. Movieland legends say that this classic film of intrigue and romance—set in North Africa but shot in Los Angeles at Warner Bros. Burbank studios—used the Burbank Airport for that last tear-wrenching moment in which Humphrey Bogart doesn't fly away with Ingrid Bergman (but instead sends her off with Paul Henreid). Actually, according to Mr. Henreid himself, the foggy Moroccan tarmac was created on a Warner Bros. soundstage. For decades, Mr. Henreid and some historians felt that the Burbank Airport might have been used for the long shot of the plane taking off. It's now been established that the shot was not done at Burbank but at the Van Nuys Airport, seven miles west. Considerably modernized and enlarged since then, the Van Nuys terminal bears little resemblance to a 1940s airport these days, whereas there's still something romantic about Burbank, with its glassed-in control tower and 1930s terminal building. They don't make airports like this any longer—just as they don't make films like *Casablanca*. "Here's looking at you, kid."

Visit www.burbankairport.com.

13. ACADEMY OF TELEVISION ARTS AND SCIENCES
5220 Lankershim Boulevard, North Hollywood

A massive silver Emmy marks the site of the Los Angeles branch of the Academy of Television Arts and Sciences, located in trendy North Hollywood, now known to insiders as NoHo. The gleaming statue and spiffy building were erected in 1991, whereas the Academy was founded in New York (still the location of its head office) in 1957. Among the Television Academy's founding members were such TV pioneers as Ed Sullivan, Walter Cronkite, Edward R. Morrow, writer Neil Simon, and writer-comedian Carl

Reiner. The name Emmy, by the way, is a feminization of "Immy," the term used for the early image orthicon camera tube. The statuette was designed in L.A. by Louis McManus, an engineer at Culver City's Cascade Pictures, who used his wife, Dorothy, as a model.

The Academy frequently screens films and TV productions at its NoHo headquarters, often with a celebrity guest speaker. For information, call 818-754-2885 or visit www.emmys.com.

14. STUDIO CITY WALK OF FAME
Ventura Boulevard, Studio City

Studio City, the San Fernando Valley community across the Hollywood Hills from Hollywood, has never gotten the acclaim it deserves in the film history of Los Angeles. Perhaps because it has always been in the shadow of Hollywood, Burbank, and Universal City—or blame it on marketing. In any event, city officials recently decided to actively promote Studio City's movie image (the town is home to the historic CBS Studio Center, originally built by Mack Sennett and later taken over by Republic Pictures) with its own version of neighboring Hollywood's Walk of Fame.

Running on both sides of Ventura Boulevard between Rhodes Avenue and Carpenter Avenue, Studio City's new star walk doesn't have any stars, but instead features eighteen-inch-square granite tiles celebrating the likes of Orson Welles (who lensed *Macbeth* here), Mary Tyler Moore (whose production company was based here), and any number of Republic Pictures' Westerns and Studio City–produced TV series such as *Leave It to Beaver, Rawhide, Gilligan's Island, Hill Street Blues, Seinfeld,* and *Will & Grace.* Hooray for . . . Studio City?

15. CBS STUDIO CENTER
4204 Radford Avenue, Studio City

His career had nowhere to go but down when Mack Sennett, "The King of Comedy," moved his studio from Silverlake to Studio City in the San Fernando Valley in 1927. And down it went: What with the triumph of the talkies as well as the ravages of the Great Depression, Sennett wound up selling his new studio in the early thirties and retiring from the industry a few years later.

Where Sennett failed, a man named Herbert J. Yates succeeded. It was in 1935 that Yates made the former Sennett studio the headquarters for his new Republic Pictures. A true motion picture factory, Republic turned out a constant stream of "B" pictures noted for their action, their surprisingly polished production values, and their predictable plots. Republic's trademark was the Western; and several of its stars of the 1930s and 1940s—Gene Autry, Roy Rogers, John Wayne—stand among Hollywood's legendary celluloid cowboys.

After Republic went out of business in 1959, CBS took over the lot and used it for many TV series, including the long-long running *Gunsmoke, Leave It to Beaver,* and *Gilligan's Island.* In the 1970s *The Mary Tyler Moore Show* ruled the lot for seven seasons, during which time and for many years afterward the studio was officially known as CBS-MTM (as in Mary Tyler Moore) Studios. So it's no surprise that the studio was home to the MTM spinoffs *Rhoda, Phyllis,* and *Lou Grant.* It's also

Outside Republic Pictures Studios in the 1940s

where such other TV classics as *Hill Street Blues, St. Elsewhere, Remington Steele, Falcon Crest, The Bob Newhart Show, WKRP in Cincinnati,* and *Seinfeld* were done. The lot's recent stars have been *Spin City, 3rd Rock from the Sun, Will & Grace, Malcolm in the Middle, Still Standing,* and *Yes, Dear.*

CBS Studio Center is closed to the public. A quick walk around the place offers a peek at its Western Street but the most interesting area to check out is the residential section of Studio City west of Radford Avenue. Here, edging tiny streets with names like Agnes, Gentry, and Ben, are lovely little homes and bungalows built to house studio personnel in the 1930s and 1940s. Another fascinating glimpse at how the real "Hollywood" once lived—and still does. For tickets to TV tapings, call 818-753-3470 and visit www.cbssc.com.

16. VITELLO'S
4349 Tujunga Avenue, Studio City

It was actor Robert Blake's regular restaurant, an unpretentious brick-and-stucco Italian place with red awnings and planters with ficus trees in front. Since the *Beretta* and *In Cold Blood* star lived just down Tujunga at 11222 Dilling Street, Vitello's was only a few minutes' drive from home. On the night of May 4, 2001, Blake and his wife of seven months, Bonnie Lee Bakley, dined here. After dinner, they returned to the car, but according to Blake, he had left something back at the restaurant—his gun!—so he left Bonnie at the car while he went off to retrieve his firearm. As the world knows, when Blake got back to the car, he found his wife dying of a gunshot wound to the head. Or that's what the actor said. The L.A. County District Attorney's office felt otherwise and ultimately booked Blake on suspicion of murder, jailing him for eleven months before he was released in March 2003 on a $1.5 million bond. Currently Mr. Blake has gone through a number of different defense lawyers and the case, at presstime, was scheduled to go to trial in late 2004.

After the incident, Blake sold his Dilling Street abode to *ER* actress Alexandra Kingston and her husband, who extensively renovated but never moved in. Instead they put the place on the market for $1.6 million. A karma thing?

17. *THE BRADY BUNCH* HOUSE
12222 Dilling Street, Studio City

It was the story of a "lovely" widow (Florence Henderson) and her three fair-haired daughters, who hitched up with a widower (Robert Reed) with three sons roughly the same ages as the girls. They lived in a comfortable suburban home; they dressed in bright-colored, odd-shaped clothing—bell-bottom trousers, shirts with huge collars; they had few problems other than the occasional dating and/or identity crisis or how to deal with six kids and one telephone in those pre–cell phone times. It was the early 1970s and never mind that the Vietnam War was still raging, here at 4222 Clinton Way, it was American Dream time 24/7. *The Brady Bunch,* which ran from 1969 to 1974, may have been what the country needed at the time. When it went off the air, however, a decidedly different family called the Bunkers had taken over the airways—and their problems, although frequently funny, were far more real.

But back to the Bradys. The home they lived in for five years was this standard-issue Studio City split-level. When the series was shot, the house appeared to have a second story, thanks to a

The Brady Bunch house, Studio City

little help from the show's art department. And although the series ended in 1974, the Bradys kept resurfacing in TV specials and feature films up until the mid-1990s, taking themselves less and less seriously. While these shows met with varying degrees of success, the solid hit remains the original series, which has achieved cult status among the late-night cable crowd.

18. CLARK GABLE ESTATES
4543 Tara Drive, Encino

In the 1930s, it was quite fashionable for picture people to have "ranches" in some of the small outlying communities of the San Fernando Valley. These ranged from vast tracts such as Jack and Harry Warner's racehorse farm in Woodland Hills to Clark Gable's more modest 30-acre estate in Encino. More a Connecticut country place than a Western ranch, the "King of Hollywood's" Encino property was his L.A. home from the late 1930s up until his death in 1960.

In 1939, Gable brought his new bride and the love of his life, Carole Lombard, to live with him in Encino. They were Hollywood's ideal couple—adored by friends and gossip columnists alike. She had been married once before, he twice—but for the couple and for the world, this was the marriage that was going to last, the one made in heaven . . . not Hollywood. And when Carole Lombard left Gable in January 1942, it wasn't for another man, but for a cause: World War II—a War Bond rally in her home state of Indiana. It was the last time they saw each other. On the flight home, Lombard was killed when her plane crashed near Las Vegas. Several months later, grief-stricken as well as angry at the war that had taken his wife, Gable became one of Hollywood's first big leading men to enlist in the armed services. It is said that on his first home leave, his grief was still so painful that he couldn't face spending the night at the ranch—so he stayed in town.

After the war, Gable did return to Encino and went on to share his home there with two more wives, Lady Sylvia Ashley and Kay Williams Spreckles. The Gable-Ashley marriage (in 1949) lasted less than two years, but the Spreckles union (in 1955) endured for the rest of Gable's life. Felled by a heart attack a few months before the birth of his son in 1960, Gable never got to see his one and only legitimate child, John Clark. (It was of-

At home in Encino: Clark Gable and Carole Lombard

ten rumored and has since been ascertained that Gable was the father of Loretta Young's natural—but supposedly "adopted"—daughter, Judy Lewis, born in 1935.)

Mrs. Gable and son stayed on the Encino ranch until the early 1970s. Since then, the property has been subdivided into an expensive housing tract that was called Clark Gable Estates when it opened in the 1980s. The houses here—neo-Tudor, neo-Gothic, Plantation-Moderne are the predominant architectural themes—are priced in the millions. Streets have names such as Tara Drive and Ashley Oaks in honor of Gable's greatest film, *Gone With the Wind*. Tucked away behind a brick wall at 4543 Tara Drive, Gable's unpretentious clapboard home still stands in wonderful seclusion. Beyond are more housing tracts, supermarkets, freeways—all a far cry from the peaceful little Encino of the 1930s where movie stars built ranches to get away from the hustle and bustle of Hollywood. Talk about gone with the wind.

19. JACKSON FAMILY HOME
4641 Havenhurst Avenue, Encino

The longtime home of one of America's most powerful and arguably most dysfunctional showbiz families lies behind well-guarded gates on the west side of the 4600 block of Havenhurst

Avenue just south of Ventura Boulevard in Encino. Although there is no visible street number, movie lovers passing by may be surprised by the relatively unpretentious character of the neighborhood. Son Michael would make up for his family's modest—by Hollywood standards—home base by building his extraordinary Neverland Ranch, complete with private amusement park, up the coast in Santa Barbara.

20. CARL'S JR.
20105 Saticoy Road, Canoga Park

"Smile, you're at Mr. Smiley's!" quips a deadpan Kevin Spacey in one of the funniest scenes in the 2001 film *American Beauty*, as he suddenly appears, in full Mr. Smiley's drag, at a fast-food restaurant's drive-in window, ready to serve his wife (Annette Bening) and her new romantic liaison (Peter Gallagher). Playing the role of Mr. Smiley's in the scene, which effectively torpedoes Bening's budding romance with Gallagher, is one of the hundreds of Carl's Jr. fast-food spots that pepper Southern California.

Mr. Smiley's location for *American Beauty*

This particular one is in the suburban west Valley community of Canoga Park. When questioned about the film recently, the current staff had no recollection of the shoot, nor had they heard of Spacey, Bening, or *American Beauty*. So much for fast-food film history.

21. MOTION PICTURE COUNTRY HOUSE AND HOSPITAL
23450 Calabasas Road, Woodland Hills

It's a pleasant place—47 green acres of gardens, plazas, low bungalow-style buildings, a chapel, and a hospital. Indeed, residents of the Motion Picture Country House have all they could ask for—except youth and, in many cases, good health. This has been the last stop in the careers of such Hollywood greats as Mary Astor, Donald Crisp, Viola Dana, Mae Clark, Norma Shearer, Ellen Corby, Bruce Cabot, Herbert Marshall, Arthur O'Connell, Eddie ("Rochester") Anderson—all of whom lived and died here. Johnny Weissmuller was here too for a while, but had to be relocated when he started roaming the halls at all hours of the day and night, often letting loose with what was left of his Tarzan yell.

For those who are well and strong enough, activities abound at the Motion Picture Country House. One of the most popular is seeing movies at the Louis B. Mayer Memorial Theater, which shows two or three different films every week. There's also a Mr. and Mrs. L. B. Mayer Dining Room, a Cinema Beauty Salon, a John Ford Chapel, and a Samuel Goldwyn Plaza with shuffleboard and putting and croquet greens. In the words of the late Mary Astor, "If you have to be institutionalized, this is the best."

Visit www.mptvfund.org.

22. LOS ANGELES PET MEMORIAL PARK
5068 North Old Scandia Lane, Calabasas

Mae West's monkey, Humphrey Bogart's cocker spaniel, Lionel Barrymore's dozen dogs and cats are all buried here, as are Tonto's horses, Good Scout and Smoke; Hopalong Cassidy's

Topper; Valentino's dog, Kabar; and the *Our Gang* dog, Pete. Besides monkeys, dogs, horses, and cats, there are rabbits, birds, and at least one African lion among the 42,000 pets that have been interred here since the 1920s.

Burials are proper, often elaborate: Caskets with satin linings are available on the premises and many families make use of the "slumber room" for open-casket viewings of their dear departed doggies. The grave markers—all must be approved by the park—are often eye-grabbing and sometimes moving: "Who Is The Most Beautiful Girl? . . . Charlie Is." Some of the gravestones have likenesses of the animals embossed on the marble; others have Christian crosses or Jewish Stars of David; occasionally, there are inscriptions in Spanish. The grounds are well tended and many of the graves are topped with fresh flowers.

The park is open from 8 a.m. to 5 p.m. seven days a week. Not all of the celebrity animals' graves are marked, but the office staff is friendly and will direct visitors to those that are. To reach the Pet Memorial Park, take the Ventura Freeway west to the Calabasas Parkway exit. Visit www.lapetcemetery.com.

23. CALABASAS PARK GOLF CLUB
4515 Park Entrada, Calabasas

Built on land that once was part of the old Warner Bros. Ranch, this private golf and country club remembers its roots by naming holes on the golf course after some of the films that have been shot here: *Showboat* (1951), *High Noon* (1952), *Calamity Jane* (1953), *Stalag 17* (1953), and *Carousel* (1956). But moviemaking was only a sideline for the brothers Warner at their ranch. The real purpose of the property was the raising of racehorses—a business that Harry and Jack Warner were passionately involved in along with Harry's son-in-law, Mervyn LeRoy of MGM. Thus when MGM needed a horsey locale for *National Velvet,* the Warner Ranch must have fit the bill perfectly. In fact, some of the barn buildings from the 1944 film can still be seen at the edge of the golf course.

Elizabeth Taylor in
National Velvet, 1944

24. PARAMOUNT RANCH
2813 Cornell Road, Agoura

An unusual and cooperative venture between the Department of
the Interior and the film industry, the Paramount Ranch is a
working movie ranch administered by the National Park Service
and open to the public. On any given weekday, visitors will not
only be able to hike, picnic, and explore the rugged Wild West
terrain of this 335-acre park, they may also catch a Hollywood
film crew at work—either shooting in the wide-open spaces of
the ranch or in its Western Town. Restored by the park, the
Western Town was designed and built with moviemaking, camera angles, and light in mind.

The ranch belonged to Paramount from the late 1920s into
the late 1940s. In those days, the studio used it for its own
movies, and also rented it out to other studios. Among the early
Paramount films shot here were a string of Gary Cooper Westerns, including *The Last Outlaw* (1927), *Nevada* (1927), *The
Virginian* (1929), and *The Texan* (1930). The Ranch also pro-

vided locales for *Morocco* (1930) with Cooper and Marlene Dietrich; Ernst Lubitsch's *Broken Lullaby* (1932) with Lionel Barrymore and Nancy Carroll; DeMille's *The Sign of the Cross* (1932) with Claudette Colbert; *Blonde Venus* (1932) with Dietrich; *Goin' to Town* (1935) and *Klondike Annie* (1936), both with Mae West. The most lavish production of all, however, was Samuel Goldwyn's 1937 *Adventures of Marco Polo,* which used some two thousand horses, a number of elephants, and a huge fortress set. Gary Cooper was the star and Lana Turner had a bit part.

Paramount sold the ranch in 1946 but subsequent owners continued to rent out part of the original acreage for films and television shows. In the 1950s, when TV Westerns scored big with audiences, the ranch was frequently a location for *The Cisco Kid, Bat Masterson, Zane Grey Theater,* and *Have Gun, Will Travel.*

Recent research has also revealed that the ranch was the principal location for the 1953 jungle-thriller *Bwana Devil,* which would be completely forgotten except for the fact that it was the first commercial feature to be released in 3-D, beating out Warner Bros.' *The House of Wax* by a matter of months.

Western Town set at Paramount Ranch, Agoura

In the 1960s and 1970s, Westerns continued to be attracted to the increasingly scruffy movie location—indeed, by 1976, it presented the perfect double for the derelict Spahn Movie Ranch, the place the Manson Family called home, in the 1976 TV movie version of Vincent Bugliosi's book *Helter Skelter.* The same era saw the ranch host the medieval jousts and banquets of the annual Renaissance Pleasure Faire for a few years.

The National Park Service acquired the property in 1981 and set to revitalizing it—especially the Western Town, which it rebuilt and which has been used by *The Fall Guy, Chips, The A-Team, Falcon Crest,* and *Trapper John, M.D.* In 1992, *Dr. Quinn, Medicine Woman* turned the ranch's Western Town into Colorado Springs, Colorado, circa 1860, where Jane Seymour was the local physician for six years. In 2003, the same set became a Depression-era Central California town for the HBO series *Carnivàle.*

The ranch is still used for features, such as the 1999 *Flintstone's Viva Rock Vegas,* where it was the site of Slag Copper Manor, and Universal's 2004 Dracula-Frankenstein saga *Van Helsing,* which shot a couple of scary nighttime sequences on the property.

The Paramount Ranch is open from 8 a.m. to sunset, daily. Movie lovers should check out the ranch's guided "From Set to Screen" tours, which focus on the site's film history and are given the first and third Saturday of every month at 9:30 a.m. Sunday evenings in summer, the ranch shows classic silent movies as part of its "Silents Under the Stars" program. For general information, call 805-370-2301. To reach the ranch, take the Ventura Freeway west and exit at Kanan; turn left at the exit, left again at Cornell Way, then bear right onto Cornell Road and continue about 2.5 miles south. Visit www.nps.gov/samo/maps/para.htm.

25. MISSION SAN FERNANDO
15151 San Fernando Mission Boulevard, Mission Hills

The Mission San Fernando Rey de España occupies a place of importance—both in the history of California and in the history of the American cinema. For California, the date of note was 1797, the year Padre Fermin Lasuen founded the mission, the

On location at Mission San Fernando in 1919

seventeenth of the twenty-one Spanish outposts in California that brought the fruits and horrors of European civilization to this part of the New World.

For film buffs, the history-making year connected with the Mission was 1910. It was in that year that the visionary American director D. W. Griffith spent his first winter in California. Here, Griffith found not only good weather—but a whole new world as far as terrain, sites, and film locations were concerned. Taking advantage of this, Griffith carefully chose the perfect Southern California landscapes to match the films he was shooting. One of the locations Griffith discovered in 1910 was the town of San Fernando, with its haunting old Spanish mission (in a state of semi-ruin at the time). For Griffith, this was the authentic Old West, and he immediately used San Fernando and its mission in *Our Silent Paths,* a drama about the hardships endured by a miner and his daughter who have traveled cross-country aboard a prairie schooner. Griffith is reported to have used the mission town of San Fernando in various other early Westerns— including *Under Burning Skies, The Sheriff's Bully, Two Men of the Desert,* and *Battle of Elderberry Gulch,* all done in 1912 and 1913. In 1914, the San Fernando Mission turned up in a movie directed by another American movie pioneer—Cecil B. DeMille's

Rose of the Rancho. The Mission's Western tradition continued with the advent of sound with films such as *Cisco Kid in Old Mexico* (1945) and Tim Holt's *The Mysterious Desperado* (1949) using it as a backdrop.

Today, the Mission San Fernando el Rey de España looks quite a bit better than it did in Griffith's or DeMille's or even the Cisco Kid's day—thanks to several major restorations (most of them after earthquakes). Besides being a magnificent tourist attraction, the Mission is still being used by film companies when scripts call for a backdrop of Spain, Mexico, South America, or early California. Television shows done at the Mission have included segments of *The Love Boat, Knight Rider, Remington Steele, The Incredible Hulk, Buffy the Vampire Slayer, Alias,* and *The Pretenders.* Feature films: *Pee-Wee's Big Adventure* (1985), *Mr. Wrong* (1996), *The Truth About Cats and Dogs* (1996), and *The Banger Sisters* (2002).

The mission is open seven days a week from 9 a.m. to 5 p.m. To reach the site, take the Ventura Freeway west to the San Fernando exit; then head south along San Fernando Mission Boulevard.

26. CEMETERY AT MISSION SAN FERNANDO
11160 Stranwood Avenue, Mission Hills

Hidden behind the historic San Fernando Mission, this formerly little-known Catholic cemetery came into the limelight recently, when it was announced that comedian Bob Hope, who died in July 2003, would be buried here. Most insiders expected him to be laid to rest, like so many other major stars of his era, at Forest Lawn in Glendale, but his widow, Delores, said that the San Fernando Mission Cemetery was in tune with her wish for "simplicity and good taste." In addition, Mrs. Hope's mother and one of Hope's brothers are also here. Hope, who was not a Catholic at birth, converted to his wife's religion in the last years of his life. His remains are currently resting in a temporary mausoleum vault, until the grotto that will be his permanent resting place is completed.

In the meantime, movie lovers visiting this cemetery can also find the graves of a few other Hollywood celebrities such as actors William Bendix, Walter Brennan, Chuck Connors, William

Ritchie Valens's grave, San Fernando Mission Cemetery

Frawley (Fred Mertz on *I Love Lucy*), comedian George Gobel, and singer Ritchie Valens, of "La Bamba" fame, who died at the age of seventeen in the same 1959 plane crash that killed fellow pop stars Buddy Holly and the Big Bopper. The 1987 film *La Bamba*, starring Lou Diamond Phillips, documented Valens's all too short life.

The cemetery is open from 8 a.m. to 6 p.m., 8 a.m. to 5 p.m. in winter. The grounds staff is helpful in finding celebrity grave sites.

27. OAKWOOD MEMORIAL PARK AND CEMETERY
22601 Lassen Street, Chatsworth

The lovely town of Chatsworth, with its horse farms and distinctive rock formations, has been used as a location for cowboy movies ever since the days of D. W. Griffith. Today, one of the town's most beautiful hillsides is graced by a small rural cemetery where movie lovers will find the graves of one of the screen's greatest duos—Fred Astaire and Ginger Rogers. Since they were said never to have been the best of buddies offscreen, it's odd that they have wound up in the same cemetery.

Blame it on family ties. Miss Rogers (1911–1995) is buried next to her mother, Lela (1890–1977), in the Vale of Memory section, whereas Mr. Astaire (1899–1987) can be found at quite some distance from his former costar up in the Sequoia section. Here, he is surrounded by his mother Ann, his sister Adele (with whom he danced in the early days of his career), and his in-laws from his first marriage to Phyllis Livingston Bull, who died of cancer at the age of forty-six in 1954. Astaire's large marker is by itself below the two families; it has no dates, just the inscription "I will always love you, my darling—Thank You." It is assumed this refers to the dancer's second wife, jockey Robyn Smith. It is also assumed that the empty space next to his will someday be hers.

While the cemetery office staff will provide visitors with a map and directions to Ginger's grave—as well as to those of *Ben Hur* star Stephen Boyd (1931–1977), sultry screen siren Gloria Grahame (1923–1981), and Hopalong Cassidy sidekick Russell

Fred Astaire and Ginger Rogers: together forever at Oakwood Memorial Park

"Lucky" Hayden (1912–1981)—they will not help in finding the Astaire plot, citing the family's wishes. Still, fans have little difficulty in coming upon the site, and the groundskeepers are usually more cooperative than the office staff.

Oakwood Memorial Park is open from 8:30 a.m. to 5 p.m. For directions, call 818-341-0344.

28. WILLIAM S. HART RANCH AND MUSEUM
24151 San Fernando Road, Newhall

"While I was making pictures, the people gave me their nickels, dimes, and quarters. When I am gone, I want them to have my home." Would that more movie stars shared the late William S. Hart's philosophy. One of the first great cowboys of the American cinema, Hart bequeathed his entire 250-acre ranch to the County of Los Angeles to be used as a public park upon his death. Hart died in 1946, and today his former ranch attracts locals who seem much more interested in picnicking or hiking than in the man who once lived here. But for anyone wishing to know about Hart and his career, they've come to the right place.

Hart, who had the soft-hard good looks of a Clint Eastwood, came to be a Western star somewhat circuitously. Born in the East, he learned about the West as a young boy through traveling there with his father, who was everything from an itinerant worker to an executive with a lumber mill, depending on the biography one reads. As a young man back East, Hart went into the theater and eventually became known for Shakespearean roles. His stage career was a long one, and he was well into his forties when he again went West—this time to Hollywood—and started making Western films with director Thomas Ince. Characterized by realistic plots and an unglamorous depiction of what the West was like, Hart's pictures did well at first but eventually were overshadowed by the more spectacular exploits of Tom Mix and Buck Jones.

Meanwhile, back at the ranch, today three of the original buildings on the Hart estate have been turned into museums. Near the park entrance, the old ranch house that was on the premises when Hart first leased them in 1918 for his William S.

William S. Hart hosts Barbara Stanwyck and Robert Taylor at his ranch in Newhall in the early 1940s

Hart Productions was formerly Hart's office and studio. It now contains photos of Hart and his friends (Calamity Jane, Maurice Chevalier, Charles Lindbergh, and Pola Negri among them), Western gear from Hart's films, period furnishings, and other mementos of his career.

Up a hill from the ranch house, the bunkhouse is a little cottage that was originally built as a movie set and which Hart later used as a place to entertain the boys. Inside, there's a roulette table, small pool table, old-fashioned Victrola, Indian rugs and skins. At the top of the hill is Hart's permanent home La Loma de Los Vientos (The Hill of the Winds), which he built after having made his final film, *Tumbleweeds,* in 1925. The handsome twenty-two-room Spanish mansion contains more old photographs, plus collections of guns, Western paintings, and Native American art and artifacts. Hanging over "Big Bill's" bed is a painting of his best friend, his pinto pony Fritz. (Fritz's elaborate grave is another attraction of the park, as is the site where Hart's many dogs lie buried.) Married just once and for a mere matter of months, Hart lived on his ranch with his sister, Mary Ellen.

She died in 1943, three years before her brother. At his death, Hart was eighty-one.

The William S. Hart Ranch is open every day from 7 a.m. to sunset. Tours of the main house are given Wednesdays through Sundays from 1 to 4 p.m., mid-June to Labor Day; the rest of the year tours operate from 10 a.m. to 1 p.m., Wednesday to Friday, from 10 a.m. to 4 p.m., weekends. Visit www.hartmuseum.org.

29. RONALD REAGAN PRESIDENTIAL LIBRARY AND MUSEUM
40 Presidential Drive, Simi Valley

No matter how you feel about President Ronald Reagan, this is a fascinating place to visit—a tribute to an American Dream that smacks a little of a Frank Capra film, where a man of relatively humble Midwestern beginnings not only becomes a movie star but the president of the United States. For the movie lover, the Ronald Reagan Presidential Museum, where the late actor-

America's movie-star president: Ronald Reagan

president is also buried, documents his Hollywood years with posters, photos, and an occasional clip. The museum also looks at former First Lady Nancy Davis's eleven-picture career through posters and stills.

But the main agenda of the museum is to present and celebrate the life and times of the fortieth president of the United States with historic documents, documentary films, and an array of fascinating exhibits. Among the most impressive of these is a full-scale replica of the Oval Office, just as it was during Reagan's presidency, in which the former chief executive's own haunting voice-over provides his personal commentary on such historic events as the freeing of the Iran hostages and the *Challenger* space shuttle disaster.

Less dramatic but no less compelling is an exhibit focusing on the Reagan's beloved Santa Barbara ranch, Rancho del Cielo, with family photos, riding gear, and other memorabilia from the former Western White House. Mrs. Reagan—known for being a clotheshorse—has donated a number of glamorous garments from her official wardrobe, including the gown she wore to her husband's second inaugural. Numerous official gifts are also on display, such as the ornate mother-of-pearl armchair given the Reagans by former Philippine First Lady Imelda Marcos.

A large section of the Berlin Wall is also here, since its fall, which took place during the first President Bush's watch, is still credited to President Reagan's efforts. What is arguably the most exciting exhibit to date debuted in mid-2004: *Air Force One*. Moved here in pieces and reassembled on the facility's mountaintop Simi Valley site, the historic Boeing 707 was used by presidents Nixon, Ford, Carter, Reagan, and H. W. Bush as their lead plane. Today visitors can now walk through it and check it out up close. It's not every day you get to walk through the Oval Office and *Air Force One*.

The Ronald Reagan Presidential Library and Museum is open from 10 a.m. to 5 p.m., daily. For directions and other information, call 800-410-8354 or visit www.reaganfoundation.org/pma.

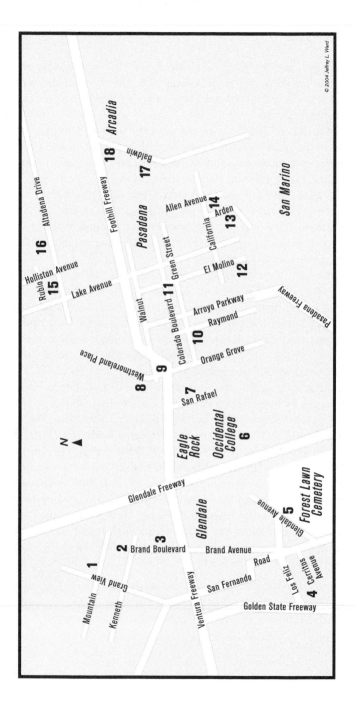

© 2004 Jeffrey L. Ward

Arcadia

Baldwin

17

18

San Marino

Altadena Drive

16

Foothill Freeway

Pasadena

Allen Avenue

14

Arden

13

Holliston Avenue

Rubio Avenue

15

Lake Avenue

Green Street

California

El Molino

12

Walnut

Colorado Boulevard

11

Arroyo Parkway

10

Raymond

Pasadena Freeway

Westmoreland Place

9

Orange Grove

8

7

San Rafael

Eagle Rock

Occidental College

6

N

Glendale Freeway

Forest Lawn Cemetery

5

Glendale Avenue

Glendale

Brand Boulevard

3

2

Brand Avenue

Road

Los Feliz

Cerritos Avenue

4

1

Grand View

Mountain

Kenneth

Ventura Freeway

San Fernando

Golden State Freeway

Pasadena/Altadena/Glendale:
Another Country

It's the first reel of *A Star Is Born*, the 1954 version. Norman Maine (James Mason) is the biggest movie star in America. He's rich, famous, powerful—and accustomed to getting anything he wants. He walks into the Cocoanut Grove looking for the young woman band singer (Judy Garland) who saved him from falling on his face in front of thousands of people at a benefit at the Shrine Auditorium earlier in the evening. The maître d' at the Grove, Bruno, tells Maine that the band left over an hour ago. Maine then checks out the available-women situation at the club. Bruno suggests several possibilities, but none is quite to the exacting Maine's liking. Except for the young girl in the green dress. When Maine expresses his interest to Bruno, the knowing maître d' shakes his head and says: "No, Mr. Maine . . . Pasadena. Leave it alone." Maine instantly understands, says no more. There are some things even a Norman Maine can't mess with—and Pasadena is one of them. Or, as Whoopi Goldberg, as a Pasadena police detective, puts it to Tim Robbins in Robert Altman's 1992 *The Player*: "This is Pasadena. We do not arrest the wrong person—that is L.A."

Only a matter of minutes from Hollywood, this ever-so-proper northern suburb of Los Angeles was always worlds away in outlook, mores, and lifestyle. Founded by Midwestern farmers in the 1870s, the city really took off several decades later when the railroads helped make it a fashionable winter resort for wealthy easterners. Many of these winter visitors became so enamored of Pasadena's gentle climate, crisp air, lush gardens, and nearby snow-capped mountains that they built fabulous winter homes here. Eventually, many of these same easterners gave up the East and became full-fledged, full-time Pasadenans. Whereas most of Los Angeles was settled by those seeking fortune and often fame, a large portion of Pasadena's population was made up of individuals and families who already had both.

Pasadena therefore has a long tradition of culture, class-consciousness, conservatism, and indeed isolationism. Needless to say, when the movies came to Southern California, they didn't wind up in Pasadena. Pasadena, however, occasionally wound up in the movies—as many of its mansions provided early production companies with the grand (and often "East Coast") backgrounds they sometimes couldn't find in L.A. Today, despite tough laws that limit filmmaking, Pasadena's mansions as well as those of neighboring Altadena and Glendale still rank at the top of many location managers' lists as prime places for shooting. For the movie lover, therefore, a visit to these communities is a visit to one of L.A.'s most important back lots.

Besides Pasadena, Altadena, and Glendale, this chapter includes the adjacent communities of Eagle Rock and Arcadia. The former is home to Occidental College, one of the most frequently filmed institutions of higher learning in L.A., whereas the latter boasts Hollywood's most historic racetrack as well as an extraordinary arboretum that's been seen in films since the 1930s. For sightseers, Pasadena, Altadena, and Arcadia can be covered in one jaunt; Glendale and Eagle Rock can be combined with Burbank or with the Los Feliz/Silverlake area of Hollywood.

1. BRAND LIBRARY
1601 West Mountain Street, Glendale

A long spectacular driveway edged with palm trees leads to this marvelous white Middle Eastern palace at the foot of Glendale's Mount Verdugo. Built in 1904 by Leslie C. Brand, the controversial character who "developed" Glendale, the palace was inspired not by Brand's extensive Asian travels but rather by a trip he had made to a world's fair in Chicago, where he had fallen in love with the East India Pavilion. Brand called his dream house El Miradero ("the lookout") and actually encouraged its use as a location for silent films since the excitement generated by these "shoots" helped publicize the town he had founded. One of the best-documented films shot here during the teens was a 1915 white-slave epic from Universal called *Under the Crescent,* which effectively used El Miradero as the palace where the heroine is held captive by an evil prince.

Besides encouraging filmmaking, Brand staged other publicity stunts at El Miradero to promote the city of Glendale. Among the most outlandish of these were his "fly-in" parties to which all guests had to arrive in airplanes. Stars helped hype these events—especially when they piloted their own planes, as Mary Miles Minter and Ruth Roland were reported to have done

Grand entrance:
Glendale's Brand Library

in 1921. Cecil B. DeMille, however, flew the most glamorous airplane, a Junkers JL-6.

When Brand died in 1925, his will stipulated that El Miradero and its grounds be left to the city of Glendale upon the demise of his wife. Mrs. Brand died some twenty years later, and by 1956 the mansion had been converted into a library specializing in music and art. Today, film companies often come to El Miradero when in need of an exotic foreign locale. Needless to say, the old *Mission Impossible* TV series loved the place. Lee Majors also must have liked it, since episodes of both *The Six Million Dollar Man* and later *The Fall Guy* were done here. More recently, the *X-Files* and *Alias* have used the library as a location. On the feature front, Sidney Sheldon's *The Other Side of Midnight* (1977) shot here—but the most memorable shoot was for the original *Naked Gun* film in 1988, when live camels were imported to turn the site into Beirut. Not quite as spectacular as old Mr. Brand's fly-ins but definitely in the same spirit.

The grounds of the Brand Library and Art Center are open from 8 a.m. to sunset, daily. Besides El Miradero, the park is home to the 1890s Victorian Doctor's House, a Japanese teahouse and gardens, and several picnic areas.

2. *GONE WITH THE WIND?*
727 Kenneth Road, Glendale

Although there seems to be little evidence to back it up, the legend persists that this impressive "antebellum" Glendale mansion was used as a location for *Gone With the Wind* for about two weeks in late 1938. If it wasn't, it certainly could have been with its columned portico, sweeping driveway, and oh-so-Southern weeping willows. While its *GWTW* connection is somewhat shaky, one of 727 Kenneth Road's recurring television roles is better documented, since it was the Florida estate seen at the opening of each episode of the early-1980s Aaron Spelling series *Flamingo Road*. The mansion, known as Bel Aire, was built in 1922 by a local business and community leader named Madison Boyd Jones and is now a historic landmark.

3. ALEX THEATER
216 North Brand Boulevard, Glendale

An architectural standout amid not-so-beautiful downtown Glendale's countless auto dealerships and sprawling Galleria shopping mall, this delightful 1925 theater (where Glendale boy John Wayne, then Marion Morrison, once sold popcorn) seemingly looked both to ancient Egypt and to ancient Greece for its design inspiration. No matter, the result—by architects G. Lindley and Charles R. Selkirk—is a classic of movie-palace-eclectic design. Made for dramatic entrances, the Alex has a long forecourt, not unlike the one at the Egyptian Theater on Hollywood Boulevard, that leads to the massive Doric-columned temple/theater. Adding to the aesthetic confusion is the pure Art Deco streetside marquee, designed in 1940 by another famous theater architect, S. Charles Lee, who also gave the theater its arresting vertical neon sign.

Despite its glamorous forecourt, the Alex was considered too far from Hollywood for major premieres. It was often used,

Glendale's Greco-Egyptian–style Alex Theater

however, for studio previews. In 1943, MGM staged an advance screening of *National Velvet* there. Evidently, Elizabeth Taylor and her mother arrived late and found every seat taken, so they were forced to stand and watch the entire film from the back of the house.

In 1993, the Alex had another major upgrade, when the 1,460-seat theater was completely restored for use mainly as a venue for live performances, special events, and as a film and TV location. In the 2002 film *Big Fat Liar*, the movie premiere sequence was done at the Alex. On TV, the theater has appeared in the series *New World* and *First Monday*; it also hosted the 2003 season of the *American Idol* TV talent contest phenomenon and is currently the home of *Steve Harvey's Big Time* variety show.

These days, too, the Alex has a vital film society, which keeps the projectors running on a regular basis. The society's motto: "Enjoy classic movies as they were intended . . . on the Big Screen!"

For information on the Alex Film Society and its programs, call 818-243-2539 or visit www.alextheater.org.

4. SOUTHERN PACIFIC RAILROAD STATION
400 West Cerritos Avenue, Glendale

It was the 10:15 from Glendale that Fred MacMurray boarded posing as Barbara Stanwyck's husband in the elaborate murder plot of Billy Wilder's *Double Indemnity* back in the early 1940s. Wilder shot the sequence—as he did much of the movie—on location. According to Wilder, he really wanted to use the Pasadena Train Station but couldn't get permission so he wound up at Glendale. He next decided to turn Glendale into Pasadena by changing the sign outside the station. That would have been fine—except that the name change caused such confusion among conductors that station officials made Wilder remove the Pasadena sign.

Besides its appearance in *Double Indemnity*, the highly photogenic Mission Revival–style Glendale station, built in the early 1920s for the Southern Pacific Railroad, often turns up in television series, commercials, and print ads. Beautifully restored in the 1990s, the station is now a vital part of L.A.'s burgeoning new Metro-Link light rail system.

Southern Pacific Railroad Station, Glendale

5. FOREST LAWN MEMORIAL PARK
1712 South Glendale Avenue, Glendale

The Disneyland of cemeteries, Forest Lawn in Glendale is one of Southern California's greatest attractions. Like many of the area's wonders, Forest Lawn was the creation of a man who dared to dream big. The man was Dr. Hubert Eaton, and in 1917, he was the new manager of the very conventional and not very well tended Tropico Cemetery. Feeling that cemeteries should inspire the living, Eaton set out to create, in his own words, "a great park, devoid of misshapen monuments and other customary signs of earthly death, but filled with towering trees, sweeping lawns, splashing fountains, singing birds, beautiful statuary, cheerful flowers, noble memorial architecture with interiors full of light and color, and redolent of the world's best history and romances."

With the same spirit and energy of the great movie moguls—for whom all things were possible—Eaton acted on his dream, and made it come true on a scale that must be seen to be believed. At Forest Lawn, there are no rows of ordinary tombstones. Instead, there are acres of gardens and courts, with names such as Slumberland, Lullabyland, Everlasting Love, Inspiration Slope, and Babyland, where flat stone markers scarcely alter the smooth contours of the green lawn. There is a swan lake. There are two mausoleums—one of which resembles a great sprawling Medieval abbey. There are churches that are full-sized reproductions of churches in England and Scotland. Not only used for funerals, these are sometimes the scenes of weddings. In 1940, for example, Ronald Reagan married Jane Wyman in Forest Lawn's Wee Kirk of the Heather.

At Forest Lawn, there is also . . . art. Here, one can see not copies but "re-creations" of some of the world's great masterpieces. The top artist whose works are "re-created" at Forest Lawn is Michelangelo. His colossal *David* stands in its own court—where a taped recording tells the story of David and Goliath. Meanwhile, there's more Michelangelo on view in the Memorial Court of the Great Mausoleum. Here, the star attraction is a gigantic stained-glass version of *The Last Supper,* which is unveiled several times a day at regular intervals complete with special lighting effects, music, and "dramatic narration." In the same room with *The Last Supper* are reproductions in Carrera

Wee Kirk of the Heather, Forest Lawn Memorial Park, Glendale

marble of Michelangelo's *Pietà, Madonna in Bruges, Medici Madonna and Child,* and various other of his better-known sculptures.

Movie lovers, however, should venture beyond the Court of Honor and over into the Sanctuary of Trust where they will find the wall crypts of Clark Gable and his wife Carole Lombard lying beside each other. Not far away is the man who produced Gable's greatest film—*Gone With the Wind*—David O. Selznick. Unfortunately, the nearby Sanctuary of Benediction is cordoned off with a low locked gate. It is here where Sid Grauman, Marie Dressler, Alexander Pantages, Irving Thalberg, Jean Harlow, and Red Skelton are buried.

Not off-limits to the public is the large memorial to another well-known Hollywood name that edges the driveway outside the main entrance to the Great Mausoleum. The name: Jean Hersholt, frequently remembered at the Academy Awards when the Academy hands out its Jean Hersholt Humanitarian Award. Hersholt, born in Denmark, made a career doing character parts in silent films and also became known in Hollywood for his charitable activities. Another Hollywood figure known for good works, although she was considerably more controversial than Hersholt, was superstar evangelist Aimee Semple McPherson. Her large flat tomb (all monuments must be approved by the Forest Lawn management) lies in front of the Great Mausoleum down the hill and off to the left; it is guarded by kneeling angels.

From the Great Mausoleum, Cathedral Drive leads to Freedom Way and ultimately to the Court of Freedom and Freedom Mausoleum. Here, a 20-by-30-foot mosaic of John Trumbull's famous painting, *The Signing of the Declaration of Independence,* sets the patriotic tone of this Forest Lawn enclave where Errol Flynn and baseball manager Casey Stengel are buried in the courtyard. Inside the Freedom Mausoleum—in the Sanctuary of Heritage—are the crypts of Alan Ladd, Nat King Cole, George Burns and Gracie Allen, Jeanette MacDonald, Clara Bow and her husband, cowboy actor/Nevada lieutenant governor Rex Bell.

On the lower level of this same mausoleum are the crypts of two of the Marx Brothers—Gummo, in the Sanctuary of Brotherhood, and Chico, in the Sanctuary of Worship—and one of the

Great Mausoleum, Forest Lawn Memorial Park, Glendale

Three Stooges—Larry Fine, in the Sanctuary of Liberation. Down here, too, is the long-forgotten silent matinee idol Francis X. Bushman, in the Sanctuary of Gratitude.

Back outside, secluded in a small walled garden just to the left of the entrance to the Freedom Mausoleum, is a marker that says Walter Elias Disney. Some Disney fans, however, don't believe that Disney's ashes are in this little garden and insist that their idol's body has been frozen and stored in a secret vault until the time when medical science can cure the cancer that killed him in 1966. Whether Disney is here or not (and it appears highly likely that he is at Forest Lawn), it seems fitting that he should be remembered in a place that has the same fantasy/reality quality of the great park that his own dreams created: Disneyland.

Forest Lawn is open daily from 9 a.m. to 5 p.m. The management does not provide information concerning where celebrities are buried. Visitors are requested to observe the same rules of decorum that they would when visiting any cemetery. Visit www.forestlawn.com.

6. OCCIDENTAL COLLEGE
1600 Campus Road, Eagle Rock

Founded in 1887, Occidental was one of the first liberal arts colleges in California. Although it lies between downtown L.A. and Pasadena, the Occidental campus with its Beaux Arts buildings and beautifully landscaped lawns and walkways has the look and feel of a small college in New England. The only giveaway that we're in California is the fact that many of the buildings have Spanish red-tiled roofs.

A longtime hit with location managers, Occidental has been used as a backdrop for more than seventy-five years, beginning with *Collegians,* a series of comedy shorts filmed by Universal in 1926–27. Other early Occidental film credits include *Horse Feathers* (1932) with the Marx Brothers; *She Loves Me Not* (1934) with Bing Crosby and Kitty Carlisle; *Change of Heart* (1934) with Janet Gaynor and Ginger Rogers; *Pigskin Parade* with Judy Garland (1936); *That Hagen Girl* (1947) with Shir-

Betty Grable, Judy Garland, Patsy Kelly, Tony Martin, and Jack Haley on the Occidental campus in *Pigskin Parade*, 1936

ley Temple and Ronald Reagan; *Goodbye My Fancy* (1951)
with Joan Crawford and Robert Young; *Pat and Mike* (1952)
with Katharine Hepburn and Spencer Tracy; *Tall Story* (1960)
with Jane Fonda and Anthony Perkins; *Take Her, She's Mine*
(1963) with Jimmy Stewart; and *The Impossible Years* (1967)
with David Niven. More recently, it's been in *Gumball Rally*
(1975) with Michael Sarrazin and Gary Busey; *Midnight Madness* (1980) with Michael J. Fox and Pee-Wee Herman; *Star Trek
IV* (1986); *Jurassic Park 3* (2000); and *Orange County* with
Colin Hanks and Jack Black (2001).

A great thing about the Oxy campus is that, depending on
how it's photographed, it can provide either East or West Coast
backgrounds. In *The West Wing,* for example, Occidental has
played Washington, D.C.'s Georgetown University, with the
camera taking care to leave those tile roofs out of the shots. But
in *Beverly Hills 90210,* where Occidental played California University, the Southern California look of the place was highlighted. The same was true in the witty 1995 film *Clueless,* an
update of Jane Austen's *Emma,* set in 1990s Beverly Hills. In the
film Occidental was used extensively as Bronson Alcott High
School, an idyllic world of way-cool skateboarders, Valley girls,
and Beverly Hills brats that could only be Southern California.

In the real world, Occidental counts a handful of alumni who
have done well for themselves in the film business: Academy
Award–winning documentary filmmaker Marcel Ophüls '50,
AFI founder George Stevens Jr. '53, producer-director Terry
Gilliam '62, and actor Ben Affleck, who attended Oxy in 1995.

Visit www.oxy.edu.

7. *TOPPER* HOUSE
160 San Rafael, Pasadena

A Pasadena classic, this glorious Gothic mansion behind the iron
gates at 160 San Rafael Avenue achieved screen fame as the
Connecticut estate of Cosmo Topper (Roland Young) in the Hal
Roach *Topper* series of the late 1930s/early 1940s. The estate is
especially recognizable in the original film, which stars Cary
Grant and Constance Bennett as George and Marion Kirby, the

two ghosts that good-naturedly drive Topper and his wife, Henrietta (Billie Burke), crazy. The same mansion was also Wayne Manor, home to Batman and Robin, in the 1960s *Batman* TV series. It was also used by director Ulu Grosbard in his 1981 film about late 1940s Los Angeles, *True Confessions,* and was home to Rocky Balboa (Sylvester Stallone) in *Rocky V* (1990).

8. GAMBLE HOUSE
4 Westmoreland Place, Pasadena

Two of America's most important early-twentieth-century architects were the brothers Charles and Henry Greene, whose Craftsman-style buildings were notable for their fine workmanship and their clean Asian lines. Like many architects of the era—such as Frank Lloyd Wright—Greene and Greene paid as much attention to the interiors of their buildings, right down to the specially designed furniture, as to the façades. One of the greatest Greene and Greene creations was a Pasadena residence built in 1908 for a wealthy Ohio family by the name of Gamble (as in Procter & Gamble). Today, the mansion, with its distinctive overhanging roofs and its sumptuous teak interiors, is

Back to the Future in Pasadena: Gamble House

maintained by the University of Southern California School of Architecture and is open for public tours on a limited basis.

Although the landmark mansion is rarely used for filming—production crews can sometimes be pretty rough on a property—an exception was made in the 1980s, when the Gamble House played a major role in *Back to the Future* as the base of operations for the mad scientist Doc, played by Christopher Lloyd, who sent Michael J. Fox back in time. Fox, Lloyd, and the Gamble House all reprised their roles in the film's two sequels (1989 and 1990).

For information on tours and special events at the Gamble House, call 626-793-3334 and visit www.gamblehouse.org.

9. THE FENYES MANSION
470 West Walnut Street, Pasadena

Typical of the many grand homes that edged Pasadena's Orange Grove Boulevard at the turn of the century, this magnificent columned mansion was built in 1905 by Los Angeles architect Robert D. Farquhar for Dr. Adalbert and Mrs. Eva Scott Fenyes. Besides being a leading social figure in Pasadena, Mrs. Fenyes was an accomplished artist and her home was a salon for painters, writers, and—which must have ruffled the feathers of her straitlaced Pasadena friends and neighbors—movie people!

D. W. Griffith was on the scene at the Fenyes Mansion as early as 1912 when he and a cast of costumed cavaliers used the place as the backdrop for a film called *The Queen's Necklace*. A few years later, Douglas Fairbanks's *Reggie Mixes In* was done here, as were films starring Harry Carey and Tom Mix. All the while, Mrs. Fenyes collected photos of the productions and made little notes on the backs of them. Typical of these is her synopsis of a "photoplay" done on her property in 1915: "An American girl who married a Turkish Prince. She was an actress and entered his harem after her marriage. Had many adventures and finally left him. Coming to America, she eventually joined the 'movies.' In a play, supposed to depict the principal events of her career, she and her company played several scenes in our grounds. This photo gives a scene supposed to take place in the harem. Her gown is a most gorgeous affair in brilliant strings of

Tom Mix in the 1916 film *Western Life*, Fenyes Mansion in the background

beads—mostly emerald green." Besides showing Mrs. Fenyes's fascination with moviemaking, the note also gives an idea of the outlandish plots of many silent films.

Several generations later, Mrs. Fenyes's estate—now the headquarters of the Pasadena Museum of History—is still being used as a location for films. In *Being There* (1979), for instance, it appears early on as the mansion where Peter Sellers is the gardener. The estate has also been used in the 1970s miniseries *The Immigrants* and *A Testimony of Two Men*, the 1980 Agatha Christie feature *The Mirror Crack'd*, Disney's *Newsies* (1992), and the 1996 HBO movie *The Ransom of Red Chief*. Its grandest role, however, was as the White House in the 1977 miniseries *Eleanor and Franklin: The White House Years.*

The house—with its priceless paintings, tapestries, antiques, and Oriental rugs—has tours Wednesdays through Sundays. For information, call 626-577-1660.

10. CASTLE GREEN APARTMENTS
99 South Raymond Avenue, Pasadena

Originally part of a lavish resort hotel—built in the 1890s to cater to wealthy easterners and midwesterners who wintered in Southern California—this eye-catching Moorish masterpiece is today one of downtown's poshest condominium complexes. The building also has a long history as a movie location—going at least as far back as 1919, when Rudolph Valentino and Dorothy Gish starred in *Out of Luck,* which was set at Castle Green.

Present-day film fans will more likely remember it from such films as *The Sting* (1973), which used the building's original game room for a card-game sequence; *The Man with Two Brains* (1983), as the Austrain hotel where Steve Martin honeymooned; *The Grifters* (1990), where the sumptuous Victorian parlor became a fancy restaurant; and *Bugsy* (1991), in which the building doubled for the legendary Hotel Nacional in Havana, Cuba.

More recently, Castle Green has made memorable appear-

Pasadena's Castle Green Apartments

ances in some less-than-memorable films such as the first four of *The Puppet Master* (1989–93) series, when through the magic of special effects, the building is transformed into a beach hotel. Then, in *Master of Disguise* (2002), the castle is the exclusive Turtle Club, where Dana Carvey arrives dressed as a turtle in a green suit. Tom Cruise's *The Last Samurai* (2003) calls on the Moorish salon to serve as a restaurant. Television has also visited Castle Green frequently, with *Judging Amy* and *Alias* two of the most recent to shoot here. In one *Alias* episode, the castle provided locations on the same day for both an elegant hotel in China and an apartment in Rome.

Most shoots are fairly uneventful, but when Jason Scott Lee arrived in 2002 to do a scene for *Time Cop: The Berlin Descision,* all hell broke loose. It seems the Castle was to be the site of a Third Reich get-together and thus the building was draped in three massive banners bearing gigantic swastikas. These could be seen all over downtown Pasadena and needless to say created quite a stir among the locals—until they realized it was only a movie.

Castle Green Apartments opens its doors to the public twice a year with a fascinating tour of the property, featuring looks at not just the public rooms but many of the apartments. The tour currently costs $20, with the proceeds going to Friends of Castle Green, a nonprofit organization concerned with the ongoing restoration of the building. All proceeds from filming also go toward maintaining the premises. For tour information, call 626–577–6765 and visit www.castlegreen.com.

11. PASADENA PLAYHOUSE
39 South El Molino Avenue, Pasadena

William Holden was "discovered" here. Tennessee Williams tried out plays here. And when Samuel Goldwyn thought a young Brit named David Niven needed a little more acting experience, he told him to head over to the Pasadena Playhouse. One of the oldest community theaters in the country, the Pasadena Playhouse was organized in 1918, inaugurated its attractive pueblo/Spanish quarters in 1925, and eventually grew to include

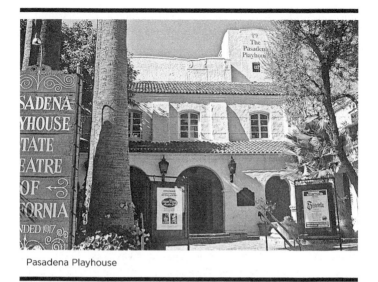

Pasadena Playhouse

five stages, a touring company, a radio and TV station, as well as one of the country's most important theater schools.

For Hollywood, the Pasadena Playhouse was an important source of talent, especially once talkies came in. Among the stars who went from the stages of the Pasadena Playhouse to the soundstages of Hollywood were Tyrone Power, Dana Andrews, Frances Farmer, James Arness, and the aforementioned William Holden. On the other hand, Eve Arden was discovered in a Playhouse production not by Hollywood but by Broadway. The year was 1933 and Arden was appearing in *Low and Behold!* (using her real name, Eunice Quedons) when she was scooped up by the Ziegfeld Follies. Eve's Hollywood career didn't begin in earnest until 1937. Raymond Burr is another star who made it to Hollywood via the Pasadena–New York–L.A. route.

In addition to the many performers who trace their theatrical beginnings to the Pasadena Playhouse, literally hundreds of established actors and actresses appeared there over the years. Indeed, for many years, the Pasadena Playhouse was one of the few centers of "live" theater in Los Angeles and therefore one of the few places where movie stars could prove that they were also serious actors. Despite its prestige, the Playhouse ran into severe financial difficulties in the sixties (some of them caused by the burgeoning small-theater scene in Los Angeles during the same decade) and was forced to close in 1970. After being dark for some fourteen years, the landmark theater was restored and re-opened in 1985 and has been going strong since then. Among the stars who have appeared at the revitalized theater, which currently presents six full-scale productions a year, have been William H. Macy, Richard Thomas, Scott Bakula, Stephanie Zimbalist, Marilu Henner, and Conrad Bain.

For information regarding what's on at the Pasadena Playhouse, call 626–356-7529 or visit www.pasadenaplayhouse.org.

12. *FATHER OF THE BRIDE* HOUSE
843 South El Molino Drive, Pasadena

In 1950 MGM had a big hit with a sweet little comedy about the trials and tribulations suffered by a father (Spencer Tracy) preparing for the wedding of his daughter (Elizabeth Taylor). The film, *Father of the Bride,* which was directed by Vincente

Father of the Bride house, Pasadena

Minnelli and which also starred Joan Bennett as Tracy's wife, did so well it gave birth to a sequel just a year later. Titled *Father's Little Dividend*, the film—again directed by Minnelli and featuring the same cast—dealt with the daughter's impending motherhood. It, too, did well.

The amazing thing is that it took four decades for Hollywood to do a film remake of the old MGM chestnut, when in 1990, director Charles Shyer had a go at it, with Steve Martin, Diane Keaton, and Kimberly Williams. History repeated itself—not only was the remake a hit, the producers, on a roll, decided to remake the sequel as well, using the same cast and the same house, a pretty clapboard number with green shutters and distinctive lattices on a quiet residential street in Pasadena. Happily, the new sequel, which also did well at the box office, abandoned its syrupy MGM title in favor of *Father of the Bride Part II*.

13. ARDEN VILLA
1145 Arden Road, Pasadena

It was the definitive 1980s prime-time soap opera: a celebration of greed, glitz, and all manner of emotional, social, and sexual excess. Set in the then petrochemical boom town of Denver, Colorado, *Dynasty* traced the tortured trajectory of zillionaire Blake Carrington (John Forsythe) and the various branches of his family and extended family. Carrington's base of operations was "a peerless forty-eight-room Georgian mansion . . . built in 1915 . . . situated on a wooded 645-acre estate . . . unquestionably Denver's finest." At least that's how the place was described in *Dynasty: The Authorized Biography of the Carringtons* (A Dolphin Book, 1984).

Don't go looking for the Carrington Estate in Denver, however—and don't go looking for just one Carrington Estate—because there were two. One, used in those dramatic aerial shots, was the National Trust Property Fioli, located some 400 miles from L.A. in the San Francisco suburb of Woodside. The other, used mainly for close-ups with actors, was, like so many great Hollywood movie mansions, in Pasadena. Surrounded by a stately iron fence and ornate gates, the Carrington main house is a magnificent Palladian structure called Arden Villa. Built in 1915, it boasts formal gardens, tennis court, swimming pool, and a lily pond that was the scene of a famous 1983 fight between Alexis Colby (Joan Collins) and Krystle Carrington (Linda Evans) in which both ladies wound up making quite a splash.

Dynasty managed to hang on until the end of the 1980s, finally going off the air in mid-1989. Besides its long run on TV, Arden Villa's impressive film credits include Buster Keaton's *Cops* (1923), the Marx Brothers' *Duck Soup* (1933), *Terms of Endearment* (1983), *Beverly Hills Cop* (1983), and *Beverly Hills Cop II* (1987). It is especially memorable in the 1998 film *Gods and Monsters*, starring Sir Ian McKellen as horror-film director James Whale, as the site of a glittering Hollywood garden party given by director George Cukor for a visiting Princess Margaret.

14. THE HUNTINGTON LIBRARY, ART COLLECTIONS, AND BOTANICAL GARDENS
Allen Avenue at Orlando Road, San Marino

One of the country's greatest museum complexes, the 207-acre former estate of railroad baron Henry E. Hungtington (1850–1927) is a must for any visitor to Southern California. The 1910 main house is a Palladian-style beauty that contains an extraordinary collection of eighteenth-century English and French art, including Gainsborough's *Blue Boy,* George Romney's *Lady Hamilton,* and Thomas Lawrence's *Pinky.* The Beaux Arts Library, built in 1920, displays among other treasures an original Gutenberg Bible, a rare early manuscript of Chaucer's *Canterbury Tales,* and Thoreau's original draft of *On Walden Pond.* A 1980s-era gallery focuses on American art.

Beyond the galleries, the vast property's gardens—Zen, Chinese, French, Rose, Elizabethan, etc.—are some of the most beautiful in the world. And some of the most photographed, since the Huntington and its gardens are constantly visited by film crews.

The property is especially popular as a venue for screen weddings—which is ironic, since it's off-limits for real weddings! Some of the most memorable cinematic nuputals have been in *Dream Lover* (1995), *The Wedding Singer* (1997), *My Best Friend's Wedding* (1997), *Path to War* (2000), *Intolerable Cruelty* (2003), *Legally Blonde 2* (2003), and *American Wedding* (2003). One surprising exception is *The Wedding Planner*

Huntington Library's Japanese Gardens

(2000), which despite the title did *not* use the Huntington for a wedding sequence but did call on its Japanese gardens to represent San Francisco's Golden Gate Park. *Anger Management* (2003) used the same gardens, this time as the entrance to a Zen monastery.

In *Legally Blonde 2*, besides the wedding scenes, the film called on the Huntington's mausoleum—where founder H. E. Huntington is buried—as the background for a Washington, D.C., dog run. The fact that the mausoleum resembles the Jefferson Memorial in D.C. is no accident—both were designed by the same architect: John Russell Pope.

Needless to say, the place is a popular TV location, having been used at one time or another in *Beverly Hills 90210, Charmed, Days of Our Lives, General Hospital, Fantasy Island, Murder, She Wrote, Star Trek, War and Remembrance,* and *The West Wing,* to mention just a few. Not just one of the country's grandest museums, the Huntington is one of L.A.'s busiest back lots.

For general information and directions, call 626-405-2100 or visit www.huntington.org.

Risky Business house

15. *RISKY BUSINESS* HOUSE?
1090 Rubio Street, Altadena

A popular property on the location circuit, this shingled colonial can be seen in *The Baby Sitters Club* (1995), *How Stella Got Her Groove Back* (1998), *Can't Hardy Wait* (1998), and as the home of Reverend Eric Camden and family in the pilot for the TV series *7th Heaven*. It is also said to have been used for additional photography on director Jon Avnet's sophisticated teen comedy *Risky Business* (1983), but Avnet's people insist that the film was done entirely in the Chicago suburb of Highland Park, where the story took place. Nonetheless, the Altadena house bears an uncanny resemblance to the Tom Cruise house that got trashed in the film.

16. THE WALSH AND LAWRENCE FAMILY HOUSE
1675 East Altadena Drive, Altadena

Another popular Altadena address, this handsome Spanish ranch house is where Brenda (Shannen Doherty) and Brandon (Jason Priestley) Walsh lived in *Beverly Hills 90210*. Before that, the

Beverly Hills 90210 house, Altadena

same spread was home to the Lawrences of the 1970s series *Family*. In a rare instance of verisimilitude, the Lawrence family supposedly actually lived in Pasadena, so the Altadena location was about as close to the real thing as things get in Hollywood.

17. LOS ANGELES COUNTY ARBORETUM AND BOTANIC GARDEN
301 North Baldwin Avenue, Arcadia

Remember "De plane . . . de plane!" that landed on the lake with the jungle and a whimsical Victorian house in the background? Welcome to *Fantasy Island*! Far from the South Pacific, the hit TV series' trademark locale was actually a public botanical park and gardens just east of Pasadena. One of L.A.'s most fantastic spots, the Los Angeles County Arboretum is a 127-acre preserve of exotic trees, plants, flowers, and birds. Among the latter, a huge population of peacocks roams freely, often begging for popcorn and other tidbits from the tourists.

The famous Fantasy Island house is not a movie set. It was

built in 1881 by real estate tycoon E. J. Baldwin as a guesthouse for his vast ranch that then encompassed the present-day arboretum property and much of the land surrounding it. The Baldwin ranch stayed in the Baldwin family until the mid-thirties, when it was purchased by a syndicate headed by Harry Chandler, publisher of the *Los Angeles Times*. It was also around that time that the movies discovered the property—with its lake and its jungly grounds—and Chandler's Rancho Santa Anita Corporation was glad to rent it all out for location shooting. Among the films lensed here then were *Devil's Island* (1938), *The Man in the Iron Mask* (1939), *The Women* (1939), *Road to Singapore* (1940), *The Lady Eve* (1941), *Anna and the King of Siam* (1946), *The Best Years of Our Lives* (1946), *Notorious* (1946), *Till the Clouds Roll By* (1946), all the Johnny Weissmuller *Tarzan*s, and a couple of Dorothy Lamour South Seas spectaculars.

When the state and county bought the property in 1947 and turned it into the arboretum, the filming didn't stop. Offering

Fantasy Island house, Los Angeles County Arboretum, Arcadia

the instant jungle, the arboretum immediately welcomed back Weissmuller, this time for his *Jungle Jim* movies of the late 1940s and early 1950s. The 1950s also saw more *Tarzan* features, now with Gordon Scott as the lead, all of which were done here. The arboretum was also used for one of the classic jungle films of all times, *The African Queen* (1951). Although most of the film was done on location in Africa and England, it is said that the famous leeches sequence had to be reshot once Humphrey Bogart was back in California. Needless to say, the arboretum was a lot closer than Africa and just as realistic.

In recent years, the arboretum has been a location for *Behind Enemy Lines* (1986), *Who's That Girl?* (1987), *Lord of the Flies* (1990), *Terminator 2: Judgment Day* (1991), *Dave* (1993), *The American President* (1995), *The Phantom* (1990), *Anaconda* (1997), and *Bedazzled* (2000).

The Los Angeles County Arboretum and Botanic Garden is open every day except Christmas from 9 a.m. to 4:30 p.m. Visit www.arboretum.org.

18. SANTA ANITA RACETRACK
285 West Huntington Drive, Arcadia

It was a glamour track from the day it opened—December 25, 1934. And much of the glamour came from its strong Holly-wood ties. One of its founders was none other than producer Hal Roach, who also served as its president for a time. Santa Anita, especially its ultraposh, ultraprivate Turf Club, lured the film world's most outstanding names and faces.

Some went to the races to be seen—feeling that horses and horseracing spelled class with a capital C. Others—like Bing Crosby, L. B. Mayer, Harry M. Warner, Raoul Walsh, Spencer Tracy, Howard Hawks, Barbara Stanwyck, Robert Taylor, George Raft, Zeppo Marx, Errol Flynn, Myron Selznick, Don Ameche, and William Goetz—went because they owned horses themselves. Finally, there were those who went because they were hooked. In fact, there was a time in Hollywood during the thirties and forties when the film colony was so obsessed with the ponies that the town's two trade papers, the *Hollywood*

Reporter and *Daily Variety,* featured racing schedules as well as tips along with news of the motion picture industry.

Santa Anita wasn't the only track with Hollywood connections. Harry M. Warner of Warner Bros. was one of the men behind Hollywood Park in Inglewood, and Bing Crosby was president and a principal owner of Del Mar near San Diego. It was during this race-crazed period in Hollywood's history that Groucho Marx is said to have gone to see an executive at MGM dressed as a jockey. Quipped Groucho when questioned about his attire: "This is the only way you can get to see a producer these days."

Picture people not only went to the races, they made movies about them. Among Hollywood's many racetrack epics, one of the funniest is the Marx Brothers' *A Day at the Races* (1937), which was shot at Santa Anita. Santa Anita also turned up in David O. Selznick's not-so-funny *A Star Is Born* that same year, as well as in the Warner Bros.' 1954 remake. In both versions, the alcoholic Norman Maine has just returned from a sanitarium where he has stopped drinking. He goes to the track, has an altercation with his former press agent, and starts drinking again— the final fatal binge. While on not-so-funny subjects, it must be noted that Santa Anita served as a detention center for Japanese Americans during World War II.

Recently the track was back on screen in a big way in the 2003 film *Seabiscuit,* which documented the career of the legendary racehorse, who scored one of his greatest triumphs at Santa Anita in 1940. Here, after a year's hiatus, following a ruptured leg ligament, an injury which many thought spelled the end of his racing career, the miracle Thoroughbred came back to win the $100,000 Santa Anita Handicap. For the race scenes in the film, the extras acting as fans in the bleachers were joined by a battery of some seven thousand inflatable dummies, which is Hollywood's latest low-tech way to beef up crowd scenes. Cheaper than real-life "background artists" (who can cost up to $200 a day) and more realistic than computer-generated crowds, these new inflatable extras were also used to pack the stands in the 2004 Kirsten Dunst tennis epic *Wimbledon* and to fill seats in the 2004 Depression-era boxing flick *Cinderella Man.*

Today, Santa Anita remains one of Southern California's premier racing centers, with its main Thoroughbred season running from December through late April. The track's Turf Club is still posh, still exclusive, still a favorite hangout of the Hollywood elite—such as TV-producer Aaron Spelling and producer-director Steven Spielberg, both of whom, in the grand old movie-mogul tradition, breed, raise, and race their own Thoroughbreds.

Visit www.magnaent.com.

Index

PHOTO CREDITS
(in order of appearance)

p. iii

Los Angeles Convention and Visitors Bureau

1. Hollywood: Birth of a Boulevard

Larry Ashmead collection; Courtesy Academy of Motion Picture Arts and Sciences; L.A. Morse; Hollywood Chamber of Commerce; Richard Alleman (RA); Bragman Nyman Cafarelli; Bragman Nyman Cafarelli; Marc Wanamaker/Bison Archives (Bison Archives); RA; L.A. Morse; Bison Archives; J. Evan Miller; RA; Jim Heimann collection; Bison Archives; Bison Archives; Historic Resources Group; RA; RA; Bison Archives; RA; RA; RA; RA; RA; RA; Whitley Heights Civic Association; RA; RA; Bison Archives; RA

2. Hollywood: Beyond the Boulevard

Bison Archives; L.A. Metro Rail; RA; Bison Archives; Bison Archives; Courtesy American Academy of Motion Picture Arts and Sciences; Courtesy American Academy of Motion Picture Arts and Sciences; L.A. Morse; RA collection; Bison Archives; RA collection; RA; RA collection; Jim Heimann collection; Los Angeles Convention and Visitors Bureau; RA; Bison Archives; L.A. Morse

3. Hollywood: The Factory Town

Bison Archives; RA; RA; Bison Archives; RA; L.A. Morse; Courtesy American Academy of Motion Picture Arts and Sciences; RA; RA; RA; RA; RA collection; RA; Bison Archives; RA collection

4. The Wilshire District: Main Street, L.A.

RA; Los Angeles Tennis Club; Courtesy American Academy of Motion Picture Arts and Sciences; RA; RA; RA; L.A. Morse; RA; J. Evan Miller; J. Evan Miller; RA; Larry Ashmead collection; RA; RA; RA collection; RA collection; RA; RA

5. Los Feliz/Silverlake/Echo Park: The Original "Hollywood"

RA; RA; Courtesy American Academy of Motion Picture Arts and Sciences; Bison Archives; Courtesy American Academy of Motion Picture Arts and Sciences; Los Angeles Convention and Visitors Bureau; RA; Courtesy American Academy of Motion Picture Arts and Sciences; RA; Bison Archives; RA; Bison Archives; RA; RA; Bison Archives; Bison Archives; RA; RA; Bison Archives

6. Downtown Los Angeles: The First L.A.

RA; Bison Archives; J. Evan Miller; J. Evan Miller; J. Evan Miller; J. Evan Miller; J. Evan Miller; J. Evan Miller; RA collection; Bison Archives; J. Evan Miller; RA; RA; RA; Courtesy Millennium Biltmore hotel; Bison Archives; Courtesy Downtown Standard Hotel; RA; RA; RA; RA; RA; Courtesy American Academy of Motion Picture Arts and Sciences; RA; RA; RA; RA collection; RA

7. West Hollywood: Border Town

Bison Archives; Bison Archives; Bison Archives; Bison Archives; RA; Bison Archives; RA; Bison Archives; RA; Bison Archives; RA; RA; RA; RA; RA; RA; Bison Archives; Bison Archives; Andrew Achsen collection

8. Beverly Hills: Hollywood's Golden Ghetto

Jim Heimann collection; Courtesy Beverly Hills Hotel; Bison Archives; Beverly Hills Convention and Visitors Bureau; RA; RA; RA; Bison Archives; Bison Archives; Beverly Hills Convention and Visitors Bureau; RA; RA collection; Beverly Hills Convention and Visitors Bureau; RA; RA; RA; Photofest; RA

9. Beverly Hills: Star Houses

Bison Archives; Historic Resources Group; RA; RA; RA; Larry Ashmead collection; RA; RA; RA; Larry Ashmead collection; RA; Larry Ashmead collection; Bison Archives; Courtesy American Academy of Motion Picture Arts and Sciences

10. The Fashionable Westside: Between Beverly Hills and Santa Monica

Kobal Collection; Courtesy Hotel Bel-Air; Andrew Achsen collection; Bison Archives; RA collection; RA; RA; Los Angeles Convention and Visitors Bureau; RA; Historic Resources Group; Larry Ashmead collection; Bison Archives; Bison Archives

11. Culver City: "The Heart of Screenland"

RA collection; Bison Archives; Bison Archives; Bison Archives; Courtesy American Academy of Motion Picture Arts and Sciences; Courtesy American Academy of Motion Picture Arts and Sciences; RA; RA; Courtesy American Academy of Motion Picture Arts and Sciences; Bison Archives; RA; RA; RA; RA

12. Venice/Santa Monica/Malibu/Long Beach: Hollywood by the Sea

Bison Archives; Courtesy American Academy of Motion Picture Arts and Sciences; Andrew Achsen collection; Bison Archives; Bison Archives; RA; RA; Courtesy The Georgian; Larry Ashmead collection; Courtesy American Academy of Motion Picture Arts and Sciences; RA; Bison Archives; RA; Ed Wanner; RA; Courtesy American Academy of Motion Picture Arts and Sciences; RA; Courtesy *Queen Mary*

13. San Fernando Valley: The Big Spread

RA; RA; Bison Archives; Larry Ashmead collection; RA; Bison Archives; Bison Archives; Larry Ashmead collection; RA; Bison Archives; Bison Archives; RA; Larry Ashmead collection; RA; Courtesy American Academy of Motion Picture Arts and Sciences; RA; Bison Archives; RA; Courtesy American Academy of Motion Picture Arts and Sciences; Bison Archives; RA collection

14. Pasadena/Altadena/Glendale: Another Country

RA; RA; RA; RA collection; RA; Courtesy American Academy of Motion Picture Arts and Sciences; Pasadena Convention and Visitors Bureau; Pasadena Museum of History; Friends of Castle Green; Bison Archives; RA; Huntington Library; RA; RA; RA

ABOUT THE AUTHOR

RICHARD ALLEMAN, a longtime contributing editor at *Travel + Leisure* magazine, is the former travel editor of *Vogue,* where he is a regular contributor on travel and entertainment. Currently living in New York City, he has carried on a longtime love affair with Los Angeles, where he lived for several years as an actor and writer.